GAMES IN ECONOMIC DEVELOPMENT

Games in Economic Development examines the roots of poverty and prosperity through the lens of elementary game theory, illustrating how patterns of human interaction can lead to vicious cycles of poverty as well as virtuous cycles of prosperity. The book shows how both social norms and carefully designed institutions can help shape the "rules of the game," making better outcomes in a game possible for everyone involved. The book is entertaining to read, intended for a broad audience, and can be accessed with little background in development economics or game theory. Its chapters explore games in natural resource use, migration, education, coping with risk, borrowing and lending, technology adoption, governance and corruption, civil conflict, international trade, and the importance of networks, religion, and identity to economic development. It illustrates concepts with numerous anecdotes from recent world events. An appendix explaining basic ideas in game theory used in the book is provided for interested readers.

Bruce Wydick is Professor of Economics at the University of San Francisco, where he has taught since 1996 after completing his Ph.D. at the University of California at Berkeley. His research focuses on applications of game theory, empirical and experimental methods to address poverty and development issues, especially microfinance. Professor Wydick has published more than a dozen articles in academic journals such as the *Journal of Development Economics*, *Economic Development and Cultural Change*, *World Development*, and the *Economic Journal*, and received grants and awards for his research from USAID, the Jesuit Foundation, the McCarthy Foundation, and the Pew Charitable Trust. He is codirector of the masters program in International and Development Economics at the University of San Francisco, has served as a consultant on a number of research projects of the World Bank, and is actively involved in both field research and development work in the highlands of Western Guatemala.

GAMES IN ECONOMIC DEVELOPMENT

BRUCE WYDICK

University of San Francisco

CAMBRIDGE
UNIVERSITY PRESS

CAMBRIDGE UNIVERSITY PRESS

Cambridge, New York, Melbourne, Madrid, Cape Town, Singapore, São Paulo, Delhi

Cambridge University Press

32 Avenue of the Americas, New York, NY 10013-2473, USA

www.cambridge.org

Information on this title: www.cambridge.org/9780521867580

First published 2008

Printed in the United States of America

A catalog record for this publication is available from the British Library.

Library of Congress Cataloging in Publication Data

Wydick, Bruce,
Games in economic development / Bruce Wydick.
p.   cm.
Includes bibliographical references and index.
ISBN 978-0-521-86758-0 (hardback)
ISBN 978-0-521-68715-7 (pbk.)
1. Development economics.   2. Game theory.   I. Title.
HD75.W94   2008
338.9001′5193—dc22
2007024357

ISBN   978-0-521-86758-0 hardback
ISBN   978-0-521-68715-7 paperback

For Dad

Contents

Figures and Tables

Figures

Game Figures

Tables

Preface

WHAT ACCOUNTS FOR the wide spectrum of poverty and prosperity in the world today? This is arguably the most important question in the social sciences, but it has also proven to be one of the most difficult. Many books written about economic development contain a plethora of macroeconomic statistics that document the widening span of the economic chasm between rich and poor. This is not one of those books. There are relatively few statistics in it. You will not find many references here to GDP, macroeconomic growth rates, inequality coefficients, or statistics about hyperinflation. This book addresses this question not by reexamining the statistics on world poverty or looking at the successes, failures, or potential of grand development schemes. Instead, it examines how patterns of human interaction form the basis for poverty and prosperity.

Game theory is a formal structure used to understand human interaction. Because human interaction is both frequent and desirable for most of us, game theory covers a lot of ground: Games occur in social relationships, during market exchange, in the fulfillment of contracts, in the use of environmental resources, in educational and technology choices, in politics, and myriad other aspects of everyday life. By analyzing human interaction in a formal structure, game theory can make predictions about how people will behave and the consequences of their behavior. This makes game theory a powerful tool. It can also give us insight into difficult questions, such as why some countries have become rich and others remain poor.

Traditional economics typically assumes that markets arrive at a single, efficient outcome. In contrast, game theory shows that many outcomes are often possible in human interaction, including economics. The study of economic development is essentially the study of how multiple outcomes in economies may arise, some better than others. In this book, I try to show how changing the incentives and rules of the game by which society operates can dramatically affect the outcome of the game and the resulting welfare of its players, creating a basis for either poverty or prosperity.

Institutions and social norms of a society establish the formal and informal rules of the game. Functioning properly, they make the good outcomes more likely and the bad outcomes less likely. Rich countries have become rich, not principally because they have abundant natural resources, or because they have exploited poor countries, or because they have been lucky. Rich countries have become rich because institutions, social norms, and patterns of behavior have emerged within them that have fostered widespread accumulation of capital, technology, and education. If you are browsing this book, trying to find its main idea before picking up something else, this is it. You have found it. You can now move on to another book.

But if you continue to read this book, you will find that it is aimed at a broad audience. I have written it for economists, undergraduate students in economics, other social scientists interested in development issues, development practitioners, and even graduate students and development economists wanting an up-to-date review of current ideas in the field. By aiming at a large audience, I have chosen to make this book fairly self-contained. This means that different readers may find parts of the book to be either too rudimentary or too challenging. Although I sympathize, I also believe that current ideas in a field should be accessible to a broad audience – one of my goals for the book.

One of the features that attracted me to development economics was that it seemed more humble than other fields in economics, less insular, and more eager to draw from other disciplines. Since then, I have become increasingly convinced that it is impossible to understand poverty issues strictly through the lens of economics. In addition, development economics has increasingly devoted itself to understanding political, social, and even psychological phenomena in poor countries as a way of trying to understand poverty. But the traditional tools of economics, which assume a set of well-functioning (and often market-based) institutions, are often not the right tools for this job. Game theory, with its more general analytical apparatus, functions more comfortably in this terrain. One of the laudable attributes of game theory is its ability to be "a uniter and not a divider," a methodology that spans academic disciplines, and it has done so increasingly in recent years. Through its use of game theory throughout, this book is fervently interdisciplinary, drawing from political science, sociology, psychology, and even animal biology and theology.

Some common themes run throughout the book. One relates to the tension between human competition and cooperation and how this affects economic development. A regrettable legacy of Darwinian theory is that academics have misapplied it in seeking to understand the development of human societies. Whatever success human beings have achieved over other species has come about not mainly through *competition* with one another but rather through *cooperation*. A large degree of altruism exists biologically at the level of the nuclear family, just as it does between bees in a common hive. But early human societies learned the advantages of broader altruism and cooperation. They adopted internal systems of reciprocity within groups that rewarded cooperators and punished cheaters. By repeated interaction with one's biologically unrelated neighbors or "clan," early societies were able to develop cooperative behavior within a larger local network. The promise of future interaction helped encourage honesty in market exchange. Reciprocal aid by neighbors in times of distress allowed households to smooth over the effects of unavoidable mishap such as illness, injury, and bad weather. These systems evolved into social norms, which came to act as guidelines for appropriate behavior.

However, the materially advanced societies have been able to construct institutions that have fostered cooperation on an even broader level. In the most economically developed societies, formal institutions provide incentives for widespread economic creativity, freedom, and exchange while simultaneously mitigating opportunism. Economic and social cooperation based on repeated face-to-face interaction has been replaced by institutions that allow for exchange between individuals who have no history (and often no future) with one another. Yet, despite their anonymity, mutual exchange benefits both.

One example I will discuss more fully in Chapter 7 involves credit markets. In developing countries, the credit contract is typically enforced through a borrower's personalized relationship with a local moneylender. The moneylender is able to curtail opportunism by the borrower (say, absconding with a loan) by virtue of his monopolistic control over the borrower, which is based on inside knowledge of his trustworthiness. Unfamiliar lenders cannot ascertain the borrower's trustworthiness, and so the borrower has few alternative options. Thus, if the borrower does not repay his personal moneylender, he loses access to credit. This keeps the borrower repaying and the moneylender lending, albeit often at usurious interest rates. In economically developed countries, however, institutions share credit information about borrowers broadly among lenders. That so many lenders have access to a borrower's credit rating lowers interest rates for borrowers via increased competition (and in the process creates a lot of credit card junk mail).

Property rights, judicial systems, bureaucracies, police, commercial law, and even international bodies such as the World Trade Organization are other examples of institutions that foster cooperation and mutually beneficial exchange on a widespread level. What remains common to all of these institutions is that their broad-based support and their perceived legitimacy are keys to their success.

A related theme in this book is the importance to economic development of institutions that act as a check on human self-interest. Economic development is fostered, and perhaps even *defined*, by the creation of institutions that allow for exchange on an impersonal, public level, rather than simply on a clan or communal level. Solving the problem of self-interest on a large scale allows an economy to realize the greater benefits of increased specialization. Some academics (especially those who are not economists) are troubled by the assumption common to game theory that players formulate strategies based on their own selfish interests, rather than the interests of others or the common good. I teach at a Catholic university, the University of San Francisco, where my students have sometimes shared this concern. My answer to them is that, unfortunately, we live and interact in a fallen world. Furthermore, in such a world, the Judeo-Christian view of human nature may offer a more useful picture of human behavior than some of the more optimistic perspectives. Although we must uphold altruism as a standard, in such a world it is unwise to assume systemic altruism, to understand the world by it, or to formulate policy based on it. As will be seen in many of these chapters, even some behavior that may appear on its face to be altruistic, when studied more carefully, may be understood ultimately to be self-interest. We are not like the angels.

Good institutions not only check our self-interest, they harness this self-interest for the benefit of the common good. Ironically, advocates of both socialism and unbridled capitalism similarly underestimate the human predilection toward self-interest. Both extremes create a set of incentives that elicit undesirable qualities in human beings: Socialism fails because it gives workers the incentive to be lazy. Unbridled capitalism fails because it gives entrepreneurs the incentive to cheat. This is because markets, which rely on "greed," require sets of formal and informal rules to curtail opportunism; otherwise, they break down. Well-functioning markets with a clear and enforceable set of rules, however, provide unparalleled welfare benefits.

A good society has formal and informal rules that induce people to do good things. Properly designed institutions establish rules of the game that foster incentives for people to act in the long-term interest of the community rather than in short-term self-interest. Yet it is crucial that individuals also *perceive* that the way to advance is through playing by these institutional rules rather than outside them. The most successful societies are ones in which the payoffs to cooperative behavior are almost universally perceived as higher than the payoffs for opportunistic behavior.

It is not necessary for readers to have studied game theory to read this book. If you are unfamiliar with game theory, you will learn the basic ideas of game theory while reading the examples in the book like someone learns about electricity while learning how to install a light switch. Although mathematically sophisticated explorations in game theory are needed to expand the frontier of the field and prove the generality of important results, most of the basic ideas of game theory can be communicated using little more than high-school algebra. Therefore, if you remember your high-school algebra, this book will not be too technically difficult for you, for it relies on nothing past this level.

Moreover, I have tried to array the chapters in an order that makes sense as a way of both presenting economic development issues and gradually introducing new concepts in game theory. Consequently, I develop the basic ideas of the Nash equilibrium and Pareto efficiency in the context of introducing a handful of well-known games in Chapter 2. Coordination games are used as a way of understanding poverty traps in Chapter 3. I introduce repeated games, especially of the Prisoners' Dilemma in discussing the relationship between natural resources and economic development in Chapter 4. Chapter 5 presents the basic principal-agent model in the context of day-labor markets, sharecropping, and traditional agricultural institutions. Chapter 6 introduces expected utility in an analysis of risk, insurance, and peasant solidarity networks. In Chapter 7, I examine credit markets through an expansion of a repeated Trust game. Chapter 8, which looks at technology adoption, uses slightly more advanced applications of Coordination games. I look at the emergence of property rights using Hawk-Dove games in Chapter 9. In this chapter, I also make use of backward induction in dynamic games more extensively and give an example that uses mixed strategies in a game in which potentially corrupt public officials must be monitored. In Chapter 10, on civil conflict in developing countries, I introduce evolutionary game theory, which is a helpful framework for understanding the underlying motives for conflict. Chapters 11 and 12 employ a variety of game theoretic concepts in examining social capital and the political economy of international trade. For interested readers, I have included an overview of some key game theoretic concepts in an appendix along with some exercises.

Many have helped me write this book. First, I am grateful to God for the opportunity to learn, teach, and write about something as important as world poverty. I can't imagine anything else that is more challenging or more rewarding, and not many people can say that about their work. I am also greatly indebted to many wonderful people who helped me directly and indirectly in writing this book. The initial chapters of this book were taken from lectures given at the University of Costa Rica and the National University of Costa Rica. I wish to thank David Solano for organizing these and the faculty and students who participated. The final chapters of the book were completed while I was on sabbatical leave at the University of California at Santa Barbara, and I wish to thank my colleagues there for hosting my stay and for the many stimulating and fruitful discussions about development issues we enjoyed throughout the year.

I owe a great intellectual debt to a number of people who have been particularly influential in my way of thinking about development economics and whose work has formed the background for this book. I owe an enormous intellectual debt to many, especially George Akerlof, Pranab Bardhan, Tim Besley, Javier Birchenall, Alessandra Cassar, Gary Charness, Alain de Janvry, Marcel Fafchamps, Hartmut Fischer, Karla Hoff, Dean Karlan, Elizabeth Katz, Michael Kevane, Tee Kilenthong, Rachel Kranton, David Levine, Craig McIntosh, Ted Miguel, Jeff Nugent, Jeff Perloff, Jean-Philippe Platteau, Jim Porter, Robert Powell, Matthew Rabin, Paul Ruud, Elizabeth Sadoulet, John Strauss, Chris Udry, and Romain Wacziarg, who through their work and conversation have helped me to better understand development economics generally, and in many cases, how game-theoretic, experimental, and empirical research methods can be used to understand poverty issues. Many of these people also took the time to look over drafts of chapters for this book, some of them took up far too much of their valuable time looking over the entire work. Much praise to my wonderful research assistants, Kim Singer and Lea Prince. I am grateful to the late John McMillan for his inspiration and for encouraging me to write this book. Economics has lost a beautiful mind.

I would also like to thank my editor at Cambridge University Press, Scott Parris. A more encouraging editor would be impossible to find. Thanks to him for shepherding this book through the many stages of publication and through offering innumerable points of advice about how to make this a better book that could be enjoyed by a broad audience. I also thank my production manager Mary Paden and her associates at Aptara Inc. for their tireless efforts in poring over my manuscript and correcting my silly mistakes and oversights.

Lastly, I would like to thank my family, particularly my wife Leanne, who has been incredibly patient and supportive during my writing as she is in other times. She is the most wonderful wife a husband could ever dream of. I also thank my little daughter Allie, who was born at about the time I started writing the first chapter, and is now ready for preschool. She provided many happy and healthy distractions the whole way through. As a former English teacher, my mother, Judy Wydick, has been engaged in an unflagging battle for me to communicate properly in my native language, a steadfast effort that began at a very early age and continues unabated. I am truly thankful for her support. My father, Richard Wydick, professor emeritus at the University of California at Davis, was with me at every step in the writing of this book, patiently and carefully reviewing every chapter and sending it back through the mail with marks on every page. He has been an unwavering support to me in my career, and especially in my writing, and I would like to dedicate this book to him.

CHAPTER 1

Economic Development, Interdependence, and Incentives

ON SEPTEMBER 5, 2006, an electoral court proclaimed Felipe Calderón to be the next president of Mexico. The court ruled that Calderón had won the election, which had taken place two months before, over his rival, Andrés Manuel López Obrador. Calderón's presidential victory was by the slimmest margin in Mexican history, igniting street protests organized by López Obrador's followers that would last for months.

Both before and after the election, the political battle between Calderón and López Obrador grew increasingly tense over the issue of corruption. As political tensions mounted, each tried to paint the other candidate as a contributor to the problem, while simultaneously presenting himself as the best solution to it. López Obrador's accusations were particularly painful for Calderón, who had campaigned under the nickname *El Sr. de Manos Limpias* (Mr. Clean Hands), pledging to eliminate the scourge of corruption in Mexico.

Presidential pledges to combat corruption, however, were not revolutionary. Vicente Fox had been elected as an anticorruption warrior six years earlier, as had been Ernesto Zedillo six years before him. The tenacity of corruption in Mexico has not kept politicians from promising to eradicate it. Because citizens correctly identify corruption at the root of Mexico's development problems, promising to break its stranglehold on society garners the votes of many. But were Calderón fully aware of the difficulties before him, he might have considered easier alternatives, like changing the national language to Swahili.

Corruption occurs at all levels in Mexico, from the mundane to the grandiose, but some of the more brazen, high-level cases of corruption have become legendary. These would include the $114 million deposited into Swiss bank accounts by Raul Salinas, brother of the former President Carlos Salinas, who shortly thereafter fled to exile in Ireland. The money was believed to have come through relationships with Mexican and Colombian drug cartels during the administration of his brother.[1] In a 2004 scandal, Carlos Ahumada, a 40-year-old self-made millionaire, was charged with giving million-peso bribes to officials of Mexico's left-of-center *Partido de la Revolución Democrática* to obtain lucrative sewer-cleaning contracts in Mexico City.

---

[1] *BBC News*, October 20, 1998.

Unfortunately, for the residents of Mexico City, Ahumada put a lot more energy into his underhanded dealings than he did into cleaning their sewers. Very creatively, he filmed many of the payoffs for the purpose of subsequently blackmailing the same government officials. But unfortunately, for Mr. Ahumada, the video footage was discovered and used for his arrest. It also led to the arrest of the finance chief of Mexico City, Gustavo Ponce, who was caught gambling in Las Vegas with $1.67 million in wire transfers traced back to Mr. Ahumada.[2]

In Mexico, they call it the "culture of corruption." The word for bribe, *mordida*, literally means "the bite," and getting bitten in Mexico is regrettably common. The *mordida* permeates every level of society, from the offices of presidents, governors, police chiefs, and mayors, down to the level of the most menial government employee. Part of the difficulty with corruption in Mexico is that it is often hard to determine where harmless cultural norms end and the *mordida* begins. For example, around Christmas time, it is customary in many areas of Mexico to provide the local postman with a "gift" for his hard work during the year, perhaps freshly baked *pan dulce* (sweet bread), some fruit, or a box of cigars. Those who fail to provide the postman with a Christmas gift often find that the number of people from whom they receive Christmas cards plummets sharply.

Some in Mexico might feel that people who refuse to provide a Christmas gift to their underpaid mailman deserve to have their mail tossed in the *basura*. But the greater problem is that people in Mexico have to pay bribes for even the most routine interactions with government officials: A 2001 study of 16,000 Mexican households by Transparency Mexico, the local arm of the corruption-fighting organization Transparency International, determined that residents of Mexico City have to pay bribes for nearly 25 percent of the basic government services they receive. They calculated the average bribe at around 100 pesos, about $10. Bribes were reportedly highest in activity related to cars: retrieving an impounded car required the *mordida* 57 percent of the time; avoiding traffic tickets (just or unjust), 56 percent of the time; and avoiding other traffic offenses, 54.5 percent of the time.[3] Bribes in Mexico are also common and indeed are often deemed necessary for obtaining business licenses and other types of permits.

Widespread corruption is not the norm in every country. Transparency International scores countries from 1 to 10 based on perceptions of corruption by businesspeople and country analysts, those closer to 10 being the most honest and closer to 1 the most corrupt. By this measure, Iceland tops the charts with a (non-)corruption score of 9.7, followed closely by countries such as New Zealand, Singapore, and Finland with scores ranging from 9.4 to 9.6.[4] Nigeria, Myanmar, Turkmenistan, and Haiti are at the bottom of the list with scores of 1.7 to 1.9. Mexico scores a 3.5. Clearly many different outcomes are possible with corruption. What accounts for these differences?

[2] *Wall Street Journal*, June 23, 2004, p. A1.
[3] *Washington Post*, October 31, 2001, p. A23.
[4] Transparency International Corruptions Perception Index, 2005.

Many of these differences are influenced by people's expectations about the behavior of others. Suppose that in a country like Mexico government officials and common citizens believed that a new campaign *would* indeed produce a significant public backlash against corruption. Officials would be more hesitant to solicit the *mordida* if they expected that irate citizens would be likely to report them. Citizens would be less willing to offer the *mordida* if they expected that officials would refuse it or maybe even report them for offering it. In this way, the phenomenon of corruption is a problem of coordination, where entire societies coordinate themselves around corruption or noncorruption. The problem in the game is that history matters; past experience shapes people's expectations about the present and future. And it is hard to expect that public officials will behave honestly if the past provides little basis for such, and hard to expect that people won't pay bribes if they always have. In this sense, Mexico remains a prisoner of its own expectations.

What makes rich countries rich and poor countries poor? Over 230 years since Adam Smith produced his (1776) classic *An Inquiry into Nature and Causes of the Wealth of Nations*, economists continue to inquire about the nature and causes of the wealth of nations. Although there is arguably no more important question in economics, the process of economic growth, the underlying causes of entrenched poverty, and the best set of development policies for reducing poverty all have remained, in many respects, unresolved mysteries.

The short answer to the question of why poor countries are poor is that, relative to the rich countries, poor countries lack capital, technology, education, and the subsequent division of labor that these factors of production naturally create. However, saying that developing countries are poor because they lack capital, technology, and education is a little like saying that some people are hungry because they don't have enough to eat – true, but unhelpful. The more important issue is *why* capital, technology, and education are so scarce in some countries, while they are so abundant in others. Absent an understanding of these underlying causes, policies that have simply tried to push more investment, more technology transfer, and more education on the developing world haven't worked very well. The poorest parts of the developing world are falling farther behind.

Unfortunately, this book is not going to provide simple solutions to the complex issues of world poverty. Instead, what I offer in this book is a framework for understanding poverty and development problems. Central to this framework is a growing understanding by economists in recent years of how social, political, and economic incentives at the micro level shape the pattern of economic development profoundly. As a result of this understanding (as well as from decades of experience with learning from past mistakes), economics is closer to understanding why poor countries are poor than it has ever been. We now recognize more fully how the incentives that influence a person's own choices are in themselves shaped by the behavior of others as we seek to understand the causes and consequences of, for example, corruption.

Individuals everywhere are part of social, political, and economic networks in which the behavior of others influences their own best choices, and vice versa. A situation in which people's choices and welfare are interdependent in this way is called a *game*. Many games, such as the interaction between a citizen and a public official, have a number of different solutions. Some of the solutions to a game may be good for everyone, some solutions may favor the powerful over the vulnerable, and still other solutions may be bad for just about everybody. The solutions to these seemingly innocuous everyday games, multiplied countless times over, largely determine what we observe as the economic outcome of a society.

What you will see in this book is that the solution to a game largely depends on the institutional framework within which the game is played. Good definitions of "economic development" are hard to come by, but a reasonable definition is one that is related to institutions and incentives. Institutions define the framework within which social, political, and economic interaction takes place.[5] Developed nations commonly have institutions that align the incentives arising from an individual's "pursuit of happiness" closely with a behavior that simultaneously promotes the common good. For example, a functional legal system creates an incentive within markets for sellers to provide goods and services to others that live up to their billing, while creating an incentive for consumers to pay for them. Underdeveloped nations, in contrast, often lack institutions that are able to protect buyers and sellers in a market effectively, check corrupt behavior, establish property rights, manage risk, hold their governments accountable, provide incentives for long-term investments, and promote the sustainable use of natural resources. A dearth of such institutions produces an incentive for short-term individual gain at the expense of the long-term common good. Is there a common perception that the best way to advance is through entrepreneurial creativity or through seeking a share of the profits created by others? Do the incentives exist to experiment with new technologies, or to be wary of them? Are there checks on utilizing natural resources to ensure that they are used sustainably, or is there a plundering free-for-all in the use of forests, grazing land, and watersheds?

This book tries to understand economic development by getting "under the hood" of economies and looking at the incentives and institutions that guide every-day, micro-level behavior. We will see that much of this social, political, and economic behavior and its effect on development can be understood in the framework of elementary microeconomics and game theory. These will be the tools we use as we explore under the hood. But first, let's begin with a short history of how economists have thought about economic development, and how this has come to influence the way we think about it today.

A Brief History of Thought

A brief history of thought in the field of development economics helps explain the long and winding road that has led to the current understanding about the causes,

[5] North (1990).

consequences, and (even possibly) cures for world poverty. From the Great Depression until the early 1980s, there was little confidence that the market left alone could do the job. Disillusionment with the free market after the Depression left little confidence that market forces, by themselves, could produce healthy economic growth in the industrialized countries, let alone in the developing world. Much of the economics profession, even in the West, was devoted to formulating economic policy that sought a middle ground between the unbridled forces of the market and the Soviet-style command economy. Moreover, in the LDCs (less-developed countries) there existed a great deal of pessimism about the ability of the nonindustrialized countries to develop properly in the context of open economic relationships with the economically advanced countries, a view articulated by leading thinkers of the day such as the Argentine economist Raul Prebisch and Hans Singer of the University of Sussex. Import protection and state-led industrial planning became the preferred solution in India, Latin America, and most other parts of the developing world.

The consensus regarding economic development policy during this period might be summarized as "get the planning right." During this middle period of the twentieth century, whole volumes were dedicated to the proper economic planning of the developing economy. Wassily Leontief's development of input-output matrices provided the technical foundations for this exercise. Works such as Albert Hirshman's (1958) *The Strategy of Economic Development* and W. W. Rostow's *The Stages of Economic Growth* (1960), with their emphasis on state involvement in the "commanding heights" (large industries) of the economy, represented the vanguard of development thought and policy. In fact, the subfield of study in doctoral programs in economics was often called Development and Planning. During the initial decades of the development-planning era, many parts of the developing world realized fairly robust economic growth rates and marked declines in poverty rates.

However, by the late 1970s, the consensus was that the full-fledged industrial planning model had begun to run its course. Infant industries in some of the Pacific Rim economies such as South Korea, Taiwan, and Singapore had grown up, been successfully kicked out of the government nest, and had become high-flying exporters, fully and successfully integrated into world markets. Some even view the relationship between state and industry in these economies, especially at the early stages, as integral to their success. Yet, in other parts of the world, what began as shiny state-sponsored infant industries in the early 1950s had grown up to be cranky, state-dependent geriatrics. Too often riddled with corruption and political cronyism, these industries became increasingly dependent on the government dole for their sustenance. This was true particularly in India, Africa, and Latin America. Always thirstier for government subsidies, these industries became sinkholes for government resources. The mother's milk of the infant industry slowly became the addictive moonshine of the aging, unproductive alcoholic. The easy solution, especially in Latin America, was to print money to keep such industries afloat. Politically this was the most convenient solution, but unsurprisingly it led to hyperinflation in many countries and chronic macroeconomic and political instability.

After being created to help repair Europe after World War II and to foster the development of the new international economy, the International Monetary Fund (IMF) and the International Bank for Reconstruction and Development (World Bank) created a new mission for themselves in coming to the rescue of these dysfunctional economies. The two sister institutions became deeply involved in many of these economies beginning in the early 1980s. The primary targets of their intervention were the state-sponsored industries, which had been protected from foreign competition by elaborate systems of domestic subsidies, tariffs, and quotas. What most alarmed the IMF and World Bank was that state-led industrial planning had produced wide gaps between domestic prices and world prices for many goods. These price distortions sent faulty signals to both domestic producers and consumers about the relative values of different goods and services. As a result, price distortions to protect domestic industry were consequently viewed as a major source of economic backwardness and instability. The mantra that emerged at the IMF and World Bank was for LDCs to "get the prices right." Economic "shock therapy" was employed in countries such as Bolivia and Peru to reduce inflation and stimulate production to bring domestic prices in line virtually overnight with the relative value of goods on world markets.

The great test for "get the prices right" was the collapse in the early 1990s of the Soviet Union. Politicians, economists, and nearly everyone else realized that stable market economies needed to be developed immediately in the former Soviet republics, most particularly Russia. Quite understandably, the West viewed the prospect of a nuclear-armed, economically destabilized Russia with great trepidation. In 1991, a shock therapy approach had been implemented in Poland with some degree of success. A team of economists worked feverishly to bring about a similar overnight change in the Russian economy, privatizing assets and freeing prices in a dizzying process of economic liberalization. As is now well known, the process was largely a failure in the absence of a supporting institutional framework. "Getting the prices right" in Russia produced an economy rife with monopoly, corruption, and organized crime. Estimates of output decline during the 1990s ranged from 25 percent to 45 percent.[6] Unaccompanied by other critical reforms, getting the prices right proved to be a disaster.

However, the best outcome from the Russian debacle was a fuller understanding of what actually makes market economies work. What was gleaned from the experience in Russia and other transitional countries during the 1990s was an understanding that effective institutions are critical ingredients to economic development. Put more broadly, we realize that it is *incentives* more generally, and not just prices, that matter. A new consensus emerged in economics that views the creation of proper incentives within both the political and economic systems as foundational to broadly based development.[7] If one were to simplify the approach of the current consensus in a phrase, it might be described as "getting the incentives right."

---

[6] Dolinskaya (2002) of the IMF, for example, lists the fall in Russian GDP from 1991 to 1997 at 40 percent.

[7] Well-known voices of this consensus would include William Easterly, Joseph Stiglitz, Amartya Sen, and others.

Although admittedly it is a bit vague, the current approach represents a more robust, as well as a more humble, framework for thinking about development problems.

Incentives and Strategic Interdependence

Incentives are shaped by the rewards that accrue from different activities, by the institutional framework within which one operates, and by one's expectations about the behavior of others. If an entrepreneur believes the only way he will get a business permit is to pay a bribe, then he will probably pay a bribe. If an inspector believes that entrepreneurs will be forthcoming with bribes, then he will probably solicit them.

To take another example, the strength of your desire for more schooling depends on the array of employment opportunities for educated people (which depends on the number of educated employers), feedback that you get from your social network about the costs and benefits of further education, and the norms with respect to schooling among your peers – you might not want to stick out. The point is that your schooling decision depends substantially on what others do, and even what you *think* others are likely to do.

This phenomenon is called *strategic interdependence:* Your optimal decision depends in part on what I do, and my optimal decision depends in part on what you do. Economic development is laden with examples of how strategic interdependence affects economic incentives. Consider investment in a machine. A woman may invest in, say, a new sewing machine if she believes that there will be a reasonable demand for new clothing in her village. The demand for clothing, however, is linked to the incomes of the other villagers. This in turn is linked to their own willingness to undertake small capital investments in other local small businesses, in agriculture, and so forth. If each villager is confident about the investment behavior of the others, each is more likely to make the required investment, and everyone is better off. If each believes that the others will hold back, then a lack of confidence in others' behavior becomes a self-fulfilling prophecy.

The twentieth century in Latin America illustrates some of the problems with incentives in a context of strategic interdependence. Free from the discipline of the market, economies in countries such as Mexico, Argentina, and Brazil evolved into self-reinforcing systems of patronage. Economic policy stifled entrepreneurialism, while the system simultaneously rewarded those who greased the palms of politicians to help themselves to a larger piece of the economic pie. Politicians rewarded their supporters with economic protection and lucrative subsidies. Creative people used their creativity to seek the surplus produced by others rather than creatively produce new surpluses of their own. Though the end was a stagnant economy rife with corruption, each behavior constituted a best response to the behavior of others, and so the mutually reenforcing behaviors continued.

Development Traps

In this way, an economy can get "stuck" on the path of economic development. Economic, political, or social behaviors emerge that are negatively self-reinforcing, causing society to be worse off than it could be and making change difficult. Some development traps affect just one aspect of behavior and are fairly benign; more serious development traps can imprison entire societies in long-term poverty.

In this chapter, I provide examples of strategic interdependence in the context of economic development. I take these examples from Mexico, Central America, and the Caribbean, the areas of the world that have been the main focus of most of my own interest and research. In each example, multiple outcomes are possible. Which outcome occurs as history unfolds is not always easy to predict, for often many possible outcomes can result from games in which there is, by definition, strategic interdependence. As I will point out later, multiple outcomes are even possible for situations with apparently similar initial conditions. What results may sometimes be generated by fine nuances in perception, small events in the past, or by what appears to be random chance.

These examples, in the form of vignettes, will serve as examples of five distinct types of games. Each of the games behind the vignettes will be explained more carefully in Chapter Two. These games will then serve as building blocks for exploring the relationship between economic development and behavioral incentives in areas as diverse as natural resource use, savings and credit, technology adoption, corruption, civil conflict, and international trade.

Understanding how each type of game differs from the others is necessary in order to understand key differences in the incentives that underlie each example. Being able to categorize different types of social behavior into the framework of specific types of games is valuable for thinking clearly about incentives and interdependence. It is also valuable for creating institutional structures that direct human energy and creativity in directions that lead to broadly based development.

Bienvenidos a Los Angeles

Many people (especially Californians) do not regard Los Angeles as a beautiful city. Its streets are lined with car dealerships, convenience stores, and tacky fast-food restaurants. The sky is brown. However, to immigrants from many developing countries, Los Angeles possesses the allure of Florence. With the number of foreign-born inhabitants equal to 3.5 million out of its population of 9.5 million, its esteem as a U.S. immigrant destination is unparalleled. What makes Los Angeles such a popular destination for immigrants?

It is tempting to point at the city's balmy weather, but this is almost certainly a pleasant side benefit, rather than the major draw. Cities such as New York and Chicago, both with comparatively uncivilized climates, also receive huge numbers of immigrants. The answer is likely that, after a point, immigration begins to feed on itself: A principal reason for the spiraling migration to the City of the Angels is that to people from certain countries, Los Angeles has become a virtual "home away from home." The city is home to 3,041,974 people of Mexican origin, making it the second-largest "Mexican city" in the world (behind, of course, Mexico City). It is also the second largest "Guatemalan city," the second-largest "Samoan city,"

Table 1.1. Population by major city and ethnic group

Ethnic group	Los Angeles	New York	Chicago	Miami
Chinese	329,352	361,531	48,058	9,869
Cubans	38,664	41,123	12,752	650,601
Dominicans	1,735	406,806	2,205	34,454
Filipinos	296,158	54,993	54,915	4,563
Guatemalans	100,341	15,212	16,765	9,676
Koreans	186,350	86,473	34,536	1,333
Mexicans	3,041,974	186,872	786,423	30,095
Puerto Ricans	37,862	789,172	130,414	80,327
Salvadorians	187,193	24,516	5,072	9,115
Vietnamese	78,102	11,334	11,325	1,383
TOTAL POPULATION	9,519,338	8,008,278	5,316,741	2,253,362

Source: Data compiled from 2000 U.S. Census, *Demographic Profile on Race, Ethnic, and Ancestry Groups* from Los Angeles County, New York City, Cook County (Chicago), and Dade County (Miami).

and the second-largest "Armenian city."[8] In some countries, it seems that nearly everybody has a friend or relative in greater Los Angeles.

This is important because once a critical mass of migrants from a certain country has settled in an area it makes it a great deal easier for those who follow. Consequently, there is a "beachhead" effect with immigration. A useful analogy recalls the Allied invasion of France, as is graphically conveyed by the opening scene of the movie *Saving Private Ryan*. As the movie portrays, life in the moment is exceptionally difficult for the first arrivals on the beach. Like the lead soldiers who take the heaviest onslaught of bullets and shrapnel, immigrants who arrive first on foreign shores lacking a social and economic network also endure great hardship.

Because of the beachhead effect, immigrants from a particular country tend to cluster together in one or two major cities. Table 1.1 gives population figures from the 2000 U.S. Census for ten large immigrant groups and four major U.S. immigrant cities. Like New York, Chicago, and Miami, notice that Los Angeles does not have large numbers of immigrants from every country. For example, there are relatively few Puerto Ricans in Los Angeles, relatively few Cubans, not to mention a paltry 1,735 Dominicans. Moreover, it is clear from the data that immigrants do not always head toward the city with the best weather, or even that which is closest to their homeland. If so, what are 406,806 Dominicans and 789,172 Puerto Ricans doing in New York or 786,172 Mexicans doing in Chicago? Arguably, Miami could have made a nicer destination for 86,473 Koreans than New York; yet, only 1,333 chose Miami.

During a field research trip to Guatemala, I returned to a village in which a rather embarrassingly large number of the microfinance borrowers I had interviewed five years before were working as busboys in Houston. One woman claimed that more than 500 men from this particular village were living in Houston, most of them in the same apartment complex. Brothers and cousins, fathers and sons, childhood friends and childhood enemies lived in this apartment complex. Each had paid a *coyote* to

[8] U.S. Census (2000).

smuggle him across Mexico into the Promised Land of Houston. Villagers told of the boisterous parties that often took place when a friend made it across Mexico, over the border, and to the doorstep of the apartment complex. Upon arrival of a fellow villager, they would kill the fatted calf in wild celebration.

Why the celebration? The rural wage in Central America is typically less than $0.50 per hour. Because of the scarcity of labor relative to capital and technology in the United States, the same workers can earn between $5 and $15 per hour as busboys, painters, construction workers, and landscapers. This leaves much to celebrate, especially for families back home. The lion's share of this wage is wired back to home country families as remittances and used to purchase land, finance small businesses, schooling, and home construction, and to buy televisions. It is said in Guatemala that the income of the 1 million Guatemalans in the United States is roughly equal to the 10 million that have stayed behind.

The immigrant network is critical to this entire (ad)venture. Those without a network are forced to struggle on the streets without moral, social, or economic support. Those within a network immediately have a place to live, can conserve on costs through shared expenses, and are quickly plugged into appropriately skilled jobs. As a result, the rewards from immigration are great if undertaken in tandem with others but small if undertaken alone. One migrant's behavior greatly shapes that of another, and vice versa, as well as the payoffs each realizes from migration. For this reason, even when the economy, weather, and amenities are viewed to be more favorable in another city, a Dominican will still head to New York, and a Salvadorian to Los Angeles.

Land Tenure in Costa Rica and El Salvador

Compared with almost any pair of countries in the world, El Salvador and Costa Rica have much in common: both populated by Spanish settlers in the sixteenth century, both originally part of the Central American Federation until 1838 (after which both gained their independence), both with size and population similar to a small U.S. state (6.4 million and 3.9 million, 21,000 km^2 and 51,000 km^2, respectively), geologically similar in the volcanically rugged yet fertile Central American landscape, both predominantly Catholic, and both heavily reliant on coffee as a predominant export commodity. Nevertheless, it is hard to imagine a greater contrast between two countries in the historical evolution of their political economy.

Much of this contrast can be traced to the historical differences between the countries in land distribution and property rights. Settlement of Costa Rica began in 1522, twenty years after Columbus originally landed on what he far-too-optimistically called the "Rich Coast." In fact, settlers were later disappointed to find very few deposits of precious minerals in Costa Rica. The lack of precious metals quickly forced the Spanish settlers of Costa Rica into agriculture. Because most of the small native population had quickly succumbed to diseases brought by the Europeans, slavery of natives was relatively uncommon. Consequently, agricultural plots were typically small-to medium-sized because farmers had to work their own land.

This proved manageable to the early settlers of Costa Rica, who tended to be of more humble origins than the Spanish nobility that had laid claim to other areas of Latin America during the colonial era. Thus, at least relative to its colonial counterparts in Central America, Costa Rica became a country of yeoman farmers.[9] In the individualistic agrarian society that developed in Costa Rica, landholdings tended to be broadly based; strong systems of property rights were developed, and the early seeds of a relatively egalitarian democratic tradition were sown.[10]

In contrast, land title in El Salvador was much more directly under control of the Spanish crown from the arrival of the conquistador Pedro de Alvarado in 1525. The Spanish gave control over most of the land to a group of fourteen elite European families, though formal land title remained with the Spanish crown.[11] On this land, the fourteen families developed large colonial-style haciendas with plantations of cotton, balsam, and indigo, enslaving the relatively large indigenous population or using slaves imported from Africa. Although formal property rights began to evolve later, the vast inequality in landholdings remained, supported by a military dedicated to upholding property rights of wealthy landowners.[12]

The late nineteenth century brought great changes to Central American agriculture. Indigo, one of the region's most important export crops, was replaced by synthetic dyes in the coloring of garments. The late nineteenth century also witnessed a great coffee boom, in which coffee quickly came to dominate Central American agriculture as an export crop. Lucrative coffee exports exerted great economic pressure on coffee exporters to increase and consolidate landholdings. The government decreed that anyone who planted coffee on Indian communal land immediately received title over it.[13] Thus during the coffee boom, the land of smaller farmers and traditional communal landholdings began to be absorbed into larger coffee plantations, creating a class of landless peasants in the Salvadorian countryside. Antivagrancy laws were enacted, which assured that displaced *campesinos* would provide an abundant labor supply for the coffee plantations. While coffee exports also surged during the mid-nineteenth century in Costa Rica along with the rise of banana plantations, land consolidations in the central coffee regions were not as severe and did not create a widespread landless class.

It is not always easy to develop a societal consensus over the process that governs how people are given rights to land: Land can be allocated by historical claim, by economic exchange, by the political process via land reform, by granting rights to squatters, or by war. The next chapter uses conflict over land rights to illustrate the more general game of conflicting claims over private property. However, for poor and uneducated rural populations who are trapped in a vicious cycle of landlessness and below-subsistence wages, rights to arable land can be worth dying for. In El Salvador,

---

[9] Paige (1997), pp. 218–20.
[10] Kraus (1991), pp. 215–7.
[11] Paige (1997), pp. 222–6.
[12] Montgomery (2000), pp. 473–9.
[13] Krauss (1991), p. 60.

the gross inequalities in landholdings proved to be politically unsustainable by the 1970s, and they were the genesis of a brutal civil war that began in 1979 and caused an estimated 75,000 deaths.[14]

Since the Chapultepec Peace Accords that finally brought peace to El Salvador in 1992, land transfers have continued to expand, but with only moderate success. In the interest of preventing recurrence of land concentration, strict laws were put into place regarding land size, rental, and sales. El Salvador now has a large problem with insecurity of land tenure, which has resulted from a series of complex land redistributions. Official title relies heavily on voluntary registration and, as a result, only about 40 percent of properties are registered, and of that, less than one-third have official public survey records, making buying and selling of land extremely difficult. To facilitate a functioning land market, the government has legalized the free sale of land and has allowed farmers to use the proceeds to reduce arrears to state agencies.[15]

Because of the more favorable land distribution in its colonial past, Costa Rica has escaped much of the region's political instability and moreover has been able to achieve a relatively efficient land registry system.[16] Costa Rica has had such a system since 1975, which has integrated the entire nation's land registration, including public survey records. Since the 1970s, disputes over land can be settled in the court system. In Costa Rica today, 80 percent of property owners hold registered land titles. The stability and effectiveness of Costa Rica's land registration policies have helped it to achieve a high level of "rule of law" in land tenure. We will see that these kinds of institutions are pivotal in solving games that involve conflict over virtually any type of private resource, such as land. As a consequence, they foster healthy markets for the exchange of resources and mitigate potentially destabilizing conflict.

Deforestation: Haiti and the Dominican Republic

Malcolm Gillis, former president of Rice University, once remarked that the border between Haiti and the Dominican Republic looks as if it had been drawn by an "acetylene torch." Gillis was referring to the massive deforestation in Haiti and the comparatively tempered deforestation in the Dominican Republic, its neighbor on the Caribbean island of Hispaniola. Over the decades since its independence in 1804, Haiti has been steadily stripped of trees, mostly for fuel and farming. Whereas nearly 99 percent of Haiti has been deforested,[17] the Dominican Republic still maintains about 33 percent forest cover, though it enjoyed as much as 80 percent forest cover in 1900.[18] The stark difference in deforestation illustrates the contrasting economic conditions between the two countries, conditions that reflect the difference between a poor country and a desperately impoverished country.

---

[14] Krauss (1991), p. 55.
[15] World Bank (1998).
[16] Trackman et al. (1999).
[17] USAID, *Haiti Country Report* (1998).
[18] World Bank (2002).

Deforestation in developing countries typically stems from the basic need for people to cultivate and cook their food. Forests are cleared to plant crops and raise cattle; wood from cleared trees is used for cooking and to heat homes.[19] It is another case of a vicious development trap: Large, uneducated rural populations exert tremendous pressure on environmental resources. The degradation of environmental resources further impoverishes the population. "We know we need trees, but we also need to eat and to cook," says 87-year-old Philis Milfort.[20] The problem in Haiti is compounded because there is no electricity outside major cities, forcing most people to rely on charcoal for fuel.

The problem worsens dramatically with the heavy rural population pressure that exists in countries such as Haiti. Though only 30 percent of its land is now suitable for agriculture (due to soil erosion stemming from deforestation), 70 percent of Haitians nevertheless depend on agriculture and small-scale subsistence farming, with the population growing at an astounding rate of 2.3 percent per year.[21]

Haiti's deforestation has been devastating to the island. Without roots from trees and bushes to hold it in place, precious topsoil has run off into the oceans, polluting rivers on the way. The Haitian soil is thus unable to absorb water quickly, and torrential flooding follows heavy rains. In June 2004, at least 1,700 people died in floods near Mapou.[22] In Haiti, 75 percent of the population lives in poverty, less than 60 percent receive primary health care, and scarcely one-half of adults are literate. With a per capita average income of just $380 per year in 2003, Haiti is by far the poorest country in the Western Hemisphere. Environmental degradation helps to keep it poor.

What accounts for the difference in deforestation between Haiti and the Dominican Republic? In countries with more educated, urban populations, fewer people compete for the resources of the forest. Though Haiti and the Dominican Republic share roughly the same-sized population, only about 36 percent of Dominicans live in rural areas (about half of that in Haiti), and only 17 percent of the population is employed in agriculture, which creates less pressure on the forests. A more highly educated urban population is one factor that has mitigated deforestation in the Dominican Republic.

A second explanation is a change in the Dominican economy from a primary reliance on sugar, coffee, cacao, and tobacco – which all require the clear-cutting of forests – into light manufacturing and tourism. Because of political instability, the Haitian economy has been unable to make this transition into economic activities that are less threatening to forests.

However, the greatest factor responsible for lower rates of deforestation in the Dominican Republic is related to simple governance issues. While the Dominican Republic by no means has a spotless environmental record, for many years governmental institutions have existed that have acted as a check on clear-cutting by indigenous farmers. Networks of forestry officials and rural police have patrolled

---

[19] World Bank (2002).
[20] "Haiti's Deforestation Allows Flood Water to Run Unchecked," *USA Today*, June 3, 2004.
[21] USAID. *Haiti Country Report* (1998).
[22] Haiti's Deforestation, *USA Today*, June 3, 2004.

agricultural areas for decades, prohibiting not only the clearing of state lands but also the clearing of land already settled.[23] In Haiti, where much weaker institutions exist, such efforts have been dramatically less effective.

The irony of deforestation is that the easiest escape from poverty for an individual peasant household is often to clear-cut a section of forestland to cultivate cash crops. In densely populated rural areas, where households live in dire poverty and restrictions on clear-cutting are weak, deforestation is the likely outcome. Yet, while the individual incentive is to exploit the common forest resource to meet individual needs, there are powerfully negative environmental effects from deforestation. The players in this game are stuck in a dilemma in which what seems good for the individual is bad for society, and in turn ultimately bad for individuals. As a result, there is a common interest in imposing strict limits on clear-cutting. The solution to this game is that society must hire a "sheriff" to keep itself from cheating. Rural welfare depends largely in part on the ecological sustainability of rural development, which in turn depends on the efficacy of the sheriff. When the sheriff is weak, everybody loses.

Microfinance in Guatemala

The most densely populated rural village I had ever seen was pressed up against the volcanic mountains on the southwest shore of Lake Atitlan, Guatemala. It was the summer of 2004; it was perhaps my tenth trip to Guatemala in the same number of years. This time my graduate students and I were carrying out a survey with funding from the U.S. Agency for International Development on sources and uses of credit within a half-dozen villages in the western highlands region. As we made our way from house to house, we inquired with local Mayan villagers about the abnormal population density. They explained to us with a story:

Apparently, many generations before in the early twentieth century, a catastrophic plague broke out in San Juan, nearly wiping out the whole Tzutuhil-speaking village of several thousand residents. During the worst part of the plague, a remnant from the village fled to the Pacific coast. There they settled and worked in agriculture for decades, existing as a Tzutuhil-speaking minority among the already present Quiché-Mayan coastal population. Around 1980, weary of living as a minority among the Quiché and facing the effects of a coastal economic downturn, the community longed to return to San Juan to resettle in their more culturally comfortable, original homeland. By this time, however, lands formally held by the emigrants had become occupied by other newcomers to the village. Nevertheless, a kind mayor at the time allotted small plots of land to each returning household, just big enough on which to build a small house.

This explained the mystery of the high population density, but another puzzle remained. In our credit survey we found that, despite ample potentially profitable entrepreneurial activities in the village, very few households had relationships with

---

[23] Sharpe (1977), p. 7–9.

formal lenders. The problem: To ensure against the possibility of a local homeless-ness problem, the land parcels were given to the returning Tzutuhil on condition that land title was nontransferable. This well-intentioned policy made it impossi-ble for these villagers to leverage their land as collateral to access credit markets. Thus, the community remained desperately poor, with weak credit access, relying on day-labor jobs in agriculture and bricklaying and occasional help from interna-tional charities.

The fundamental problem in any credit transaction is that, as a lender, one can never be 100 percent sure that a borrower will repay. The quality of any given loan is fundamentally based on the willingness and ability of a borrower to repay the loan. Unless a lender has built up a reservoir of trust over previous lending experiences with a borrower, obtaining a loan typically requires a costly screening process. The cost of this screening process is worthwhile only for large loans, where the differ-ence between the interest rate and the lender's own cost of capital can be multiplied over a large principal, such that lender profits are generous. To most lenders, these screening costs make small loans simply not worth the effort – unless, of course, a borrower can offer an easy and attractive form of collateral against a loan, such as a land title. Consequently, poor borrowers are often forced to turn to local mon-eylenders, who often charge exorbitant rates of interest. In Guatemala, for example, I have seen moneylenders slinking around public markets, collecting as much as 10 percent interest per *week* on small loans to vendors of pants and shirts. Apart from the moneylenders, there is sometimes little alternative.

The good news in Guatemala is that many other villages enjoy much greater credit access than San Juan La Laguna, though this is clearly a great source of frustration to the moneylenders. A swarm of microfinance institutions have blanketed many parts of the country with access to small loans. Institutions such as Génesis Empre-sarial, FUNDAP, Ban Rural, and *Fe y Alegria* (Faith and Joy) have offered low-income entrepreneurs with little or no collateral a chance to unleash the income-generating power of their own creativity through starting or expanding small businesses.

How do microfinance institutions overcome the traditional problems in credit transactions? Essentially, they make small loans available to poor borrowers by solv-ing the confidence game associated with credit transactions. By lending to small groups of mutually liable borrowers, microfinance institutions claim to be able to harness the *social* capital within a village, rather than the *physical* capital, to pro-vide the proper incentives for loan repayment. Because social capital, the network of trust between members of local communities, is often abundant in develop-ing countries, this offers a great advantage to microfinance institutions. Because microlenders know that a defaulting borrower will hesitate to disappoint his com-panions by saddling them with the debt from his unpaid loan, lenders can be more confident about making the loan in the first place. The result has been repayment rates consistently over 90 percent realized by most major Guatemalan microfinance institutions and tens of thousands of jobs created in small enterprises.

How does game theory help us to understand such issues? By allowing us to clarify the incentives involved in a particular context of human interaction, we are often able to make predictions about people's behavior. This is not only fun and interesting, but when things are going wrong, it also helps us to diagnose *why* things may be going wrong. It also helps us in the development and fine-tuning of new institutions that can expand economic opportunity. For example, game theory has been instrumental in the understanding and continued development of group-lending schemes, such as those operating in Guatemala. This and many other applications begin in the next chapter.

CHAPTER 2

Games

No man is an island . . .

– John Donne, Meditation XVII

ADAM SMITH'S CONCEPTION of the "invisible hand" postulated that a market consisting of self-interested individuals would yield an outcome that was best for society simply through the natural course of free exchange. One of the most striking contributions of game theory has been to demonstrate that the benevolence of the "invisible hand" is merely a special case, rather than a general truth about the fruits of economic self-interest. We will observe a number of cases, in fact, where the invisible hand can become an angry, malevolent hand, punishing players for their selfish behavior. What we will see is that self-interest is sometimes good for society, but often it is not. Indeed, self-interest may yield very poor economic outcomes outside the discipline of well-functioning institutions.

Game Theory

The origins of game theory are fascinating, and they help us to understand how such important insights came about. The work of French economist Augustin Cournot revealed the earliest glimpses of a formalization of strategic behavior in the 1830s. Cournot developed a famous model of strategic competition between two firms that foreshadowed some of the later insights of game theory. But Cournot was never able to generalize his concept of an equilibrium solution to other contexts, and for many decades, his results were regarded as insightful as applied to only a restricted type of competition between two firms.

The seminal work in game theory is considered to be *Theory of Games and Economic Behavior* (1943) by Princeton mathematicians John Von Neumann and Oskar Morgenstern. Von Neumann and Morgenstern are considered to be the founding fathers of game theory. They proved that there is an equilibrium solution to any zero-sum game, a class of two-player games in which a victory by one player implies an equivalent loss to the other. (French mathematician Emile Borel had argued that such games do not necessarily have a solution.)

Yet arguably, the most important consequence of Von Neumann and Morgenstern's seminal work was that it laid the foundation for the far-reaching insights of

John Nash and others who followed him. Nash, whose celebrated life and work are brilliantly portrayed in Sylvia Nassar's biography *A Beautiful Mind* (1998) and in the 2002 Academy Award–winning movie of the same title starring Russell Crowe, was a graduate student at Princeton University when he derived the greatest single result in the theory of games and formal modeling of social behavior. His 1950 and 1951 papers "Equilibrium Points of N-Person Games" and "Non–Cooperative Games" contain his now famous Nash equilibrium. His pathbreaking insight generalized the result of Von Neumann and Morgenstern to include a much broader category of social interaction that is not necessarily zero sum.

Part of the power of Nash's solution is its almost childlike simplicity. To begin to understand the Nash equilibrium, remember that every game contains three elements: (1) two or more players, (2) a set of potential strategies for each player, and (3) payoffs, a function of the combination of strategies employed by each player. *A set of strategies is a Nash equilibrium if the strategy by each player in the game is a best response to the strategies of all of the other players*. That is, given what every other player is doing, no player wants to do anything else. (For readers unfamiliar with the Nash equilibrium concept, a more detailed introduction to the Nash equilibrium and other concepts in game theory used in this book is provided in the appendix.)

A simple example of the Nash solution concept is a game in which two cars simultaneously approach an intersection, one from the West, the other from the North.[1] Suppose the strategies available to each are to Proceed or Yield. If both Proceed, they get into a wreck, and both receive a low payoff. If each Yields, then both drivers waste time making frantic hand gestures at one another, deciding who should go through the intersection first. There are two Nash equilibria in the game: one in which North Yields while West Proceeds, and a second in which West Yields while North Proceeds. Both are Nash equilibria because both constitute a best response, given the behavior of the other.[2]

Why do we expect that a solution to any game should be a Nash equilibrium? The first and most important argument is a simple proof by contradiction: If a particular outcome were not a Nash equilibrium, then it would be in the interest of someone to deviate from it. In addition, if a game has a single Nash equilibrium, it forms an intuitive outcome to a game that well-reasoning players are likely to anticipate. Such anticipations then create a focal point for play and become self-reinforcing. The Nash equilibrium can also be justified as a stable "prescription" for play. If, for example, a social norm, a tradition, or a third party suggests a behavior for players, creating an expectation about play, neither player will want to deviate from these prescriptions. Last, if players experiment with strategies over time on a trial-and-error basis, the final settling point in the game should constitute a Nash

---

[1] I will use capitals to delineate players and strategies in games throughout the book.
[2] It makes sense to codify one of the two Nash equilibria into law. In the United States and many other countries, West would have the right-of-way since it approaches to the right of North, an arbitrary distinction but one that induces the efficient behavior by fostering behavioral expectations that promote safer and quicker transitions at intersections.

equilibrium in which players develop a mutually reinforcing best response to one another's behavior.

Perhaps not coincidentally, as Nash languished in a schizophrenic haze for several decades after his major breakthrough, game theory also languished, with few major advances in interesting economic applications. Thomas Schelling's *The Strategy of Conflict* (1960) and Garret Hardin's application of Albert Tucker's now-famous Prisoners' Dilemma in the *Tragedy of the Commons* (1968) are two major exceptions. By the 1980s, however, economists had begun to understand the power and generality of the Nash equilibrium concept. In fact, much of modern microeconomic theory by then was beginning to be recast in the language of game theory. This has continued such that in economics today, there is hardly an issue of any mainstream academic journal that does not contain the phrase "Nash equilibrium." Almost miraculously, by the late 1980s Nash began to emerge from mental illness. Moreover, in recognition of his revolutionary solution concept (as well as his work on bargaining models), Nash received the Nobel Prize in 1993 with Reinhard Selten and John Harsanyi, who extended the Nash equilibrium to include dynamic games and games with imperfect information, respectively. The 2005 Nobel Prize in Economics was also given for work in game theory, to Thomas Schelling and Robert Aumann, who pioneered important extensions and applications of Nash's basic solution concept.

The Nash equilibrium is a powerful tool for understanding development problems. As is now commonly understood, most economic behavior is not zero-sum. For example, economic exchange nearly always falls into the category of "win-win" (though some may not "win" as much as they would like). Other phenomena, such as environmental degradation or economic corruption, are often ultimately "lose-lose." As a result, the Nash equilibrium is helpful for understanding the incentive structures that end up producing unhappy outcomes.

Let us now return to our five vignettes from Chapter One . We can model each of these as a simplified two-player, two-strategy, normal-form game. A game in normal-form (sometimes called *static* form) uses a payoff matrix with one horizontal player, Player 1, choosing strategies by row, and a vertical player, Player 2, choosing strategies by column. In the normal form, players choose strategies simultaneously or at least independently of the other's knowledge. The payoffs in the lower left of each cell are to Player 1 and those in the upper right of each cell are to Player 2.

Coordination Games: The Battle of the Sexes and the Stag Hunt

Consider a Businessman from the bribery and corruption story in Chapter One. A model of this game in normal form appears in Figure 2.1. Suppose that he needs to get a business license to open a branch office in the capital city. Arriving at the window at which such licenses are issued, he must choose between an Honest Behavior and a Corrupt Behavior. Either he can expect the official to process his application expeditiously without a bribe or knowing that a little speed money will help grease the wheels of the bureaucracy, he can slip a fifty-dollar bill under the window with his application. The Public Official likewise can dutifully process the

Public Official

		Honest Behavior	Corrupt Behavior
Businessman	Honest Behavior	1 3	-2 0
	Corrupt Behavior	0 -2	3 1

Figure 2.1. Battle of the Sexes/Corruption Game

permit application or suggest to the businessman that the permit can be "expedited" for a special "rush fee" of $50.

A culture of corruption contains reinforcing behaviors that form a Nash equilibrium in the cell located in the intersection of the bottom row and right column. The Public Official expects a bribe and the Businessman comes prepared to oblige. The Businessman receives the payoff of 1 in the lower-left corner of this cell, and the official receives the payoff of 3 located in the cell's upper right. Neither will choose to deviate given the behavior of the other. Failing to obtain a permit leaves the Businessman with a payoff of zero, whereas he receives a payoff of 1 through bribing. The Public Official receives a payoff of 3 by taking an offered bribe and zero if he does not. If either player were to act honestly in the face of dishonesty by the other player, it would increase the chance of prosecution to the dishonest player so that the latter's payoff falls to −2. But the payoffs do not dictate such a response because the inconvenience of this action reduces the payoff of the honest player to zero. Thus cultural expectations can create an outcome in which people expect to pay bribes and officials expect to receive them, producing a Nash equilibrium of (Corrupt; Corrupt).

However, another equilibrium also exists in this game: the corruption-free Nash equilibrium, (Honest; Honest). The Businessman approaches the window expecting to pay the normal processing fee and no more. The Public Official has little reason to expect that the Businessman will offer him a bribe; perhaps bribes have seldom been offered in the past. A bribe may be regarded as out of the norm or, possibly, as an insult. No fifty-dollar bill changes hands. The Businessman's payoff is 3 and the Public Official's payoff is 1. If either were to deviate from honesty, then his payoff would fall to −2, hence the outcome is self-sustaining.

Consequently, two Nash equilibria are possible in the game.[3] This is true in all two-strategy Coordination games. In the general case of m players in an n-strategy Coordination game, there are typically n Nash equilibria (not m). Which Nash equilibrium actually occurs is often difficult to predict, but past play tends to govern

---

[3] There is actually a third Nash equilibrium that occurs in "mixed strategies," in which players are honest some of the time and corrupt some of the time. We will consider only "pure strategy" Nash equilibria for now, until we examine the mixed strategy case in Chapter Nine.

future play. All that we know for certain about a Coordination game is that players will ultimately coordinate on a similar behavior. Other examples of Coordination games in everyday life include, time and spatial measurements, currency, different types of software programs, electrical plugs, fashion (e.g., neckties, turbans, droopy pants). The list is endless. The game in which I write this book in English and you read it in English is a Coordination game.

The game presented in Figure 2.1 is a particular type of Coordination game often called a Battle of the Sexes game. It has this curious title because a common prototype of the game depicts a couple deciding where to go on a date, wherein one activity is favored by the man and the other by the woman. The game assumes that the couple is enamored with one another, so that they prefer to be together even if it means one of them has to endure his or her second-favorite activity.

As a two-player Coordination game, the Battle of the Sexes has two Nash equilibria, but each is favored by one of the two players. If I wrote this book in English even though you would have preferred to read it in Spanish (but will read it in English anyway), we have a Battle of the Sexes game. It would have taken longer for me to write it in Spanish, but this might have made life easier for you. (Although given the level of my written Spanish, this is clearly questionable.) In the corruption game in Figure 2.1, the businessman is better off in the honest equilibrium, and the public official is better off when there is corruption.

Let's turn now to the migration story discussed in Chapter One. Contrast the Nash equilibria in the corruption game with the migration game depicted in Figure 2.2. In the migration game, consider two peasants, Ronny and Jaime, lured by the lucrative wages of *el norte*. They consider migration to the United States, where currently few of their countrymen have settled. If they Stay, they both earn low rural wages in their home country and receive a payoff of 1. If they both Go (migrate), they can form a small network in which they can share living expenses, help each other to find jobs, and have somebody to talk to in their own language. The payoff when they both migrate is 3. If only one Goes, lonely times dictate a payoff of −2 for him who Goes and one for him who Stays.

Like the corruption example, this is also a Coordination game with two Nash equilibria, (Stay; Stay) and (Go; Go). However, unlike the corruption example in which the businessman prefers the (Honest; Honest) Nash equilibrium and the official prefers (Corrupt; Corrupt), in the migration example *both* prefer (Go; Go) over (Stay; Stay). The migration example is also a particular type of Coordination

Figure 2.2. Stag Hunt/Migration Game

	Jaime	
	Go	Stay
Ronny Go	3 / 3	1 / −2
Stay	−2 / 1	1 / 1

game called a *Stag Hunt* (sometimes called an Assurance game). The game gets the Stag Hunt name from Jean-Jacque Rousseau's reflection on two hunters deciding whether to individually pursue a Hare (safe, but a small meal) or jointly pursue a Stag (dangerous, but more filling). Stag Hunts capture strategic interdependence when coordinated cooperation between players yields a superior equilibrium, but a safer equilibrium exists in which players pursue their independent interests; that is, a solitary hunter is more likely to be speared by the stag but is unlikely to be overwhelmed by a hare.

Stag Hunts have one Nash equilibrium that is better than the others, but players will choose it only if they believe that the other player(s) will do the same. Otherwise, by choosing it, the player may get burned with a low payoff. For example, in the migration game in Figure 2.2, if one player Goes while the other Stays the migrating player gets burned with a payoff of -2. Yet in the same game, if both players Go, they receive a payoff of 3, which is better than the payoff of 1 if they both Stay.

In economics, we say that the strategy pair (Go; Go) is *Pareto superior* to (Stay; Stay). This means that (Go; Go) is best for all the players, or at least one player is better off while the other is no worse off than the alternative. (Here both happen to be better off.) Any set of payoffs that is not Pareto inferior to another set of payoffs is said to be *Pareto efficient*. Pareto efficiency is a critical idea in applying game theory to economic development because Pareto inefficient equilibria are often associated with development traps.

In other types of Coordination games like a Battle of the Sexes game, the Nash equilibria cannot be Pareto ranked, or ranked in terms of Pareto superiority. In the corruption game in Figure 2.1, for example, if we move from the (Corrupt; Corrupt) equilibrium to the (Honest; Honest) equilibrium, the businessman is better off, but the official is worse off. Because one Nash equilibrium is preferred by each player in the game, the equilibria cannot be Pareto ranked. In such cases, there remain n Nash equilibria in games with n strategies available to each player, and each Nash equilibrium may be Pareto efficient; that is, no equilibrium will be Pareto superior to the others.

A third type of Coordination game is one of *pure coordination*, in which payoffs to players are equal in the different Nash equilibria. One example from the previous list might be language: Can one say that coordinating on Romanian as a common language is better or worse than Swedish? If a society emerges all speaking one or the other, the payoff is essentially the same. Unlike when there is one Nash equilibrium that is Pareto superior to others, in a game of pure coordination there is no a priori reason to expect one particular Nash equilibrium as more likely than the rest. Other Coordination games fall into none of these categories but still have as many equilibria as there are strategies.

Nash equilibria in any type of Coordination game are often "focal points" that evolve around social norms. The term *focal point* was originally used by Nobel Laureate Thomas Schelling to describe the way people gravitate toward one particular coordinated type of behavior. In an experiment reported in *The Strategy of Conflict*, Schelling polls a large number of East Coast college students, asking them where and when they would meet someone in New York City if no prior place or time had been arranged. An overwhelming number in the sample gave the same answer: at noon under the big clock in Grand Central Station. The point is that "noon at Grand Central Station" may be no better than anywhere else in New York. It is simply a best response given the conjecture of players regarding where they think others think that they would show up to meet them.

In Coordination games, communication can be vital. Taking the previous example, the ability of two people to communicate before choosing a rendezvous point and time helps the players to reach a Nash equilibrium in a game of pure coordination. Thus, in Coordination games, and particularly in Stag Hunts in which Nash equilibria can be Pareto ranked, leadership is key and involves communicating the Pareto-superior strategy to all players. In a Battle of the Sexes game like the corruption example, one player may try to make the other player *believe* that he will play the strategy that corresponds with his own preferred Nash equilibrium outcome. For example, an official may try to convey to a businessman that "nothing ever gets done around here" without a little tip.

Nash equilibria in all types of Coordination games are also notoriously "sticky." Once a Nash equilibrium in a Coordination game is established, it is often difficult to move to another equilibrium, even if the alternative is Pareto superior. In economic development, this is called a *coordination failure*, an idea that will be explored more thoroughly in Chapter Three. A simple and well-known example is the QWERTY key arrangement on computer keyboards. Why should relatively rarely used letters like *j* and *k* (not to mention ";") be situated in the most convenient locations, whereas one needs to reach for important vowels like *e* and *i*?

Paul David, a well-known economic historian at Stanford, chronicles the answer in a 1985 article. In the earliest days of the typewriter, salesmen would impress potential customers by rapidly hammering out the word *typewriter* on the machine. The typewriter keys were placed such that the hammers would not jam as "typewriter" was quickly typed. (Notice that the letters in "typewriter" are located along a single row on the QWERTY keyboard.) In the days before we were all forced to do our own typing on computers, firms hired typists from typing schools, where the QWERTY arrangement had been adopted and taught. Thus, it made no sense for firms to stock any other type of keyboard as an alternative. This is ironic given the existence of the Dvorak keyboard, developed back in 1932, which contains vowels and other common letters in handy places, which some have claimed to type up to 30 percent faster.[4] The QWERTY keyboard continues as an example of a coordination failure to this day, a result of a historical accident and is an example of a lock-in process that has created a Pareto-inferior Nash equilibrium.

---

[4] The unquestioned superiority of the Dvorak keyboard has been challenged in "The Fable of the Keys," a well-known article by Stan Leibowitz and Stephen Margolis (1990) who argue that Navy tests documenting Dvorak's superiority were flawed, and even that Dvorak himself had a financial stake in the results. Still, nearly everyone acknowledges the QWERTY design to be less than optimal and its perpetuation attributed to some degree of path dependence.

We will see that games in economic development can take societies down a path in which their level of development ends up resembling a QWERTY keyboard. A combination of strategic interdependence, historical processes, and deeply rooted social norms can cause societies to become entrenched in a Nash equilibrium that is inferior to what could be achieved – as shown in the example of Mexican corruption and elsewhere.

Hawk-Dove Games

Many games in economics involve a conflict over something. The particular something may be a piece of land, food, a potential spouse, or a private good that only one person or one group of people can possess, enjoy, or consume. The essence of such conflicts is captured in a Hawk-Dove game (sometimes called "Chicken"). In Coordination games, the more people engaged in a certain behavior, the more attractive that behavior becomes to the individual player. Hawk-Dove games are precisely the opposite. The more that other players are devoted to a given type of behavior, the more the individual player wants to do something else. Suppose that two (fastidious) backpackers suddenly discover that they have only one toothbrush between them. Both would like to use the toothbrush but not if the other is using it. What is certain is that the toothbrush will be used by someone. However, a toothbrush is a personal hygienic tool. Although each backpacker would ideally like to use the toothbrush exclusively, each would also prefer that the other use it than to share it. In the Nash equilibrium, only one person will use the toothbrush.

Consider the numerous other situations like the toothbrush: Two oncoming cars approach a one-lane bridge; which should defer and which should proceed? A pair of firms would each like to enter a market of limited size, but with high fixed costs of entry. Given the limited size of the market, there is only room for one profitable firm. Which firm will enter? A government agency agrees to provide a village with a well if the villagers can decide where the well should be sunk; which families will get the well closest to their property? The common element in Hawk-Dove games is conflict over a scarce resource.

Conflict over land tenure is a classic and common problem in development. Land is most productive when it is worked by an individual or individual household. Rights to land have been the source of innumerable civil wars in developing countries, especially in nations with a legacy of colonialism. Well-defined property rights were a common feature of many European societies before, during, and after colonization, from the sixteenth to nineteenth centuries. Many indigenous societies, in contrast, traditionally viewed land as held in common, something inappropriate for individuals to own. Consequently, during the colonial era, Europeans and their descendants often laid claim to vast areas of land that had no apparent "owner." Since that era, descendants of those who first *occupied* the land have often viewed the early European claims as illegitimate. Such has been the genesis of conflicts over land tenure in less-developed countries, especially throughout Central and South America and in many parts of Africa.

		Landlord	
		Put Cows on Land ("Hawk")	Put Cows Elsewhere ("Dove")
Peasant	Live and Work on Land ("Hawk")	-10 -10	-5 5
	Live and Work Elsewhere ("Dove")	5 -5	0 0

Figure 2.3. Hawk-Dove/Land Tenure Game

The essence of the conflict over land rights as presented in Chapter One can be illustrated through the Hawk-Dove game shown in Figure 2.3.

Like Coordination games, two-player, two-strategy Hawk-Dove games are characterized by two pure Nash equilibria. The "Hawk-Dove" name refers to the idea that players can play either aggressive (hawkish) or passive (dovish) strategies. The difference between the two types of games lies in the pattern of their Nash equilibria. With Coordination games, Nash equilibria occur when all players do the same thing. In Hawk-Dove games, the equilibrium occurs with players each doing different things. In the example in Figure 2.3, Nash equilibria occur between the Peasant and the Landlord on (Live and Work on Land; Put Cows Elsewhere) and (Live and Work Elsewhere; Put Cows on Land).

With the payoff so low to players in the conflicting strategy profile (i.e., (Live and Work on Land; Put Cows on Land)), how does one ensure that one of the two Pareto efficient Nash equilibria will occur? Robert Sugden (1986, 2004) in his celebrated work *The Economics of Rights, Co-operation and Welfare* suggests that disputes in the Hawk-Dove games over goods such as property are resolved through the establishment of "conventions." Conventions are established in games through the exploitation of *asymmetries* in the roles of players. For example, consider a conflict over a piece of land in which one player has possessed the land for a number of years but is faced by a challenger who wants the same piece of land. The convention "if Possessor, play Hawk; if Challenger, play Dove" always leads to one of the two Pareto-efficient Nash equilibria of the game. Seldom does a player take the same role of Possessor or Challenger in all conflicts. Typically, a player will take different roles in different situations; the convention prescribes the proper strategy for each role that facilitate a (Hawk; Dove) or (Dove; Hawk) Nash equilibrium. These conventions prevent the conflict associated with (Hawk; Hawk) and the economic waste associated with (Dove; Dove). Irrespective of what role a player takes in a particular situation, provided that his opponents follow the convention, then it is in each player's interest to follow it. Sugden, moreover, argues that formal law emerges from such conventions (perhaps from which comes the idea that possession is 9/10 of the law!).

Children, for example, learn even as toddlers about two types of conventions that can give them claim over a toy. We can call these *possession* and *sharing*. A child may be told that she has claim over a toy if she "had it first" but also if it is "her turn" to play with it, sometimes even if the toy is in the possession of the other child. Conflict occurs between children when one convention butts up against another, such as when one child has been playing with the toy for a long time while the other has coveted it. In such cases, the child without the toy is likely to invoke the latter convention, claiming "It's MY turn!" while the child with the toy will invoke the former convention, "I had it FIRST!".

Like the toy example, conflict occurs similarly in developing countries when different groups have different views of what convention should apply. Another convention, for example, might dictate that land ownership should be egalitarian. Under an egalitarian convention, asymmetry in the game would occur between those with more and those with less land, those with less land being prescribed to play Hawk, and those with more land to play Dove. Thus conflict, in the form of Pareto inefficient (Hawk; Hawk) play, could occur between one party who favors a "first-possession" convention and another party who favors an "egalitarian" convention.

Nevertheless, even when there is a shared understanding over a particular convention such as first-possession, arguments may linger concerning which party is indeed the rightful first-possessor. A group of people of indigenous ancestry may dispute the convention that the first to claim property rights over a piece of land should occupy the role of Possessor if land was previously possessed, perhaps communally, before formal property rights were bestowed on a later claimant. The Israeli-Palestinian conflict also seems to apply here. Does first-possession in modern history trump first-possession in ancient history? We will explore the subject of conflict more closely in Chapter Ten.

Conventions help determine how a broad array of resources is allocated in society: Should a given lump of government expenditure be spent where it is most efficiently utilized or where poverty is greatest? A limited number of tickets are available for sale at a counter. Should they be allocated to those first waiting in a line or to those who can most aggressively shove themselves toward the window? A business started by a member of a poor extended family becomes lucrative. Who is entitled to share in the good fortune? Economic development is hampered when a consensus over basic conventions has failed to emerge in society, creating an atmosphere of conflict and unpredictability.

The Prisoners' Dilemma

The story of deforestation in Haiti and the Dominican Republic in Chapter One is but one of the countless instances of environmental degradation in the developing world. Insight into the vexing problem of environmental degradation is one of the many applications of the famous Prisoners' Dilemma game.[5] The Prisoners'

---

[5] Albert Tucker at Stanford University is credited with the original Prisoners' Dilemma game in an unpublished manuscript. In his game two suspects are charged with a joint crime, and are held separately by the police. Each prisoner is told the following: if one prisoner confesses and the other one does not, the

Rochelle-Marie

		Restrain Cutting	Cut Down Maximum
Jean-Pierre	Restrain Cutting	3 / 3	4 / -1
	Cut Down Maximum	-1 / 4	0 / 0

Figure 2.4. Prisoners' Dilemma/Deforestation Game

Dilemma illustrates how individually rational people can collectively do irrational things, and it has vast applications across the social sciences. The game has yielded insights into issues as diverse as arms races, marital cooperation, commodity cartels, price wars, bidding strategy, voter participation, cooperatives, international trade policy, and the provision of public goods, as well as the degradation of natural resources. Some scholars such as Robert Axelrod (1984) have even used the game to develop general theories about the emergence of social order from anarchy.

The general characteristic of a Prisoners' Dilemma game is that it consists of two or more players who are each able to engage in either "cooperative" or "defecting" types of behavior. Each player benefits from the cooperative play of others, but individually each has an incentive to defect. The Prisoners' Dilemma is a game rich in irony. Because each player is better off defecting regardless of the behavior of the others, the game yields a unique Nash equilibrium in which *all* defect and are worse off than if each player had played cooperatively. Moreover, agreements between players *not* to defect are notoriously difficult to enforce, particularly in one-shot plays of the game. No matter what they agree to, each player knows that in the end he will be better off by defecting. Therefore, each does defect, to the detriment of everyone. In this regard, the Prisoners' Dilemma represents a divergence between individual and collective rationality.

The structure of the Prisoners' Dilemma can be seen in a representation of the Haitian deforestation problem of Chapter One in Figure 2.4.

Notice that whether or not Rochelle-Marie restrains cutting firewood, Jean-Pierre's best response is to cut as much firewood as he can. Cut Down Maximum is therefore a *dominant strategy* for Jean-Pierre. Since the game is symmetrical, Rochelle-Marie likewise has the same dominant strategy. The ensuing Nash equilibrium is the (Cut Down Maximum; Cut Down Maximum) deforestation payoff, in which the mutual payoff is zero and the hillside is left barren.

As Garret Hardin (1968) famously observes in the *Tragedy of the Commons*, Prisoners' Dilemma problems occur in many, if not most, situations that call for some

former will be given a reward of 1 and the latter will receive a fine equal to 2; if both confess, each will receive a fine equal to 1; if neither confesses, both will be set free. These payoffs establish the basic payoff structure for the game's many applications.

kind of collective sacrificial restraint or action. For example, individual conservation of common-pool resources, such as forests, fisheries, and grazing lands, typically yields a total public benefit that more than compensates each individual for his own restraint. Individual restraint in littering; in air, water, and noise pollution; in respect for private property; even in self-control while resolving disputes, make up only a fraction of other examples. Nevertheless, the underlying incentive in these situations lies in gaining an individual advantage through a lack of individual restraint.

Like individual *restraint*, individual *action* can produce benefits to society and to each individual that more than compensates each individual for his own effort. These are circumstances in which a group of individuals can collectively produce a public good, to be shared by all, that is worth more than the sum of the individual efforts. The Prisoners' Dilemma problem is manifest, for instance, in the incentive structure of cooperatives. A quick numerical example illustrates the point: Suppose a group of n people establish an onion cooperative in which each agrees to work a given number of days planting, weeding, harvesting, and then selling the onions in a local market. All contribute their effort to the onions and then share in the collective bounty. A basketful of onions, selling for $10, is produced for every day each person contributes to the cooperative effort. The incentive for a co-op member to be a slacker is evident: "Calling in sick" for a day reduces a member's take by only $10/$n$, whereas a person working independently would lose the full $10 for a missed day. If the value of doing something else for a day besides farming onions lies between $10/$n$ and $10, the co-op member has an incentive to slack off that an individual onion farmer would not have.

The overuse of common-pool resources such as forests or fisheries and the incentive to slack off as a member of a cooperative are symptoms of the "free-rider" problem in collective action. Prisoners' Dilemma games capture a broad class of settings in which the welfare of the individual and the welfare of the group are in conflict with one another. This contrasts with a Coordination game, in which a player may have an incentive to act cooperatively, provided the others do the same.

The relative importance of communication is another difference between the Prisoners' Dilemma and Coordination games. Communication can be vital in a Coordination game, but it is worthless in a single play of the Prisoners' Dilemma. Households in a village may agree that they should restrict tree cutting in a common forest, but the incentive remains to cut as much wood as one needs. Members of a cooperative may agree that each should give 100 percent effort in the work of the cooperative, but the incentive to slack off still exists. "Talk is cheap" in Prisoners' Dilemma games.

The relationship between self-interest and group welfare in a Prisoners' Dilemma also contrasts with normal market exchange. Economists have shown (under a standard set of assumptions[6]) that as individuals pursue their own self-interest in the course of market exchange, they generate an outcome that is Pareto efficient – a

---

[6] The conditions include full information between many buyers and sellers, that each consumer's well-being is unaffected by the consumption choices of another, an absence of transaction costs and externalities, and that some technical assumptions about the preferences of buyers and sellers are satisfied.

result known as the First Theorem of Welfare Economics. This is essentially a proof of the benevolence of Adam Smith's invisible hand, that greed can be harnessed for the common good of society. But in a Prisoners' Dilemma, greed is bad. Unbridled self-interest leads to an outcome that is worse for everyone, that is Pareto *in*efficient.

All of this seems a bit depressing. How can the Dilemma be resolved? As we will see in many of the following chapters, Prisoners' Dilemma problems are solved principally by two means. In traditional societies where the same people interact frequently, Prisoners' Dilemma problems are often solved through *reciprocity*. In other words, an implicit social contract may prescribe people to help others who have helped them in the past. Likewise, a traditional society may sanction those who fail to help others in the group or who fail to display the proper restraint in using public resources. In such cases, the threat of future punishments will often deter short-term opportunism.

In modern societies, where interaction between individuals is frequently nonrepeated and anonymous, society must devise ways to deter defections in one-shot plays of the Prisoners' Dilemma. A modern society with strong governance structures can impose a series of punishments on certain behaviors (e.g., overfishing, deforestation, littering, making too much noise) that will keep antisocial behavior in check. The establishment of formal laws, police, courts, and prisons helps to deter Prisoners' Dilemma–type defections (at least for most people). A system of penalties for defective behavior can turn a Prisoners' Dilemma into a Coordination game, in which cooperative behavior can be a Nash equilibrium.

Trust Games

In economic transactions, one party often has an opportunity to take advantage of another. A peasant farmer rents a mule from his neighbor, overworks it, and returns it exhausted, limping, and hungry. A woman buys from a merchant on credit and never bothers to repay. A day laborer, paid to herd goats to a remote mountain area for fresh food and water, spends the day in the mountains indeed – taking a nap. Because of the dynamic sequence of many economic transactions, they frequently involve some element of trust.

Stanford game theorist David Kreps (1990) captures this element of second-stage vulnerability in what is now commonly referred to as a Trust game. Trust games involve one player taking a preliminary action in which she is vulnerable to a second player acting in his selfish interest. If the second player were to restrain from selfish behavior, both would benefit from the transaction. But understanding the incentives of the second player, the first player eschews the transaction at the outset. Consequently, unless the incentive problem of the second party can be somehow resolved, the transaction never happens. This results in a Pareto-inefficient outcome in which both players are worse off than if somehow the second player could commit to honoring the transaction.

A credit transaction involves an exchange of money for a promise to repay it back in the future (with interest, of course). A number of problems plague credit

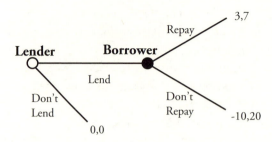

Figure 2.5a. Trust/Lending Game (Extensive Form)

transactions, which we will examine in more detail in Chapter Seven. But one very basic problem is simply the problem of enforcing the promise to repay. Especially in developing countries, where resources are scarce and needs are so often over-whelming (sick children, low crop yields, etc.), there are a thousand decent excuses one could make to justify failing to repay a loan. If it is impossible to enforce loan repayment, then how can a lender lend? If lenders do not lend, how can a low-income economy grow?

The credit transaction in Figure 2.5a illustrates a Trust game, where the game is presented in *dynamic* (sometimes called *extensive*) form. Payoffs are given in order of (first player, second player), in this case (Lender, Borrower). Here we take the example of a $10 loan that is able to generate a 100 percent return on investment. Assume the interest rate is 30 percent, so that $13 is due back to the Lender at payback time. Notice that the Lender is happy to lend the $10 to the borrower, provided the Borrower repays; this yields a payoff of $3 to the Lender, and $7 to the Borrower.

By using a technique appropriate to extensive-form games called *backward induction*, we see that in the second and final stage of the game the borrower has an incentive not to repay. With no recourse against the borrower, the lender in this case would lose not only the interest but also the principal. By backward induction, the lender, understanding the incentives of the borrower in the latter stage of the game, chooses not to lend. This results in a Pareto-inferior (Don't Lend; Don't Repay) solution to the game, and a solution by backward induction is always a Nash equilibrium.

At its most basic level, this story explains one reason so many of the poor in developing countries are left without access to credit. Collateral requirements are one of the most common mechanisms used to solve the Trust game in a lending transaction. But the poor, who arguably have the greatest need for credit, are the least likely to possess the kind of assets needed to secure a loan. (In Chapter Seven, we will see how the lending game can be resolved without collateral!)

Presenting the lending game in normal form in Figure 2.5b shows the similarities and differences between a Trust game and a Prisoners' Dilemma.[7] Both games have

---

[7] At least, theoretically, every extensive-form game can be represented as a normal-form game and vice versa. However, it is typically more convenient to represent games that involve dynamic play, or sequences of moves in extensive form and to represent static games in normal form.

Borrower

		Repay Loan	Don't Repay
Lender	Lend	3 7	20 -10
	Don't Lend	0 0	0 0

Figure 2.5b. Trust/Lending Game (Normal Form)

a single Pareto-inferior Nash equilibrium. However, in a Trust game, the incentive to defect is one sided. (In fact, some refer to such games, especially when presented in the normal form, as a one-sided Prisoners' Dilemma.) Unfortunately, given the structure of the game, it takes two to play, and an incentive for even one player to defect brings about the sad result. This creates a "market failure" in which two parties each have something to gain in a transaction, but flaws in the market prevent it from happening.

We will explore in Chapter Six how rural labor and land markets in developing countries are often characterized by traditional institutions that have evolved to solve Trust games. Distribution of land ownership is often highly unequal, creating a substantial demand for labor among large landowners and a substantial supply of labor among landless or near-landless peasants. A natural solution would be for peasants to sell their agricultural labor at a fixed wage to landowners. However, once a worker is promised a fixed wage, he has an incentive to shirk if his wage doesn't depend on what he produces for the landowner, creating the underlying incentives of a Trust game. One alternative would be for workers to rent parcels of land from the landowner, taking a surplus from the land equal to the revenue from the crop minus land-lease and other costs. But because of the uncertainty of crop yields, a land rental contract may burden a peasant with an unacceptable level of risk. We will see that the common solution to this problem is sharecropping, a contractual mechanism that mitigates the problem of shirking (though not completely) while saddling a peasant with less risk than a land rental contract.

Three factors can help curtail the enforcement problem in Trust games. First, as in Prisoners' Dilemma games, repeated interaction can be crucial. In developed and developing economies alike, reputation matters. The desire to maintain access to credit may induce a borrower to repay a loan. The desire to remain employed may be enough to keep workers from shirking their responsibilities. The desire for repeat business is often enough to keep shops from passing off shoddy goods to their customers. We will study the importance of repeated games repeatedly in this book, beginning in Chapter Four.

Second, legal systems play a pivotal role in facilitating economic transactions because, like Prisoners' Dilemma games, Trust games are also games of "cheap talk." Holding payoffs constant, promises and pregame communication are ineffective since they do not eliminate Player 2's incentive to cheat. However, a credible threat of civil action can alter the payoffs in a Trust game enough to make the second player's promises credible. In the frequently one-shot and anonymous transactions in advanced industrialized economies, legal systems are critical for dealing with the enforcement issues in a Trust game. For example, a firm may have a short-term incentive to hawk shoddy merchandise and make off with a customer's money. But in industrialized societies, buyers are made to feel reasonably confident about even first-time purchases of goods and services. Volumes of tort law, reasonably efficient courts, and an abundance of lawyers sharpening their fangs for lucrative civil lawsuits provide ample incentive for most suppliers to make their goods and services conform to their claims. Paradoxically, the ability of the first player to take civil action against the second player results in a benefit to the second player as well as the first: It may allow for a mutually beneficial transaction to occur that would not occur otherwise. The importance of well-functioning legal systems, until recently, has been a long-neglected component of economic development, and is a subject that we will examine in Chapter Nine.

Third, a strong and broadly based set of ethical norms is critical. Most people don't cheat others, not for fear of being thrown in jail, but because they genuinely feel bad about cheating. Ethical norms help to internalize a concern for the welfare of those aside from the self and are typically established through religious institutions, the community, and the family. The importance of this to economic development will be discussed in more detail when we analyze the importance of *social capital* in Chapter Eleven.

CHAPTER 3

Development Traps and Coordination Games

Just then there was a strong wind. It blew Toad's list out of his hand. The list blew high up into the air. Help! Cried Toad. "My list is blowing away. What will I do without my list?" "Hurry!" said Frog. "We will run and catch it." "No!" shouted Toad. "I cannot do that." Why not?" asked Frog. "Because," wailed Toad, "running after my list is not one of the things that I wrote on my list of things to do."
                                                          – Arnold Lobel, *Frog and Toad Together*

ECONOMIC DEVELOPMENT, AS we know it, is a relative newcomer to human society. For most of history, the world languished in a kind of economic limbo. Centuries after the early Roman era, world per capita income hardly changed, lingering around $400 per year in both the rich and poor areas of the world.[1] (Ironically, for centuries it remained slightly higher in what is now considered the "developing world.") The world economy was dormant, technological change was slow, and advances in human welfare were virtually imperceptible, bringing to mind the ageless and changeless millennia of J. R. R. Tolkien's *Middle Earth*. By the time of the Renaissance, however, per capita income in Europe slowly began to grow – to around $700 by 1500, creeping to $1,100 by the eve of the Industrial Revolution, the beginning of a spectacular economic takeoff.

What finally got the economic ball rolling? The answer, according to many, was the Big Push. The Big Push idea was originally conceived by Paul Rosenstein-Rodan (1943) as he pondered the economic fate of postwar Eastern Europe. However, the first Big Push took place during the Industrial Revolution in Great Britain, later spreading to parts of Western Europe and the United States. Among other factors, such as important innovations in technology and education, the American Big Push involved a combination of investments in key industries – steel, textiles, coal, and railroads. Feeding off one another, investments in these interlinked sectors generated the economic momentum necessary to escape the gravitational pull of the low-equilibrium trap.

Central to the Big Push is the idea of strategic interdependence among the economy's different players. Investment and growth in one area of the economy depend on the actions of other economic players and, equally importantly, on *expectations*

---

[1] Madison (2001).

about the behavior of the others. Because of strategic interdependence among economic actors, in the world of the Big Push, *complementarities, coordination*, and *confidence* are everything.

Looking at the example of early American economic growth, economic historians W. W. Rostow (1960), Robert Fogel (1964), and Albert Fishlow (1965) each studied the relationship between the development of the American railroad system in the nineteenth century and the emergence of the coal, steel, agricultural, and textile industries. Though a lively debate existed between the three over the extent to which railroads were the *leading* sector of development, there was little debate over the high degree of backward and forward linkages between railroads and other key industries. To cite Rostow:

> The path to maturity lay in a complex of industries whose possibilities were, in part, unfolded by the nature of the railway take-off . . . steel flowed from the railroads, as the railroads had flowed from the requirements and consequences of modern cotton-textile industries. But once cheap, good steel was available, many further uses unfolded, including the efficient boiler and the modern steel ship; the machine-tool; new equipment for heavy chemical manufacturers; and new forms of urban construction. (Rostow 1960, p. 61)

Thus, while forward linkages existed from the nascent textile industry to the railways, backward linkages existed from the railways to the steel and coal industries. Western agriculture also benefited tremendously from railway introduction.[2] The steel and coal industries themselves benefited from the railroads, not only from backward linkages, but through forward linkages as railways facilitated the transport of coal and steel.[3]

Forward and backward linkages create *complementarities* between industries. Complementarities often exist between industries, and in many other aspects of everyday life. For example, bartenders eagerly push free bowls of peanuts and popcorn in front of their customers, understanding that the complementarity between salty snacks and fermented beverages induces patrons to guzzle down more beer than they might otherwise. In the context of industry, linkages give rise to complementarities in which investment in Industry A makes investment in Industry B more attractive, leading to more investment there as well. On the other hand, a lack of investment in Industry A lowers returns to investment in Industry B, thereby reducing investment in B. As a result, complementarities in the economy can lead to virtuous cycles of prosperity as well dreary cycles of economic malaise.

Complementarity between industries is what makes one Big Push advantageous over a series of little, independent pushes. In a low-income economy, demand may be so weak that investment in a solitary industry may doom it to failure, especially when there is limited scope for international trade. When such industries exhibit economies of scale, strong demand for their output by complementary industries may be critical to their economic viability, since higher output lowers

---

[2] Fishlow (1965), p. 205.
[3] Fogel (1964), p. 221.

their average cost of production. As a result, coordination and timing of investments matter.

Simultaneous investments in industries that have strong complementarities can jump-start economic growth. Here, each component is necessary for the success of the whole. Consider the roles of a screenwriter, director, and lead actor in the production of a film. Performance by each role is necessary, but none alone is sufficient for a film's success. Any one of the three who excels helps the other two to shine; their roles are complementary. No matter how strong the other two, failure by any of the three will send critics howling and moviegoers sprinting to the exits.

Confidence is also critical to a Big Push. When complementarities exist, the confidence that investors are active in complementary industries induces others to do the same. A lack of such confidence can lead to what economists call a "coordination failure." A coordination failure occurs when economic actors are unable to coordinate on a set of complementary economic activities. Coordination failures are responsible for a common type of development trap whose root is a chronic lack of confidence in the economy.

Though the Big Push idea originated with Rosenstein-Rodan in the 1940s, it was discounted for many years, probably because critics associated it with the disillusionment over development policies based on central planning. (As the idea was put into in practice, it was often corrupt and inept governments that ended up doing most of the pushing.)

Yet, in their zeal to point out the shortcomings of central planning, and the subsequent dependence of industries on the government dole, some astute young economists saw that critics had tossed out a gold nugget of economic insight along with the pyrite. The Big Push was resuscitated in a series of important academic papers, most influentially that of Murphy, Shleifer, and Vishny (1989), all then at the University of Chicago. Since then the "coordination failure" concept has flourished as a way of explaining how economic growth blossoms in poor countries, and even fluctuations in economic growth.

An abstract illustration of a coordination failure is given in Figures 3.1a and 3.1b.[4] Picture an economy made up of a large number of identically sized entrepreneurs, who produce an individual level of output y_i. From the perspective of an individual entrepreneur, each of the rest of the entrepreneurs in the economy produce output y. The solid line in Figures 3.1a and 3.1b is a *best response curve*, showing the optimal strategy for the individual entrepreneur, y_i, as a best response to y. The curve is upward sloping: If complementarities exist, higher output by others increases the demand for the output of each individual enterprise, and lower output by others decreases it. A Nash equilibrium occurs when the best response curve crosses the 45° line, where $y_i = y$, where none of the entrepreneurs wants to change from his existing level of y_i given the output of the others.

Figure 3.1a represents the case where only a single Nash equilibrium exists (reminiscent of the type of economy described by the traditional classical economic

----

[4] This model is a simplification of Cooper and John (1988) taken from Romer (1995).

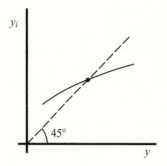

Figure 3.1a. Coordination Failure (Single Equilibrium)

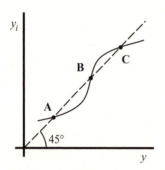

Figure 3.1b. Coordination Failure (Multiple Equilibria)

models). Figure 3.1b, however, shows an economy in which multiple levels of equilibrium economic output (and development traps) are possible. If each entrepreneur expects others to produce at output level at A, the individual entrepreneur's best response is likewise the lower level of individual output at A, and similarly for points B and C.

Notice that the Pareto inefficient point A is a *stable* Nash equilibrium. At levels of y below point A, the best response of the individual entrepreneur is $y_i > y$, thus inducing overall production to increase toward point A. Levels of y between points A and B, where $y_i < y$, bring the economy backward toward point A. In this respect, the unstable equilibrium at point B represents a threshold level of economic activity, or even *confidence* about economic activity. If individual entrepreneurs begin to produce at a level even slightly above point B, perhaps because this is what they think others are doing, the economy converges to the Pareto superior point C, also a stable Nash equilibrium.

Because of its flexibility and integration of complementarities, coordination, and confidence in the economy, the coordination failure idea and its numerous complex variations may be among the best thinking tools economists have today for understanding how economies actually work.

Let's relate this idea to the early American development example with pivotal sectors being coal, steel, and railroads. Steel uses coal as an input, and steel is used to make railroads. Railroads use coal and steel as inputs, and are used to extract coal and haul it to steel mills for smelting. Here we have an example in which complementarities abound. To produce profitably, each industry requires inputs as

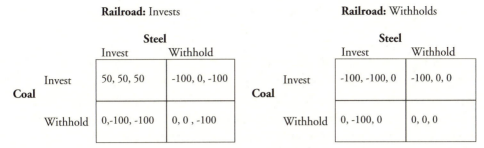

Figure 3.2. Coordination Failure/Coal, Railroad, and Steel Investment

well as a source of demand for its output. Suppose that the fixed costs of investment in each of the three industries equal 100, giving the industry the capacity to produce 150 units of output at a variable cost of 1 each. Suppose also that each industry charges of price equal to 2 and that output demand is equal to exactly the same 150 units. This coordination game yields the payoff matrices in Figure 3.2.

Payoffs in the three-player game are given to the row player (Coal), the column player (Steel), and the matrix player (Railroad), respectively. There are two important Nash equilibria in the game. The first (Invest; Invest; Invest) occurs when each industry has access to the necessary inputs and output demand and receives a payoff of 50. In the second (Withhold; Withhold; Withhold), no investment occurs and each receives a payoff of zero. In all other strategy combinations, at least one player withholds investment to avoid being left out on a limb by the others. If any industry believes that another is unlikely to invest, it also withholds investment, leading to the unfortunate noninvestment equilibrium.

Like the game in Figure 2.1, this particular coordination game is a Stag Hunt, in which all players would like to take the risky action, but only if they are confident that they won't get burned. In fact, the more you study economics, the more you understand that confidence is an essential ingredient to economic growth. Stag Hunt games capture this idea succinctly.

Starting at economic ground zero, potential investors will invest in any one of our three industries only if they feel confident that investment will take place in the other two complementary industries. How confident must they be? Because the payoff to noninvestment is zero, the expected payoff from investing must be positive. Using the inequality that must hold, $50p + (1 - p)(-100) > 0$, we know that players won't invest unless they believe there is at least a two-thirds probability that investment in both of the other industries will occur.

Where does such confidence come from? Particularly, in the context of developing countries with a history of poverty and underinvestment, confidence may be in short supply. Sometimes a positive technology shock, such as the widespread introduction of computers or a new communication technology can serve as the necessary confidence builder. Occasionally, major political changes can serve as a catalyst for economic optimism. Aware of the implications of confidence for economic (and political) success, political leaders sometimes try to generate confidence through catchy, confidence-inspiring slogans. In still other cases, confidence grows when the government actively supports a vital sector of the economy, such as the support of nascent manufacturing industries in South Korea and the information technology industry in India.

This brings us to the issue of what role the state should have in a Big Push.[5] Many economic advisors, especially in the few decades after World War II, cast government in the starring role of Big Pushes. The tide has turned on this issue, but there remains a vigorous academic debate over the respective roles of the *visible* hand and the *invisible* hand as effective coordinators. Both sides contain persuasive arguments: Governments, some argue, are better coordinators because their deeper pockets allow them to better establish credibility that investments in key industries will indeed occur. Proponents of governments as Big Pushers further argue that governments, ostensibly with a bird's-eye view of the economy, are able to see "the forest and not just the trees," and are thus able to take maximal advantage of potential spillover effects between industries.

Many others argue that private economic actors should fill the leading role because they face a healthier set of economic incentives. In his 2006 book *The White Man's Burden*, New York University's Bill Easterly distinguishes between "Planners" and "Searchers." He argues that Planners, who tend to favor large, simultaneous, state-coordinated spending in aid and industry, lack the feedback and accountability mechanisms for appropriate responses to economic opportunity. Searchers, who individually seek profitable or welfare-improving opportunities in the economy from the ground level, are more directly accountable for their efforts through economic and political markets. According to this view, the most successful Big Pushes may be elicited not by government planners, but by a simultaneous and widespread confidence among individual economic agents that an economy is ripe for a barrage of related, but not centrally coordinated, investments. Many would argue, nevertheless, that the state can play a major role in creating the stability and public infrastructure that inspires economic agents with this kind of confidence.

A good question is then why private actors in the economy such as Easterly's Searchers don't simply coordinate their economic investments and reap the ensuing rewards. The issue is that no single investor wants to be caught with his financial shorts down (if you can pardon the pun). At some point, whether coordinated or not, investments must yield real returns. This occurs only if in the end, something useful is created for consumers. There is an analogy here in the stock market: Hardly a day passes in which equity investors do not pine for a bull market that would drive stock prices ever more heavenward, showering equity holders with riches. But unless a confidence-driven bull market is supported by the creation of real value in the economy, confidence-induced bubbles eventually pop, causing painful losses for many. Because individual agents remain accountable for losses as well as gains, they are constantly on guard against these risks.

---

[5] For an excellent resource on this debate, see Yergin and Stanislaw (1998, 2002).

In the debate between the relative merits of the visible versus invisible hand in solving coordination failures, economists have tried hard to make sense of the take-off in economic growth that has occurred in East Asia. Not surprisingly, those with a free-market bias tend to attribute the East Asian economic success to its economic openness and savvy trade in global export markets.[6] Others have highlighted the role that governments in countries such as Singapore, Taiwan, and South Korea have played in the strategic coordination of industries.[7] If there does exist a consensus in the debate over the source of growth in the Asian takeoff, it is perhaps that governments in the booming Asian economies have played *some* kind of helpful role, and maybe a pivotal role, in the coordination of education, infrastructure, and export industries. Congruent with some of this line of thinking, most economists today would maintain that at the very least there is a Big Push role for Planners in facilitating investment in all levels of education and in the provision and maintenance of physical infrastructure, public investments that are likely to realize dividends across the economy, while leaving the risks and rewards of private industry to the Searchers.

Education as a Coordination Game

Along with other American children growing up in 1970s TV rerun-land, one of my two favorite after-school heroes was Daniel Boone, who built his own house, killed his own meat, and wore clothes and a coonskin cap made from the same animals he shot and ate. The division of labor being what it was on the wild frontier, he was the definitive economic generalist. Aside from a few fur trades here and there, Boone was his own economy. Another of my heroes was Maxwell Smart (Agent 86), the comic creation of scriptwriting geniuses Buck Henry and Mel Brooks, and a specialist in Cold War espionage. Though he was an inept klutz in most things, Agent 86 could, however, stealthily operate a spy-phone disguised as a bologna sandwich. Although being a generalist (at least on TV) seemed more exciting than being a specialist, an economy full of generalists is often an economy that is stuck in a development trap.

The complementarities phenomenon affects educational decisions, and as a result, coordination failures in education can lead to development traps. Some of the most striking features in any statistical comparison between developing and industrialized countries are differences in education and literacy, such as those in Table 3.1. Moreover, these statistics undoubtedly underestimate the true correlation between poverty and educational underachievement since there are also tremendous variations within countries. Poor regions within individual countries are nearly always associated with education levels that are below the average of even a poor country.

The traditional remedy for such savage inequalities has often been to fix the problem on the supply side by increasing the number of schools and teachers. Certainly this does make it easier for many families to keep their kids in school. For a moment,

---

[6] For example, Bhagwati (2003).
[7] See, for example, Amsden (1989), Wade (1990, 2004), and Rodrik (1995, 1996).

Table 3.1. Education and literacy by world region

Region	% School enrollment[a]	Literacy
Sub-Saharan Africa	44	62.4
South Asia	54	56.3
East Asia/Pacific	65	87.1
Latin America/Caribbean	81	89.2
Arab States	60	60.8
C&E Europe/fmr. USSR	79	99.3
OECD Countries[b]	87	99.0

Notes: [a]Combined primary, secondary, and tertiary enrollment ratios.
[b]United States, Canada, Western Europe, Japan, Australia, and New Zealand.
Source: UNDP, *Human Development Report*, 2003.

however, let's focus on the demand side, an increasing feature of recent research.[8] Is there a reason that families in impoverished regions might *rationally* choose a low level of education for their children? In a world of complementarities, the unfortunate answer might very well be yes. In education, we have an area in which complementarities abound: My optimal level of education is positively related to what I expect yours to be, and vice versa. Where there are complementarities, there is strategic interdependence in which multiple Nash equilibria and development traps are possible, and where coordination and confidence matter.

Education, like the construction of a factory, is an investment in which current resources are sacrificed in exchange for future benefits. Although numerous personal and social spillover benefits are associated with higher educational levels, the monetary rewards to education depend heavily on the division of labor in society. As the division of labor increases, likewise does the return to acquiring specialized skills.

In my field survey work, I have had the opportunity to personally interview hundreds of households in rural Central America, most of whom are parents with kids. The majority of these parents withdraw their children from school around age 10 to 12, even when more schooling is available. Many expect their children to live the rest of their lives in the same impoverished village, working as they have, in subsistence agriculture. Little Central American children, like other little children, are not especially productive on the farm; they can be kept in school, especially if it is free, at little cost to the household. But as they grow older and more knowledgeable about agricultural tasks, the opportunity cost of their education increases. Given the thin market in rural Central American villages for biology degrees, tax accounting skills, and perhaps even secondary-school-level numeracy and literacy, the number of households that withdraw their children from school at an early age is unsurprising. They grow up to be generalists, creating an economy of Daniel Boones in rural Central America. They are Jacks and Jills of all trades for which skills are abundant but masters of little requiring skills that are scarce. As a result, most rural regions

---

[8] See, for example, Coady and Parker (2004) on the PROGRESA antipoverty schooling program in Mexico.

in Central America are stuck in a development trap: Everyone is a generalist and no one is a specialist, and as long as everyone expects the situation to remain the same, no one has the incentive to do anything different.

Coordination failures in education arise because the returns to education depend on how many other people in the same economy are educated. Individual choices about education are not made in a vacuum; they are made in the context of the relevant society and its corresponding division of labor. My first experience working in a developing country, the Dominican Republic in 1988, helped me to understand this point. Despite the embarrassingly large number of years I had logged in school, many of my Dominican neighbors, though lacking a high school education and living in relative poverty, were better at doing more things than I was. Doubtless, I held a considerable advantage in solving economic and statistical problems. Nevertheless, from the perspective of the Dominicans, I lacked a number of essential skills. Foremost among these were the ability to fix a broken carburetor, repair an old shoe, slay a chicken, and, most importantly, connect a hidden wire to a special place on the nearest telephone pole to receive free ESPN. I was a specialist; the average Dominican was a proud generalist. In the Dominican Republic, my specialized skill set was a mismatch for the market.

Put simply, parents rationally give their children about the same amount of education as they expect from other children in their community. Those who overinvest in education get burned by a low division of labor in that community, which reduces the demand for specialized skills. Those who underinvest in education lose out when there is a high division of labor, because the demand for nonspecialized skills is low. This is illustrated by the game Figure 3.3.

Assume that there are three strategies in our simplified two-family economy. Each family, Postigo or Lora, can choose for its children a mere primary school

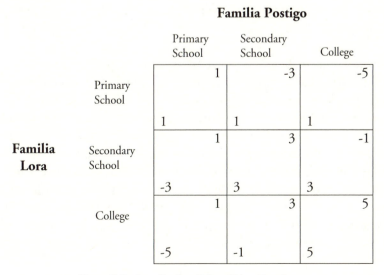

Figure 3.3. Coordination Failure/Education Game

education (in which only basic skills are acquired), a secondary school education, which may include some vocational education (in which a moderate degree of specialization occurs), or college, (which produces greater specialization). Notice the three Nash equilibria in the coordination game corresponding to matching educational choices. The equilibria can be Pareto ranked: All are better off in the example if everyone chooses college, but again, expectations matter. Lacking the confidence that others will choose anything but primary school, primary school becomes a best response for everyone. Once more we have an example in which an individual choice that may be rational in the context of one's environment may not be collectively rational from the perspective of society.

In most developing countries, when children are not in school, they are typically working, either for their parents, or somebody else. Child labor has probably existed since the dawn of civilization, persisting even through the beginnings of modern industrialization, including the now infamous abuse of British children in the early decades of its industrial revolution. It continues today throughout the developing world. The International Labor Organization estimates that in 2000 there were 211 million children aged 5 to 14 engaged in economic activity, including 123 million in Asia, 48 million in Africa, and 17 million in Latin America and the Caribbean.[9]

Economists have studied child labor for years, but in the last decade, they have made breakthroughs by viewing child labor as a type of coordination game. Perhaps the most celebrated work in this area is that of Cornell University's Kaushik Basu and former student Pham Hoang Van (1998). They describe the following vicious circle: The presence of children in the labor market increases the supply of labor, making wages for adults decline. Parents, who might ordinarily like to keep their children in school, are forced to send them into the labor market simply because their own reduced wages make the family unable to reach subsistence consumption solely on the adult family labor. Thus, the trap: Low adult wages, caused significantly by child labor, create even more child labor. And hence, the solution: Every family could remove its children from the labor market all at once, driving up wages and removing the impetus for child labor in the first place, the epitome of a Stag Hunt.

As is often true for Stag Hunts stuck in a bad equilibrium, with education there is a potentially strong role for government. Mandatory educational requirements could at least theoretically solve the coordination failures involving child education and child labor simultaneously. The problem is that despite stringent laws on the books, parents customarily ignore the laws, and it is impossible (and undesirable) for the government to punish everybody. Moreover, where the absence of income from children could push a family below subsistence with low adult wages, which family will go first? An important implication: It is necessary not just to change educational *laws*; the state must also change the individual *perceptions* about the extent to which everybody else will actually obey the law.

---

[9] International Labor Organization (2003).

Coordination Failures and Globalization

Let's consider now how coordination failures affect the development of low-income countries in a globalized economy. India has been welcomed as the most recent member of the Asian high-growth club, having taken spectacular advantage of modern communications technologies. The astonishing growth of the business services and software industries in Indian cities such as Bangalore and Hyderabad is fascinating, partly because it appears to have awakened a dormant economic giant from a very long slumber. But it is also fascinating because it illustrates the resolution of a coordination failure involving both human capital and physical capital investment in the context of an open economy.

With its independence from Britain in 1947, India steadfastly rejected large-scale participation in the greater world economy, doggedly clinging to an import-substitution policy. Outward economic contact was eschewed as India turned inward. High domestic tariff rates nearly asphyxiated foreign trade, while the Indian government appeared to go out of its way to make things as difficult as possible for foreign investors.[10] In the postindependence years, India's economic ennui produced a stagnant economy, where per capita GDP growth lagged at only 1.5 percent per year.[11] U. C. Berkeley's Annalee Saxinian describes the environment faced by Indian high-tech companies a generation ago:

> Prior to 1984, the Indian software industry operated within the framework of a highly regulated, autarkic model of import-substitution-led industrialization (ISI) and the ideology of self-reliance that guided the Indian economy. This stifled entrepreneurs and isolated India from the global economy. As a result, efforts to promote software exports during the period never took off. Policies that permitted the import of state-of-the-art computers in exchange for a guarantee to export a certain amount of software were not enthusiastically received. Import procedures were cumbersome, duties were high, and obtaining foreign exchange for business expenses was difficult.[12]

After the 1984 national election, the new administration of Rajiv Gandhi would begin to implement a set of coordinated policy changes that continued with his successors, and ultimately affected both India and the information technology industry ever after.

First came the recognition by the Gandhi administration of software as an official "industry," which under Indian law allowed it to receive special treatment from the government, including special credits for investment and reduced import duties on critical inputs such as computer hardware. In 1986, the government passed the Computer Software Export, Development, and Training Policy, which facilitated the flow of venture capital to new startup firms, and invited foreign direct investment from abroad.[13] An early association of software firms convinced the government to finance a telecommunications network that paved the way for the electronic export of low-level programming services to overseas clients. Not long after, the

---

[10] See Yergin and Stanislaw (2002), ch. 8.
[11] Krueger and Chinoy (2002).
[12] Saxenian (2002).
[13] Saxenian (2002), p. 172.

Indian Department of Electronics introduced software technology parks, which gave export-oriented software firms tax exemptions and guaranteed them access to high-speed satellite links and reliable electricity.[14] Moreover, Indian public universities and polytechnic institutes began to churn out profuse numbers of graduates in software engineering and computer science fields. By the late 1990s, India was graduating 220,000 software and computer science engineers annually. Bangalore alone produced about 25,000 per year, almost as many as the United States.[15]

This set of coordinated policies paved the way for the first multinationals to set up shop in Bangalore. Texas Instruments established a small software center in 1986; Hewlett-Packard later followed, and others began to trickle in. The trickle soon became a flood: By 2004, the number of multinationals located in Bangalore alone had grown to 450, including Cisco Systems, Intel, SAP, Cadence, JVC, Oracle, Analog Devices, General Electric, Wipro, Kodak, and Sun Microsystems, employing in total more than 170,000 workers. New domestic startups began to form around the multinationals; soon the number of software and outsourcing companies had burgeoned to more than 1,300 in Bangalore alone.[16]

Hyderabad, in the neighboring state of Andhra Pradesh, has witnessed similarly breathtaking growth in information technology. Led by Andhra Pradesh's techno-savvy chief minister, Chandrababu Naidu, Hyderabad, home to more than 1,000 registered software companies, has created a vast infrastructure to support not only low-level outsourced programming and technology support services, but also software research and design.[17] Naidu's original goal was to create 1 million jobs in technology industries and technology-related customer call centers.[18] The city is well on its way: Among other developments, Hyderabad is host to a twenty-eight-acre Microsoft campus with capacity for 1,600 programmers and other employees.[19]

The phenomenal growth of the information-technology sector in India makes sense viewed through the lens of coordination failures. Indeed, India's experience is consistent with theoretical work in coordination failures by Harvard University's Dani Rodrik.[20] In an influential paper, Rodrik describes a coordination failure in which multiple equilibria exist for developing countries that are poorly endowed with physical capital, but that possess a reasonably educated labor force. Two outcomes are possible: specialization in high-tech or low-tech goods. If there are economies of scale in intermediate goods markets, the state can solve the coordination failure with coordinated policies that attract a large quantity of foreign investment, which increases the demand for (and hence lowers the cost of) a wide array of specialized intermediate inputs, such as producer services or workers with specialized labor qualifications.

---

[14] Saxenian (2002), p. 173.

[15] "Calling Bangalore: Multinationals Making it a Hub for High-tech Research," *Business Week*, June 25, 2002, p. 52.

[16] "Bangalore: Tech Eden No More," *Business Week*, November 1, 2004, p. 57.

[17] *BBC News*, Friday, September 8, 2000.

[18] "Cyber City Tested by High-Tech Downturn," *San Jose Mercury News*, February 8, 2002.

[19] *New York Times*, November 16, 2004, p. W1 (Late East Coast Edition).

[20] Rodrik (1995, 1996).

Rodrik's theory, though developed out of the experiences of South Korea and Eastern Europe, can help us understand the recent Indian experience. While each of India's policies may have been insufficient alone, complementarities in coordinated policies favoring large-scale foreign investment, infrastructure, and continuing investments in technical education all appear to have been critical in generating the dramatic growth of the Indian information technology sector.

Moreover, the Indian experience points to a role for political leadership in solving coordination failures and creating the expectations of a new and improved equilibrium. In some cases having a Naidu may not be sufficient, or even necessary, when economies are able to coordinate by themselves, such as the technology industry in California's Silicon Valley. But a charismatic leader who is perceived as being wise and beneficent by a large number of people may help to create a focal point Nash equilibrium for key economic players that could be unachievable otherwise.

Complementarities in International Capital and Labor

A misconception today is that the most foreign direct investment flows into developing countries to build sweatshops that take advantage of low wage rates. The popular picture is of a giant race to the bottom, where the lowest wages and the laxest environmental laws always win. Clearly this cannot be the whole truth; if it were, then all of the world's foreign direct investment would be headed for countries like Burma, Chad, and Haiti. In fact, the truth is closer to the opposite. Every year, more than two-thirds of all foreign direct investment flows into the richest economies, in the United States, Japan, and the European Union. Thus what exists is typically more like a frenzied race to the top. For the developing countries, often starved for foreign investment, this begins to smell like a development trap. What accounts for this? Can't multinational firms recognize a good deal when they see one?

Again, the explanation lies with complementarities. Complementarities at the firm level are created when the existence of a large cluster of firms in a region makes it advantageous for new firms to locate there as well. Some benefits may come from lower costs of production due to experienced and conveniently located suppliers of intermediate goods. Other benefits are more esoteric, such as the transmission of ideas, innovations, and know-how between business people in pubs, coffee houses, and social gatherings.[21] All together these things are referred to as *agglomeration economies*. When agglomeration economies are present, producers stumble over each other to get to where the action is.

Returning to the Indian example for a moment, the location of an overseas technology campus in India was undoubtedly more difficult for Texas Instruments in 1986 than for Microsoft in 2004. By the time Microsoft decided to build its campus in Hyderabad, agglomeration economies were strong enough in the Indian high-tech cities to ease the entrance of yet another firm. Such agglomerations, of course, have long existed and been the source of incalculable investment in the prosperous regions of industrialized countries.

[21] For more on this, see Saxenian (1996).

Investment naturally flows to places where its productivity is augmented by complementary skills and know-how. A reasonably well-functioning infrastructure helps too. Investment typically moves to a low-cost region only after a long process in which wage rates, housing prices, and the general cost of living have finally been bid up so high (see Silicon Valley) that the cost of plant location at long last begins to outweigh the benefit of agglomeration economies. Investment then begins to look for a new, cheaper location with a sufficient level of existing complementary assets, where the process starts all over again.

This story of international *capital* movement also applies to international *labor* movement. Another popular economic misconception today is that immigrants to industrialized countries are by-and-large poor and uneducated, the huddled masses in the immigration line. A more accurate picture is of immigrants waiting in line with graduation caps, cell phones, and personal digital assistants. The reality of emigration from poor to rich countries is the Brain Drain. Migration to countries like the United States brings the greatest rewards to those who match their more advanced skill set with the capital and technology existing in economically advanced countries.

This matching in the labor market may occur simply because of the wider division of labor in industrialized countries. Harvard's Michel Kremer, however, suggests that it may be due to production processes that differ from the traditional way that economists have learned to think about the relationship between inputs and outputs. The traditional way of thinking sees quantity and quality of labor as essentially being substitutable, so that the value of, say, twenty-five productive workers equals the output of seventy-five slackers who are only one-third as productive. Kremer's (1993) "O-Ring Theory of Economic Development" posits that the traditional view is misleading when mistakes by unproductive workers are costly to a firm. His theory breaks down production by a firm into a given number of "tasks," where the value of the firm's product is maintained if each of the tasks is carried out successfully. However, when a worker makes a mistake carrying out her task, the product is ruined. (The name of his well-known paper comes from a single mistake in the design of an O-Ring in the engineering of the Space Shuttle Challenger, which caused it to explode 73 seconds after its January 1986 liftoff.)

"O-Ring-type" production may apply to many types of industries: The value of an otherwise expensive pair of pants falls to zero with a bad zipper. The value of a meal at a restaurant created by a prize-winning chef falls to zero when a clumsy waiter spills it in a customer's lap. Kremer shows that with this type of production, productive firms with existing high-quality workers (who make fewer mistakes) have an incentive to pay a premium for other high-quality workers. Less-productive firms with less-productive workers will be out-bid by the high-quality firms for high-quality workers, and so will be stuck with hiring lower-paid less-productive workers. Kremer shows that this kind of assortative matching process may explain why wage and productivity differences between countries are so enormous. It also explains why a high-skilled worker from a developing country has an especially strong motivation to emigrate to a more economically advanced country, despite the fact that his skill may be more scarce at home. Bill Easterly describes it well in *The Elusive Quest for Growth* (2001):

> What if skilled workers can move across national boundaries? The matching story helps explain the brain drain of some skilled workers from the poorer countries to the rich countries. A star chef in Morocco knows that he can match with more highly skilled restaurant people in France than in Morocco, and thus will be paid more in France. A surgeon from India will be paid more when she can match up with the highly skilled nurses, anesthesiologists, radiologists, medical technicians, bookkeepers, and receptionists. The highly skilled surgeon from India would prefer to move to United States, were other highly skilled workers can be found. (p. 158)

The astonishing size and sucking power of the Brain Drain is portrayed in detail by William Carrington and Enrica Detragiache (1999) of the International Monetary Fund. Their study, using 1990 U.S. Census data, finds that only one-half million out of a total of 7 million U.S. immigrants had less than a secondary school education. People from a second group, consisting of about 2.7 million, were immigrants with secondary school educations, coming mainly from Mexico. A third group of about 1.5 million people consisted of university-educated immigrants from Asia and the Pacific. Moreover, they found that 74 percent of immigrants to the United States from India and 75 percent of immigrants from Africa were university educated. In some countries, the power of the Brain Drain is so strong that it hardly leaves any college-educated people behind. For example, in Jamaica and Guyana, 67 percent and 77 percent of residents with tertiary educations, respectively, had immigrated to the United States! Carrington and Detragiache conclude that

> Our estimates show that there is an overall tendency for migration rates to be higher for highly educated individuals. A number of countries – especially small countries in Africa, the Caribbean, and Central America – lost more than 30 percent of this group to migration. We have also found a sizable brain drain from Iran, Korea, the Philippines, and Taiwan. These numbers suggest that in several developing countries the outflow of highly educated individuals is a phenomenon that policymakers cannot ignore.

Clearly, there are both winners and losers from the Brain Drain, with some of the winners being relatives who remain behind to collect remittances sent by the migrants. Taking remittances into account, if highly skilled workers from developing countries are more productive after immigrating to developed countries, those left behind should theoretically have more resources to invest in their own education if their overseas relatives are generous. Some research has indicated that this may indeed be the case.[22] Nevertheless, the more powerful forces of the Brain Drain indicate a world in which complementarities provides strong incentives for the skilled to match with the skilled, leaving the unskilled behind with the unskilled.

A simple game illustrates this idea. Imagine that there are n as yet unlocated high-technology workers spread out over the United States and the rest of the world. Each has complementary skills with other high-tech workers such that each is made more productive (and therefore is paid a higher wage) by working among those

---

[22] See Beine, Docquier, and Rapoport (2003).

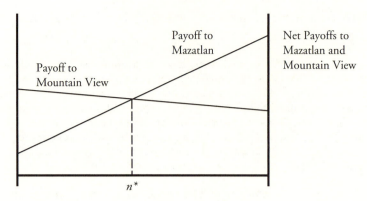

Number of high-tech workers locating in Mazatlan.

Figure 3.4. Coordination Failure/High Tech Migration Game

with complementary high-tech skills. At the same time, each also would prefer, all else equal, to locate in an area in which high wages have not already bid up the general price of everything. Suppose that there are two regional centers of high-tech employment: Mountain View, California, and Mazatlán, Mexico, both having highly desirable amenities and climates. However, a very large number of similar high-tech workers already exist in Mountain View, but very few as yet exist in Mazatlan.

Because of the large number of high-tech workers already in Mountain View, the highest payoff to any one of the n (as yet un-located) workers is to join the large mass of high-tech workers in Mountain View. However, as the game is presented in Figure 3.4, if all of the n workers were to decide to simultaneously locate in Mazatlán, agglomeration economies created by the mass tech-migration to the area, the mutual complementarities of their skills, along with the lower existing costs of living, would yield a higher payoff to them in Mazatlán. The critical mass required to induce any to relocate to Mazatlán is denoted by n^* in that for any of the n high-tech workers to relocate to Mazatlán, she must expect at least n^* of the others to do so. But because the decision made by each of the n workers is made individually and not collectively, each will decide to locate in Mountain View. In the absence of some almost unimaginable level of communication between these dispersed tech workers, each is likely to believe that the others will locate in Mountain View anyway; it is a far more likely focal point than Mazatlán. This decision results in a lower payoff to the newly locating workers, further exacerbates the cost of living and congestion in Mountain View, and causes Mazatlán to remain relatively poor.

In this kind of world, we begin to have something that looks less and less like the well-behaved world of classical economics in which the scarce resource stays put to reap its rewards, and more like the brutal assortative matching process of high-school clique formation. Is it only the stumbling block of immigration laws and other frictions associated with the psychological costs of leaving family and friends that prevent a nearly complete exodus of skills and human capital from the developing world? The point is that in a world of complementarities, productive resources go where productive resources are, and this can leave the poor behind.

CHAPTER 4

Rural Poverty, Economic Development, and the Environment

If you ignore the environment, it will go away.
— Berkeley Bumper Sticker

EASTER ISLAND IS one of the most isolated spots on earth, lying 2,100 miles to the west of Chile and 4,000 miles to the southeast of Hawaii. The island is renowned for its massive stone faces that stoically gaze over the Pacific, the *moai* statues, carved by the native Rapanui half a millennium ago during the zenith of an ancient and mysterious civilization. This same thriving island civilization of perhaps 10,000–15,000 inhabitants once survived on cultivation of sweet potatoes, yams, bananas, domesticated chickens, and, of course, fishing. But by the arrival of Dutch explorers in 1722, the Rapanui had dwindled to a few thousand; by 1877, the entire population of Easter Island had plummeted to just 111 half-starved natives.[1]

In his book *Collapse* (2005), UCLA geographer Jared Diamond explains the principal blunder of the Rapanui civilization: deforestation.[2] Trees and timber had been vital to the ancient Rapanui. Trees prevented crop erosion and provided a native habitat for birds and animals important for supplementing the local diet. Wood provided raw materials for hand tools, logs used in the erection of the *moai* statues, fuel for warmth during cool and rainy nights, and most importantly, for constructing fishing canoes.[3] Since Easter Island receives only 50 inches of rainfall per year (scanty by tropical standards), trees grow slowly, leaving the island's inhabitants more vulnerable to the "tragedy of the commons."

Careful study by archaeologists of the ancient Rapanui's rubbish dumps has shown that by the time island forests began to disappear around 1500, fish likewise began to disappear from diet of natives: Large trees, once used for canoe-making, had vanished. Crop yields began to fall from soil erosion, so that nuts, apples, and other wild fruits dwindled as a food source. Lacking a natural habitat, native birds and animals became extinct on the island. When Captain Cook arrived in 1774, he described the islanders as "small, lean, timid, and miserable."[4] By the eighteenth

---

[1] See Van Tilburg (1994).
[2] Diamond (2005), pp. 79–120.
[3] Diamond (2005), pp. 107, 108.
[4] Diamond (2005), pp. 108, 109.

century, the Rapanui were reduced to feeding on rodents and, later, to cannibalism. As Diamond relates, an inflammatory taunt in the latter days of the civilization became "The flesh of your mother sticks between my teeth."[5]

The relationship between economic development and the natural environment is one of the most critical relationships in the development process, but it is also a peculiar one. In many indigenous cultures, such as the native Rapanui, humans often live in tandem with their environment and thus directly rely on it for their subsistence. However, in the initial phases of economic development, significant degradation of the environment can occur as population pressure and modern technology induce society to sacrifice natural resources and environmental quality for higher income. This pattern occurs regularly across most parts of the developing world. During this period, critical intermediate institutional structures often fail to regulate this early exploitation of environmental resources.

The strongest protection of environmental resources is typically found in the high-income countries. A rich society becomes increasingly eager to pay for a clean environment, and it begins to demand that the state take a leading institutional role in natural resource regulation and protection. Consequently, economists generally view the relationship between per capita income and environmental quality as being U-shaped.[6] Thus depending on the stage of development and the quality of institutional structures that regulate the use of the commons, economic development can be the natural environment's best friend – or its worst enemy.

The depth of the environmental plunge in the intermediate phases of development depends on the health of local institutions that exist to govern the environmental commons. The health of these institutions is shaped by an array of factors related to human social organization and the science of environmental resource sustainability. It is thus one of the very few areas of serious investigation in which economists, political scientists, anthropologists, biologists, and legal scholars actually communicate with one another, and simple game-theoretic models have become a principal means of this communication.

The outcome in the real world, resulting from the interplay of these different human and environmental factors, is far from straightforward. A bewildering assortment of outcomes exists, ranging from comprehensive environmental destruction, to instances in which environmental resources are efficiently and sustainably utilized, enjoyed, and preserved.

This chapter focuses on the use (and abuse) of environmental resources such as forests, water, fisheries, and grazing lands. These are all examples of *common-pool resources* (CPRs), which share a pair of common characteristics: (1) their consumption is *rival*, but (2) it is *nonexcludable*. Rivalry means that consumption by one party precludes consumption by another. For example, the fish that I catch, fry, and eat is one that you can't. Excludability means that it is easy to control access to a resource, and to exclude others from consuming it. I can exclude you from

---

[5] Diamond (2005), p. 109.
[6] The relationship is often referred to as the "*Environmental Kuznets Curve*," mirroring a similar pattern to the relationship between economic growth and income equality discovered by Kuznets (1955).

	Excludable	Non-Excludable
Rival	**Private Goods** *e.g.* banana, toothbrush	**Common-Pool Resources** *e.g.* forests, fisheries
Non-rival	**Club Goods** *e.g.* cable TV, honor society	**Public Goods** *e.g.* lighthouse, national defense

Figure 4.1. Categorization of Goods by Rivalry and Excludability

eating my fish, but not from using my lighthouse to guide your boat to safety. The characteristics of CPRs relative to other goods are shown in Figure 4.1.

The combination of rivalry and nonexcludability is what creates the individual incentive to exploit a common-pool resource for personal gain, collectively leading to a Pareto inefficient outcome for society – often called the *"tragedy of the commons."* As the Danish economist Ester Boserup (1965) observed, population pressure among the rural poor in developing countries is another critical ingredient in the commons tragedy. Lacking a fairly dense population, a commons tragedy is unlikely, if not impossible. As Boserup argued, it is rural population pressure that not only leads to the development of formal agriculture and property rights, but also the need for institutions that regulate conflict over CPRs. Because the rural poor in less-developed countries tend to be heavily dependent on the local availability of common-pool resources (such as firewood for cooking and for heating the home), the lack of institutional controls can lead them to collectively overexploit a natural resource as each household attempts to satisfy its short-term needs.

Addressing this predicament, however, is a problem of *collective action*. A group of people may understand that they will be better off by placing communal limits on fishing or cutting down trees in a forest. But the temptation of each individual to free-ride on the goodwill of others may create a set of individual incentives that leads to the collectively inferior outcome. Unless there is some device to enforce cooperative agreements between individuals, individual *rationality* can produce collective *irrationality*.

This is the essential argument laid out in Mancur Olson's (1965) *The Logic of Collective Action* captured in the Prisoners' Dilemma. The Prisoners' Dilemma in general form is given in Figure 4.2a, where s is the payoff to shared and "sustainable" use of the CPR, t is the commons "tragedy" payoff, r is the payoff to the "rogue" who Plunders the resource while the other player Conserves, and v is the respective "victim" of the rogue who Conserves while the rogue Plunders.

With payoffs ordered $r > s > t > v$, the game forms a Prisoners' Dilemma. (The relative payoff values are easy to remember because they are in alphabetical order.) The Nash equilibrium in a one-shot play of the game is the regrettable (Plunder; Plunder) outcome in which each player receives only t when mutual payoffs of

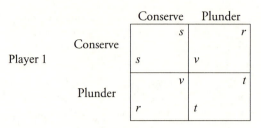

Figure 4.2a. Resource Conservation Game

$s > t$ are possible. Fortunately, the (Plunder; Plunder) outcome is by no means the *only* possible outcome to a CPR game. Much of the remainder of this chapter will discuss why it need not be so.

Repeated Interaction

One way that the commons tragedy might be averted is if the commons game is played repeatedly between the same players. Consider Zeke and Deke, two Appalachian bachelors living in remote huts on opposite ends of a small lake. Every day, each goes down to his dock to fish for his dinner, and every day each can choose to either Conserve or Plunder the fishing commons. Let's assume that both Zeke and Deke can observe the other's catch at the end of each day, and that neither plans to relocate "any time soon." (These are crucial assumptions, as you will see later.)

Now suppose that one evening Zeke invites his neighbor Deke to imbibe a little moonshine in the rocking chairs on the front porch of his hut. They talk about fishing. Through a puff of smoke from his corncob pipe, Zeke offers Deke a deal: He will never plunder the lake if Deke never plunders, but if Deke ever does, Zeke will plunder in response for n days thereafter. Deke enthusiastically nods in agreement, and promises the same. Is it possible that such an agreement could avert the tragedy of the commons? The Folk Theorem of Repeated Games tells us yes. The Folk Theorem, in a nutshell, says that when a game between players is repeated infinitely, and players are sufficiently "patient," just about any type of Nash equilibrium behavior is possible.[7]

To understand why, we need to embark on a short diversion to understand how we can represent the difference between the value of an early payoff and a later payoff. It generally makes sense to assume that for any positive payoff that, "now is better than later." Therefore, let us assume that both Zeke and Deke discount any payoff they receive one period into the future by a factor of δ, where δ is some number lying between 0 and 1. The parameter δ is subject to different interpretations. As δ becomes closer to 1, it may reflect (a) a measure of a player's increasing *patience*, defined as his value of obtaining payoffs one period into the future

---

[7] It is called the *Folk Theorem* because a number of game theorists seem to have thought up the idea at roughly the same time in the early 1970s, but none was brazen enough to claim it for his own.

relative to the present; (b) the probability that a repeated game continues to the next period; (c) the frequency of player interactions, where δ closer to one means that little time separates episodes of interaction between players; or (d) a combination of any of these. A payoff of x received one period later is therefore equal to δx, two periods later equal to $\delta^2 x$, and so forth. One interesting fact we will use often (which is demonstrated in the Appendix) is that the value today to a player of receiving a payoff of x in every period forever is equal to $x/(1 - \delta)$; if x is received forever starting one period from now, the value is $\delta x/(1 - \delta)$, two periods from now $\delta^2 x/(1 - \delta)$, and so forth.

The possibility of obtaining the cooperative (Conserve; Conserve) outcome is greatly enhanced in a repeated-game context, particularly if a game is repeated with no end in sight.[8] In an infinitely repeated game, a player may adopt a strategy of sustained cooperation, provided that the other player responds in kind. However, if the other player defects, the open-ended nature of the interaction makes retribution possible. Of course, there can be various degrees of nastiness in response to defection. One of the tamer responses is a brave Tit-for-Tat strategy, in which a player "bravely" starts with cooperation. Cooperation by the other player is rewarded with cooperation, but a player responds quickly to every defection with her own one-period defection. One can think of this kind of strategy as similar to the Old Testament's "eye-for-an-eye," which, incidentally, Biblical scholars have come to view as a *limit* on retaliation, not as a *license* to retaliate in kind.[9] The opposite extreme on the scale of vengeance is the "Grim Trigger" strategy. Playing the Grim Trigger, a single defection by a player mercilessly triggers defection forever. Creative intermediate responses to defection can involve reprisals of various lengths, threats of only intermittent future cooperation, and so on.

Let's suppose, for illustrative purposes, that Zeke and Deke desire to play the hardball "Grim Trigger" strategy, where the reprisal length, n, is equal to infinity. In this case, Zeke or Deke will choose to Conserve (the fish) if $\frac{s}{1-\delta} > r + \frac{\delta t}{1-\delta}$, or $\delta > \frac{r-s}{r-t}$. Thus, the higher the value the bachelors place on future episodes of fishing (higher δ), the more likely is (Conserve; Conserve). Again, this may reflect either their patience, their belief that future repeated plays are likely, and/or that they will occur frequently. Thus in stable, tightly knit communities, conservation is more likely. Conservation is also more likely with a higher s, the payoff to sustainable resource use, and the lower are r and t, the rogue and tragedy payoffs. With a lighter punishment, such as Tit-For-Tat, the requirements on the parameters lie in the same direction, but are stronger, because the threatened punishment is weaker.

The Folk Theorem is one of the most important ideas in game theory, and helps to establish a framework for conditions under which sustainable use of CPRs might

---

[8] There are problems with obtaining cooperation in game such as the Prisoners' Dilemma when play is repeated a finite and predictable number of times. Promises to play cooperatively in the last stage of the game are likely to be noncredible in the penultimate stage, thus inviting defection. If players expect defection in the penultimate stage, then promises of cooperation are noncredible in the previous stage, and so forth, such that, at least at a theoretical level, the game unzips from its back end. Infinite (or at least some probability of) future repetition solves this problem.

[9] Miller (2006), p. 21.

be possible, even when there are more than two players.[10] Nevertheless, it is probably insufficient in itself to explain the diversity of what we observe in the myriad experiences with CPR conservation in the real world. Although the theorem does predict that cooperation is *possible* in an infinitely repeated Prisoners' Dilemma, so is virtually any other outcome; cooperation is anything but assured.

To obtain the cooperative outcome, Paul Seabright of the *Université de Toulouse* argues that an element of initial trust may be critical in order to establish cooperation as a habitual pattern of group behavior.[11] Moreover, what precisely establishes this trust in the beginning rounds of the game can be somewhat of a mystery. Wherever these beliefs come from, however, they have a tendency to be self-fulfilling, establishing a pattern of either trust and cooperation – or distrust and defection. In this way, players in a repeated Prisoners' Dilemma can become subject to virtuous or vicious circles in which beliefs about the trustworthiness of others rely on past interaction, which in turn can lead to self-fulfilling prophecies about future cooperation, or lack thereof.[12] The whole process can become driven by the level of "optimism about optimism" regarding cooperation.

A further limitation of the Folk Theorem is that it predicts that the good outcome is possible when players can make strategies contingent upon the past strategies of other players. As a result, information about other players' actions is essential. There also must be a positive probability of the game continuing to the next period at every point in the game. Thus, the Folk Theorem is probably most applicable in the context of CPR use when the number of resource users is small and unchanging. The broad range of potential outcomes from the Folk Theorem lead Ostrom, Gardner, and Walker to remark that

> Consistent policy prescriptions cannot be based solely on the Folk Theorem. It is a gigantic leap of faith to deduce that, simply because a mathematical solution exists to an infinitely repeated CPR dilemma, appropriators will automatically find such a solution and follow it . . . The challenge for theory is to predict when appropriators outcomes will approximate those given by the Folk Theorem outcomes, and when not. (1994: p. 18)

The Folk Theorem is a good reference point for understanding the dynamics of repeated interaction in CPR use. But some have questioned why nonviolators should choose to retaliate against a defector by likewise breaking the rules during the next period, when this type of retaliation could very well jeopardize the whole CPR management scheme.[13] Moreover, it is very difficult to find real-world examples of CPR retribution schemes that have the explicit characteristic of self-sabotage.

Tit-For-Tat and Grim Trigger–type punishment schemes are much more common in the context of a *parallel game* involving the ongoing social relationships between CPR users. Jean-Marie Baland and Jean-Philippe Platteau at Belgium's *Universataires Notre Dame de la Paix, Namur* cite a study of a fishery in the Solomon Islands

---

[10] See Myerson (1991) pp. 331–7.
[11] Seabright (1997), p. 293.
[12] Seabright (1997), p. 305.
[13] For example, Baland and Platteau (1997), p. 320.

Player 2

		Conserve	Plunder
Player 1	Conserve	s $\quad s$	v $\quad r\text{-}f$
	Plunder	v $\quad r\text{-}f$	$t\text{-}f$ $\quad t\text{-}f$

Figure 4.2b. Resource Conservation Game with Sheriff

where those who employ prohibited fishing methods or harvest protected species are subject to a series of graduated Tit-for-Tat-like social sanctions aimed at creating personal shame. In the extreme, notorious poachers face a Grim-Triggeresque form of social excommunication in which the community permanently revokes the offender's status as a kinsman, a particularly harsh punishment in the local culture, in which there is a strong desire to avoid relational conflict.[14] Taking the point back to our example, Deke may refrain from plundering the fish, not because Zeke would plunder forever after in response, but because it might jeopardize happy hour on Zeke's porch. *Anger*, as an emotional response, may be useful in this context. It induces players to carry out punishments that otherwise might not be in their interest, making punishments more credible against prospective violators and helping to foster cooperation.

Governing the Environmental Commons: The Top-Down Approach

What happens when CPR use involves a large number of parties with short-term interests in resource exploitation? One possible method of preventing environmental degradation is a "top-down" approach by a strong central state with a long-term interest in future resource needs. In such an approach, the state steps in to penalize private parties for nonconservation of CPRs. Although the state allows open CPR use, it employs a "sheriff" to ensure individual compliance congruent with a long-term conservation strategy. While the sheriff may be unable to monitor CPR use perfectly, the top-down approach can prevent resource degradation if the expected penalty for Plundering exceeds any benefit from it.

Suppose that the sheriff monitors CPR users, and catches violators with some fraction of the time equal to m, and if they are caught, they are immediately slapped with a fine, F, making the expected fine equal to $mF = f$. This changes the payoffs from the game in Figure 4.2a to those in Figure 4.2b. If the sheriff is sufficiently adept at monitoring and fines are sufficiently stiff such that $r-f < s$, then (Conserve; Conserve) is a Nash equilibrium, even in one-shot plays of the game. If $t-f < v$ also, then (Conserve; Conserve) becomes the *unique* Nash equilibrium. Thus if the state is strong and ubiquitous enough to carefully monitor resource use, a top-down

---

[14] Hviding and Baines (1994), p. 24, cited in Baland and Platteau (1997), p. 197.

approach may be able to promote sustainable CPR use even when a large number of parties with short-term interests are involved.

An example of this top-down approach is relayed by Jared Diamond about Japan during the years of the Tokugawa shoguns from 1603 to 1867.[15] Deforestation had started in Japan as early as 800 A.D. in the Kinai Basin, spreading to the island of Shikoku by 1000 A.D. as a gradually growing population increased the demand for wood used in houses, monuments, and ships. By 1550, about one-quarter of Japan's total area had been deforested.[16] The shogun, or "chief of the warrior estate," was granted extraordinary powers by the Japanese emperor in 1603 to rule over the nation, a time that happened to coincide with a large construction boom that lasted from about 1570 to 1650. When the great Meireki fire occurred in 1657, the resulting need for timber to begin reconstruction highlighted the extent to which deforestation had ravaged Japan.[17]

Immediately this led to a change in policy, upheld by a series of successive shoguns, placing strict limits on the use of Japanese forests. Early evidence of this policy was a proclamation by the shogun in 1666 "warning of the dangers of erosion, stream siltation, and the flooding caused by deforestation."[18] Government decrees regulated the use of common-pool resources, particularly forest products. Over the following decades, shoguns and their regional deputies, the *daimyo*, enacted a series of laws that established monitors on roads and rivers to ensure that timber harvesting rules were being obeyed. Forest patrols vigilantly guarded against unauthorized logging, inflicting severe punishments on violators. Subsequently, rules were enacted specifying the quantity of timber a family could use in building its house. Detailed laws were laid down that even regulated the type of wood to be used in box making and New Year decorations.[19] Moreover, the shoguns encouraged plantation forestry by urging people to plant seedlings, helping to forge the custom as an integral part of Japanese culture.

The combination of top-down restrictions on forest use and the increasing practice of plantation forestry began to reverse deforestation trends between 1750 and 1800. Today, despite a population of over 127 million people, almost 80 percent of Japan's land area consists of forested mountains, whose management is so thorough that they flourish even though they continue to be used as a valuable resource for timber.[20]

Self-Governance and the Sheriff

The primary problem with top-down CPR regulation, especially in developing countries, is nearly always the monitoring problem: It is often too costly for the state to hire enough monitors to catch violators often enough such that plundering the

[15] Diamond (2005), pp. 294–308.
[16] Diamond (2005), p. 298.
[17] Diamond (2005), p. 299.
[18] Diamond (2005), p. 300.
[19] Diamond (2005), p. 302.
[20] Diamond (2005), p. 294.

Herder 2

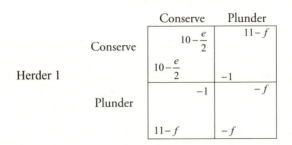

Figure 4.3. Sheep Herder Game

commons doesn't pay. And even this sets aside the governance question over who monitors the monitors. Elinor Ostrom proposes an alternative structure for CPR regulation that instead relies on the informational advantages of local CPR users themselves.[21] Let's examine a slight variation of her game in which we consider the example of two local goat herders who share a common grazing pasture. Because the grazing pasture is a common-pool resource, each is tempted to allow his goats to graze longer than he should, endangering the health of the pasture. Suppose that from the previous example we have the payoff values $r = 11, s = 10, t = 0,$ and $v = -1$, reflecting a Prisoners' Dilemma. Mindful of the dilemma, the herders establish a binding contract in which they agree to a monitoring scheme to police the common pasture. The cost of the scheme is equal to e, contingent upon conservation, assumed to be split equally between the herders.

The game is represented in Figure 4.3. Note first that with $e = 0$ and $f = 0$, the herders remain stuck at the unfortunate (Plunder; Plunder) Nash equilibrium. However, for critical values of e and f, the herder's monitoring scheme is able to avert the tragedy of the commons. First, the cost of the monitoring scheme, e, must not be greater than 20, the total surplus that the herders receive when the commons is used sustainably. Second, as before, the fine that can be credibly extracted from a potential Plunderer, f, must exceed, or at least equal, the benefit from Plundering, in this example $11 - 10 = 1$. Given that the values of these parameters are satisfied, the commons tragedy can be averted even in one-shot or finitely repeated plays of the game.

Ostrom notes that in some instances self-governance may involve the communal hiring of a "sheriff," while in others it may be easier for local commons users to take up the task of monitoring and sanctioning amongst themselves. Particularly when local users have informational advantages over outsiders in monitoring and the ability to enforce sanctions (social or otherwise), the value of e may be smaller, and f may be larger when group members themselves carry out monitoring and punishment. Nevertheless, this leaves open the possibility of "free-riding" by members in both the monitoring of neighboring users, and in the application of sanctions – if individuals find sanctioning others against their own interests. For this reason it

---

[21] Ostrom (1990), p. 15.

may be better in some cases to delegate such tasks to a more objective outsider. (For example, when dealing with a noisy neighbor, other neighbors often find it easier to call the police than confront the offending neighbor themselves.)

Robert Wade, political scientist at the London School of Economics, provides an apt example of this kind of local management of the commons. He reflects on his study of Kottapalle, India (population 3,000), a village of peasant farmers located in Andhra Pradesh, 300 miles south – and two worlds away – from Hyderabad.[22] The economy of Kottapalle revolves around the cultivation of rice and sorghum, both essential subsistence foods, both requiring large and constant supplies of water. Irregular rainfall necessitates irrigation from a nearby canal. However, because Kottapalle lies downstream from other villages with access to the canal, even irrigation involves uncertainties.[23] The supply of water that reaches Kottapalle must be painstakingly allocated among users.

Wade describes a fascinating institutional structure developed within the village itself that oversees this allocation of water. Central to this institutional structure is the village council, consisting of nine members chosen by the community each year.[24] The Village Council administers the village's *standing fund* from which it provides essential services to the village: an animal clinic, schools, road repair, and keeping the village clear of monkeys.[25] Along with these other public goods, the Village Council represents the village in obtaining the necessary supply of water from the government-run canal, and employs a work group of *common irrigators*, charged with maintaining the public irrigation systems and monitoring the distribution of water among the village fields. The common irrigators report water-use violations to the Village Council, which imposes fines upon the perpetrators. The fines are collected by village *field guards*, who receive a fraction of the fines as part of their salary. [26]

Kottapalle's local institutional structure has functioned remarkably well in helping to overcome the potentially contentious issues associated with water allocation. This proved true even during a local drought, in which rainfall ebbed and the canal ran low. During the drought, cases of farmers taking water out of turn rose to two or three each day, including abuses by two of the Village Council's own members.[27] But in response to the crisis, the Council appointed extra common irrigators, and deployed them earlier in the season. The Council exerted collective pressure against abusers and levied the appropriate fines. Village leaders also lobbied the Supervisor of Irrigation (with meals, drink, and expensive cigarettes) to increase the flow of water down the canal.[28] In short, Kottapalle represents an example of how local indigenous institutions in developing countries can effectively regulate the use of a vital natural resource through a combination of local "sheriffs" and self-monitoring.

---

[22] Wade (1987).
[23] Wade (1987), p. 91.
[24] Wade (1987), p. 6.
[25] Wade (1987), p. 7.
[26] Wade (1987), p. 91.
[27] Wade (1987), p. 91.
[28] Wade (1987), p. 94.

The Big Leader

A more-or-less homogeneous group of CPR users such as those in Kottapalle has distinct advantages in governing the environmental commons.[29] They are likely to have congruent interests, and be able to monitor and sanction one another effectively. On the other hand, in a homogeneous group of small users none may have a vested interest that is large enough to ensure that the commons is preserved. For example, in the game in Figure 4.3 suppose that it is impossible to enforce a contract between members that ensures equal contributions, and $e = 14$. In this case, herders not only free-ride on the commons, they free-ride in their contributions to police their own commons free-riding problem. This is obviously inefficient since monitoring costs are less than the difference between the total surplus of the herders in the Conserve and Plunder outcomes, that is, $14 < 20 - 0$.

Thus sometimes the CPR dilemma can be resolved if one Big Player exists with a lot to lose if everything falls apart. In such cases, the Big Player may have an incentive to shoulder the entire burden of solving the CPR dilemma for the entire group. Picture a situation like Elinor Ostrom's goat herders, but in which the goat herders are heterogeneous. The herds are of equal size, and the goats eat the same amount of grass, but one herder has a herd of prize goats whose fur is used to make upscale cashmere sweaters sold at the finest salons of Paris. The other herder's more humble goats are exported as pet meat. Let the s and r payoffs to the former be equal to 20 and 21, while the respective payoffs to the latter remain at 10 and 11.

Begin with the top game of Figure 4.4. If both herders Contribute to the cost of monitoring the CPR, then we assume that they receive the (Conserve; Conserve) Nash equilibrium payoffs as in the basic game in Figure 4.3 when $f > 1$. If neither herder Contributes, we assume that they receive the (Plunder; Plunder) Nash equilibrium that exists for $f = 0$. Observe the other two possible outcomes in the top game: If Pet Meat Contributes, but Cashmere doesn't, we move to Game A, in which the Nash equilibrium payoffs to the players are -4 and 20, respectively. If Cashmere Contributes, but Pet Meat doesn't, we move to Game B, in which the Nash equilibrium payoffs to the players are 10 and 6, respectively (in both cases assuming $f > 1$). Plainly, Pet Meat has an incentive to free-ride on Cashmere in the contribution round, letting him shoulder the cost of the monitoring burden alone. This is a clear example of what Mancur Olson (1965) referred to as "the exploitation of the strong by the weak" in the problem of collective action. Those with the greatest interest in preserving the commons may end up shouldering the burden alone.[30]

Herd Behavior and the Commons

In the real world, the incentives that affect how people relate to the natural environment are in a significant way shaped by the behavior of others. This is true both

---

[29] See, for example, Ostrom (1990), Wade (1987), and Baland and Platteau (1996).
[30] This phenomenon brings to mind the United States in the role of the "world's policeman." Does the United States have more to lose if the system breaks down?

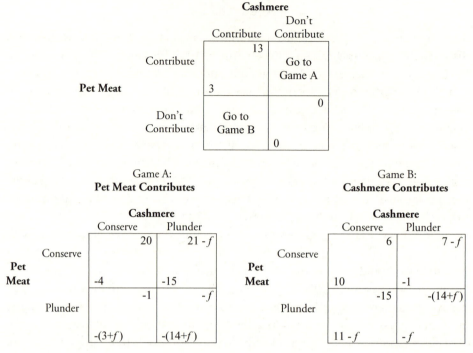

Figure 4.4. Sheep Herder Game with Leader

in developing and industrialized economies. For example, in the United States, the Keep America Beautiful antipollution campaign, made famous by the "Crying Indian" television public service announcements that debuted in 1970, resulted in enormous changes in social norms about the evils of water pollution, air pollution, and littering. Many in the American environmental movement credit the campaign for creating a public perception that isolated polluters as engaging in antisocial behavior.

Baland and Platteau thus argue that in many instances the tragedy of the commons may not always be best represented as a Prisoners' Dilemma, but as a Coordination game, where the incentives to Conserve depend on how many others Conserve.[31] The reasons that payoffs change with herd behavior can be both complex and mysterious (and something we will examine more closely in Chapter Eight). In this context, suffice to say it may stem from number of sources: (1) A sense of social norms changing the internal psychological costs to players from engaging in behavior contrary to the common good; (2) the increased fear of social sanctions as a result of standing out as a Plunderer; or (3) the increased likelihood of being caught by those obeying the rules.

To illustrate, let's extend the basic game to eight players. Assume the payoff to Conserve is constant at ten, but that the payoff to Plunder declines as the number

[31] Baland and Platteau (1996), p. 94.

Number of *other* players Conserving:	$n = 0$	$n = 1$	$n = 2$	$n = 3$	$n = 4$	$n = 5$	$n = 6$	$n = 7$
Payoff to Conserve:	10	10	10	10	10	10	10	10
Payoff to Plunder: ($= 17 - 2n$)	17	15	13	11	9	7	5	3

Figure 4.5. Coordination Game in Resource Conservation

of Conserving players increases, so that the payoff to Plunder is, say, equal to $17 - 2n$. Notice from Figure 4.5 that from the perspective of any one individual player, if a majority of players Plunder, the incentive is to do the same, but as a majority of the other players play Conserve, the incentive is to Conserve. The result is that there are two Nash equilibria, one in which the commons is Plundered and one in which it is Conserved.

Again we have an example in which leadership in CPR use is critical. However, note the dissimilarity: In the Cashmere–Pet Food example, leadership entailed a willingness and ability to incur sole responsibility for the state of the commons. It is like the "leadership" of the man who habitually tidies up the mess in front of his house left by other neighbors' dogs, as well as from his own (a suburban tale of the commons tragedy?). In contrast, the second example of leadership involves effective communication. If the leader can convince a critical mass of CPR users that sustainable practices will be followed, the resource use settles into the Pareto efficient Nash equilibrium of Conservation.

A distressing example illustrating the absence of either type of leadership is given by Elinor Ostrom. She relays the story of Bodrum, a Turkish village lying beside the Aegean Sea.[32] Historically, Bodrum had been the center of a prosperous fishing industry, when in the 1970s some fishermen began to switch to large trawling vessels, and moreover began to disrespect the three-mile coastal fishing limit.[33] In the short-term, this competitive edge proved quite lucrative. This of course induced others to bring large trawling vessels into the area, quickly eliminating the temporary windfall. Adding to the chaos, tourism began to boom in Bodrum, creating a market for chartered fishing boats full of tourists and an emergent spear-fishing industry.[34]

Distraught over the impending devastation of their traditional livelihood, groups of local fishermen hastily formed a fishing cooperative to try to regulate the local fishing industry. Less than a decade later, however, the cooperative had broken down. Lack of leadership, lack of communication between competing fishing interests, an absence of monitoring, and nonenforcement of fishing limits were all to blame.[35] Especially lacking was a comprehensive institutional structure to regulate

[32] Ostrom (1990), p. 144.
[33] Berkes (1986), p. 79, cited in Ostrom (1990), p. 144.
[34] Ostrom (1990), p. 145.
[35] Ostrom (1990), p. 145.

use of the common fishery during a period of strong economic development. The vast heterogeneity between resource users made it tricky to establish a set of rules that could govern the commons, since any single set of rules would be likely to benefit one group of users over another. The sad result: Everyone believed that everyone else was plundering the fishery, providing everyone with the incentive to do the same.

Assignment Rules in CPR Usage

The Bodrum example illustrates another important issue in the regulation of the commons: the clear assignment of rules. Consider the example of a fishery with a number of discrete fishing spots, where some of the spots are more alluring than others from the perspective of a fish. Even if there are an equal number of fishers as fishing spots, fights are likely to break out over who gets the best spot, and who is stuck with the worst. Recreational fishermen may be content to rely upon simple social norms such as "the best spot to the first; the last gets the worst."

Such informal mechanisms may be reasonably efficient. The fisherman who wants the best spot the most, will be willing to pay the highest price (in terms of rousing himself out of bed the earliest) to secure it. Nevertheless, inefficiencies may arise, say, between two fishermen both wanting the prime spot, struggling to get up earlier and earlier each morning to beat the other to it. If only one of them will end up with the coveted spot anyway, both would be better off using an assignment rule. This rule could be something such as "Zeke gets the good spot on even days, and Deke gets it on odd days." In large-scale fishing operations, where there is more at stake, such rules may be critical.

Suppose that there are two desirable fishing spots on the lake of our Appalachian fishermen, but of the two best spots, the fishing spot "on top of the Granite Rock" enjoys a higher yield than the spot "near the Mud Hole." (To simplify, assume for now that sustainability requirements are satisfied.) Now see that in Figure 4.6 that if both fight over the Granite Rock they split the high yield, k_G. If they fight over the

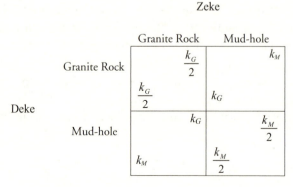

Figure 4.6. Assignment Rules and Resource Rights

Mud Hole, they split the low yield, $k_M < k_G$. With separate spots, each obtains the respective yield of that spot.[36]

There are two interesting cases in the game. The first case is when $k_M > \frac{1}{2}k_G$, which makes the incentives characteristic of a Hawk-Dove game rather than a Prisoners' Dilemma. Both fishermen will settle in separate spots. This is the outcome to the game that produces the greatest total payoff for the fisherman, $k_G + k_M$. The second case is when $k_M < \frac{1}{2}k_G$, where the Granite Rock spot is radically better than the Mud Hole. In this case, the incentives are for both fishermen to locate on the Granite Rock. This produces a sub-optimal outcome for the players, in that the total catch is equal to k_G instead of $k_G + k_M$. An assignment rule in which Zeke and Deke took alternate spots on alternate days would result in an average catch per day for each of $\frac{k_G + k_M}{2}$ instead of $\frac{1}{2}k_G$.

Elinor Ostrom illustrates the importance of assignment rules in CPR use with an example of a more fortunate Turkish fishery, Alanya, also located on the Aegean, 250 miles east of Bodrum. She relays Berkes's (1986) account of how in the early 1970s members of Alanya's local fishing cooperative began to implement a clever set of allocation rules for local fishing spots.[37] Because Aegean fish stocks slowly migrate to the west between September and January and to the east from January until May, local fishermen have an incentive to follow the migration of fish and crowd one another in areas where fish concentration is highest. Based on the rules of the cooperative, however, each begins with an assigned location, and from September to January, they rotate east to the next spot daily; from January to May each rotates to the west. This arrangement gives the fishermen equal opportunities at the best spots during each season, and promotes sustainable catch levels. Because fishermen have the incentive to arrive early on days when they are allotted the best spots, cheating the system is difficult and rare.[38]

Privatization of Rights over CPRs

Because ambiguities and conflicts sometimes remain with informal assignment rules over a natural resource, in some instances the state has encouraged privatization of CPRs. As with any allocation mechanism, privatization of a CPR has advantages and disadvantages, which can be both understood at a theoretical level and in practice. Two main arguments favor CPR privatization: First, if individuals take a long-term view of resource use, privatization should ostensibly be linked to an incentive for sustainable resource use and hence some form of conservation. In this respect, privatization reduces the short-term incentive to engage in the Plunder strategy. Rendering the resource "excludable" for the sole use of a single private party eliminates resource-degrading "catch as catch can" behavior by multiple users.

Second, many economists advocate privatization of resources on Pareto efficiency grounds. The roots of this lie in Ronald Coase's (1960) famous theorem,

[36] The game is an application of Ostrom, Gardner, and Walker (1994), p. 59.
[37] Ostrom (1990), p. 19.
[38] Ostrom (1990), p. 20.

which argues that Pareto efficiency in resource use can be achieved if private property rights over the resource can be created and if bargaining between parties is costless. For example, suppose that two villages share use of a river. The first village, Alto, lies upstream, and Alto residents use the river to bathe and wash their clothes (using soap). The unfortunate downstream village, Bajo, tries to use the river to fish, despite declining levels of fish in the sudsy water. Suppose the value to Alto of using the river for washing is X, the value to Bajo of fishing in a clean river is Y, and the cost to Alto of using a pollution-free soap is Z. If Y is greater than either X or Z, then no matter which village starts out with river rights, the Coase Theorem says that the two villages will end up with a pollution-free outcome. For example, if rights over the river are given to Alto, then Bajo can pay Alto X or Z (whichever is less) to eliminate the pollution, and Bajo ends up better off while Alto is no worse off. If Bajo has river rights, Alto is forced to pay the lesser of X and Z to clean up its act. If Y is less than both X and Z, irrespective of who has the property rights, the value of fishing to Bajo is insufficient to entice Alto to clean up. Even if Bajo has river rights, Alto can pay Bajo an amount equal to Y in place of reducing its pollution, leaving Bajo no worse off and Alto better off than if it stopped washing in the river or began using the pollution-free soap.

The elegant results of the Coase theorem notwithstanding, there are reasons to question whether the effects of privatization of CPRs should be unambiguously positive, especially in the context of developing countries. First, if many parties are affected by use of the resource, bargaining may be so logistically cumbersome that the costs of reaching a solution may overwhelm any benefit that might be derived from it.

A second set of caveats related to privatization are related to problems of wealth distribution. Take the example of a multinational firm that makes a profitable chemical resin, but in so doing, dumps noxious waste into a common-access lake used for subsistence fishing by local residents of a developing country. Even if the multinational has been granted property rights to pollute, it may be impossible for local residents to purchase rights to the lake from the multinational if they are extremely poor, or do not operate in a cash economy – even if lake pollution results in a tremendous local welfare loss for them. This is so because the bargaining cannot occur over of units of welfare, which are not transferable, but must occur over a common measure of value such as currency.

Some have argued that privatization can also worsen an existing income distribution.[39] The idea is that when a resource such as an open-access pasture is privatized, a drop in the intensity of CPR usage implies a general drop in the demand for CPR labor. Consequently, those left outside the privatization scheme may be worse off, although the natural resource may in the end be used more sustainably under privatization. Some have argued that this was the result of the eighteenth-century English enclosure movement, when aristocrats were given property rights over previously open-access pastures.

---

[39] See, for example, Weitzman (1974).

The poor may be adversely affected in other ways. Jean-Marie Baland and Patrick Francois (2005) demonstrate that privatization may have a particularly adverse effect on the poor if they use natural resources as a kind of fallback employment insurance in hard times. For example, households in crisis may use forestland to forage for fruits and vegetables, wild game, and building materials. In this way, Baland and Francois suggest that the commons can act as a kind of "employer of last resort." In particular, they show even when privatization can be carried out costlessly and is perfectly egalitarian, that privatization can be worse off for everyone if households are sufficiently averse to risk.

Paul Seabright (1993) highlights a number of other difficulties related to privatization. He notes that privatization may undermine previously existing informal institutions that facilitated resource conservation. Though privatization may bring title of a land or water resource to an individual owner, it may not render the CPR completely excludable in practice from use by others. As a result, it may be impossible to prevent encroachment by individuals not holding rights to forestland, but privatization may dampen the incentives for the trespassers to practice conservation. Moreover, the people who might tend to use such lands sustainably, such as indigenous forest dwellers, may be most able to monitor sustainable use of a forest to keep others from overexploiting it. Prohibiting such people from access to the land may actually make it more susceptible to encroachment by those with only short-term interests.

Seabright also illustrates how, in a context in which resource use had been sustained via the incentives in a repeated Prisoners' Dilemma, privatization can actually make all parties worse off. Suppose, in the game in Figure 4.2a, that the payoff from the (Plunder; Plunder) outcome to the player who is given rights to the resource increases from t to t' under privatization. This increases the requirement on δ to achieve the (Conserve; Conserve) outcome under the Grim Trigger strategy from $\delta \geq \frac{r-s}{r-t}$ to $\delta \geq \frac{r-s}{r-t'}$. This, Seabright argues, implies that there may be cases in which potential landowners may actually be better off (and natural resources used more sustainably) under informal common-access arrangements rather than under privatization.

Finally, benefits of privatization can be lost if privatization is carried out in one resource but not in a complementary resource. An example is the privatization of Mongolian sheep and goat herds that began in the early 1990s. The typical Mongolian herd is mixed, often consisting of sheep and goats as well as horses, cattle, yak, and camel. While the Mongolian government privatized ownership of herds, most grazing land remained communal. Because of herd privatization, herd sizes increased during the 1990s, putting tremendous ecological pressure on Mongolian grazing lands. Degraded pastureland has had negative effects on herd animals. One study by Dutch researchers found that due to the pasture degradation, body weights have fallen and mortality rates have risen for sheep, goats, and other herd animals.[40]

---

[40] Van Hezik (2002).

Empirical Studies on Commons Sustainability

What has empirical evidence shown about characteristics of informal institutions that promote sustainable use of the commons? A number of studies have sought to test Olson's (1965) hypothesis, that inequality among resource users promotes resource sustainability. Interestingly, many of these studies have suggested that the relationship between sustainable CPR use and inequality in wealth between users may instead be U-shaped. [41] Studies using data from Mexico, India, and Pakistan indicate that extreme equality as well as extreme inequality are good for sustainable commons use. It appears that only a middle ground of asset heterogeneity is conducive to the poor free-riding on the rich.

Seeking to test Olson's hypothesis from a different angle, Juan-Camilo Cardenas (2003) carried out an experimental study that employed a simulated forestry game among residents in three Colombian villages. In the experiment, each subject chose optimal "months in the forest" to cut wood. Cardenas used both blind and face-to-face settings with his subjects. He found that inequality in wealth negatively affected cooperation in sustainable forest management, particularly in the face-to-face setting, thus presenting further evidence that contradicts Olson's theory.

The vast experiences of different groups in different regions of the world vary greatly, but even so, research has drawn together some common elements from the larger studies of sustainable CPR management. Yale political scientist Arun Agarwal (2002) reviews the major empirical work carried out on the environmental commons during the previous decade and a half, focusing on the large empirical studies of Ostrom, Wade, and Baland and Platteau.[42] First, he finds that smallness of CPR size and well-defined boundaries around a CPR tend to promote sustainability in resource use. Second, he finds that small group size, clearly defined membership, shared social norms, past successful experiences, interdependence between group members, low levels of poverty, and heterogeneity of endowments (but homogeneity in identity and interests) are all characteristics of successful groups sustainably utilizing CPRs. He also notes how institutional rules matter: Sustainable CPR use is facilitated by rules governing the use of the commons that are simple and easy to understand, that are locally devised, and that are easily monitored and enforced. Agarwal's findings about the importance of monitoring, social sanctions, clearly defined rules, and leadership are fascinating because they are consistent with what even very simple games predict about behavior in environmental resource conservation.

---

[41] See Bardhan and Dayton-Johnson (2002), Bardhan (2000), Dayton-Johnson (2000), and Khwaja (2000).

[42] Agarwal (2002), pp. 62–3.

CHAPTER 5
Risk, Solidarity Networks, and Reciprocity

Two are better than one, because they have a good return for their work: If one falls down, his friend can help him up. But pity the man who falls and has no one to help him up.
        – Ecclesiastes 4:9,10

RISK IS UNDESIRABLE to most people, especially risk involving household income. However, for the rural poor in developing countries, fluctuations in income pose a particularly grave danger. Suppose the income of a typical North American family fell abruptly by $1,000. Although certainly unwelcome, it would be of little real consequence, perhaps vacation plans changed from a hotel stay to a camping trip. But an income loss of $1,000 for a rural Central American family would be devastating. It would probably necessitate the sale of assets, such as land, that are crucial to the household's long-term livelihood. It could force the migration of a family member. It might even force a change to a cheaper and less nutritious diet: more tortillas, fewer meats and vegetables.

The irony is that while the consequences of risk are more disastrous in developing countries, risk is also more prevalent. To continue the example, despite a far lower base of wealth, an abrupt $1,000 loss in income is arguably more likely for the rural Central American household than for the household in North America. This may be true for several reasons. First, risk inherently follows the uncertainties that surround rural households in developing countries. Indeterminate factors such as weather, pests, and the availability of inputs such as water, labor, and draft animals at critical times bring volatility to agricultural crop yields. A dearth of preventative medical care renders people more susceptible to the sudden onset of disease and less likely to be treated effectively when they become sick. Poor roads and rickety vehicles make accidents more common.

Second, because risk-mitigating devices such as burglar alarms, building codes, airbags, and quick-and-ready firefighters are scant in the developing world, various kinds of misfortune such as theft, earthquakes, and fire tend to be more common and their effects more severe. A day laborer riding in the back of an old truck is more likely to be injured in a road accident than an American suburbanite riding in a new Volvo where cushy airbags soothe the impact of a crash from every angle.

Third, a large portion of the vast resources of industrialized countries is spent on formal means of mitigating risk. Most households in industrialized countries purchase insurance policies for home, automobile, life, and health. These formal insurance mechanisms are almost completely absent in the poorest rural areas of developing countries, exposing households to the capricious acts of man and nature.

Consider, for example, the disparate human impacts of Hurricane Mitch, which struck Central America and the Caribbean on October 26, 1998, and Hurricane Andrew, which struck the southeastern United States, mainly in Florida and Louisiana, on August 24, 1992. It would be difficult to determine which of these hurricanes was more ferocious. Although neither represented the violent assault on a densely populated urban area of 2005's Hurricane Katrina, both were Category 5 hurricanes that hit their respective coasts at full strength with 175 mile per hour winds. Both Andrew and Mitch hit highly populated *rural* areas.

The difference in their destructive impact, however, was striking. Hurricane Mitch left an estimated 19,000 people dead and 2.7 million homeless in Honduras, El Salvador, Nicaragua, and surrounding countries, while causing an estimated $5.4 billion in damage (BBC, 2000). It has been estimated that it may take up to twenty years for the areas most affected to recover from the disaster. In contrast, Hurricane Andrew resulted in twenty-three deaths, destroyed 25,524 homes, and damaged 101,241 others. The total damage from Andrew has been estimated at $26.5 billion by the National Oceanic and Atmospheric Administration, about five times the damage done by Mitch (mostly because of higher U.S. home values). Yet, Andrew caused only a small fraction of the homelessness and relocation and, most notably, a tiny fraction of the deaths. Moreover, of the $26.5 billion in damage from Andrew, $15.5 billion was insured losses.[1] Better building codes, more sophisticated warning systems, and a huge insurance infrastructure worked together to mitigate the worst potential impacts of Andrew. The *human* devastation from Mitch was incalculably greater.

Differences in behavior toward risk between the rich and the poor originate from the law of diminishing returns, which applies to income as well as just about everything else. A landless peasant who misplaces the equivalent of $50 is devastated; one who stumbles on $50 by dumb luck like feels like a king. Microsoft Chairman Bill Gates could absentmindedly spend $50 on a lunch he doesn't even remember. Thus, a concave relationship generally holds between household utility and income in which increases in income increase utility but at a diminishing rate. An easy way to model this relationship is, for example, to make the utility of a household equal to the square root of its income, as seen in Figure 5.1.[2]

This relationship between utility and income produces two seemingly contradictory behaviors by the poor about risk. On the one hand, a poor household has a much lower tolerance for a given level of variability in its income than does a rich household. Consider two Indian households, both in environments where incomes are uncertain. The first is a poor household, whose uncertain monthly income

---

[1] However, Andrew bankrupted nearly a dozen major insurance companies and caused such deep financial hardship to others that it led them to geographically diversify their own future exposure to hurricane and earthquake risk.

[2] Another common way of describing the relationship is to make utility equal to the natural log of income.

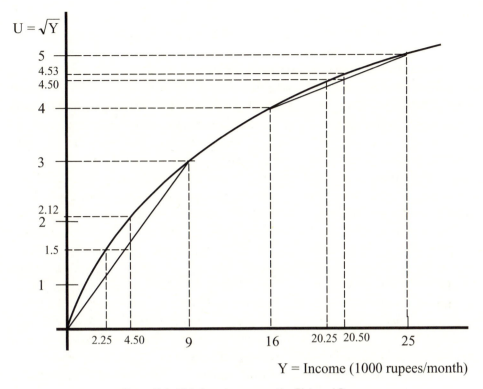

Figure 5.1. Risk Aversion among the Rich and Poor

(in thousands of rupees) is equal to either 9 or zero, with 50 percent probability, so that expected *income* for the poor household, taken along the horizontal axis, is $\frac{1}{2} \cdot 0 + \frac{1}{2} \cdot 9 = 4.5$. The second is a wealthy household, where income is equal to 25 or 16, also with 50 percent probability, so that expected income for the wealthy household is $\frac{1}{2} \cdot 16 + \frac{1}{2} \cdot 25 = 20.5$.

Figure 5.1 illustrates the difference in the aversion to risk between the wealthy and poor households. Given the uncertainty faced by each, the expected *utility* of the wealthy household (taken along the vertical axis) is simply the utility of each possible level of income, weighted by its respective probability. Thus the expected utility of the poor household is $\frac{1}{2}\sqrt{0} + \frac{1}{2}\sqrt{9} = 1.5$. As Figure 5.1 shows, this expected utility of 1.5 yields the same utility as a *certain* income of 2.25. In other words, the 50% gamble between having an income equal to 9 or zero provides the same level of utility as an income of 2.25 for sure. The wealthy household's expected utility is $\frac{1}{2}\sqrt{16} + \frac{1}{2}\sqrt{25} = 4.5$, yielding a level of utility corresponding to a certain income of 20.25.[3]

It is easy to see in the example why poor people dislike variability in their income more than rich people do. Though both households face an equal uncertainty involving 9 units of income, the wealthy household is willing to give about 1.2 percent of its expected income to remove the underlying uncertainty, 0.25 of 20.50.

---

[3] This kind of utility function with probabilities is referred to as a Von Neumann–Morgenstern utility function; in any game that we study in this book, payoffs to players are Von Neumann–Morgenstern utility payoffs, not necessarily monetary values.

In contrast, the poor household is willing to give up to *half* its expected income, 2.25 of 4.50, in order to eliminate this uncertainty. Without a doubt, this is one of the world's great injustices – those least able to deal with risk are often willing to give up the most of what they have to eliminate it.

However, the idea that the poor are heavily risk averse would seem to contradict certain behaviors that we systematically observe among the poor. The idea may be particularly incredulous, for example, to those who have ridden in the back of taxis in poor countries, where taxi (and bus) drivers often seem to be willing to incur tremendous risks to ensure that their passengers arrive at their destination in a brief amount of time. The increased risk of accident, injury, and death presented by stunning velocities and white-knuckle passes around blind corners have simultaneously terrified and mystified foreign visitors from richer countries.

This apparent tolerance of other types of risk is difficult to attribute to cultural norms (for example, a desire to for drivers to appear *macho*) because passengers also appear to incur startling risks to get from point A to point B. Traveling once by public bus in Haiti, I was amazed to see clusters of children and adults hanging off the top and sides of the vehicle, often by one hand and one foot, grinning at the passengers inside as the bus aggressively negotiated bumpy mountainous roads adjacent to perilous cliffs. What those from rich countries would regard as risky behavior is by no means limited to transportation: The poor in LDCs appear to make many other decisions that marginally increase the chance of total loss in order to conserve income or time: using cheap electrical wiring in shower water heaters,[4] cutting corners with safety in the workplace, establishing dwellings in areas prone to flood and landslides, and so forth.

How is this seemingly intentionally risky behavior by the poor consistent with their risk aversion? The answer is that the poor, relative to the rich, have more to gain and less to lose by taking risks that are likely to result in small increases in income, provided that the increased probability of total loss remains relatively small. Consider the following example: A bus driver with a route between two towns can increase his monthly income by 1 (thousand rupees) by driving sufficiently "fast and furious" that he can squeeze in an extra round trip each day during his shift. However, suppose the higher speed at which he must drive to squeeze in the extra run increases his chance of having a disabling accident from zero to some (still relatively small) probability $p > 0$. If he gets into a wreck, he is disabled and his income falls permanently to zero. Assuming again that $U = \sqrt{Y}$, the extra speed is worth it if $(1 - p)\sqrt{Y + 1} > \sqrt{Y}$. If p is small, then a little algebra shows that a bus driver will choose to drive fast and furious if $p < \frac{1}{2(Y+1)}$. For example, a poor bus driver with $Y = 9$ will drive recklessly provided that $p < 1/20$. A rich bus driver with $Y = 24$ will risk driving recklessly only if $p < 1/50$, because he has more to lose and the marginal utility of the added income from the risky behavior is smaller. Consequently, if the probability of an accident falls between $1/50$ and $1/20$, the poor bus driver drives

---

[4] In many places in Latin America, such showers, where the water is heated by an unprofessionally wired electrical circuit in the showerhead are aptly called *hacerviudas*, or widow-makers.

recklessly and the rich one drives safely. Thus, safety like most other things is a "normal" good, something whose demand increases as people become richer.

Risk-Sharing in Peasant Cultures and Repeated Games

Nevertheless, although the poor may intentionally take relatively small risks in order to secure marginal increases in income, they find larger, uncontrollable risks highly undesirable. Indeed, it is impossible to understand the behavior of the poor in developing countries without understanding the ways that they seek to mitigate these kinds of risks. Many decades ago, researchers who began formal studies of peasant economies, such as the Russian social scientist A. V. Chayanov (1926), were puzzled at anomalies in peasant behavior, which they deemed as irrational, or even "self-exploiting."[5] In his now classic book *The Moral Economy of the Peasant* (1976), Yale anthropologist James Scott provided an underpinning rationale for much of what academics had previously believed to be irrational concerning peasant behavior. Scott portrays a moral economy in which altruistic behavior between members of a peasant society follows logically in the context of an uncertain agricultural environment. Solidarity networks, between peasants and wealthy patrons and among peasants themselves, are created by social norms of reciprocity and mutual aid, in a constant effort to keep consumption levels above subsistence.

A debate emerged between Scott and fellow anthropologist Samuel Popkin over whether the kind of reciprocity observed in peasant societies was truly altruistic, or the product of rational, utility-maximizing behavior. In *The Rational Peasant* (1979), Popkin argued for the latter, citing numerous and convincing examples of shrewd, calculating behavior in Southeast Asian peasant societies. What emerged from the debate was an insightful harmonization of these views in work by Oxford economist Marcel Fafchamps (1992) and Stephen Coate and Martin Ravallion (1993) at Cornell and the World Bank, respectively. Their contribution was to apply game-theoretic models, specifically the theory of repeated games, to uncover the rationality behind open-ended altruistic behavior observed in traditional peasant societies.[6]

The essence of their argument is the following: It may be consistent with self-interest to withhold aid from a needy individual in an isolated transaction, in a one-shot play of a mutual-assistance game after which the players don't interact with one other again. However, solidarity with a needy comrade may be congruent with self-interest in the context of a repeated game, where after every interaction some probability of an additional interaction remains, and where negative shocks are frequent and can affect anyone at any time. This mirrors the environment of traditional rural societies, in which uncertainty is ubiquitous, and repeated economic and social interaction is the norm rather than the exception but contrasts strongly with the often anonymous, one-shot transactions in industrial societies.

---

[5] Chayanov (1926) describes a type of self-exploitation in which peasants work startlingly long days to eke out tiny increments in production to reach subsistence levels of consumption.

[6] As Pranab Bardhan notes, "Development economics is full of examples of how apparently irrational behavior may be successfully explained by an outcome of more complex exercises in rationality, particularly with deeper probes into the nature of the feasibility constraints or preference patterns" (1989, p. 42).

Insurance in Patron-Client Relationships

The need for some kind of insurance arrangement for those living close to subsistence is obvious, but as economists have long understood, insurance arrangements are fraught with problems. One such problem is the sequential action endemic to any kind of Trust game. How does the victim of an unfortunate mishap enforce his claim to insurance after the mishap occurs? How does the insurer keep the insured from making false claims or undertaking action that increase the probability that a claim will be made? These problems occur even with the "sophisticated" insurance contracts in industrial societies: Your car is stolen and the insurance company wants to lowball the insurance payout. A person with health insurance spends too much time eating fatty foods in front of the television. People buy automobile insurance and then drive too fast. A landlord procrastinates in replacing old wiring in a fire-insured apartment. The temptation to engage in this kind of free-riding behavior within developing societies is no less strong. Yet as Scott notes in *The Moral Economy of the Peasant*,

> There is an entire range of networks and institutions outside the immediate family which may, and often do, act as shock absorbers during economic crises in peasant life. A man's kinsmen, his friends, his village, a powerful patron, and even – though rarely – the state, may help tide him over a difficult period of illness or crop failure. (1976, p. 27)

One commonly observed insurance network in rural areas of less-developed countries is the patron-client relationship. Patrons exist in almost every traditional rural society. In Mexico, for example, this kind of person is called the *cacique*; in India, he is called the *sarpanch*. The patron will often serve numerous clients, and can, though wealth accumulation, even become the hub through whom all insurance within the network flows. But how is such insurance provided within the traditional society without inducing free-riding behavior?

Consider the Patron-Client insurance game in Figure 5.2 that is a variant of the Trust game presented in Figure 2.4a. In this game, an afflicted peasant-client seeks the help of a patron. In contrast to modern societies, where people pay insurance premiums *before* a calamity strikes, the informal insurance arrangements of traditional societies are often "back-loaded," with compensation for help occurring

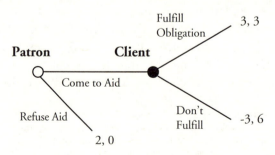

Figure 5.2. Patron-Client Trust Game

after the shock occurs. How can a wealthy Patron offer this kind of shock-contingent insurance, expecting that the Client will fulfill his part of the bargain?

See that the Nash equilibrium by backward induction is (Refuse Aid; Don't Fulfill) in a one-shot play of the Insurance game in Figure 5.2. But how would the solution change if the game were played repeatedly?

It is easy to see in the context of a repeated game how the threat by a Patron to withhold future aid can bring about cooperation in the insurance game of Figure 5.2. To keep things simple, let us define the length of one period as the expected length of time between negative shocks. Suppose that the Patron rewards a Client's fulfilled obligation with help in the future but vows to withhold help forever in response to an unfulfilled obligation. This makes the payoff to the Client for failure to fulfill his obligation to the Patron equal to $6 + \delta 0/(1 - \delta) = 6$. In contrast, the payoff to the Client from repaying the Patron is getting a payoff of 3 forever, or $3/(1 - \delta)$. Thus, for any discount factor $\delta > 0.50$, the Client prefers to repay the favor to the Patron. Consequently, the Client is more likely to fulfill his obligation (a) the more "patient" he is; (b) the more likely patron-client interaction is to occur in the following period; and (c) the shorter the time period between negative shocks and interaction between the parties. Thus, frequent, repeated interaction within a society where agricultural shocks are commonplace lead the peasant-client to fulfill his obligation at his point of decision, and persuade the Patron to provide insurance in the first place.

Exploitation in Patron-Client Relationships

Though a reciprocating relationship with a wealthier patron may offer more security to a peasant than a relationship with others at a similar level of poverty, the added security may come at great cost to the peasant. Moreover, what the peasant often gives up in exchange for help from the patron in time of need is a source of much controversy. The peasant typically trades away a higher level of average income for stability at a lower level of income, which some (Marxist scholars for instance) interpret as a form of exploitation. Though what actually does and doesn't constitute exploitation is often difficult to pin down, the provision of insurance from a patron to a peasant-client achieves a Pareto improvement in that it makes both parties (at least weakly) better off than without it.

Let's return to the example of the two Indian households in Figure 5.1, one wealthy, one poor. The poor household, whose household head we will call Ravi, lives in the same village as the wealthy headman, Sukhbir. To keep things simple, assume that states of nature are the same for all villagers. In the good state of nature (good crop weather), Ravi's household realizes income equal to 9 thousand rupees, which provides household utility, $U = \sqrt{9} = 3$. In the bad state of nature (floods), the household has no income, and $U = 0$. Thus while Ravi's expected income is equal to 4.5, his expected *utility* is $\frac{1}{2}\sqrt{0} + \frac{1}{2}\sqrt{9} = 1.50$ as seen in Figure 5.1, while Sukhbir's expected utility is $\frac{1}{2}\sqrt{16} + \frac{1}{2}\sqrt{25} = 4.50$.

Ravi's dislike of risk leads him to approach Sukhbir, the lone provider of insurance and credit within the village. Sukhbir is well-known for aiding village residents;

yet, for this security, Sukhbir demands a price: working his crops in the harvest season, when labor is most scarce. He is willing to provide for the needs of Ravi's household up to 2.3 thousand rupees during the bad times, but Ravi's transfer of labor to Sukhbir's land means a transfer of 6.7 thousand rupees to Sukhbir in the good state of nature, leaving Ravi with 2.3 thousand rupees in good times and bad. Under their agreement, Sukhbir's expected *income* thus rises by 2.2 ($= 0.5(9) -$ 2.3) thousand rupees while Ravi's expected income falls by an equal amount. Ravi, however, reluctantly accepts the contract since the constant income of 2.3 thousand rupees leaves his household with a slightly higher expected utility ($\sqrt{2.3} = 1.52$) than his expected utility ($\frac{1}{2}\sqrt{0} + \frac{1}{2}\sqrt{9} = 1.50$) under uncertainty.

Sukhbir's gain in utility from the arrangement is substantially greater than Ravi's. Half of the time Sukhbir pays out 2.3 thousand rupees, while the other half of the time he receives labor services from Ravi equal to 6.7 thousand rupees. Thus, Sukhbir's income in the good state of nature becomes 31.7 whereas in the bad state of nature it falls to only 13.7. Consequently, the expected utility of Sukhbir rises from 4.50 to $\frac{1}{2}\sqrt{13.7} + \frac{1}{2}\sqrt{31.7} = 4.67$.

This inequitable result is more common than one might think. The relative scarcity of wealthy individuals in peasant societies gives them considerable leverage in patron-client transactions. Because they have little need for insurance, their relative economic power ensures that they are amply compensated for their good deeds. Consequently, the lack of a competitive market for insurance can make the rich richer and the poor poorer. Moreover, what is not taken by the patron in direct economic compensation is accumulated in the form of communal status, social prestige, and the devotion of the client. Thus, while the patron-client relationship undoubtedly provides a useful function that should never be overlooked, it entrenches a rural hierarchy with little scope for class structure mobility.

Peasant Solidarity Networks

Insurance within the traditional rural economy occurs not only through the vertical relationship between a patron and peasant-client but also through the web of horizontal relationships among the poor. According to Scott:

> As soon as a peasant leans on his kin or his patron rather than on his own resources, he gives them a reciprocal claim to his own labor and resources. The kin and friends who bail him out will expect the same consideration when they are in trouble and he has something to spare. In fact, they aid him, one might say, because there is a tacit consensus about reciprocity, and their assistance is as good as money in the bank against the time when the situation is reversed. (1976, p. 28)

This kind of peasant solidarity network is represented in the game in Figure 5.3. Suppose that Ravi has a cousin, Ashok, in the village. Ravi cultivates rice and benefits when Nature causes it to rain; without rain, his rice withers. In contrast, Ashok is an artesian; he makes clay pots that need to dry in the sun. When it rains, his clay pots wilt. Assume that it is either rainy or sunny, each with probability one-half.

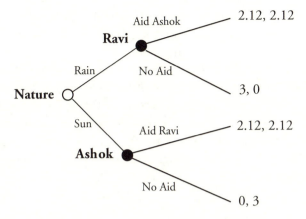

Figure 5.3. Reciprocity in a Solidarity Network

In this game, we assume that both players are vulnerable to the positive and negative shocks from Nature. Suppose that peasants' income structures are identical in that each receives the income of 9 (thousand rupees) in the advantageous state of nature, but an income of zero in the disadvantageous state of nature (as in Figure 5.1). If the fortunate player shares half of what he has with the less fortunate player, the payoff to each is equal to $\sqrt{4.5} = 2.12$. However, because $2.12 < 3$, the Nash equilibrium in any one-shot play of the game, as in the Patron-Client game, is noncooperation. Each has an incentive to cheat in good times.

But suppose that in a repeated game, each plays the Grim Trigger strategy, implying that refusal to provide aid in any period means that from the next period forward, the player receives only the expected utility available under autarky, $\frac{1}{2}\sqrt{0} + \frac{1}{2}\sqrt{9} = 1.5$, or what he could get outside the network. Thus by refusing to come to the aid of his kinsman, a peasant would gain a utility payoff of 3 in the present, but an expected utility of only 1.5 each period thereafter, or $3 + \frac{\delta 1.5}{1-\delta}$. This payoff can be compared to the payoff from cooperation in every period, $\frac{2.12}{1-\delta}$, the latter of which is preferred for sufficiently "patient" players with $\delta > 0.59$.[7] Therefore, given sufficient patience on the part of players, or a sufficiently short time between plays of the game, a solidarity network can emerge.

The poorer people are, the more incentive they have to be part of such a network. Poverty fosters solidarity between individuals. Continuing with our numerical example from Figure 5.1, suppose our wealthy patron, Sukhbir were part of a similar solidarity network with Sunil, head of an identically wealthy household, realizing utility of 5 ($=\sqrt{25}$) in the good state of nature and a utility of 4 ($=\sqrt{16}$) in the bad

---

[7] Although the most simple strategy to use for illustrational purposes, one should notice that the Grim Trigger strategy may lack credibility, as the punishment also hurts the punisher by forcing him also into perpetual autarky. Consider an alternative strategy, a punishment-accepting form of Tit-for-Tat, in which an offending player allows the affected player to keep any income generated by either of them in the period after a defection. The payoff from defection is then $3 + 0(\delta) + 2.12\delta^2/(1-\delta)$, which allows for cooperation if $\delta > 0.415$. This Tit-for-Tat strategy is a more credible threat than the Grim Trigger because the threatened punishment actually benefits the punisher rather than harms him!

state of nature. For consistency assume that in the solidarity network they play the same Grim Trigger strategy – defection by a partner means the end of all cooperation. Continuing to aid the unfortunate member incurring the negative shock in each period would yield a payoff of $\frac{4.53}{1-\delta}$ (since $4.53 = \sqrt{20.5}$); refusal to aid a partner in need would yield $5 + \frac{\delta 4.50}{1-\delta}$. Note that the difference between the solidarity payoff and the autarky payoff, 4.53 versus 4.50, is so small that even the strictest solidarity pact (i.e., the Grim Trigger strategy) cannot assure cooperation for any level of δ less than 0.94. This contrasts with the requirement that δ be greater than only 0.59 in the low-income solidarity network. Although poverty breeds *inter*dependence, wealth fosters *in*dependence.

Breakdowns in Insurance Networks

What can cause networks to break down? Oddly, both wealth accumulation and wealth depletion can be the genesis of solidarity breakdown. As Marcel Fafchamps (1992) observes, wealth accumulation by individual households yields both advantages and disadvantages for solidarity networks. One household in the network rejoices in the wealth accumulation of another – but only to a point. When one individual household accumulates wealth, the network initially benefits because the added store of wealth creates a bigger buffer against bad states of nature. But too much wealth accumulation by one household begins to make the others nervous. At some point, the wealthy household may pull out of the insurance network if gains from reciprocity no longer outweigh the costs. Its own wealth creates a self-sufficiency that allows the household to ride through the storms of life independently. Friendships sometimes operate in a similar manner: We root for the success of our friends but may feel threatened if an overabundance of success might lead them to invest less in the relationship.

Wealth depletion can also either increase or decrease solidarity within the network. It can cause a growing solidarity and interdependence because at lower levels of wealth, shocks are more harmful. However, if increasing poverty renders some individuals so destitute that they can no longer contribute, it can lead to their exclusion.

The concept of the *core*, which is often used in cooperative game theory, is useful for understanding solidarity network breakdown. The idea is that when a group of individuals form a cooperative coalition, that coalition is able to produce a "surplus value" among its members, such as through transacting commodities or sharing risks. An allocation of benefits among a group of individuals lies within the *core* if there is no subcoalition existing within the original group that could achieve a higher surplus value for its members by forming its own separate arrangement.

A related concept in cooperative game theory is the *Shapley value*. The Shapley value reflects the average added benefit any player brings into the possible coalitions to which he could belong, given that each size coalition is equally likely. A player with a high Shapley value is able to exert greater bargaining power within any coalition to which he belongs and thus should expect to receive a bigger share of the surplus created by the coalition. One with a lower Shapley value brings less bargaining power. This is, of course, what we generally observe in the real world: Those who could be valuable additions to lots of different "teams" command a high price for their allegiance; those who add less, receive less.

Viewing peasant solidarity networks as coalitions, an increasingly wealthy household becomes a more valuable member of the network because of its greater ability to help the group weather financial storms. However, in light of its rising Shapley value, it may also demand more exacting terms from the poorer households for remaining in the network. This can foster social pressures or jealousies against wealth accumulation in traditional societies, since growing inequality may threaten the very existence of the network, or may shift the bargaining power within the network against the more vulnerable members.

Fafchamps considers the plight of the destitute, the sick, or the old for whom the expected contribution (Shapley value) within a solidarity network may be low, especially during a negative aggregate shock such as a famine. Sadly, the destitute, the old, and the sick may no longer be attractive partners for others. As the original network no longer lies in the core, a subcoalition may break off from the original group that excludes the weaker members.

To understand this idea more concretely, suppose that Ravi and Ashok are joined by a third peasant in their network, Quezar, who grows ornamental flowers. Now we will introduce three states of nature each with probability 1/3: hot, cool, and rainy. Ashok's clay pots dry only when it's hot, Quezar's flowers flourish when it's cool (droop when it's hot and become moldy in the rain), and Ravi's rice needs rain. Each of the three's projects yields 9 in its favorable state of nature, but zero in the other two. Utility for each remains equal to the square root of income and $\delta = 0.9$.

Can a solidarity network hold together under a Grim Trigger strategy? Yes, because a cooperating player receives $\frac{\sqrt{3}}{1-\delta} = 17.3$, while a defecting player gets $\sqrt{9} + \frac{0.33(\sqrt{9})}{1-\delta} = 13$. Now suppose one member, say, Ravi, is sick and his rice yields a zero even when it rains. Does the coalition of three in the solidarity network continue to lie in the "core"? No, because when they maintain Ravi as part of the network, each of the three receives $\frac{0.67(\sqrt{3})}{1-\delta} = 11.6$. By excluding Ravi, Ashok and Quezar receive $\frac{0.67(\sqrt{4.5})}{1-\delta} = 14.2$. Sadly, for Ravi, the other two are better off without him, and the original coalition of three no longer resides in the core.

Solidarity Networks in Transitional Economies

Solidarity networks are not limited to peasant economies. John McMillan and Chris Woodruff (2002) explore the emergence of entrepreneurialism in transition economies when formal institutions are weak. Their study began with the administration of surveys to merchants, traders, and service providers in Russia, China, Poland, and Vietnam. Surveys contained questions regarding profit and other data related to their businesses, and their relationship to other entrepreneurs and the state.

Results from the surveys confirmed that during the early years of economic transition to a market economy, governments in the transition economies did little in these countries to support small business activity. Legal guaranties of property rights were insecure. Contract law was nascent, and enforcement of contract law was unreliable. Entrepreneurs enjoyed little protection from swindlers, organized criminal elements, and the generally dishonest. In particular, McMillan and Woodruff asked,

> How did the entrepreneurs succeed in overcoming the lack of market-supporting institutions? Ongoing relationships among firms substituted for the missing institutions. Firms relied on the logic of incentives for cooperation to arise in playing a repeated game. Where courts and laws are unreliable for settling disputes, firms trust their customers to pay their bills and other suppliers to deliver quality goods out of the prospect of future business. (2002, p. 159)

McMillan relates one particular story from this study in his excellent (2002) book *Reinventing the Bazaar: A Natural History of Markets*. Vietnam had begun a series of reforms to its economy during the mid-1980s intended to spur growth in small manufacturing businesses. As with many economies transitioning from socialism, the state allowed local forms of entrepreneurialism but essentially left firms to fend for themselves in enforcing business contracts. Only a few years later, these enterprises were booming but with almost no institutional support from the Vietnamese government. As McMillan writes,

> Disputes (among Vietnamese entrepreneurs) were prevented partly by the threat of loss of future business. The sanction for nonpayment of a debt was to cut off further dealings with the debtor, though the entrepreneurs tried to prevent disputes form getting to this point. If a debt was not paid, one manager said, he "negotiates patiently." Getting money repaid, "is an art, which is very difficult to explain." (2002, p. 58.)

To avoid the schemes of hucksters and the noncompliant, entrepreneurs relied on a network of buyers and suppliers with whom they engaged in a long series of repeated transactions. Furthermore, information was shared about dealings among different buyers and sellers during social gatherings between network members. McMillan continues,

> People in the same line of business would meet each other every day in teahouses and bars. An aluminum-goods producer said that when he meets fellow producers, they discuss the reliability of particular customers. Another, making steel products, said he meets other businesspeople everyday to exchange information about customers. These regular meetings, he said, "create an ethic in doing business which helps the market work." If a customer cheated a manufacturer, the others would hear about it and might blacklist the debtor. (2002, p. 59.)

In the same way that solidarity networks in peasant economies substitute for formal insurance institutions, networks of entrepreneurs in transitional economies use the incentives of a repeated game as a surrogate for institutions that guarantee contractual enforcement. Consider the relationship between a retailer and a wholesale supplier. The retailer who makes a bulk purchase of goods from a wholesaler typically pays on credit, a promise to pay his invoice within, say, thirty days. On the

Vladimir

		Swindle	Comply
Boris	Swindle	0 / 0	-2 / 5
	Comply	5 / -2	3 / 3

Figure 5.4. Market Exchange Game

other side of the transaction, the retailer may be unable to ascertain the true quality of the goods sold by the wholesaler; the true quality of the goods may not be clear until long after he buys them. Thus, the retailer may obtain goods on credit, and fail to pay. And even if the retailer pays, the wholesaler may fail to send the goods, or send the retailer shoddy goods. We can represent this game as an application of the Prisoners Dilemma as seen in Figure 5.4.

In a one-shot game, both Boris and Vladimir have dominant strategy to Swindle; the defecting behavior is a best response regardless of the action taken by the other. In a repeated-game context, however, cooperation becomes possible. Consider again a Grim Trigger strategy by both players. If one player cheats another, he is cast out of the "circle of trust," swindled forever after. Faced with a Grim Trigger strategy by Boris, Vladimir can receive $\frac{3}{1-\delta}$ by dealing honestly, but gets $5 + \frac{\delta \cdot 0}{1-\delta}$ for swindling. Because the game is symmetrical, the same incentives apply to Boris. In this example, cooperation is possible within the network for any $\delta > 0.40$. Thus, given sufficient patience on the part of the players, honest business behavior can emerge spontaneously, even absent formal legal mechanisms to enforce it.

Limits to Solidarity Networks in Industrialized Economies

A natural question at this point might be the following: If cooperation naturally arises within solidarity networks, then why bother with the formal institutions of developed economies? The problem is that while solidarity networks operate among business associates at some level in nearly every kind of economy, a total reliance on them as a surrogate for formal legal institutions is not conducive to long-term economic growth, causing an economy to underperform to its potential. Solidarity networks require a relatively small number of individuals within which reputations circulate freely, the discount factor δ being related to the frequency of interaction between individuals. If interactions are infrequent, by definition δ falls, and cooperation becomes more difficult. Because advanced economies must be characterized by a high degree of specialization and the frequent need for one-shot interaction, they require a web of transactions that extend outside the boundaries of a local solidarity network.

Rachel Kranton at University of Maryland argues in a well-known (1996) paper that systems of reciprocity tend to break down as the number of participants increases, which happens as an economy grows. As the number of participants in the network rises, threats of relationship termination for deviant behavior become less worrisome; there are too many other alternatives. Moreover, when individuals or firms desire access to a larger variety of goods, systems of reciprocity and solidarity networks fair poorly, as a larger number of traders enter the system. In both cases, solidarity networks tend to dissolve in favor of formal markets and enforcement mechanisms, where large numbers of buyers and sellers exchange with one another on a more impersonal basis.

It turns out that this is almost precisely what McMillan and Woodruff observe in their transitional economies. While solidarity networks and reciprocity are helpful in the early stages of development, they find that pressure begins to develop in the transitional economies that favors the emergence of formal markets and market-regulating institutions. As businesses expand during the normal process of economic development, they typically attract a greater number of consumers and require a greater number of suppliers. Moreover, in the early stages of transition to a market economy, profits are often high for new businesses, but profits always attract competition. As the number of competing enterprises in an industry increases, the implicit threats needed to sustain cooperation in the repeated game become less meaningful.

It is in this context that entrepreneurs and other business interests exert political pressure in the transitional economies for legal means of enforcing contracts, a subject we will pursue in Chapter Nine. Strong legal protection of property rights and contracts dissuade Prisoners' Dilemma–like defections, even in less-personalized, one-shot interactions, and in this sense are more broadly able to curtail opportunistic behavior. Individual reputations and accountability move beyond a small network of friends and associates as entrepreneurs develop a relationship with the market as a whole. This transition from personalized transactions to a more impersonal market structure, whether for better or for worse, is a key characteristic of economic development. Although long-term relationships may remain important after the transition, the primary means of enforcing agreements becomes the state, rather than the social network. Thus, we see that an important characteristic of a developed economy is that individuals are able to enjoy a similar level of confidence entering into a transaction with someone outside the network as they do with a familiar face within the network.

CHAPTER 6

Understanding Agrarian Institutions

When the cat's away . . . the mice will play.
– Old Saying

WHAT DO TEENAGE ice-cream scoopers, taxi drivers, door-to-door salesmen, and peasant day laborers all have in common? The answer is, at least at work, they all can be difficult to monitor and motivate. Economics considers a fundamental problem in which a *principal*, who needs a task carried out, hires an *agent* to carry out the task. The problem is that once the agent is hired, the agent's interests may not match those of the principal. As any supervisor of human resources can attest, a hired worker left unmonitored and unmotivated is a worker tempted by the twin evils of sloth and self-indulgence. The labor supervision problem is a definitive example of moral hazard, the incentive for an agent to act in his own interest rather than the interest of the principal when the agent's actions are hidden. As a result of moral hazard in labor markets, the principal may never offer a labor contract in the first place unless he can design a contract that sufficiently lines up the agent's incentives with his own.

In this chapter, we will examine three different types of contracts between principals and agents: fixed-wage, fixed-rent, and share contracts. We will explore how these different types of contracts address the issues of moral hazard and risk sharing in the context of some industrialized country labor market examples, and then analyze how they shape the agrarian institutions that order rural economic life in developing countries.

Fixed-Wage Contracts

When I was 16, I made my grand entrance into the world of work as an ice-cream scooper at the downtown Baskin-Robbins of Davis, California. My boss was retired Air Force lieutenant Jack Nunn, whom my father wryly called the "Ice Cream Man." Though always fair-minded, Nunn took his role in the community seriously as a provider of early teenage employment, and he approached his managerial task with a stern countenance. We were all hired at minimum wage, and promised a raise of 15 cents an hour for every six months on the job. As teenagers, we were certainly interested in making money, but this was, of course, only one of many interests.

Among these other interests was being somewhat more generous with our scoops, especially to our friends, than the Baskin-Robbins ice-cream manual suggested.

During training, Nunn had rigorously emphasized the 2.5-ounce scoop dictated by the manual, which, in our view, was rather too close to the size of a Ping-Pong ball. As he left the store to run errands, our scoops would magically grow, often approaching softball size and beyond. No scooper likes to see a disappointed expression on the face of an ice-cream cone recipient, especially that of a teenage peer. As a result of our generosity, friends visited the store with abnormal frequency, to the point that the store became a haven for ice-cream starved teenagers and others who had missed an important meal.

Though the Ice Cream Man did his best to supervise us, constant monitoring was out of the question, for he wore other hats. One monitoring tool was a statistic he meticulously calculated and labeled the "gross scoop index," ice-cream tub purchases divided by gross sales receipts, which he tracked weekly on a chart stapled to the back room wall. The index often hovered at mysteriously high levels. Yet it was difficult to identify who the overscooping culprits were with precision. Rumor had it that sometimes he would pretend to leave in the evening but secretly observe us behind the steering wheel of his truck in the parking lot, shrouded by darkness, sipping on an ice-cream soda while monitoring the size of our scoops through old Air Force binoculars. Others believed that it was Nunn himself who strategically circulated the rumor to make us *think* that he was always watching, like a kind of omniscient Deity.

With any fixed-wage contract, the role of the principal can be complicated and taxing. Tragically, he passed away not many years after my short tenure there, and it was hard to believe it merely a result of his high-glucose snack habit. Military service must have seemed easy compared with supervising teenagers at work. I think we wore him out.

Because fixed-wage contracts are ripe with the potential for moral hazard, they are typically used only when the principal can easily monitor agents. A fixed-wage contract usually includes some explicit or implicit understanding that if a worker is caught slacking or behaving dishonestly too many times (or maybe even once), she may be fired. Berkeley's Carl Shapiro and Nobel laureate Joseph Stiglitz have used this threat of termination under a fixed-wage contract to explain the persistence of unemployment in market economies. Their efficiency wage theory is that an employer (principal) offers a fixed-wage contract that pays the worker (agent) something in excess of the market-clearing wage. This gives the agent something to lose if she is caught shirking. Meanwhile, both employers and employees understand that if a worker shirks, she will be caught only some fraction of the time because monitoring of workers is imperfect. The intuition of their theory is that if it is worthwhile for one firm to offer this kind of contract to workers, then it must be worthwhile for *all* firms to do so. However, this leads to a labor market in which the prevailing wage is greater than the wage at which supply equals demand for labor, meaning that an excess supply of workers results in the market, *i.e.* unemployment. But in the framework of Shapiro and Stiglitz, this pool of unemployed workers operates to the employer's advantage. The threat of being cast into this pool of the unemployed helps discourage workers from shirking, hence the title of their renowned 1984 paper: "Equilibrium Unemployment as a Worker Discipline Device."

For such a scheme to keep a lid on shirking, however, the expected penalty for getting caught (the probability of getting caught times the value of lost wages) must be greater than shirking's benefits (the probability of not getting caught times the bliss of shirking on the job). Clearly, if monitoring is poor, a fixed wage would have to be very high to prevent shirking, maybe even so high that the principal won't be able to hire the agent with a fixed-wage contract at all.

Fixed-Rent Contracts

The impossibility of preventing shirking in a fixed-wage contract is recognized first-hand by taxicab companies everywhere. While monitoring ice-cream scoopers may pose its challenges, monitoring cab drivers is nothing short of impossible. Because the nature of cab drivers' work requires them to roam around urban areas in perpetual pursuit of riders, one can only imagine the creative ways cab drivers might spend their time if they were paid a fixed wage independent of ridership. As a result, they often work off a fixed-rent contract, where cab drivers (the agents) pay a flat rate to a firm (the principal) to lease their taxis. Their net income then is what they are able to bring in from riders in fares and tips less gasoline costs and the rent payment paid to the cab company.

Lease rates for taxis in the United States depend on a number of factors, including the particular urban area but generally fall in the range of $50 to $100 per day. Samuel Singh of "Friendly Yellow Cab" in Berkeley, California, says that he and his co-workers pay $60 per day to lease their taxis. In exchange, the cab company maintains the vehicles, and the drivers receive radio dispatches from the cab company's central office, though not as many as Singh would like. (A good deal of the time they are forced to waste time chatting and playing cards with one another as they wait for passengers near public transit stations.) Lease rates for some cab companies fall to as low as $250 per week, but this rate doesn't come with dispatch service. Asked how much he is able to clear per day, he replies "Usually about $100, sometimes less; maybe $200 on the best days when there are lots of students."

In contrast with a fixed-wage contract, a fixed-rent contract provides ample incentive for hard work. For example, drivers in the San Francisco Bay Area often work 12–16 hours a day just to clear $100, sometimes averaging less than the U.S. minimum wage.[1] How much they take home at night in fares and tips substantially depends on their developed hunches about where passengers may be waiting, their intimate knowledge of a city, and their navigational acumen.

Remarkably, biologists at the University of London found that the self-motivated rigors of urban cab driving actually causes taxi drivers' "grey matter" (brains) to

---

[1] Mike Cassidy, "Yellow Cab 4 Show Courage But Lose Jobs," *San Jose Mercury News*, September 6, 2005. Article available online at www.mywire.com/pubs/MercuryNews/2005/09/06/992231?extID = 10037&oliID = 229

enlarge as they become forced to store an enormously detailed mental map of their cities and solve complex navigational problems. They found that, relative to other people, experienced cab drivers grew a larger *hippocampus*, the frontal area of the brain associated with navigational skills.[2] Startled by the findings, taxi driver David Cohen of the London Cab Drivers' Club remarked: "I never noticed that part of my brain growing – makes you wonder what happened to the rest of it." [3]

Although it clearly addresses the moral hazard problem, a fixed-rent contract leaves the agents, who are typically risk averse, with large swings in their incomes. No matter how their day goes, they still owe the cab company its $60. Fortunately, for taxi drivers, these swings in income occur on a daily basis, allowing the vacillations to average out nicely over the weeks and months. Consequently, a fixed-rent contract may not be as unattractive to taxi drivers as to, say, peasant farmers, whose incomes vary not on a daily basis but rather on a yearly basis. Thus, we would expect to see fixed-rent contracts in instances where monitoring is difficult for the principle, and swings in income over a larger season are not too severe.

Share Contracts

One of the most common examples of the principal-agent problem occurs between a principal who wants something sold but needs someone else to do the selling. Whether one is selling shoes, cosmetics, advertising space, or vacuum cleaners, it is easy to be passive about selling someone else's product. A really good sales job takes not only time but also sensitivity, energy and creativity, which may be more naturally directed toward one's more personal interests. Consequently, salespeople, acting as agents of a principal, nearly always receive contracts flush with incentives for closing the deal with customers. A typical salesperson receives a relatively low fixed wage and a commission on each sale that is a percentage of the item's final selling price. Usually the more difficult it is to monitor the salesperson, the greater the percentage of the salesperson's income is composed of commission. When monitoring by the principal is easier, the fixed-wage component may be higher, while still providing some incentive for an enthusiastic sales effort.

The supervisors of door-to-door salespeople face a double dose of difficulty that surpasses that of the ordinary principal. First, they face the ordinary problem of motivating their sales staff to interact persuasively with customers. But unlike a salesperson selling shoes or cosmetics in the confines of a physical retail space, they face a colossal monitoring problem due to the ambulatory nature of their sales staff. In practice, the supervisor simply can't monitor the salespeople at all. As a result, door-to-door salespeople labor under contracts that often pay no fixed wage whatsoever, with their income entirely consisting of a share of their gross sales.

In 1906, Alfred C. Fuller founded a legendary door-to-door sales enterprise, the Fuller Brush Company. Fuller began the company, renowned for its distinctive collection of home and personal care products, by establishing three basic rules for

---

[2] "Taxi Drivers' Brains 'Grow' on the Job," Sci-Tech Section, *BBC News*, March 14, 2000.
[3] Ibid.

his products: make it work; make it last; and guarantee it "no matter what."[4] His company took off quickly. Fuller became something of a folk hero, and the traveling Fuller Brush Man became an American folk icon. Early Walt Disney cartoons cast Donald Duck in the role of a Fuller Brush Man.[5] In Disney's rendition of the Three Little Pigs, the Big Bad Wolf appeared at the little pigs' front door disguised as a Fuller Brush Man before he huffed and puffed and tried to blow their houses down.

Fuller Brush products, which include everything from floor brushes, brooms, and household cleaners to lotions, fragrances, and hair-care aids, are manufactured at a plant in Great Bend, Kansas. However, they are sold, in large part, by a virtual army of door-to-door salespeople. From the company's beginning, salespeople have worked on commission only, with no base salary. The origins of this contract came from Fuller's own boyhood experience in his home Nova Scotia, where he picked strawberries for a neighbor, earning 1 cent per quart. He was known to pick up to 30 quarts a day. He wrote later,

> If I had picked strawberries on an hourly wage, I would have eaten most of them, and quit early to swim in the enticing river that was never out of view. I know what would have happened to me – I'd be in Nova Scotia yet, gazing at my weedy fields and wondering why times were so hard, bitter against a world which had not given me something for nothing.[6]

According to sales office personnel, Fuller Brush salespeople today begin with what is essentially a share contract that gives them 20 to 24 percent of the retail price of a sold product, rising to 26 to 46 percent with higher sales volume.

Incentives matter and can powerfully effect people's work ethic and behavior. Contracts, specifying these incentives, are powerful enough to alter work personalities. The incentives created by different types of labor contracts explain why post office workers are often surly, waiters are often polite, and salespeople are often aggressively polite. A properly structured share contract may elicit a strong sales effort, but it can also create moral hazard problems of its own. Specifically, it can motivate a pushy sales behavior that may marginally increase the chances of an immediate sale from a gullible client but damage the image of the company in the eyes of other potential customers, thus reducing the chances of a future sale captured by another salesperson. For example, Internet blogs and discussion groups overflow with disaster stories of Kirby vacuum cleaner salesmen, infamous for their unyielding sales techniques. The following is an excerpt of one such story relayed by "Bob's Brain" of Yexley.net:

> (My wife) and I were just sitting on the couch watching a little bit of TV talking about going to bed early because we were tired, and here comes this guy knocking on our door. I got up and walked to the door and he looks at me and says "You must be Bob" – thinking to myself "OK, how in the . . . do you know my name stranger? He explained that he was there to give us our demo. So I said to the guy, "At nine o'clock at night?!"

---

[4] "Alfred C. Fuller: The Original Fuller Brush Man," company website www.myfullerbrush.com/history.htm. (Accessed 10/15/2005.)

[5] Ibid.

[6] Ibid.

He continues on to explain that it "won't take long" and that they'll "be out of 'hair' in no time." Alright, come on in. Anyway, to make a long story short, this guy spends the next HOUR giving us this stupid Kirby vacuum cleaner demonstration while his rookie partner just sat there in our chair watching the TV that was on mute . . . The whole time this guy is asking us these stupid questions with ridiculously obvious answers like "Do you like to save money" and "Do you like being healthy" and various other insulting stuff like that. Then he asks us if we have any salt, so I give him a can of it and he proceeds to pour HALF OF IT into a pile in the middle of our carpet and then grinds it all down into our carpet. I'm sorry, there's no WAY he (vacuumed) all of that salt up after as much as he dumped down there and ground all down into it. I was pretty torqued . . .[7]

Since agents are rewarded based only on their own sales, they have no incentive to internalize the negative consequences of their "nonsales" behavior. Thus, a strict share contract can create a divergence between the interest of the agents and the principal. We will see that this phenomenon exhibits some parallels with the behavior of peasant farmers who are given high-powered, short-term productivity incentives but lack the long-term incentives to promote sustainable land use.

When would we expect to see principals use share contracts? Share contracts provide stronger incentives for agents than fixed-wage contracts, though, as we will see later in this chapter, they lack the strength of incentives embodied in a fixed-rent contract. Share contracts also distribute risk between the agent and the principal and in this way are more attractive to a risk-averse agent than a fixed-rent contract. Thus, we should observe share contracts when monitoring is difficult for the principal and when agents are risk-averse and susceptible to idiosyncratic shocks to their incomes – events that affect their productivity but are out of their control, like moody customers.

Land and Labor Contracts in LDCs

Imagine an agrarian society in which land was distributed perfectly evenly across households. Assuming there were no economies of scale in agriculture, there would be little need for land or labor contracts. This imaginary (and somewhat utopian) agrarian society would consist of a multitude of self-employed family farmers, each working their own uniform plot of land. In practice, land distribution varies considerably between countries in the developing world, and in many areas, it is brutally unequal. Speaking in general terms, in the Asian countries the distribution of land tends to be more uniform: 92.5 percent of farms and 90.1 percent of land is owner-cultivated, and 70 percent of farmland is made up of small farms of less than 5 acres in size. Contrast this with the savage inequalities of Latin America, where owner cultivation falls to 68.5 percent of farms, and farms of less than 5 hectares make up less than 10 percent of all farmland. [8] In Africa, where private property rights are far

---

[7] "Bob's Brain," www.Yexley.net/blogs/bob/archive/2004/06/08/KirbySucks.aspx. (Accessed 11/26/05.)
[8] Camara (2004) (data from FAO 1990 World Agricultural Census) and Otsuka et. al. (1992) (data from FAO 1970 World Agricultural Census.) See de Janvry (1981), chapter 2 for details on the historical inequalities in land ownership across Latin American countries.

less defined, a great deal of agricultural land is communally owned, only about 5.2 percent of farms and 9.2 percent of land is owner cultivated.[9]

Any time there is an imbalance in land ownership in an agricultural economy, it creates a demand for labor among the land abundant, and a demand for land among the landless. In other words, those with an excess of land will tend to hire labor, and they also may rent out (or sell) land. Those with a shortage of land will tend to enter the labor market, and they also may rent (or buy) land. The formation of any of these markets – land rental or purchase and labor rental (we will rule out labor purchase, i.e., slavery) – will release the natural pressure to equalize the labor/land ratio across agricultural landholdings. Whichever market functions better will probably be the one that does the job.

Unfortunately, the market for land *sales* in a poor economy, where households are continually strapped for cash, depends heavily on well-functioning credit markets. It is difficult for households living close to subsistence to self-finance the purchase of a big asset such as a tract of land. But because credit markets function notoriously poorly in developing countries (a phenomenon we will explore in depth in the next chapter), the market mechanism tends to operate through land rental markets and the market for hired agricultural labor. In these two markets we commonly observe fix-rent contracts for land, fixed-wage contracts for labor, and the hybrid institution that has evolved in numerous and diverse regions of the world, *sharecropping*.

Because of its highly unequal land distribution, agricultural production in Latin America has historically occurred on large plantations, or *haciendas*, where land-less peasant laborers are employed in often serf-like conditions by a landlord, or *patron*.[10] Because there tend to be economies of scale in monitoring workers (e.g., it takes less than ten times the effort for a supervisor to monitor ten workers as it does to monitor one worker), large-scale landholdings have historically facilitated the widespread use of landless or semi-landless laborers in agricultural production across Latin America.

Many currently existing agricultural institutions originate from *labor tenancy*, a quasi-feudal agrarian arrangement in which a *patron* allows peasants to live on and cultivate a portion of his land. In return, the patron provides a subsistence living for the peasant, often coming in the form of small amounts of cash, payment in crops, and help in times of distress. Some social scientists have disparaged labor tenancy as a particularly backward agrarian institution, partly because it appears to have evolved after the abolition of slavery in the eighteenth and nineteenth centuries, but in practice can be difficult to distinguish from it. Nevertheless, as pointed out by Berkeley's Elizabeth Sadoulet (1992), labor tenancy is an institution that serves at least two important purposes. It provides a form of security and insurance to peasant laborers, while simultaneously reducing the default risk for landlords that accompanies fixed-rent contracts. Sadoulet argues that these properties appear to have explained its persistence, for example in Chile, long after fixed-rent contracts

---

[9] Otsuka et. al. (1992).
[10] de Janvry (1981), pp. 73–85.

had become available. But labor tenancy has generally declined in Latin America, both as a result of increasing opportunities for labor and as a result of agrarian reforms enacted across Latin America in the 1960s and 1970s. In Chile, for example, legal labor tenancy came to a halt in the late 1960s when the government passed a law requiring estate owners to pay their tenants a minimum cash wage. [11]

Sharecropping does exist in Latin America, notably in Chile and Colombia, but represents only about 16 percent of all of agrarian tenancy arrangements.[12] Share-cropping is also practiced in Africa but in a relatively limited context in which it is used for gaining access to additional land if land access via rights to tribal property is insufficient to meet household consumption needs. As a result, sharecroppers in Africa are often referred to as *strangers* because they are usually migrants. These migrants are not necessarily landless but have often left their home communities due to population pressures on their own tribal lands.[13]

Two other types of sharecropping in Africa can occur when one household with excess land lies near another household with excess labor or with draft animals. One form of sharecropping (called *tetebani* in Ethiopia) typically results in the payment of one-fourth to one-half of the harvest from the labor- or animal-owning household to the landowning household. A related form of sharecropping, called *haresti riba'e*, involves an animal and landowning family providing *all* inputs except labor into a plot of land, for which they typically received three-fourths of the output from the work of a tenant laborer.[14]

Sharecropping is much more common in southern Asia, where it is the contract of choice in the vast majority of tenant occupancies (almost 85 percent), including 91 percent in Bangladesh, 60 percent in Indonesia, 79 percent in the Philippines, and 48 percent in India.[15] One of the best-known empirical studies on land tenancy and sharecropping, undertaken by Radwan Shaban (1987), investigates the contractual characteristics of 7,811 different plots across eight different Indian villages.[16] Shaban finds that while 80.9 percent of the plots are owner-cultivated, the vast majority of nonowner tenancies (17.5 percent of the remaining 19.1 percent) were at least partially under share contracts, while only 1.6 percent had pure fixed-rent contracts.

Pranab Bardhan (1980) presents data on sharecropping from 334 randomly chosen villages in four states in northern and eastern India: West Bengal, Bihar, Uttar Pradesh, and Orissa. Of the many striking findings from the study is the frequency that 50–50 is the preferred share contract, witnessed in more than two-thirds of the observations in the survey. Moreover, corresponding with what theories of risk-sharing would predict, he finds that sharecroppers who cultivate (somewhat more risky) high-yield-variety rice paddies tend to be rewarded with contracts that give

[11] Lastarria-Cornhiel and Melmed-Sanjak (1999), pp. 20–25.
[12] Otsuka et. al. (1992).
[13] Lastarria-Cornhiel and Melmed-Sanjak (1999), p. 36.
[14] Ibid., p. 38.
[15] Otsuka et al. (1992).
[16] The villages are from the ICRISAT (International Crops Research Institute for the Semi-Arid Tropics) study covering Aurapalle, Dokur, Shirapur, Kalman, Kanzara, Kinkheda, Boriya, Rampura, located in the Indian states of Maharashtra, Andhra Pradesh, and Gujarat.

them higher shares, as do tenants who use new, but potentially risky, chemical inputs. Why sharecropping so dominates South Asian land tenancy arrangements, and the effect of sharecropping on economic growth in rural areas, are issues that we will investigate further in this chapter.

Wage and Land Contracts in Agricultural Tenancy

Every type of principal-agent contract must meet two requirements from the perspective of the principal. First, the contract must satisfy a *participation constraint*. This means that the contract offered by the principal must induce the agent to sign on the dotted line; it must offer a better deal for the agent than his best alternative. If the expected utility under the proposed contract falls below the agent's best alternative, his "reservation utility," the agent will take his business elsewhere. Second, the contract must satisfy an *incentive constraint*. The terms of the contract must induce the agent to work diligently in the interest of the principal rather than work lackadaisically or direct his energy toward other ends.

The extensive-form game in Figure 6.1 shows participation and incentive constraints in a wage contract. The players include a Landowner (the principal), who owns more land than he himself can work. Assuming that he chooses not to sell, his excess land motivates him to either enter the labor market as an employer, or offer his land in the rental market. In either case, he seeks the services of a laborer who I will call the Tiller (the agent), to work his extra land.

Let's suppose that the Landowner considers a wage contract. At the outset of the game, the Landowner can propose a wage to the Tiller, who can either accept or reject the contract. If no contract is offered or accepted, then both receive their reservation utilities, $\overline{U}_L$ and $\overline{U}_T$, respectively. If the Landowner offers and the Tiller accepts, the Tiller then chooses a level of effort to exert in preparing the land, planting, watering and weeding, and finally, harvesting. To keep things simple, suppose that he chooses between just two levels of effort: "Toil" (work hard), and "Shirk" (slack off). Toiling is unpleasant and costs the Tiller e units of his utility. Shirking allows the Tiller to

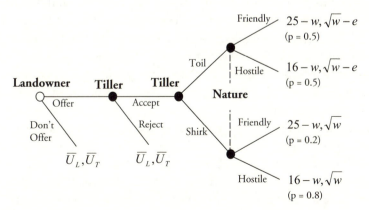

Figure 6.1. Principal-Agent with Fixed-Wage Contract for Tiller

catch up on some well-deserved rest, costing him zero units of utility. Nature also has a hand in determining whether things turn out well or poorly, but the probability that Nature is "friendly" rather than "hostile" to the crop is greater if the Tiller toils rather than shirks. If the Tiller toils, there is a 50 percent chance that the crop will yield a bountiful harvest of 25 and a 50 percent chance that it will yield only 16. If the Tiller shirks, there is only a 20 percent chance the yield will be 25, and an 80 percent chance that the yield will be 16. Although hard work, applying the proper amount of herbicide, protecting the crops against wind and rain damage, and so forth, reduces the threshold at which Nature turns from friend to foe, there is not a perfect correlation between the effort of the Tiller and the final yield of the crop. Even if the Tiller works hard, bugs may eat the crop, a fungus may break out, or weed seeds may blow in from a neighboring field. Moreover, because perfect monitoring of the Tiller's effort is impossible, the Landlord is unable to discern whether a bad crop was caused by an unavoidable act of Nature or a lazy Tiller. As with teenage ice-cream scoopers, it is hard for the boss to tell if the ice cream is disappearing by accident, on purpose, or a combination of both.

Assume for now that the Tiller is risk averse in income, but the ostensibly richer Landlord is risk neutral so that the payoff to the Landlord is equal to Y, where Y is the crop yield minus wage expenses, w, and the payoff to the Tiller is $\sqrt{w} - e$, where e again is effort – again, equal to zero in the case of shirking.

If you examine Figure 6.1 closely, you will notice that this game is really just a fancy version of a Trust game – with a little bit of imperfect information thrown in. The Landlord would like to offer the Tiller a wage contract, but any time shirking is more fun than toiling, the Tiller has an incentive to shirk in a one-shot play of the game, since $\sqrt{w} > \sqrt{w} - e$. Even a relatively hard-working Tiller has an incentive to shirk, since e could be small, but is always likely to be greater than zero. Because of moral hazard, in a one-shot play of the game the landlord will never offer any fixed-wage contract where the Tiller's wage is so high that $0.2\,(25 - w) + 0.8\,(16 - w) < \overline{U}_L$. However, when $0.2\,(25 - w) + 0.8\,(16 - w) \geq \overline{U}_L$, by using backward induction, we see that a Nash equilibrium does exist in which the Landlord offers a fixed-wage contract that is accepted by the Tiller if it satisfies the Tiller's participation constraint that $\sqrt{w} \geq \overline{U}_T$. But in this one-shot play of the game, the Nash equilibrium involves shirking, and thus while it is a Nash equilibrium, it fails to satisfy the incentive constraint. If his business is good enough, and alternatives for hired labor are bad enough, the principal may simply end up hiring a slacker. Even though a contract may be offered in this case, the Landlord obviously prefers that the Tiller would Toil rather than Shirk because it improves his chances of receiving the residual profits from a more bountiful harvest.

The moral hazard problem endemic to a fixed-wage contract may be resolved by switching to a fixed-rent contract (as seen in Figure 6.2), in which the consequences of any shirking are borne by the Tiller himself. Nevertheless, as in the theory of Shapiro and Stiglitz, the moral hazard problem may also be addressed by offering the fixed-wage contract in the context of a repeated-game. A wage contract is offered, but may (or may not) be renewed in subsequent periods. Here, the enticing carrot

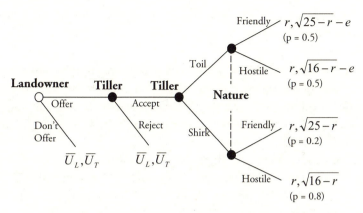

Figure 6.2. Principal-Agent with Fixed-Rent Contract for Tiller

of future contracts is dangled in front of the agent, while the stick of termination threatens from behind. But such a scheme works only if there is some positive probability of the agent getting caught slacking on the job. Let's denote as m the monitoring ability of the Landlord, where m is the probability that the Tiller gets caught if he shirks, which we incorporate as part of the repeated play of our one-shot game in Figure 6.1. For example, if $m = 0.27$, then any time the Tiller shirks, there is a 27 percent chance that the Landlord catches him shirking.

Suppose that the Landlord employs a kind of Grim Trigger strategy: He renews the Tiller's fixed-wage contract each period (which may be an agricultural season) if the Tiller is not caught shirking, but if the Tiller shirks and is caught, he is fired immediately without pay, and never rehired by the Landlord, thereafter receiving his reservation utility, $\overline{U}_T$.[17] Clearly the Landlord must give the Tiller something of a bonus over and above his reservation utility to ensure his faithfulness. And depending on the ability of the Landlord to keep an eye on the Tiller, it may be better for the Landlord to offer a fixed-wage contract in the context of a repeated game instead of a fixed-rent contract, which would internalize the consequences of shirking completely. However, the Tiller may not be willing to pay very much rent, because a fixed-rent contract saddles our risk-averse Tiller with considerable risk. How difficult will monitoring have to be so that the Landlord begins to prefer the fixed-rent contract over the repeated fixed-wage contract?

Suppose that $\overline{U}_T = 1.80$, the discount factor of a Tiller, $\delta = 0.90$, and that for now we set $e = 0.50$ for all Tillers. From the perspective of the Tiller, the worst *fixed-rent* contract he would accept would be one that gives him his reservation utility, that is, a contract in which the Landlord charges him r to rent part of his land, where r satisfies the equation $0.5\sqrt{25-r} + 0.5\sqrt{16-r} - 1 = 1.80$. Solving for r, we find that a rent of $r = 14.25$ barely meets the Tiller's reservation utility of 1.80, thus satisfying

---

[17] In the framework of Shapiro and Stiglitz, the reservation utility could equal the long-term value of being unemployed for a spell and then later being rehired at the higher "efficiency" wage needed to prevent shirking.

his participation constraint. Any rent above this demanded by the Landlord will be rejected by the Tiller.

Therefore, provided he is able to satisfy his own reservation utility, the Landlord is willing to offer a fixed wage that gives him a payoff at least as high as the fixed-rent payoff of 14.25. We can calculate this wage by setting the Landlord's expected utility from the fixed-wage contract equal to 14.25 and solving for w, that is, $0.5(25 - w) + 0.5(16 - w) = 14.25$, where we obtain $w = 6.25$, the maximum fixed wage the Landlord is willing to pay a Tiller.

As monitoring becomes more difficult, at what level of m will the Landlord revert to a fixed-rent contract instead of a repeated fixed wage? The Tiller will Toil rather than Shirk if $(1 - m)e + m(\overline{U}_T - \sqrt{w} + e)\left(\frac{1}{1-\delta}\right) \leq 0$. A shirking Tiller gains the present benefit of shirking, e, with probability $(1 - m)$, but loses the future discounted benefits of a higher (toiling) wage with probability m. This net benefit from shirking must be no greater than zero. Solving for m shows that our Tiller will Toil if $m \geq \frac{e(1-\delta)}{(\sqrt{w}-\delta e-\overline{U}_T)}$. Using our hypothetical values for $\overline{U}_T$, e, and δ, while plugging in $w = 6.25$ in this expression, we find the critical value of m to be 0.20. This means that the Landlord will offer repeated wage contracts to the Tiller if he is able to catch a shirking Tiller at least one out of five times, but when the Landlord's ability to monitor falls below 20 percent, a fixed-rent contract is better for him than a fixed-wage contract.

Short-Term versus Long-Term Tenancy

Although one-shot, fixed-rent contracts provide ample incentive for hard work on the plot, they are susceptible to other types of inefficiencies and indiscretions. Some of these are the result of the moral hazard that by nature occurs in rental markets. Vacationers, for example, often subject their rental cars to more wear and tear (and driving bravado) than they would their own vehicles. Who has ever dutifully changed the air filter in a rental car, or carefully touched up flaky paint in a hotel room? For short-term renters, these kinds of investments of time and money simply do not pay sufficient future dividends. For this same reason in developing countries, rental markets for draft animals are typically very small or nonexistent (Bardhan, 1984). Owners of draft animals know that those using the animal on a one-time basis have an incentive to underfeed and overwork it.

It can be the same with land. A tiller operating under a fixed-rent contract may overapply chemical fertilizers with negative long-term side effects or fail to prepare the land after harvest properly for next season. Short-term fixed-rent tenancy may induce a tiller to undersupply inputs that maintain the long-term fertility of agricultural land. Like the high-powered incentives behind the Kirby vacuum salesman, a fixed-rent tiller has incentives aplenty to bring a full effort to his task, but his incentives may conflict with the long-term interests of the landlord.

The idea that long-term tenancy is good for productivity has empirical support. Abhijit Banerjee at MIT, Paul Gertler at Berkeley, and Maitreesh Ghatak at the London School of Economics (2002) study the effects of "Operation Barga," a major property-rights reform initiative undertaken by a left-wing government that was elected in the Indian state of Bengal in 1977. Under the reforms, sharecropping tenants were guaranteed permanent and inheritable tenure on the land they farmed, provided they hand over at least a 25 percent share of their crop from each harvest to the landowner. The authors propose two possible effects from this kind of more secure land tenancy: Because the reforms made it nearly impossible to evict a tenant, even for shirking, the lack of the eviction option potentially reduces the incentive for hard work. At the same time, stable, long-term tenure creates an incentive for investment by the tenant, which could increase productivity. They claim that the second effect appears to dominate and that the reform led to an increase in aggregate crop yields of 20 percent. Using a more disaggregated farm-level data set, however, Bardhan and Mookherjee (2007) estimate the increase in aggregate crop yields due to Operation Barga to be only about 5 percent, a significant but more modest effect from the tenancy reform.[18]

World Bank economists Hanan Jacoby and Ghazala Mansuri (2003) study manuring by peasant cultivators in Pakistan. Manuring of land, spreading farm-animal dung over fields and working it into the soil, is smelly, laborious, and unpleasant. But it is also an activity that typically enhances land productivity for at least three years after application. Consequently, it only makes sense to manure your field if you expect to cultivate the same field for a long time. Controlling for a wide variety of outside factors and potential biases in their estimations, Jacoby and Mansuri find that tenants operating under fixed-rent contracts manure less than owner-cultivators. The most egregious undermanuring in their sample was among Pakistani tenants who had operated under fixed-rent relationships with short duration at the time of the survey. When tenant duration was longer, the rental contract was viewed as more stable, perhaps offering evidence of an implicit repeated-game relationship played between landlord and tenant. Tenants who had cultivated the same plot of land for a longer period manured at a rate more closely approximating owner-cultivators.

The problems with short-term land and labor contracts help explain the widespread use of family labor in traditional agricultural economies. The intensive use of family labor in agricultural economies is ubiquitous in developing countries, and there are several reasons why it makes sense that agricultural households should prefer to hire or rent land to family members rather than outsiders. First, by nature family relationships are long term, and not only embody a repeated-game within the scope of the given activity, but in myriad other aspects of the relationship as well. Consequently, moral hazard in agricultural work may be kept in check in a family context by an endless list of potentially undesirable repercussions. Greater than normal work effort may also be motivated in many cases by interfamilial altruism. Second, children have an added incentive to care for land, equipment, and animals because these may form part of an eventual inheritance from their parents. A worker

---

[18] Bardhan and Mookherjee moreover find that superior to the impact of Operation Barga was a contemporaneous program of government subsidization of farmer credit and local irrigation facilities, which displayed much larger increases on agricultural productivity.

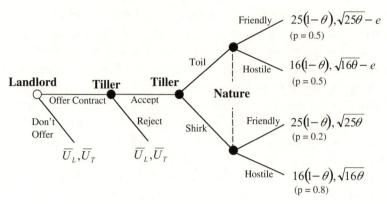

Figure 6.3. Principal-Agent with Share Contract for Tiller

tends to avoid abusing what may actually be his in the long run. Third, congruent with the observation of the University of Chicago's Gary Becker (1975), enterprises have an incentive to invest in the training of their workers only if they expect workers to remain within the enterprise for the long haul. Because the long-term health of the agricultural enterprise may require landowners to invest in the skills of their workers, families will be more apt to impart skills to their children rather than to outsiders, who may pack up and take these skills elsewhere.

Labor tenancy, in which landless laborers more or less permanently dwell on the land of a patron for whom they work, can be most optimistically viewed as a kind of second-tier familial relationship that is similarly able to mitigate myriad forms of moral hazard in the context of a repeated-game. Labor, valued highly in the peak agricultural seasons, is traded by the tenant to the landlord in exchange for housing, payment-in-kind, credit, and different forms of insurance in the case of emergencies. The arrangement allows for landlords to gain what they value most highly – labor in the peak agricultural season – and the arrangement reduces risk for the tenant in an inherently risky environment.

Sharecropping

A sharecropping contract represents a compromise between the fixed-wage contract and the fixed-rent contract, not providing incentives as strong as fixed-rent (but more insurance) and not providing as much insurance as a fixed-wage (but better incentives).[19] The payoffs from a sharecropping contract are given in Figure 6.3.

Let's focus on the advantages of the sharecropping contract in terms of risk sharing. Returning to our example, suppose the Landlord is only able to catch a shirking Tiller 20 percent of the time (our borderline case between the Landlord offering a

---

[19] A concise way to generalize these three contractual forms is to see that any contract represents a transfer from the principal to the agent of $F + \theta Y$, where F is a fixed payment (which may be negative) and θ is a share of output Y. Thus, we have a fixed-wage contract ($F > 0$ and $\theta = 0$), a fixed-rent contract ($F < 0$ and $\theta = 0$), and a pure-share contract ($F = 0$ and $0 < \theta < 1$).

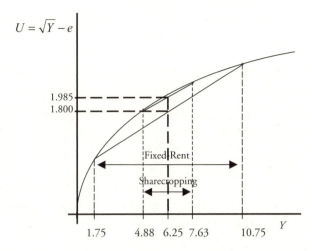

Figure 6.4. Sharecropping vs. Fixed Rent

fixed-wage and fix-rent contract that meets both incentive and participation constraints). Under the fixed-rent contract, a toiling Tiller earns an expected *income* of $0.5(25 - 14.25) + 0.5(16 - 14.25) = 6.25$, giving him an expected *utility* equal to $0.5\sqrt{(25 - 14.25)} + 0.5\sqrt{(16 - 14.25)} - 0.5 = 1.80$, his reservation utility. What share given to the Tiller would make the Landlord indifferent between offering a fixed-rent contract and a share contract? We can determine this share, θ, by setting $0.5(1 - \theta)25 + 0.5(1 - \theta)16 = 14.25$ (the payout to the Landlord from the share and fixed-rent contracts, respectively) and solving, where we obtain $\theta = 0.305$.

Notice in Figure 6.4 how under this share contract, with the Tiller receiving 30.5 percent of the output, the Tiller's expected utility increases from 1.80 to $1.985 (= 0.5\sqrt{25 \cdot 0.305} + 0.5\sqrt{16 \cdot 0.305} - 0.5)$, while the Landlord's utility remains unchanged at 14.25. If the Tiller's share fell to 26.2 percent, the Landlord's utility would rise from 14.25 to 15.13, while the Tiller's utility from income remained at 1.80. The exact share that will result depends on the relative bargaining power of the Landlord and Tiller. In practice, crop shares are usually one-half and otherwise virtually always one-third or two-thirds, a fact that still remains a puzzle to some development economists.

From a risk-sharing perspective, sharecropping consequently represents a Pareto improvement over a fixed-rent contract. Relative to a fixed-rent contract, either the Tiller can be better off without hurting the Landlord, the Landlord can be better off without hurting the Tiller, or *both* can be slightly better off if the share (in our example) falls somewhere between 0.262 and 0.305. The advantages of sharecropping become even greater when the Landlord and the Tiller are *both* risk averse. In this case, sharecropping allows for a more efficient dividing of risk between the two parties. This Pareto superiority of sharecropping holds, however, with one caveat – that it is possible for the Landlord to enforce the high-effort level. These are the essential insights of a seminal (1974) paper on sharecropping by Joseph Stiglitz.

But as Stiglitz and many others before him have noted, the problem with share-cropping is that it is not as shirk-proof as a fixed-rent contract. This observation was made early on by Adam Smith (1776), who commented about the incentives to maintain land under sharecropping, which was widely practiced in France during his time:

> It could never, however, be to the interest even of this last species of cultivators to lay out, in further improvement of the land, any part of the little stock which they might save from their own share of the produce, because the Lord, who laid out nothing, was to get one-half of what ever is produced. (1776, Vol. I, pp. 414.)

The great British economist Alfred Marshall, famous for his formalization of classical economic theory, identified the weaker incentives associated with sharecropping and viewed them as contributing toward economic backwardness. He remarked:

> For, when the cultivator has to give his landlord half of the returns to each dose of capital and labor that he applies to the land, it will not be to his interest to apply any doses the total return to which is less than twice enough to reward him. (1890, Book VI, Chapter IX, pp. 644)

In our current example, the fixed-rent contract is shirk resistant (satisfies the incentive constraint) in a one-shot contract for any Tiller with cost of effort coefficient $e < 0.59$. However, the sharecropping contract (keeping the Tiller's share, $\theta = 0.305$) satisfies the incentive constraint in a one-shot contract only for any $e < 0.17$. If we altered our game to allow for a continuum of levels of effort, we would find that sharecropping results in a general underallocation of effort relative to both owner cultivation and fixed-rent contracts. The intuition is straightforward: As the Tiller allocates effort until the marginal cost of additional effort is equal to its marginal benefit, his optimal level of effort falls if he receives only some fraction θ of the benefit for every additional amount of effort.

Whether sharecropping causes tillers to reduce effort in practice is an empirical question, and the results are frustratingly mixed. Radwan Shaban (1987) presents a creative empirical study in which he analyzes input and output statistics on the plots of Indian households. To control for any systematic differences between landowners and sharecroppers, he studies households that both own land *and* are party to sharecropping contracts. He finds striking differences in both inputs and output on sharecropped land relative to owned land: Input levels ranged from 19 percent to 55 percent higher on owned land than on sharecropped land, and output levels were 32.6 percent higher. Mohamed Matoussi and the late Jean-Jacques Laffont (1995) present data on 100 agricultural households from the region of El Oulja in Tunisia. They find that the production efficiency of sharecroppers declines with the tenant's share of output. Both of these studies, along with other studies (Bell [1977] with data from Bihar, India; Acharya and Ekelund [1998] with data from Nepal) seem to confirm the existence of Marshallian inefficiency in sharecropping. Still, other studies, such as Hayami and Otsuka (1993), Bliss and Stern (1982), and Braido (2005) find that sharecropping contracts exhibit no significant diminutive effect on productivity. In fact, Braido's research claims the observed differences in productivity between sharecropping and owner cultivation are simply because owners work their best land and sharecrop their less productive land.

But if sharecropping does involve some degree of reduced effort (albeit less than a fixed-wage contract), then why is it so commonly found across countries? Aside from the risk-sharing argument, other theories have been put forth to explain the widespread prevalence of sharecropping. David Newbury at Cambridge has argued that if there is uncertainty in the wage market (mainly from rising and falling commodity prices) as well as uncertainty involved with output (mainly due to weather), sharecropping can optimally share these dual risks between landlord and tiller.[20] Others have argued that any moral hazard endemic to sharecropping can be compensated for by the cost sharing of inputs between the two parties. If the landowner contributes to the cost of purchased inputs in the same proportion as the crop share, then the use of inputs by the tiller should return to the efficient level (Adams and Rask, 1968). Though this theory has been subject to a number of challenges, including the nature of cost sharing and the ability to monitor inputs, it remains one plausible explanation for the continued existence of sharecropping.[21]

Another theory, initially put forth by William Hallagan at Washington State University (1978), is that the existence of sharecropping facilitates a screening and segmentation strategy of workers by landlords. Suppose there exist differences in ability between potential tillers, where some are very productive, others only average, and still others hardly productive at all, but it is impossible for the landlord or anyone else to tell the difference between them. But while the landlord might lack the power to see into a tiller's soul at the time of contracting, he may have the market power to offer take-it-or-leave-it contracts to them. Within this scenario, it is possible for a cunning landlord to offer a menu of contracts such that the high-ability tillers will naturally choose a fixed-rent contract, the average tillers will choose a sharecropping contract, and the low-ability tillers a fixed-wage contract.

This kind of self-selection into contracts can be illustrated in our example. Let's say that if a high-ability tiller "toils" earnestly, the chances of the good agricultural yield (25) are 75 percent, and the bad yield (16) only 25 percent. For the average tiller the perspective percentages are 50 and 50, and for the low-ability tiller, only 25 percent and 75 percent, respectively. Keeping the focus on self-selection effects, let's assume that whether through monitoring and repeated interaction, the landlord is able to induce the full effort by tillers. Notice in Figure 6.5a how the tillers self-select into the three categories, here assuming our previous wage and rent values, with a share contract of one-third.

Why would a landlord want to segment his tillers in this manner? If the landlord offered only a fixed-wage contract with wages high enough to satisfy the participation constraint for the low-ability tiller, he would forgo the surplus to be gained from a sharecropping contract with the average-ability tiller. The sharecropper is willing to accept a share contract that makes him only a little better off than the wage

---

[20] See Newbery (1977).
[21] See, for example, Bardhan (1984), chapter 7, and Braverman and Stiglitz (1986).

Prob. of good/bad yield:	0.25/0.75	0.50/0.50	0.75/0.25
	Low-ability	Avg.-Ability	High-Ability
Fixed-Wage = 6.25	**2.00**	2.00	2.00
Share = 0.33	1.94	**2.09**	2.23
Fixed-Rent = 14.25	1.31	1.80	**2.29**

Figure 6.5a. Hallagan's Screening Model

Prob. of good/bad yield:	0.25/0.75	0.50/0.50	0.75/0.25
	Low-ability	Avg.-Ability	High-Ability
Fixed-Wage = 5.35	**1.81**	1.81	1.81
Share = 0.265	1.69	**1.82**	1.95
Fixed-Rent = 15.60	0.74	1.35	**1.96**

Figure 6.5b. Hallagan's Screening Model with Optimizing Landlord

contract, but the landlord is then able to reap the added benefits of his higher productivity. Likewise, he offers a fixed-rent contract with the rent set just high enough to induce the high-ability tiller to prefer it to a share contract. This surplus-maximizing segmentation strategy is shown in Figure 6.5b, where the landlord simultaneously offers a fixed-wage contract of $w = 5.35$, a share contract with $\theta = 0.265$, and a fixed-rent contract with $r = 15.60$. In his optimal contract menu, our cunning landlord offers a set of contracts in which makes a tiller at each ability level barely prefer his own contract over the type of contract chosen by the tiller of the next-lowest-ability level. Hallagan's explanation for sharecropping, then, is that it represents an intermediate form of contract that can increase the landlord's surplus in this kind of self-selection strategy if there exist three or more different "types" of tillers. If there are n types of tillers, then the lowest-ability type get wage contracts, the highest-ability type will receive a fixed-rent contract, and the intermediate types will each receive different share contracts.[22]

None of this, however, explains the puzzle over why shares are so often 50–50. Pradeep Agarwal (2002) explains the widespread existence of the 50–50 share by a model that minimizes the costs of risk, supervision, and any residual shirking by the tiller. He uses a series of simulation exercises to show that sharecropping is an optimal contract for a wide variety of risk-aversion levels and supervision costs. What is more, he finds that the U-shaped curve representing the sum of these costs across different share parameters is relatively flat under most scenarios near the 50–50 sharing area. Thus even though 50–50 may not always be *precisely* optimal, it is often very *close* to optimal. Because it is often so close to an economically efficient share, it may be frequently chosen because it represents an attractive focal point that reduces haggling costs, especially when combined with the intuitive appeal of a 50–50 split based on fairness and equity considerations.

[22] Similar explanations for sharecropping and formal models of the self-selection dynamic have developed by Newbery and Stiglitz (1979) and Reid (1976, 1977). For a formal presentation of the necessary conditions for surplus maximization through a segmentation strategy, see Singh (2000), p. 47.

With properly functioning credit markets, the rationale for institutions such as sharecropping, labor tenancy, and agricultural wage contracts becomes more limited: When peasants can lend and borrow freely, they are able to purchase plots of land, allowing for owner cultivation as an alternative to working the land of others. In the next chapter, we will examine the causes of credit market failure, its effect on developing economies, and potential means of overcoming these issues to provide credit access to the poor.

CHAPTER 7
Savings, Credit, and Microfinance

Acquaintance (def.): A person whom you know well enough to borrow from, but not well enough to lend to.

— Ambrose Bierce

IN THE 1960s, Walter Mischel at Stanford University carried out an experiment to test the effects of delayed gratification in children. The subjects of his study were a random sample of 4-year-old children. The children were led into a plain room, one-by-one, where Mischel presented each with a marshmallow on a plate. Children were told that they were free to eat the marshmallow, but any child who waited to eat the marshmallow until Mischel returned from an errand, would receive *two* marshmallows.

Some of the children immediately crammed the marshmallow into their mouth with Augustus Gloop–like voracity as soon as the researcher left the room. Others were able to wait for a few moments, but then succumbed to the overpowering temptation of the marshmallow. Another group of children engaged in a variety of self-distraction exercises: covering their eyes so they could not see the marshmallow, walking over to sit in a corner, singing, and playing clapping games with themselves. When Mischel returned, he rewarded these children with their second marshmallow. Then he waited for the children to grow up.

What he found fourteen years later was astonishing. The children who had waited for the second marshmallow scored an average of 210 points higher on the SAT than those who couldn't wait. The two-marshmallow children grew up to be better adjusted, more able to get along with peers, and, by most measures, more successful young adults. In contrast, the grown-up one-marshmallow children were more likely to be stressed, disorganized, and generally less successful, not only in school but in other activities and relationships.

A good part of economic development is about not eating the marshmallow. Economic development is the product of countless decisions to restrain consumption in the present in favor of activities that yield returns in the future. The unprecedented levels of per capita capital and technology realized in industrialized nations such as the United States, Europe, and Japan didn't come about by accident but from generations of saving and investment. Wealthy economies such as these have a high level of capital and technology per person. This makes labor in these economies scarce relative to capital and technology, creating high wages and high material standards of living.

Savings and investment, and the institutions that channel savings into investment, are critical to capital formation in a developing economy. A strong financial system redirects capital from those who wish to save to those with productive investments, returning part of the profit from these investments to savers in the form of an interest rate. Banks and other financial intermediaries play key roles in this process, and the difference in the interest rates for saving and borrowing, less administrative expenses, becomes their profit.

Banks and Saving

Astonishingly, formal borrowing and lending have existed for nearly four millennia. Archaeologists have found stone tablets of primitive loan contracts written during the peak of the Babylonian Empire around 1800 B.C. Banking became more developed in ancient Greece around 200–300 B.C., when credit and even deposit-taking emerged as a mainstream facet of Greek entrepreneurial culture. After the Roman conquest of Greece, the Romans copied much of Greek society and culture, not overlooking Greek innovations in banking. By 100–150 B.C., the Romans had incorporated many facets of Greek banking practices into their own patterns of business and trade.[1]

Peter Temin of MIT (2006) has documented how commonplace and relatively sophisticated lending and borrowing had become in Roman society by the early first century, where loans commonly financed consumption, production, and even international trade. He even cites a document written by a well-known figure of that time, Columella, who advised Roman viticulturists to view the opportunity cost of investment in a vineyard in terms of the foregone interest benefits from a perpetual annuity – an observation that if made today by a student of finance would make any professor proud. But as the Roman Empire and its economy began to slowly implode, the demand for banking likewise declined. This decline in banking was hastened during the early middle ages as the church began to exert greater influence over economic life at a time when usury was widely viewed as a sin.

Modern banking appears to have evolved from the trade of gold and silver smiths in the late middle ages in larger European cities, particularly London. The smiths discovered that they could earn additional income by storing precious coins for wealthy citizens in their safeboxes in exchange for a fee. Several subsequent innovations to this arrangement led to the development of banking as we know it today.[2] First, nearly everyone began to realize that it was easier to carry around a deposit receipt from the local smith than wear out his pockets with a collection of heavy and unwieldy coins. These "notes" of deposit came to be accepted widely and exchanged along with coins and thus paper money was born.

---

[1] For excellent references on early money and banking systems, see Davies (1994) and Millett (1991).
[2] Kidwell, Peterson, and Blackwell (1993).

Around the time of the Renaissance, usury became less frowned upon and the smiths began to lend some of their deposits to borrowers at interest. Moreover, some particularly shrewd smiths discovered that they could amplify their earnings by printing notes from scratch that represented claims on their coinage, floating them to their borrowers as interest-bearing instruments, while holding only a fraction of these debts in reserves as real coinage. In this way, modern reserve banking emerged, a new innovation which brought tremendous benefits – provided, of course, that depositors didn't demand their money all at once.

The problem occurred, however, when depositors *did* wish to withdraw their money all at once. Reserve banking created the possibility of bank runs, panics when many depositors wish to withdraw funds simultaneously, but the bank holds insufficient reserves to meet everyone's demand for liquidity. Many bank runs have purely psychological roots. Even a rumor of a bank run can start a bank run. Conversely, if no one has reason to think a bank run should occur, it usually doesn't. Bank runs are the quintessential self-fulfilling prophecy.

This is clearly a game with multiple possible outcomes, and it is illustrated in Figure 7.1 with two fourteenth-century London depositors, Alasdair and Chauncey. Suppose each deposits 10 crowns into "Goldsmythe Banke." The bank holds only 40 percent of its assets as coin reserves. The other 60 percent is loaned out, where it fetches a return of 33 percent per year. Thus, when Alasdair and Chauncey deposit their 20 crowns, the bank immediately lends 12 crowns to an eager borrower, Angus Hereford, who uses the money to buy some bullocks to graze until slaughter a year from now. Goldsmythe holds the other 8 crowns in reserves in the safebox. The 12 crowns become 16 crowns after one year via the interest paid by Angus, so in order to at least break even, the yearly interest the bank then can pay on deposits is 20 percent. Let's say the bank is expected to operate for two years until Goldsmythe retires. If both Alasdair and Chauncey can keep their deposits for one year, the value of each of their accounts increases to 12 crowns. If they keep their deposits for the second year, compound interest allows each of their accounts to grow to 14.4 crowns.

However, what if shortly after depositing his money, Chauncey gets cold feet. Perhaps he becomes worried about Angus's bullocks (they seem to look a little sniffy), and fears that Angus will never pay back Goldsmythe Banke its 12 crowns, much less the 16 it owes with interest. He resolves to withdraw all of his crowns from the bank immediately. Of course, he can't do this, for much of his money is tied up in Angus's bullocks. But he can demand the 8 crowns that are held in reserves, which, as he sees it, is better than losing *everything*. Alasdair, who knows a little more about bullocks, knows that Chauncey's preoccupation is over no more than the ordinary bullock nasal discharge. Alasdair is unconcerned about the bullocks, but he is concerned about Chauncey. If Chauncey attempts to liquidate his entire account, the bank will go bust, and he will be left with nothing. For him, getting four of his crowns is certainly better than nothing, so he too rushes to the bank to withdraw.

The panic causes a bank run in which everybody suffers. As seen in Figure 7.1, a bank run in the first year of our game yields a payoff to each of four, in comparison to a payoff of 14.4 if they had waited to withdraw after two loan cycles. There are several

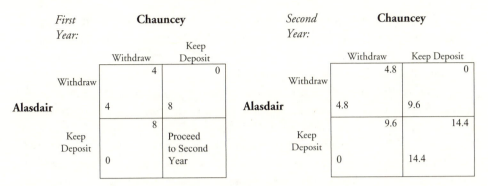

Figure 7.1. Bank Run Game

Nash equilibria to the bank-run game: There is one in which a bank run occurs in the first year and both Alasdair and Chauncey lose 60 percent of their initial deposit. Another Nash equilibrium exists in which both keep their deposit the first year but panic and withdraw during the second year. Alasdair and Chauncey are scarcely better off in this case because with a payoff of 4.8, they still lose 52 percent of their initial deposit. A third equilibrium occurs when both keep their deposits until the end of the second year, when each receives a 44 percent total return on their deposit in a payoff of 14.4.

With a bank operating for n periods, there exist n possible Nash equilibria in which a bank run can occur. Clearly, this kind of instability is undesirable. Optimism and pessimism about the economy will wax and wane over time, but it is obviously problematic that episodes of pessimism should degenerate into self-fulfilling prophesies of collapse.

Fortunately, there is a relatively straightforward institutional solution to the bank-run problem. This solution emerged from the horrendous experiences with bank runs during the Great Depression in the United Sates, in which over 4,000 banks failed between 1929 and 1933.[3] The crisis led to the 1933 Banking Act (often called the Glass-Steagall Act), which immediately established the Federal Deposit Insurance Corporation (FDIC). The act originally provided insurance of deposit accounts up to $5,000 in exchange for the right of federal regulators to monitor the activity of state-chartered banks not already directly regulated by the Federal Reserve. It was immediately successful: The year after the FDIC was established only nine banks failed.[4] In 1980, the U.S. government extended FDIC insurance to cover up to $100,000 per account.

Deposit insurance is amazingly effective at preventing bank runs. That one's account is insured means that mere economic pessimism provides little basis for panic. And knowing that others have no reason to panic over the security of their account means that no individual has any reason to panic either. Institutions that provide deposit insurance now exist commonly in most industrialized countries and

[3] Helfer (1999).
[4] Ibid.

many developing countries, including Kenya (since 1985), Nigeria (1989), Colombia (1985), and Brazil (1990).[5] In many other developing countries, governments bail out busted banks only on an ad hoc basis, if political pressures deem it necessary, or if the bank is judged to be too big to fail.

The main drawback with deposit insurance is that it may create a moral hazard. If accounts are insured, depositors have less incentive to monitor the lending activity of their bank. Also, banks may engage in riskier lending activity if their accounts are protected by the insurance safety net. The prescribed solution to this is for government regulators to ensure that banks maintain sound lending practices, a system that has worked well in most instances, the U.S. savings and loan crisis of the 1980s being one glaring exception. Nevertheless, viewed in light of game theory, the development of depository insurance is a particularly strong example of an institution that is able to solve a game (in this case, a Stag Hunt) in favor of a Pareto-superior Nash equilibrium.

Banks and Lending

On the lending side of financial transactions, there is a problem in the market for loans: Credit markets do not work the same way that most markets work. The difference between buying an apple and lending money illustrates the problem: When someone goes to a market to buy an apple, he can examine it for bruises, rotten spots, and wormholes. A bad apple is easy to spot. The same is not true for a bad *promise*. And at its most basic level, a credit transaction is an exchange of money for a promise to repay, with the desirability of the transaction to the lender depending upon the quality of that promise. Moreover, the quality of this promise is often hard to ascertain.

As a result, a credit transaction is fraught with at least three different types of problems.[6] First is an *adverse selection* problem in credit transactions. Because a borrower receives money now in exchange for a mere promise to repay in the future, it creates an incentive for risky (or dishonest) borrowers to enter the market. These borrowers may indicate a willingness to pay a higher interest rate than safe (or honest) borrowers on loans that they may never intend to repay anyway. Second is the *moral hazard* problem in credit markets; it is possible that the borrower may borrow the money and use it to bet on a proverbial three-legged horse – in other words, a risky investment, but one with a potentially spectacular payoff. If limited liability laws partially shield the borrower in the event of an inability to repay, borrowers may have the incentive to invest in riskier projects than the lender would like them to. They also may consume part of a loan rather than invest it productively, thus increasing the chances of default. Third is the *enforcement* problem. Even if the investment project turns out fine, the borrower may simply refuse to repay. Each of these shortcomings puts the lender at a disadvantage in credit transactions.

---

[5] Mas and Tally (1990).
[6] See Hoff and Stiglitz (1990) for detail on problems endemic to credit markets.

Because of this inherent disadvantage, the lender may not enter into the transaction in the first place, therefore hurting the borrower as well.

These are the essential insights of George Akerlof, Michael Spence, and Joseph Stiglitz, the 2001 winners of the Nobel Prize in Economics, who demonstrated that certain markets, such as the markets for credit and insurance, are plagued by asymmetric information. If it is common knowledge that one party holds an informational advantage over the other (knows something that the other party doesn't know), and can therefore take advantage of the other by virtue of that advantage, the disadvantaged party simply refuses to enter into the transaction. Consequently, a transaction that potentially could be mutually beneficial often just doesn't happen. And in the context of credit markets, this means that many potentially profitable projects will be left unfunded.

One piece of this research has been particularly influential in our understanding of the problems with credit markets, a famous article by Stiglitz co-authored by Andrew Weiss (1981), that has become one of the most cited and celebrated articles in economics. Its insights are worth reviewing, for they illustrate the fundamental conflict between the interests of borrowers and lenders. The key insights of the paper are shown in the two graphs in Figure 7.2 that represent the payoffs to a borrower and lender (in bold, respectively) as a function of the gross return to a borrower's investment, R, from a $1 loan.

In the diagrams, r represents the interest rate charged by the lender to the borrower on the $1 loan. Suppose there are two types of investment projects. The first is a safe one that yields a gross return of $\overline{R}$ for sure. The second one is risky. It also has an expected value of $\overline{R}$ but yields $\hat{R} > \overline{R}$ with probability $0 < p < 1$ and is a total disaster ($R = 0$) with probability $(1 - p)$ so that $p\hat{R} = \overline{R}$. If $R = 0$, we will assume the loan is unsecured and the lender loses the $1 principle and the borrower's profit is zero.[7] Though a borrower's losses are limited to zero when R falls below $1 + r$ (assuming the lender has first claim on any returns to the investment), when R is high, the borrower earns $R - 1 - r$.

Looking at the problem from the lender's perspective, he is fully repaid if the project yields greater than $1+r$. But notice that while the borrower has a *lower limit* on losses, the lender has an *upper limit* on gains: Assuming a zero cost of capital to the lender, the maximum that he can earn on this $1 loan is r.

Stiglitz and Weiss demonstrate how the different shapes of these payoff functions to the borrower and the lender create divergent interests over the choice of risky and safe projects. Notice in Figure 7.2, that the convex shape of the borrower's payoff function makes the risky project more appealing: Whereas the expected payoff to the borrower from the safe project is $\Pi^B = \overline{R} - 1 - r$, it is $\Pi^B = (1 - p)0 + p(\hat{R} - 1 - r)$ from the risky project. We know the latter is higher for the borrower, since $p\hat{R} = \overline{R}$ and $-(1 + r) < -p(1 + r)$. The lender, in contrast, wants the borrower to undertake the safe project that pays $\Pi^L = r$, entailing a higher payoff to the lender than the

---

[7] Stiglitz and Weiss assume that the loan carries collateral between zero and the value of the loan. To keep the example more transparent, here we will assume no collateral, fairly common with loans to the poor in LDCs.

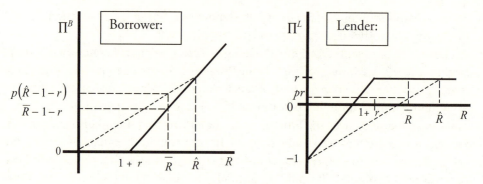

Figure 7.2. Stiglitz & Weiss: Borrower and Lender Incentives

risky project, which only allows the lender to obtain r with probability p, such that $\Pi^L = pr$.

Stiglitz and Weiss show that this basic result has several important implications. First, it means that there will be *adverse selection* in the credit market. A borrower with a risky project will be willing to pay an interest rate up to $\hat{R} - 1$ and still break even, whereas a borrower with a safe project is only willing to pay $p\hat{R} - 1$. What this implies is that if the risky projects are sufficiently risky, lenders will hesitate to raise interest rates to a potentially market-clearing level even if there is excess demand for capital, because by doing so it would drive safe borrowers out of the market and reduces lenders' profits. This is one widely accepted explanation for why shortages of credit seem to be so common, especially in developing countries: Not everyone who wants a loan can get one at the prevailing interest rate since the interest rate cannot be increased to eliminate shortages as prices do in a normal market. Their results also explain why moral hazard exists in credit markets. Take the example of a business with a project with a safe gross return $\tilde{R}$ that is somewhere between $\overline{R}$ and $\hat{R}$, meaning that its expected return is higher than the expected gross return of the risky project, $p\hat{R}$. If the interest rate lies between $\tilde{R} - 1$ and $\hat{R} - 1$, the business will choose the risky project, even though it offers a lower expected return!

While Stiglitz and Weiss provide an excellent framework for thinking about the causes and implications of credit market failure, in practice it is rare in developing countries to observe cases in which the poor find it in their interest to undertake risky investment projects. This is primarily because their model assumes that lenders and borrowers are risk neutral, whereas in developing countries the poor are notoriously risk averse. Consequently, what is more common in practice is for poor borrowers to increase risk to the lender by diverting part of a loan toward consumption rather than the promised investment. This kind of behavior may very well increase the utility of a poor borrower, for whom immediate consumption needs may be paramount, but it decreases the probability that the remaining invested capital will generate sufficient returns to repay the loan.[8] In my own experience in surveying hundreds

---

[8] For details of consumption-based moral hazard in credit markets, see Wydick (2001).

of borrowers taking loans from microfinance programs, I have observed only one clear-cut case of a low-income borrower intentionally investing in a risky project: a sidewalk vendor, who intentionally invested a disproportionate share of his loan in umbrellas, apparently gambling that rainy weather could result in a deluge of profitable sales but running the risk of high inventory carrying costs in the event of dry weather.

But regardless of the specific nature of the behavior, the asymmetric information problems in credit markets necessitate careful screening by lenders in order to ascertain whether a loan is likely to be repaid. In this process any *large* investment project warrants special attention, since the interest rate spread multiplied over a large loan represents a significant amount of profit to a lender. The large profit on such loans more than justifies screening costs. It is applicants for smaller loans that end up the victims of the process because the relatively small profit to lenders from such loans fails to justify these screening costs. Moreover, because it is usually the poor who require small loans, it is usually the poor who are left out of formal credit markets.

As a consequence, many investment projects of the poor must be self-financed. However, it is the poor who are least able to self-finance their investment projects because, by definition, the difference between income and consumption among those living close to subsistence is small. Yet, without access to credit, it is only through investing this difference between income and consumption that capital accumulation among the poor can occur. This forms a classic development trap – those with the least need for credit can most easily obtain it, and those with the greatest need for credit can least easily obtain it. Similar to what is witnessed in the absence of formal insurance mechanisms, the rich get richer and the poor stay poor, victims of a critical asymmetric-information-induced market failure.

How the Lending Game is Solved in Wealthy Economies

The problem with credit market transactions is solved in two important ways in more advanced economies. The first is that these economies often have sophisticated networks of credit information. Three major credit-reporting agencies in the United States, Equifax, Experian, and TransUnion, compile data on hundreds of millions of credit transactions. If a borrower is negligent in repaying a loan, it shows up in her credit score. The market as a whole becomes somewhat more wary of lending to that borrower, and loan terms she can get (interest rate, size of the loan, etc.) are less favorable the next time. In this way, a comprehensive web of credit reporting systems helps to bridge the gap of asymmetric information between borrower and lender in most advanced economies, holding borrowers accountable for their actions, and giving lenders more confidence in making loans.

The second way that more advanced economies solve the lending game is through well-established systems of property rights. In his well-known book *The Mystery of Capital* (2000), Hernando de Soto argues that property rights are the key that unlocks the power of capital markets. When the person has legal title to property, his property not only serves a functional purpose in that on it he can build a house, cultivate a farm, or establish a business. The property, and particularly the title to the property, serves as collateral in the credit market. This, de Soto maintains, is one of the most overlooked functions of property rights in general, and land titles in particular. They facilitate a kind of leveraged capital accumulation and economic growth that would be impossible otherwise. In this light, de Soto maintains that the granting of land titles to, for example, early American settlers was one of the factors most responsible for strong historical economic growth in the United States. Yet, in most developing countries, the poor typically lack title to land on which they live and work, almost the very definition of the *informal* sector. De Soto argues that granting land title to the poor is one of the most important conditions for broadly based economic growth in developing countries.

The use of collateral in credit transactions solves even one-shot plays of the lending game, where here we focus on the enforcement problem. You can see this through a simple modification of the lending game in Figure 2.4a, in which a borrower takes a loan with principal equal to 10, owing 13 to the lender upon repayment (an interest rate of 30 percent). Continue to assume that the investment yields a 100 percent return. Suppose that the borrower offers a piece of land as collateral that is worth 14, and a bank incurs a cost of 2 for the legal hassle of repossessing the collateral. This changes the payoffs in the lending game as seen in Figure 7.3.

Now, by backward induction, (Lend; Repay) becomes the new Nash equilibrium. The bank lends because it receives a higher payoff through repossession of the collateral even if the borrower fails to repay. De Soto's point, seen in light of the game in Figure 7.3, is that the lack of formal land titles may push the value of borrower collateral to something less than 10, the principal value of the loan. This creates two problems: One, because the borrower has less to lose, it creates a disincentive to repay the loan in the first place. Two, if indeed the borrower *doesn't* repay, the bank is worse off than it would have been if it had never made the loan. In this respect, the property rights that are so commonplace in industrialized societies create security for credit transactions that makes promises to repay far more credible, thus unleashing the potential for economic growth through leveraged investments. Of course, such transactions are commonplace as well in the formal sector among the middle and upper classes in developing countries, for whom property rights and

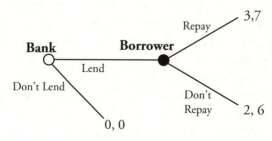

Figure 7.3. Basic Lending Game

land titles are clear. But de Soto's point is that broadly based economic growth will remain stifled without broadly based titles to land.

How the Lending Game Is Solved in Developing Economies

Often lacking formal credit reporting systems and even systems of fully defined property rights, economies in developing countries must to resort to more creative and informal means of solving the lending game. During the past twenty years, development economists have devoted a great deal of time and energy into understanding the nature of informal credit markets in developing countries. Finding the secret to channeling capital into the hands of entrepreneurial types in developing countries, many argue, may be one of the most important keys to alleviating world poverty.

Informal moneylenders are a vital source of credit in the informal economy. These characters are often stereotyped with gold-tooth smiles and scary-looking henchmen. Though a roughly accurate picture in some cases, it is important to understand the important role that moneylenders fill in the informal economy, and from whence arises the source of their power over borrowers.

For most moneylenders, moneylending is not their regular day job, as the typical moneylender is a commodity buyer, landlord, or merchant. Moneylending is often a side activity. What gives the moneylender market power in his village or urban neighborhood is that often by virtue of his profession, say as a trader or merchant, he has created a large pool of liquid wealth or gained access to formal financial markets. Via the latter, the village moneylender can serve as a conduit between the formal and informal financial systems.

In their (1997) research on moneylenders in the Philippines, Maria Floro, at the American University, and Debraj Ray, at New York University, describe the role of rice traders as intermediaries of credit to farmers in the Philippines. Called *marketing agents*, these traders engage in moneylending as a means of profiting from local rice production. Floro and Ray show how the rice traders, by virtue of their relational and informational advantages within their respective pools of farmers, serve as conduits of credit from the formal financial system into the rural, agricultural areas of the Philippines. These trader-moneylenders hold substantial advantages over other lenders from their repeated interaction with farmers through their main role as marketing agents, which also gives them an advantage in enforcing repayment.

Moneylenders tend to solidify their power in a local credit market through acquiring an informational advantage about borrowers that grows over time. As with Floro and Ray's rice traders, moneylenders often begin with the advantage of some inside information over their potential client pool originating from other types of transactions. They then frequently start clients with "test loans," and upon successful repayment, augment both the size of the loan and the types of credit offered to the borrower. Using Floro and Ray's example, a rice trader may begin by offering a farmer an advance on his harvest. If successfully repaid, the trader-moneylender may agree to a small loan to finance a new draft animal, or a new roof for the farmer's

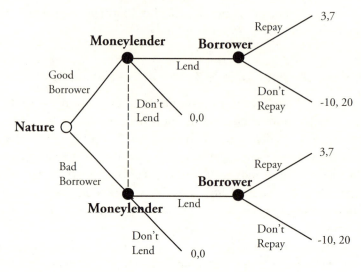

Figure 7.4. Lending Game with Moneylender

house. In this way, the moneylender is able to overcome adverse selection problems in credit markets, the difficulty with screening potentially good borrowers from bad ones. This process can be represented by an extension of the basic lending game, shown in Figure 7.4.

Suppose that there are two types of borrowers in a rural village: "good borrowers" and "bad borrowers." The good borrowers are good (from the lender's perspective) because they are patient. They have a high discount factor, δ, equal to 0.9, meaning that they place a relatively high value on the future, specifically in the future of a long-term credit relationship distinguished by borrowing and repayment. The bad borrowers are bad because they are *im*patient, possessing a discount factor of only 0.5. They care relatively more about the present benefits of absconding with borrowed capital, while heavily discounting the future repercussions of their behavior.

Though from previous dealings the moneylender possesses some inside information about borrower quality, he cannot be certain about whether nature has presented him with a good or bad borrower. (The dashed line in Figure 7.4 is typically used in game-theoretic modeling to represent a lack of information, the fact that the player does not know whether he is at one node or the other.)

Consider a sequence of loans of the same size equal to 10, and assume that the moneylender rewards a repaid loan with a subsequent loan, but withholds future loans when a loan is unpaid. Suppose the moneylender inadvertently grants a loan to a bad borrower. The bad borrower would receive a discounted payoff of $7/(1-\delta) = 7/0.5 = 14$ from repaying, but a discounted payoff of $20 + \frac{\delta \cdot 0}{1-\delta} = 20$ from not repaying. Consequently, the bad borrower doesn't repay, but doesn't get another loan either. In contrast, a good borrower receiving a loan gets a discounted payoff of $7/(1-\delta) = 7/0.1 = 70$ from repaying, but the same payoff of $20 + \frac{\delta \cdot 0}{1-\delta} = 20$ from not repaying. Thus, the good borrower repays, and the bad borrower doesn't.

The moneylender's first advantage is that he knows more than other potential lenders about the local clientele. This inside knowledge gives him a relatively higher probability that he is dealing with a good borrower on an initial loan, meaning that he is operating within the upper part of the game in Figure 7.4. If p is the probability that the moneylender is dealing with a good borrower on an initial loan, and $(1-p)$ a bad borrower, for the moneylender to expect this loan to be profitable, then $3p + (-10)(1-p) > 0$, or $p > 0.77$. Previous dealings with a potential borrower may push his trust over this threshold.

But after actually granting loans, the added discovery of which borrowers are truly good and bad is valuable information. (It is also costly information, as each bad loan costs 10 to the moneylender.) Since good borrowers continue to receive loans, and bad borrowers are quickly eliminated from the portfolio, a moneylender may begin with a small informational advantage, but he can build a portfolio over time that exhibits very high levels of repayment. Competing moneylenders from outside are placed at a distinct disadvantage: they do not know the clientele, and they suffer many painful defaults resulting from their ignorance.

As a result, what one observes when studying informal credit markets is the formation of "credit islands," with moneylenders serving a fixed pool of clients. Let's think in more detail about how this happens: Suppose a small handful of moneylenders offer credit in a given area. As before, a moneylender believes that with a first loan he is lending to a good borrower with probability p and a bad borrower with probability $(1-p)$, making his profit from an initial loan of 10 is equal to $10rp - 10(1-p)$, where r is his interest rate. Thus to break even on a first loan, he must charge $r = (1-p)/p$. However, after an initial loan is repaid, the moneylender knows he is facing a good borrower. Moreover, the borrower knows the moneylender knows that he is a good borrower, and knows that this is valuable information to the moneylender. As a result of passing the test, the good borrower may demand something of a discount on his next loan. Thus, continuing to assume that the cost of capital is zero to the moneylender, the borrower will negotiate an interest rate r on subsequent loans that falls between zero and $(1-p)/p$. The moneylender will not charge more than the latter because he does not want to lose a valuable client, and cannot charge less than the former and still break even. The quality of the deal between these two extremes that the good borrower receives depends on his bargaining skills relative to those of the moneylender. The point, however, is that once the moneylender discovers a good borrower, there is little incentive for him to leave this good borrower wanting for credit or for the good borrower to seek credit elsewhere where his quality is unproven (and face a higher interest rate). The two are stuck with each other.

This kind of exclusivity in lending is consistent with the field studies carried out by Irfan Aleem (1990) in the Chambar area of Pakistan. In his study, Aleem found that vast proportions of the portfolios of village moneylenders were made up of repeat clients that remained faithful to their lender over numerous transactions. (Apart from this phenomenon is the desire of lenders to remain the sole source of credit to any borrower so that they can remain as first claimant in the event of a problem loan.) In such situations, if there exists a limited number of lenders with access to formal credit relative to the number of borrowers than need credit, it gives strong market power to lenders over clients.

The fact that moneylenders often *interlink* credit contracts with other contracts also can augment their market power and the surplus they receive from their borrowers. Pranab Bardhan (1984) provides an analysis for the underlying rationale and consequences of interlinked credit contracts. An employer, for example, may offer a contract to an employee that interlinks a wage for a particular type of work with a loan available at a certain interest rate. By virtue of the moneylender's dual role as the borrower's employer, it may make it easier for the lender to address the moral hazard endemic to credit transactions, as the lender can threaten to fire the borrower to enforce repayment. In other cases, an employer-moneylender may offer a day laborer a cash advance for living expenses during the off-season that is repaid in the form of a lower wage in the peak season. Bardhan and others have demonstrated in theoretical models how this type of interlinked contract can yield a greater surplus to the moneylender than individual wage and credit contracts. Intuitively, by charging interest indirectly in the form of paying lower wages, the moneylender continues to be able to induce the employee-borrower to take a large loan from him without having to lower the price of it. In a similar way, commodity buyers can extract maximum surplus on loans to farmers by offering them an interlinked contract that offers subsidized credit at the cost of lower prices paid for their output.

Sometimes in developing countries it is difficult to tell when a credit contract stops and when insurance starts. Christopher Udry at Yale University undertook a pathbreaking (1994) study on credit relationships in Northern Nigeria. In the study, he found that what existed among his sample of 400 households were not pure credit contracts, but an informal hybrid between credit and insurance arrangements. Carefully recording instances of negative shocks such as illnesses and other misfortunes to households during the term of credit contracts, he discovered that the terms of the credit contract were adjusted upon repayment to account for these shocks. He observed that the terms of borrower repayment were not only eased downward after borrowing households had experienced a negative shock but also that terms of repayment were often adjusted *upward* when the household of the *lender* had experienced a negative shock, making such contracts remarkably efficient in terms of borrower and lender welfare and the sharing of risks.

Rotating Credit and Savings Associations

Other types of indigenous institutions that mobilize credit in traditional societies have intrigued development economists. One well-known institution of this kind is the Rotating Credit and Savings Association (ROSCA). ROSCAs appear to have evolved spontaneously in many otherwise seemingly unrelated cultures in Africa, Asia, Latin America, and even among numerous ethnic communities in the United States. In Senegal, for example, they are called *tontines*, in Bolivia *pasanakus*, in India *chit funds*, in Korea *kye*, and in China *Hui*. ROSCAs are everywhere.

The arrangement works in the following way: A group of individuals agrees to make monthly (or sometimes weekly) contributions into a kitty. A ROSCA of n members meets n times for one go-round. At each meeting, each of the members takes turns receiving the entire sum contributed by the members into the kitty. Typically, a member can only win the kitty once during a ROSCA cycle. The arrangement is primarily economic, but also social. The winner of the kitty often uses part of her winnings to pick up the tab for food, drink, and festivities at the meeting. No matter who the fortunate winner happens to be, showering one member with riches can create a good excuse for a party.

Timothy Besley, Stephen Coate, and Glenn Loury (1993) analyze two different mechanisms for deciding who gets the kitty each period. The first is a *random* ROSCA, in which one member's name is drawn out of a hat each meeting. The lucky winner (especially if one's name is drawn in one of the early rounds) is then able to use the collective contributions to finance some kind of large expenditure. This could be a capital investment, such as a new machine or other equipment for a small business, or a personal expenditure such as an anniversary or wedding. The drawback with a random ROSCA, of course, is the very nature of its randomness: the time one becomes the winner may not match up well with when a member is most anxious to take home the kitty.

One alternative is a *bidding* ROSCA. In a bidding ROSCA, each period the members make either open or sealed bids, with the highest bidder taking the kitty for that period. Bids can either come in the form of higher subsequent contributions to the ROSCA or through side payments made to the other members. The advantage of the bidding ROSCA is that the kitty goes to those with the greatest willingness to pay for it. When members have heterogeneous levels of desire to win the kitty, Besley, Coate and Loury argue that the bidding ROSCA may offer greater benefits, but when groups have more or less homogeneous needs, they show that a random ROSCA may be better. The fact that most ROSCAs are random, they note, may reflect a great deal of homogeneity among their participants.

A final, and somewhat less common, type of ROSCA allocates the kitty to members based on immediate need. This type of ROSCA functions more like informal insurance than informal credit. In such an arrangement, members all contribute each meeting, allocating the kitty by consensus to the member who has suffered a great misfortune or who faces an important event such as a wedding (or perhaps both).

It would seem that those who have been winners of the kitty in early rounds would have a disincentive to continue to contribute to ROSCAs. In practice, however, this does not appear to be the case because ROSCAs are typically made up of tightly knit groups of extended family members, friends, and associates with strong social ties. The social ties that surround ROSCAs create ample incentives against defection. Since most ROSCAs are not onetime events, but are recurring in the context of a close community, moral hazard is kept in check by the repeated-game nature of the ROSCAs themselves, which in turn occur in the context of the repeated social interaction of the community. We will explore this theme as we examine the potential for microfinance to harness this social cohesion to make credit available to the poor in developing regions of the world.

Microfinance

The growth of microfinance as a movement in international development has been both astonishing and unprecedented. The Microfinance Summit under the Clinton administration in 1997 kicked off a major effort to reach 100 million impoverished households with microfinance by 2005. By 2006, this effort resulted in 113,261,390 households taking microloans from 3,133 institutions worldwide, 81,949,036 of whom were among the poorest in their country when they took their first loan.[9] Even the Internet has joined the movement, permitting profit-minded investors and philanthropists alike to lend directly to developing country entrepreneurs via Web sites such as Kiva.org. The phenomenon has been the result of a strong consensus in influential policy and nonprofit circles that views microfinance as a key tool in the fight against world poverty and of empowerment to participate in markets.

Part of this consensus is political. Those on the rightish side of the political spectrum are attracted to microfinance because it helps people lift themselves up by their bootstraps by fostering entrepreneurialism and self-reliance, arguably in a self-sustaining manner without huge government giveaways. Those leaning toward the left are attracted by the grassroots nature of microfinance, its empowerment of women, and its ability to promote indigenous culture through the financing of artisans and other producers of locally made products. Moreover, compared to large-scale industrial investment, microfinance also tends to be blissfully neutral on the environment. Everybody loves microfinance.

Economists are not to be left out in this regard. Part of the intrigue of microfinance to economists is how it has apparently been able to harness the social ties within traditional societies to overcome the aforementioned difficulties with credit transactions, that is, solve the lending game. Two institutions have been studied particularly closely in this respect. The first is the Grameen Bank in Bangladesh, founded by the Vanderbilt-trained economist Muhammad Yunus, winner of the 2006 Nobel Peace Prize for his work in microfinance. The bank now boasts a portfolio of over 2 million borrowers, over 90 percent of whom are women. The Grameen Bank has been the flagship institution of the microfinance movement.

A second well-known institution is Bolivia's BancoSol, which was able to replicate some of the key lending methodology of the Grameen Bank in a Latin American context, and has now dispersed over US$1 billion in capital to low-income entrepreneurs in La Paz and 35 other secondary regions throughout Bolivia. BancoSol is best known for being the first major microfinance institution to become privatized, and indeed, it has been issuing dividends to shareholders since 1997.

The secret to the success of any microfinance institution is being able to solve the lending game at minimal cost in administrative overhead, since margins on

---

[9] Microcredit Summit, March 2007, available at www.microcreditsummit.org. (Accessed 8/15/2006.)

microfinance loans are very small. The Grameen Bank and BancoSol have achieved high repayment rates because they understand what makes indigenous credit markets work. Several tools are important to microfinance institutions in inducing high repayment rates, and through the implementation of these tools, a great many microfinance institutions have been able to achieve remarkable repayment rates, even on small loans to the poor, that often exceed 95 percent.

The first is the use of *dynamic incentives*, the carrot of future loans dangled from a stick before the borrower. As mentioned previously, village moneylenders use a version of dynamic incentives to address moral hazard issues in credit transactions by engaging clients in a repeated lending game. This works particularly well when a microfinance institution has monopoly power in a region and borrowers have scant access to alternative sources of credit. However, when credit alternatives emerge, the carrot of dynamic incentives loses its allure, and repayment discipline may break down.

A second tool is the creative use of incentive contracts for credit officers, who are responsible for their own borrower portfolios in a particular geographical region in which they typically serve between 100 and 300 borrowers. The structure of their incentives compares to the traditional American paperboy, who delivers newspapers in a defined neighborhood, advertises the paper (and his services) in the area, and prospers when the density of his customer base increases. Microfinance institutions typically compensate credit officers based on the performance of their portfolio, paying them a (fairly low) base wage but adding contractual incentives for the number of borrowers they are able to serve, the total loan assets managed in their portfolio, and borrower repayment rate. Properly structured incentive contracts induce credit officers to carry large portfolios (but not too large), and address repayment difficulties promptly. The precise nature of these contractual incentives matters: Although contractual bonuses for repayment and total portfolio assets align the incentives of credit officers sharply with the objectives of for-profit microfinance institutions, this may come at the expense of serving the poorest borrowers. Structuring credit officer incentives for institutions who want to lend to the poorest is more difficult.[10]

A third important tool in the microfinance practitioner's tool kit is *group lending*. Institutions have borrowers form self-selected groups of typically three to eight borrowers. A specific loan is granted to each member in the group, but each member of the group is financially liable for the loans to each of the other members, forming a kind of financial chain gang. Various theories have been put forth to explain the advantages of group lending over individual lending. The theories are not mutually exclusive, and each probably tells part of the story.

The first is simply economies of scale in lending. Because the idea is not very exciting, it has attracted little attention from economists, but nonetheless may be important. The simple argument goes like this: It takes x amount of time for a

---

[10] Theoretical work on this and other problems involved with credit officer contracts is found in Aubert, de Janvry, and Sadoulet (2004).

loan officer to attend to an individual borrower, but it simply takes less than $8x$ of time to attend to a group of eight borrowers. Based on my own experience in Central America, one credit officer can manage a portfolio of perhaps 150 individual borrowers, but often upward of 300 group borrowers. Here, time is money and less time in administrative overhead allows a nonprofit lender to reach more poor borrowers with small loans.

Most of the more interesting theories regarding the success of group lending focus on its positive effects on loan repayment. Some such as Maitreesh Ghatak (1999) have proposed that it is the self-selection of members among individuals well known to one another that is responsible for the high repayment rates observed in many group-lending schemes. Ghatak's explanation is rather like the reason that car insurance companies offer discounts to married drivers: If I am a reckless man, women may be less likely to want to marry me; the fact that I am married means I can't be *too* reckless (at least for one woman). In the context of group lending, one would expect that in the formation of jointly liable groups, safe borrowers would seek, and be allowed to join, a group with other safe borrowers, but that a group of safe borrowers would reject a risky borrower. Risky borrowers could potentially join a group only with other risky borrowers, but even a risky borrower has no interest in becoming liable for other risky borrowers' loans. (Even a reckless woman may not want to hook up with a reckless man and vice versa.) Hence, the fact that a group of people has promised to be jointly liable for one another's loans sends a signal to the lender that the group is likely to consist of safe borrowers. In his paper, Ghatak then demonstrates how this assortative matching process allows for more efficient credit contracts to be offered to the clients of microfinance institutions.

A second group of theories focuses on the benefits of group lending after group formation. Joseph Stiglitz (1990) and others have argued that the benefits of group lending accrue primarily through peer monitoring. Since it is costly for banks to supervise the use of borrowed capital, they argue that group lending encourages members to monitor one another in order to reduce the risk of group default. Mansoora Rashid and Robert Townsend (1992) claim that group lending increases repayment because it fosters the development of miniature self-insurance networks. When one member is subject to a negative shock that makes it difficult for him to repay, another member can make up the difference. Still others, such as Timothy Besley and Stephen Coate (1995), have argued that in traditional societies, it is the potential for social sanctions between borrowing group members that can create strong incentives for repayment.

Some of my own work on group lending (2001) argues that when group lending works well, it utilizes a combination of the repeated-game relationship between microfinance institutions and borrowing groups, and the social fabric that exists within a community of borrowers. Because there are so many factors at work in most group lending schemes (group selection, peer monitoring, social sanctions, the potential for self-insurance, repeated games, etc.), game-theoretic models of group lending can become complicated very quickly. However, a rough sketch of

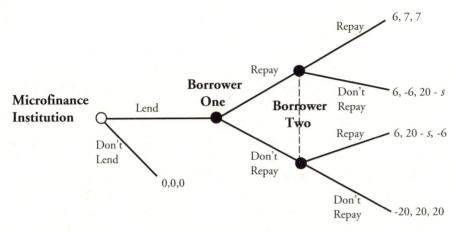

Figure 7.5. Group Lending Game

this idea is represented as a kind of hybrid between a Trust game and a mutant form of the Prisoners' Dilemma as appears in Figure 7.5.

Payoffs in the game are to the lending institution, the first borrower, and the second borrower, respectively. For simplicity, assume that all investment projects are successful, so that here we focus on the enforcement problem inherent to loan repayment. As before, assume that the lender provides loans equal to 10, this time to a group of two borrowers, where again successful projects yield a 100 percent return (a gross profit of 10). The group is jointly liable for repaying two loans of 10 each plus interest of 3 on each loan, or a total group liability of 26. If a member uniquely chooses not to repay, she receives a monetary payoff of 20 but incurs the wrath of social sanctions from the other member (and perhaps other members of the community as well) equal to $-s$. Stuck with a defecting partner, if the remaining member chooses to repay, she must repay the entire group loan, leaving her with a payoff of -6.

It makes sense that a group member might choose to repay for another member, because in order to continue receiving credit from the microfinance institution, the entire group loan must be paid off, not just a fraction. When a member has intentionally defaulted on a loan, that member is typically ejected from the group and replaced, and the group continues to receive credit, provided all previous group loans have been paid off. The repeated nature of the lending game is just as important with group lending as it is with individual lending. Now consider the incentives for a member to either repay or default on a loan; they depend both on the patience of borrowers (to refrain from eating the marshmallow), and on the potential wrath of their peers from sticking their fellow members with their unpaid debt.

Provided the other member repays, a borrowing group member will also repay if the discounted payoff from repayment, $7/(1-\delta)$, is greater than the discounted value from not repaying, $20 - s + \frac{\delta \cdot 0}{1-\delta}$. Thus either a sufficiently high level of social sanctions, s, or sufficiently high level of patience, δ, or combination of the two will induce repayment.

A *very* patient borrowing group member will repay even when her fellow group member fails to repay. Paying off a fellow member's debt results in a payoff of −6 today, but allows the faithful member to continue to receive credit in future periods, yielding a total discounted payoff of $-6 + \frac{\delta 7}{1-\delta}$. If this is greater than the payoff of 20 from joining the delinquent member in absconding with the loan, the group loan will be repaid. Perhaps this is why microfinance institutions often place a premium on strong leadership within borrowing groups. Strong leaders are likely to weigh the long-term rewards of continued partnership with the institution especially heavily relative to the short-term gains from defection, and are likely to be willing to cover for defaulting members in order to sustain their own credit access. The leader may then rally the group to replace a negligent member with a more responsible member (i.e., one with a higher discount factor). Based on what I have observed in Latin America, I have maintained that the best way to view borrowing groups is as *dynamic peer review committees*, expelling members whom they judge to have been negligent with their loans, while adding members that they judge to be better risks. Group lending therefore mitigates the moral hazard in credit transactions by placing it in the context of two repeated games: First, microfinance institutions offer the promise of future loans to groups who are functional enough to make timely payments. Second, it embeds the credit transaction in the context of the repeated game of social interplay already occurring within a closely knit community; defaulters may pay not just a pecuniary price, but also a social price for their defection.

Which of all of these theories appears to be most important in practice? Unfortunately, relatively little empirical work has been done to test the relative importance of different potential advantages of group lending. Yet, there is some empirical evidence that the ability of group lending to harness existing social ties has a positive effect on repayment. Mark Wenner (1995) of the Inter-American Development Bank found that screening of borrowers appears to have positive effects on loan repayment in Costa Rican borrowing groups. Conducting empirical tests on Guatemalan borrowing groups, I found (Wydick 1999a) that peer monitoring does appear to have some positive effects on loan repayment, but that close social ties can work both ways: They can both foster repayment but also make it hard for members to pressure one another to contribute.

Recent work such as Xavier Giné et al. (2005), Alessandra Cassar et al. (2007) and Cassar and Wydick (2008) has delved into the realm of experimental economics in search for answers. In this type of research, potential microcredit recipients play simulated "microfinance games" in the context of a controlled experiment in order to isolate how variables such as social cohesion, trust, and dynamic incentives influence loan repayment. In the latter research project, our research team from the University of San Francisco carried out a simulated group lending experiment at sites in five developing countries: India, Kenya, Guatemala, Armenia, and the Philippines. We calibrated the laboratory experiments to test how ethnic and religious homogeneity, personal trust, monitoring, and self-selection of borrowing groups each affect the repayment performance of borrowing groups. Evidence from this larger body of experimental research is mixed but seems to indicate that personal trust, homogeneity of group members, and dynamic incentives all play positive roles in group-loan repayment.

Beyond group lending, other types of institutions have attempted to harness social ties in traditional societies to make credit available to the poor. *Village banks*, such as those used by FINCA International, consist of 20–50 members and both accumulate savings from members as well as disperse loans. Loan amounts are based largely on savings; the more a member saves, the more she can borrow. In this way village banks rely not only on external sources of funding from a government ministry or NGO (nongovernmental organization) as do many group lending schemes, but also on mobilizing the internal capital of their members.

Credit cooperatives often function in a manner similar to village banks, but they often provide other benefits for their members as well, such as marketing of commodities, or low-cost access to inputs such as fertilizer and seed. The collective gain or loss realized within the cooperative is then distributed in some manner to its members. Cooperatives have often been formed by NGOs and local governments to protect rural peasants from the market power and potential exploitation of moneylenders and commodity buyers. The recurrent problem with cooperatives, however, is that their underlying incentive structure mirrors a Prisoners' Dilemma, as discussed in Chapter Two; this kind of incentive structure invites "free-riders" and often makes leadership in a cooperative difficult.

Although researchers generally believe the impact of microfinance to be modest, but positive, obtaining specific measures of its true impact is more difficult than it would seem. There is a problem in simply comparing those who have been taking microloans for a period of time with those who haven't. Borrowers have undergone a double self-selection process that separates them from nonborrowers. Not only have they had the desire to borrow to finance the growth of a household enterprise (not all people even have this desire), but their request for a loan has been approved by the microfinance institution. Thus relative to the general population, microfinance borrowers tend to be "winners," potentially showing relative improvements in many measures of welfare over time even without microfinance. Moreover, borrowers may choose to take loans at a particular time when especially profitable opportunities present themselves. This makes it hard to separate the effect of microfinance from the positive effect that this opportunity may have bestowed on the borrower anyway. All of these factors present challenges in obtaining razor-sharp estimates of microfinance impacts.

There have been various strategies to try to control for these issues: the use of instrumental variable estimations,[11] constructing a field experiment,[12] and the use of program eligibility requirements to identify those who might have had similar characteristics to those who took credit, but were ineligible. Khandker's (1998)

---

[11] An instrumental variable is used in econometric studies to isolate program impacts by obtaining estimates of a treatment (such as microlending) that are a product of a third variable that is uncorrelated with welfare outcomes. See Wydick (1999b) for an example in trying to estimate microfinance impacts.

[12] See Coleman (1999) for a study in Thailand where credit was withheld from borrowers in some villages temporarily while provided to others. He finds modest impacts on those chosen to receive the credit first.

Fighting Poverty with Microcredit is the most well-known empirical study on the impacts of microfinance, and takes the latter approach. He finds significant effects from program participation on enterprise variables such as production and income, as well as on welfare variables such as child schooling, child nutrition, and household consumption, particularly when loans were made to women, where household consumption increased 18 taka for every 100 taka in lending. His later study in 2003, which is able to examine household differences using an additional round of data, finds consumption effects to be somewhat more modest, closer to 8 taka per 100 taka loaned.

Future Developments of Credit Markets in LDCs

As the number of microfinance institutions has proliferated across developing countries, competition has increased among them. Because competition in the marketplace nearly always benefits the consumer, one would suppose that competition between credit providers would be similarly beneficial. Craig McIntosh at University of California at San Diego and I (2005) argue that this may not be the case.

Our argument for the way microenterprises enforce borrower discipline is best understood by the way eBay is able to enforce discipline within its vast multitude of participating borrowers and sellers. Since its founding in 1995, eBay has dominated the online market for person-to-person transactions of people's unwanted junk that they believe may be someone else's treasure. As goods are bought and sold through eBay's online auction process, incentives arise for buyers to cheat sellers by failing to pay up, and for sellers to cheat buyers by not delivering the goods, either figuratively or literally. What keeps participants honest is an internal rating system in which buyers and sellers have the chance to rate each other after every transaction. Because of the obvious opportunity to cheat, frequent users safeguard their eBay rating like a precious jewel. They understand that it inspires other eBayers with confidence in dealing with them, a big advantage in an impersonal market. For example, a buyer knows that a seller with a 99 percent positive rating over 1000 transactions has much to lose by cheating on a single deal. But what would happen if there were not one eBay, but numerous eBays out there, online markets where goods could be bought and sold? A deceitful seller, for example, could simply renege on an eBay transaction and begin to sell in another online market. The fact that eBay is a focal point for such transactions helps to mitigate moral hazard in the market.

Similar to eBay's virtual monopoly in secondhand goods, many microfinance institutions have operated as virtual *local* monopolies in semiformal credit. Much of what keeps borrowers from succumbing to the temptations of moral hazard is the threat of having the microfinance tap turned off by their sole provider of affordable loans. But when the number of microlenders in a given region increases, the lenders' power to induce borrower repayment (via Grim Trigger–like strategies in a repeated game) diminishes. This happens because in many parts of the world, borrowers are now presented with a dazzling new array of credit opportunities.

And why should one repay Peter when he can always borrow from Paul? One result of the overwhelming proliferation of microfinance institutions in places such as Bangladesh, East Africa, and much of Central America is some entrepreneurs who have gained newfound access to credit. But we document that this has also caused credit market chaos in many of these areas; as lenders have multiplied, repayment rates have declined.

Regions such as these are at an intermediate phase in credit market development. In many cases, the borrower's personalized relationship with the moneylender has been replaced with a personalized relationship with the microfinance institution. Although few doubt the sincerity of the NGOs involved in microlending, a personalized lending relationship with a single microfinance institution still leaves the undercapitalized borrower in the position of either being exploited or patronized. Paradoxically, the maximum economic benefit to these types of borrowers occurs when lenders can share information among themselves about the behavior of borrowers. This is a key characteristic of how credit relationships evolve during the process of economic development: The credit relationship changes from a private, *personalized* one, to a more public relationship with a more or less impersonal credit *system*. Accountability for credit behavior is encapsulated in a credit rating, where multitudes of lenders compete for a borrower's business, given his publicly perceived level of risk.

Such systems have been implemented recently in a number of countries with dense microfinance activity, such as Bangladesh, Bolivia, El Salvador, Guatemala, and Nicaragua, and in many ways are a bellwether of financial development. Credit information systems have several interesting effects when they are implemented in developing countries. A screening effect mitigates adverse selection problems at the outset by kicking out high-risk borrowers with poor credit records. Moreover, when borrowers become aware that the entire market of lenders is observing their repayment performance, it produces an incentive effect against moral hazard that causes them to be more careful with their loans. A third effect of these systems, however, is that when lenders become more confident about the quality of their borrowers, they allow them access to larger loans, which partially counteracts the first two effects and tends to *increase* default problems.

In McIntosh and Wydick (2007) we use a field experiment designed around the staggered rollout of a new microfinance credit information system in Guatemala, where some borrowers were randomly informed about the new system but not others, uncovering evidence of each of these three effects. Even the screening effect alone from implementation of the information system appeared to lower default rates by about two percentage points.[13] This has important implications for the poor: When lenders compete having strong information about borrowers, lower default rates imply better loan terms to low-income borrowers, and broader access to financial services.

---

[13] See also Luoto, McIntosh, and Wydick (2007) and de Janvry, McIntosh, and Sadoulet (2006).

CHAPTER 8
Social Learning and Technology Adoption

Imitation is the sincerest flattery.

                       – Mahatma Gandhi

IN 1968, SOCIAL psychologist Philip Zimbardo conducted a novel experiment. With the assistance of his graduate students from New York University, he bought a used 1959 Oldsmobile and left it on the street in the Bronx, hood up and license plates removed. The same experiment was repeated near the Stanford University campus in Palo Alto, California.

From a hidden position behind a nearby apartment window, Zimbardo and his students continuously monitored the abandoned car in the Bronx. What they observed over the next sixty-four hours astounded them. Within ten minutes, the Oldsmobile encountered its first, and rather unlikely, group of assailants: a family of three – father, mother, and 8-year-old son. While the mother acted as a lookout, the 8-year-old helped his father remove the battery and the radiator. Shortly after, a steady procession of passersby proceeded to remove the air cleaner, radio antenna, windshield wipers, chrome strips, hubcaps, and other sundry parts and accessories. After about nine hours, random destruction of the Oldsmobile began: A couple of laughing teenagers ripped off the rearview mirror and hurled it at the windshield and headlights. Reminiscent of a scene from *Lord of the Flies*, a group of smaller children began indiscriminately smashing the car's windows and slashing its tires. At the end of the sixty-four hours, the 1959 Oldsmobile was a mere shadow of its former self, a useless carcass of twisted metal, the victim of no less than twenty-three incidents of theft and vandalism. All of the perpetrators were well-dressed, clean-cut whites, who might as Zimbardo says, "under other circumstances be mistaken for mature and responsible citizens demanding more of law and order" (*Zimbardo* 1969).

The Stanford car was also carefully monitored from a distance and, at least initially, attracted little attention. Zimbardo notes that the "releaser cues" (license plates removed and hood up), which were sufficient in New York to initiate theft and destructive behavior, were insufficient in Palo Alto. For a week, the car remained strangely unmolested, and one kind person even lowered its hood when it began to rain. At this point, Zimbardo and his students decided to initiate destructive behavior themselves to see what would follow. After one of his students began smacking the side of the car with a sledgehammer, other nearby students quickly joined in the aggression. In short time, one passing student after another begged for the sledgehammer. As Zimbardo writes,

> Once one person had begun to wield the sledgehammer, it was difficult to get him to stop and pass it to the next pair of eager hands. Finally they all attacked simultaneously. One student jumped on the roof and began stomping it in, two were pulling the door from its hinges, another hammered away at the hood and motor, while the last one broke all the glass he could find. They later reported that feeling the metal or glass give way under the force of their blows was stimulating and pleasurable. Observers of this action, who were shouting out to 'hit harder' and 'smash it,' finally joined in and turned the car completely over on its back, whacking at the underside. (Zimbardo, 1969; pp. 290–2)

The added propensity for human beings to engage in violent behavior when others around them are doing so is well known among social psychologists. Although the precise mechanisms behind the phenomenon are still a subject of much research, it is virtually undisputed. Moreover, the "Broken Window Theory" has given rise to entire strategies of crime-fighting, cracking down on small offenses (such as fare-evasion and graffiti) to preserve a sense of order that deters bigger crimes.[1] Imitative behavior is not unique to violence; it is manifest in countless other realms of social life.

Malcolm Gladwell, celebrated author of "The Tipping Point" (2000), explains how fashion, specifically what is deemed to be "cool," emerges and spreads within popular culture through a similar dynamic.[2] He tells how in the early 1990s, sales of the classic brushed-suede Hush Puppies had gradually fallen over the decades to barely 65,000 pairs per year. Hush Puppies management, rightfully concerned that their shoes had developed a somewhat nerdy reputation, had been considering the idea of dumping the suede-casual look altogether in favor smooth leather "active casuals." But it was at this fateful Hush Puppies moment when people began to report sighting them on the feet of hip club-goers in the stylish Soho district of Manhattan. Because Hush Puppies were nerdy, they became trendy. All of a sudden, secondhand shops in New York could not keep the classic Hush Puppies, the "Duke" and the "Columbia," on their shelves. Hush Puppies had advanced from the ranks of the banal to the chic nearly overnight. Hush Puppies were cool.

Gladwell tells the story of fashion designer Joel Fitzpatrick, who immediately began converting space in his Los Angeles store into a Hush Puppies retail department, complete with a twenty-five-foot inflatable Bassett Hound on the roof. But even before Fitzpatrick had finished putting up shelves and painting, who should amble into his store but pop comedian Pee-wee Herman, asking for a pair of Hush Puppies. Thousands followed as the Hush Puppy trend spread like wildfire. Sales increased to 430,000 pairs in 1995, rising to 1,600,000 pairs in 1996.

---

[1] For more on the Broken Window Theory, see Wilson and Kelling (1982). The theory was instrumental in the formulation of successful anticrime tactics in New York City in the 1990s.

[2] Gladwell (1997) relays the story *The New Yorker* and in his well-known (2000) book.

Gladwell breaks down the spread of "cool" in the Hush Puppies example into *innovators* (20-something clubbers in Manhattan), *early adopters* (like Pee-wee Herman), the *early majority* (who are very trend sensitive and take their cues from early adopters such as Herman), and the *late majority* (who make up the bulk of sales but take their cues from the early majority). How the spread of such behavior begins, however, is exceptionally difficult to nail down. Moreover, Gladwell explains, the spread of "cool" is a process that is hard for firms to manipulate to their advantage.

What accounts for these patterns of behavior? Why was the Bronx Oldsmobile looted and destroyed right away, while the one in Palo Alto lasted until Zimbardo and his students began smashing it first? How were Hush Puppies transformed from being the focus of *nerd* behavior to *herd* behavior practically overnight? More generally, what effect does the behavior of peers have on the choices of the individual? And more specific to our concerns, how can a better understanding of imitative behavior influence the way we understand the myriad choices people make about technology, and the effects of these choices on poverty and prosperity?

While these questions are familiar to social psychologists, they have become fresh meat for the technical tools of economists. Traditionally, economists assume that agents make optimal decisions from an internal calculus based on individual preferences that are "stable," or unaffected by the preferences and choices of others. This framework is commonly employed, not because it reflects the actual behavior of human beings in the real world, but because it makes microeconomic models easier to work with from a mathematical standpoint. Often such assumptions are innocuous, but many believe that this dependence on individualistic rationality has caused economics to fall short as a genuinely *social* science. Fortunately, a new generation of economists has grown increasingly keen to bring the "social" back into the "science" without compromising the methodological rigor of the field. Much of this chapter is devoted to a review of this work, and its application to economic development.

Some Definitions and Terms

One immediate challenge in studying the effects of group behavior on technology adoption is that the academic literature uses a multiplicity of terms to describe very similar phenomena. Social learning, neighborhood effects, peer effects, imitative behavior, herd behavior, and information cascades are terms with relatively fine shades of meaning (if any) that separate their precise definitions. I will attempt to provide slightly tighter definitions to some of these terms. *Social learning* is perhaps the general term most widely used by social scientists for copycat behavior, although *imitative behavior* is equally general. ("Social learning," however, tends to refer to *process*, while "imitative behavior" refers to a *result*.) "Neighborhood effects" conveys a similar meaning, but most often refers to imitative behavior occurring within a geographical space, or neighborhood. But it also often refers to the influence of environmental factors on behavior as well as the tendency of behavior to replicate itself. *Peer effects* more commonly refers to the behavioral influence of similar *persons* as opposed to persons residing in a similar *space. Herd behavior* is the frequent result of all of the above phenomena, which can result from an "information cascade," the (at least partial) forsaking of one's private judgment about the usefulness of a behavior or technology in favor of a decision based on the actions of others.

So what motivates people to copy one another? In truth, there are many reasons why one person might want to do what someone else is doing. These reasons, however, can be broken down into broad classifications. Peyton Young of Johns Hopkins University (2001) classifies motives for imitative behavior into three broad categories: (1) pure conformity, (2) instrumental conformity, and (3) informational conformity. *Pure conformity* occurs when individuals adopt a particular behavior simply because they desire to be like other people. No one wants to be the first at the pool to wear a skimpy bathing suit, but if others are doing so, one may not want to feel left out (though other factors may play an important role in this decision). *Instrumental conformity* occurs when conforming, coordinated behavior fosters mutually beneficial and tangible gains to all who conform. For example, international academic conferences are virtually always carried out in English, which prevents Tower of Babel–like chaos from erupting at such meetings. *Informational conformity* occurs through a learning process when individuals face uncertainty about the rewards of new choices. Movie viewing is a prime example. People often wait for others to see a movie and then based on the response of early viewers, the herd follows. Let's examine Young's categories in turn and explore what impacts each might have on the adoption of behaviors and technologies.

Pure Conformity

Should someone eat with his fingers, chopsticks, or a fork? Ride a bike or a horse? Offer a dowry with their daughter in marriage? Vaccinate a child? Use birth control? In most instances, people want to conform to the behavior of those within their social network. *Why* they do remains a subject of much research by social psychologists. But conformity makes sense if we think the prospects for our individual survival depend on being perceived as "part of the group" rather than outside of it.

Instances of pure conformity arise when people adopt a behavior simply because others have adopted it. In Guatemala, most Mayan men have shifted to jeans and shirts during the last generation, while women continue to wear the traditional clothing, with its brightly colored patterns. In most rural villages, men would feel self-conscious wearing the traditional clothes, but women would feel self-conscious if they didn't. Guatemalan baby girls, in contrast to their North American counterparts, usually wear pierced earrings from the time they are a few weeks old. Why? *Solo es como se hace aqui.* (This is just how it's done here.) Likewise, when leaving a restaurant, one turns to the other guests with a boisterous "*buen provecho*," (literally: "make good use of it!"), an act that would turn one's dining companions ashen if performed in the United States. With pure conformity, something is done merely because, in a particular social group, that's the way it's done.

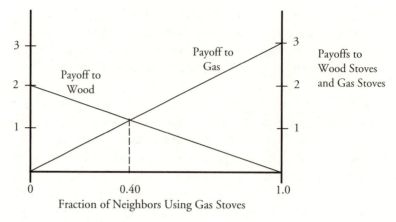

Figure 8.1. Technology Adoption Game

Consider the adoption of portable gas stoves as a new technology. To help combat deforestation problems, governments and non-government organizations (NGOs) have tried to introduce gas stoves in many rural areas of less-developed countries because they reduce the local population's dependence on firewood. Moreover, the household smoke produced by wood-burning stoves is associated with emphysema and other lung diseases, so that introducing gas stoves may also bring significant health benefits. Although gas stoves have a number of advantages over wood stoves, people may feel uncomfortable using the new technology unless their neighbors do the same. Few people desire to feel odd.

The following framework is helpful for understanding the spread of technology adoption in geographical space, *i.e.* neighborhood effects.[3] Suppose that purely based on the desire of households to conform to the behavior of their neighbors, the payoff from using either wood or gas is a linear, an increasing function of the fraction of their neighbors using that particular technology. However, the maximum payoff from using gas is equal to 3 (when all of one's neighbors are also using gas), but the maximum payoff from using wood (when all of one's neighbors are also using wood) is only equal to 2. The minimum payoff, if a household were to choose a technology when none of its neighbors were using the same technology, is zero for both gas and wood as seen in Figure 8.1.

Let's pretend our households live in an imaginary neighborhood made up of 36 households in a two-dimensional 6 × 6 lattice as seen in Figures 8.2a–8.2d. In this imaginary neighborhood each household associates only with the households next to it, the household to its immediate east, west, north and south (but not to its diagonal). It is only these adjacent households, which we will consider to be "neighbors" of any single household. Thus, all households in the neighborhood have four neighbors, except the households on the edges of the neighborhood who have three neighbors, and the corner households who have only two neighbors.

---

[3] The model is adapted from Young (2001) and Blume (1993).

Figure 8.2a. Gas Stove Adoption Scenario #1

Figure 8.2b. Gas Stove Adoption: Nash Equilibrium #1

Suppose that a local NGO has convinced a certain number of households in the neighborhood to try using the gas stoves. Figure 8.2a shows eight households using gas (gray) while the other twenty-eight (black) use wood. Notice that this is not a Nash equilibrium. Consider the following possibility: The household in the second row and third column switches to gas since half its neighbors are also using gas, greater than the 40 percent critical point to adopt the new technology. Likewise, the household in the third row and second column, fifth row and sixth column, and sixth row and fourth column switch to gas. However, the household using gas in Figure 8.2a in the first row and fifth column will revert to using wood. This causes the house in the northeast corner (first row, sixth column) to also to revert to wood. A Nash equilibrium from this initial state can be seen in Figure 8.2b where we see two small gas-using "enclaves" within the larger neighborhood.

In Figure 8.2c, the NGO has convinced fourteen of the thirty-six households to try using gas stoves instead of wood. Like the other initial state of technology introduction in Figure 8.2a, this also is not a Nash equilibrium. Enough households have been introduced to gas that gas begins to spread via neighborhood effects to some wood-burning households. Again, consider the following possibility: All of the households in columns 1 and 6 switch from wood to gas because, in each of their

Figure 8.2c. Gas Stove Adoption Scenario #2

Figure 8.2d. Gas Stove Adoption: Nash Equilibrium #2

cases, all of their neighbors are using gas. Likewise, all the households in columns 2 and 5 switch from wood to gas because at least half of their neighbors are using gas (again, above the 40 percent critical level). See how the initial state in Figure 8.2c can yield an enclave of households who remain wood users. In fact, the household in the first row and fourth column switches back to wood from gas, as does the household in the household in the sixth row and third column. What remains in Figure 8.2d is a wood-using enclave made up of all the households in the third and fourth columns. Why does this enclave stick with the "backward" technology? Because in the resulting Nash equilibrium, less than 40 percent of the neighbors of these households are using gas. They lack enough exposure to the new technology to give them a desire to switch. Notice that this (like the case in Figure 8.2b) represents a Pareto-inferior outcome. All of the wood-using households would be better off if they all had switched to gas.

This kind of model can help us to understand the existence of enclaves in geographical space characterized by perpetuation of Pareto-inefficient behaviors, that is, ghettos and slums where "cultures of poverty" may exist. Consider similar choices such as dropping out of school versus continuing in school, teenage sexual activity versus abstinence, taking or not taking illegal drugs, and so forth. These behavioral choices, whether positive or negative, tend to be geographically clustered.[4] Given the powerful influence of neighborhood effects, we can discover an element of rationality behind many destructive behaviors, which on the surface may appear irrationally self-defeating when they serve to perpetuate vicious cycles of poverty. Everyone would be better off if everyone else made different choices, but given the choices everyone else is making, the community gets stuck in a behavioral trap. (We will see in Chapter Eleven that *identity* may also play a role in this phenomenon.)

For example, few women in a Muslim country such as Bangladesh want to be the first to take a microloan. It takes but a small scholarly leap for a conservative interpreter of the Koran to judge female microborrowing (and entrepreneurial activity in general) to be a violation of the Koran and a woman's divinely ordained role in society. Many local imams have taken that leap, and the first female microfinance borrowers are often chastised and treated harshly.[5] However, women have taken comfort from the safety found in numbers. When many women in a village become micro-borrowers, it is easier for late adopters to follow.

David Bevan and Paul Collier of Oxford University have called this the *copying effect*, which they show to be critical in the adoption of new, high-return activities, especially among women in developing countries.[6] The copying effect operates both on *states* and *decisions*, meaning that the willingness of people to adopt a new activity depends on both the current number of people already engaging in the activity as well as the number of new people switching to it. Evidence points to the effect of the latter being significantly more powerful based on their empirical research on women's technology adoption in Africa.[7]

The copying effect is one reason why the Grameen Bank signs up women in large groups (usually at least forty at a time), and not individually. Like the soldiers storming the beaches of Normandy, life is easier as part of a large, overwhelming cohort. In the Grameen case, after a critical mass of women in a village begins to take microloans, local imams have been found to justify a somewhat more liberal interpretation of the text.[8]

Instrumental Conformity

In cases of instrumental conformity, people will conform to the behavior of others, not simply because they feel more comfortable doing so, but because conformity produces tangible economic benefits. An example provided by Peyton Young (1998) is the adoption of currency as a medium of exchange by ancient civilizations. Barter was the earliest form of economic exchange, but its inconveniences and inefficiencies induced people to adopt primitive forms of currency. Shells, beads, grain, and

---

[4] See Sampson, Morenoff, and Gannon-Rowley (2002) for an excellent survey of research that has explored the neighborhood effects of drug and alcohol abuse, disorder, gang activity, violent crime, and teen sexual activity.

[5] For example, see Wagener (2006).

[6] See Collier (1988) and Bevan, Collier, and Gunning (1990).

[7] Collier (1988).

[8] Kessey (2005).

Seller's Currency

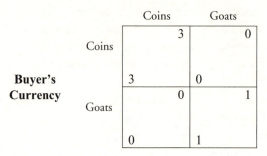

Figure 8.3. Currency Coordination Game

goats were all commonly used as well as more creative commodities such as giraffe tails and woodpecker scalps.[9]

Evidence of early coinage has been found between the first and second millennium B.C. in many parts of the world, including Europe, the Middle East, and China. But around 650 B.C. formal coinage began to emerge in Lydia (located within modern-day Turkey) and was quickly copied by the Greeks and later by the Romans. Silver and gold coins became a standard medium of exchange in the Greco-Roman world shortly thereafter. The adoption of coins as a medium of exchange yielded great advantages over earlier forms of currency in the ease of economic exchange and the development of markets, not to mention the great sense of relief experienced by giraffes and woodpeckers.

Consider the game presented in Figure 8.3. Let's suppose there are many Buyers and Sellers of different types of goods who meet in a central market somewhere in the Fertile Crescent around the fifth century B.C. Suppose that the traditional medium of exchange has been goats, but coins are beginning to be adopted in nearby areas. Both buyers and sellers must be prepared to travel to or from the market with a single medium of exchange, hoping that the corresponding buyer or seller deals in the same currency. As seen in Figure 8.3, using goats as currency is better than each using different currencies, but compared to a handful of silver coins, traveling to or from the market with a herd of bleating goats is less desirable than with a pocket full of coins. Thus, coordinating on coins as a medium of exchange is Pareto-superior to coordinating on goats. Like the previous example of stove technology, the game in Figure 8.3 represents a Coordination game in which (Coins; Coins) is a Pareto-superior Nash equilibrium.

A Buyer prefers to stick with goats unless a critical mass (fraction) of Sellers have adopted the coin technology. If the fraction of Sellers adopting coins is p, then a Buyer will strictly prefer the coins over goats only if $3p > 1(1 - p)$, or $p > 1/4$. Because the payoffs are symmetric, the sellers behave in the same way; they will stick with goats unless the fraction of Buyers rises above one-fourth, in which case they

_____

[9] Dalton (1965) and Lictheim (1973).

switch to coins. There is a coordination issue. Both Buyers and Sellers may prefer the coin technology, but unless each is confident that the other will reciprocate, they remain with the inferior technology of goats. As a result, even with the introduction and widespread availability of the new technology, two Nash equilibria exist. That Sellers and Buyers might stick with the Pareto-inefficient goat technology remains a possibility.

If both technologies are available, what leads to one equilibrium or the other? Let's change the assumptions in our game slightly and say that a new marketplace develops somewhere in our Fertile Crescent, and neither Buyers nor Sellers have any prior beliefs about the fraction of corresponding players using goats or coins as currency. Suppose also that they will play the game repeatedly, traveling to the market frequently over a long span of time. If any player enters the game "blind" in this manner, she may begin by choosing one of the strategies randomly in the first period and then learn which is the preferred medium of exchange based on past transactions.

One common framework for thinking about how people learn in this type of repeated interaction is through the concept of "fictitious play," developed in 1951 by Berkeley mathematician Julia Robinson (who later became the first female member of the mathematical division of the National Academy of Sciences). Her idea was that each player tallies the frequency distribution of the actions of corresponding players over his history of play in the game and then chooses a best reply in the *next* stage of the game according to this experience. In our current example, if in past plays of the game a Buyer had encountered Sellers who had demanded coins less than one-fourth of the time, his optimal response would be to bring goats. If a seller had encountered buyers who had demanded coins more than one-fourth of the time, then she should bring coins.

The dynamics of the movement towards one technology or the other from fictitious play can be seen in Figure 8.4. This movement may follow a variety of paths. If, for example, the fraction of Buyers using coins is greater than one-fourth, but the fraction of Sellers using coins is less than one-fourth, the dynamics of the system

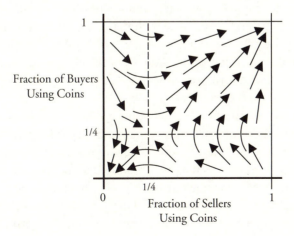

Figure 8.4. Dynamics of Currency Coordination Game

move toward the southeast, potentially shooting into the northeast quadrant, that leads to the coin equilibrium, or to the southwest quadrant, which leads to the goats equilibrium. If the fraction of Buyers using coins is less than one-fourth, but the fraction of sellers using coins is greater than one-fourth, the dynamics of the system move northwest, also potentially leading to either equilibrium. Whether the system ultimately winds up at coins or goats depends in part on the initial conditions, which are based on experiences in early-period plays of the game.

The area in the northeast quadrant of the diagram as well as adjacent areas in the northwest and southeast quadrants that feed into it serve as the *basin of attraction* to the (Coins; Coins) equilibrium. Notice that if the number of buyers and sellers using coins both become greater than one-fourth, then the dynamics are certain to converge to the sole use of coins. Similarly, the area in the southwest corner and the adjacent areas of that feed into it serve as the basin of attraction to the (Goats; Goats) equilibrium. The latter has a smaller basin of attraction because using goats as currency is less attractive than coins.

New technologies that facilitate market exchange occur in industrialized as well as developing economies. For example, not long ago if one wished to buy or sell a used car, the appropriate place to advertise it was in the classified ads of the local newspaper. Although countless used cars have been bought and sold through the local newspaper, the newspaper has never been the ideal medium to sell or buy a used car. The ability of a two or three line classified ad to convey all the necessary information about a particular car is limited. Moreover, the market in the local paper for any particular model is usually thin. If you are looking in the local newspaper for a forest green 1968 Porsche 912, you can bet it won't be there. The adoption of online technology has greatly expanded the market for buying and selling used cars.

Online car advertisements are superior first because they are more informative than the classified ads in the local newspaper. They have space for ample descriptions of automobiles, explanations for dents and dings and other shortcomings, and they also usually include pictures of the car. Moreover, while today the typical large metropolitan newspaper might contain a few hundred listings for used cars (significantly less than a decade ago), the largest online site, Atlanta-based Autotrader.com, has hundreds of thousands of listings. In the search for their dream machine, consumers can efficiently choose a specific year, maker, model, color, and transmission type. On Autotrader and other similar Web sites, the chances of finding the specific amenities one is looking for improve spectacularly, even down to the color of the seats. In the online market, one can search locally (within a given radius of a zip code) or nationally. In virtually all respects, the online market is a superior technology for car buying than the local newspaper, and it is unsurprising that in recent years buyers and sellers of used cars have begun to abandon the local newspaper in favor of the online market as the preferred medium of used-car exchange.

However, this transition to a new car-buying technology did not occur at once, and in fact is still occurring. (Using our currency example, it is probably somewhere in the northeast quadrant of Figure 8.4, moving steadily toward the northeast (Coin; Coin) corner.) But if a buyer expected most sellers to list their cars in the newspaper, a buyer would probably choose to search in the newspaper. If a seller expected most buyers to look in the newspaper rather than online, that is probably where a seller would list the car. Like the coin technology, the existence of the better online technology is a necessary, but insufficient, condition for its adoption. Individuals on one side of an exchange must be confident that those on the other side are adopting it as well.

Like the previous (Goat; Goat) equilibrium, (Newspaper; Newspaper) is also a Nash equilibrium. So how did the American used-car market move from the newspaper equilibrium, toward the online equilibrium? Three factors influenced the movement to the new technology: (1) the superior payoffs to buyers and sellers caused by the widening of the market; (2) the superiority of online advertisements over conventional newspaper ads in bridging information gaps between buyers and sellers; and (3) a large and expensive yearlong advertising campaign launched by Autotrader, culminating in TV ads aired during Superbowl XXXIV in January 2000 before 135 million viewers.

To get unstuck from a Pareto-inefficient equilibrium like (Goats; Goats) or (Newspaper; Newspaper), it takes a critical fraction of players to change their expectations about game play all at once. Similar to our game in Figure 8.4, the threshold of (Newspaper; Newspaper) is lower the worse the old newspaper technology is relative to the new online technology. Consequently, Autotrader gambled that its advertising blitz could convince enough buyers and sellers to adopt the online technology that the system would tip to the new equilibrium. Here are excerpts from a press release from January 22, 2000:

> At the National Automotive Dealers Association convention, AutoTrader.com today announced the Super Bowl as the launch event for the company's multi-million dollar nationwide branding and advertising campaign. . . ."The Super Bowl is a spring board into an aggressive year-long campaign designed to make AutoTrader.com a recognized brand and household name synonymous with smart used car buying and selling" said Chip Perry, president and CEO of AutoTrader.com. . . .With the use of high-tech digital effects, the commercial visually demonstrates to the viewer that the AutoTrader.com Web site is quick, responsive and easy to use. In addition, it emphasizes the unsurpassed selection of used vehicles and resources available for the consumer, designed to empower buyers and assist them in finding the perfect car at the right price.

The strategy worked. Since its founding in 1997, the number of private sellers listing at one time on *Autotrader* had grown to 250,000 by 2007, while the number of dealers had grown to 40,000. The total number of concurrent listings had grown to over 3 million.[10] Meanwhile, newspapers have faced shriveling classified ad sections. In August 2005, Knight Ridder, which at the time owned thirty-two major metropolitan newspapers, reported a 7.1 percent decline in classified advertising from only a year earlier.[11] Revenues from classified advertising have declined steadily since 2000 to the point that some newspapers, such as the *San Diego Union-Tribune* have begun

---

[10] Company website, Autotrader.com (accessed 8/5/07).
[11] David Washburn, "Union-Tribune to Offer Free Classified Advertisements to Readers," *San Diego Union-Tribune*, August 25, 2005.

Table 8.1. Automobile statistics by selected country

Country	Motor vehicles per capita (1 000)[a]	Kilometers of road per capita[a]	Gasoline price $US per gallon[b]
Brazil	88	11.02	$3.12
Venezuela	94	3.09	$0.12
United Kingdom	400	6.45	$5.79
France	494	13.00	$5.54
Germany	405	7.64	$5.57
Russia	87	1.81	$2.10
Japan	469	7.56	$4.24
China	5	0.45	$2.01
Nigeria	30	1.43	$0.38
United States	758	22.29	$2.20

Sources: [a]2004 World Development Indicators.
[b]CNN Survey, March 2005.

to give away classified advertising free in hopes of maintaining readership.[12] The move would seem to be futile: Consumer adoption of the online technology has passed the tipping point.

Sometimes political factors shape instrumental conformity and the adoption and diffusion of technology, particularly when use of the technology involves the creation of public infrastructure. Many new technologies require a supporting infrastructure that is often a public good. Computers without the internet are reduced to being word processors and calculating machines. Cars without roads are inferior to horses. Phones without landlines, cells, or satellites are play toys. The supporting infrastructure of a technology is often expensive to implement and maintain, and the question is always who pays for it: only the users of the technology, or everybody?

Consider the adoption of the automobile as a transportation technology. Different societies have decided differently on who should pay for the necessary highway infrastructure that makes owning a car worthwhile. In most European countries, such as Britain, France, and Germany, the answer has been that car owners should pay through taxes on gasoline – and pay they do. Table 8.1 shows pump prices of premium gasoline in March 2005, a time when American consumers were wringing their hands as United States gasoline prices rose to an average of $2.20/gallon. At that time, gasoline prices were over $5.50 in most of Europe, including $5.79/gallon in the United Kingdom, primarily a product of taxes levied on gasoline to maintain highway infrastructure.

As Table 8.1 shows, the cheapest gasoline is not, however, found in the United States. In petroleum-rich Venezuela in March 2005, the Chavez government had fixed prices such that gasoline was available at the basement-bargain price of $0.12/gallon. In Nigeria, the price was $0.38/gallon. Other countries, such as Russia

[12] Ibid.

and China, had lower gasoline taxes, making the price level closer to that of the United States.

Motor vehicles per capita and kilometers of road per capita in the United States dwarf that of other countries, reflecting the combination of both cheap gas and a highly developed economy. But is the more widespread adoption of the automobile as the primary transportation technology in the United States the *result* of cheap gasoline or the *cause* of cheap gasoline? The following game helps us to understand how the dynamics of political economy can create multiple equilibria in technology adoption, where a country can end up with high gasoline taxes and fewer cars per capita, or low gasoline taxes and cars everywhere.

The easiest way to see how this works is to imagine a small, island country of five citizens with a democratic, market-based political economy, such as exists in the United States or Europe. Let's call the five citizens Alice, Bob, Cindy, Doug, and Ethan, who differ in the benefit each receives from owning an automobile. The road infrastructure cost required to support automobile transportation is equal to C. This cost can be shared equally by the 5 citizens through an income tax (let's say that all their incomes are the same), or it can be paid for through a gasoline tax, meaning that only those who own cars pay for the roads. The private benefit B Alice receives from owing a car (the convenience and pleasure of driving minus the price of a car itself) is less than zero, so that even if all citizens pitched in equally to pay for roads through an income tax, she would choose to be car-less. Ethan, on the other hand, needs to drive. In fact, driving is so economically valuable to him (he transports coconuts and other island produce) that his benefit from driving is greater than C. Bob, Cindy, and Doug are in the middle. For these three $0 < B < C/2$, the private benefit from owning a car is greater than zero but less than $C/2$. That is, if everyone had to pay for the cost of the roads anyway through the income tax, each would buy a car, but if the cost of the roads were shared by only two car owners or less through a gasoline tax, car ownership would not be worth it for Bob, Cindy, and Doug. All five of the citizens get to vote on whether to finance the road infrastructure through an income tax or through a gasoline tax.

Discovering the different equilibrium outcomes in this political economy game involves two steps. The first step is to see that anybody who decides to own a car will vote for the income tax, and anybody who votes for the income tax will own a car, making the two decisions one and the same. Any citizen who owns a car will vote for the income tax because with the income tax a car owner pays only $C/5$, whereas with a gasoline tax, a car owner pays at least $C/4$ (since Alice will never drive). Moreover, any citizen who doesn't own a car will never vote for an income tax to pay for roads because for a car-less citizen the cost of an income tax would be $C/5$, but under a gasoline tax the car-less citizen would pay zero.

The second step is to see the different Nash equilibria that exist when the citizens make their choices. Notice that the car decision/voting decision game only involves three players (Bob, Cindy, and Doug) because we have already seen that Alice won't own a car (and vote for a gasoline tax) and Ethan will (and vote for an income tax), no matter what the other players do. Taking all this into account, consider the game

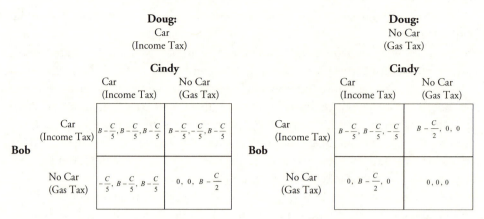

Figure 8.5. Technology Adoption with Public Investment

in Figure 8.5 involving Bob, Cindy, and Doug, where payoffs are given to the three players. Certain combinations of strategies are clearly not Nash equilibria, because at least one citizen-player will deviate. For example, if Bob plays Car (and income tax) and Cindy does the same, but Doug plays No Car (and gas tax), income tax wins over gas tax 3–2 (counting Alice's and Ethan's votes as well). In this case, Doug will buy a car (and vote for an income tax) since his benefit, B, is greater than zero, and the income tax is essentially a sunk cost. He might as well get a car given the actions of the other players, even if his resulting payoff, $B - C/5$ were to be negative; in the Nash equilibrium everybody except Alice has a car and votes for the income tax. Another strategy combination that is not a Nash equilibrium is one in which two of the three middle players, say Bob and Cindy, choose No Car (and gas tax) while Doug doesn't. In this case, Doug deviates to No Car (and gas tax) since $B - C/2 < 0$.

The two Nash equilibria to the game are when all three middle players together either adopt the car as their transportation technology and vote for the income tax to finance the road infrastructure, or collectively reject the car and vote for the gas tax. Adoption of a new technology does not guarantee Pareto superiority. In comparing the two equilibria we know that the Car equilibrium is worse for Alice and better for Ethan than the No Car equilibrium. But even from the standpoint of the middle players, we cannot say whether one Nash equilibrium is Pareto superior to the other without knowing the value of B for each of them. If $B > C/5$, then the No Car equilibrium would be worse than the Car equilibrium for 4 out of the 5 players. It is possible, however, that the equilibrium in which everyone except Alice owns a car and votes for the income tax is worse than the No Car equilibrium for 4 out of the 5 players, if for each of the middle players the value of a car is lower than their share of the road costs, that is, $B < C/5$.

The (4 out of 5) Car/Income tax equilibrium may be Pareto inferior to the (4 out of 5) No Car/Gas tax equilibrium particularly if we include the possibility of negative pollution externalities associated with automobile driving. Suppose if by owning a car, any citizen emits pollution that has a social cost of E, but the cost is spread over the population, so that the pollution cost borne by any citizen from her *own* driving is just equal to $E/5$. If $B > E/5$, then a middle player will choose to own a car and vote for the income tax if the other two choose the same. But the resulting Car/Income tax equilibrium in which players receive payoffs of $B - \frac{1}{5}C - \frac{4}{5}E$ may be worse off for all players than the No Car/Gas Tax equilibrium. Even Ethan may be worse off. If his benefit from driving is only slightly greater than C, he is worse off in the Car equilibrium if for him, $B - \frac{1}{5}C - \frac{4}{5}E < 0$, or $B < E$.

It is clear that the high car-ownership Nash equilibrium is closer to the American experience, and the low car-ownership Nash equilibrium is closer to, say, the British experience in which per capita car ownership is only half that of the United States. What might account for the different outcomes? Any answer is somewhat speculative, but one contributing factor may have been the mass-production automobile technology introduced in the United States during the early part of the twentieth century. In fact, by the late 1920s, 86 percent of all cars in the world were produced in the United States.[13] Henry Ford's low-cost assembly-line production lowered prices and helped promote popular adoption of the automobile by the American masses, which would increase the value of B in our model, perhaps making the high car-ownership equilibrium more likely in the United States. In Britain, however, early carmakers such as Morris, Rover, and Austin, favored a more artesian approach to production, in which cars were constructed by skilled craftsmen to suit individual tastes and preferences.[14] Higher costs of production and prices may have reduced the private benefit of car ownership in Britain relative to the United States, thereby influencing the subsequent politics of automobile taxation.

Informational Conformity

I watch my 18-month-old daughter Allie play in our living room with her friends, twins her age from down the street. (Even economists can learn much from observing toddlers because their uninhibited behavior reveals many of our own basic instincts.) Normally, nothing bores Allie more than a basket full of toys. As a rule, she prefers climbing on furniture, sliding down slides, chasing things, and playing with boxes more than with the toys that came in them. But one of the twins selects a toy from the basket, and immediately the toy begins to capture Allie's interest as well. The twin puts down the toy and searches for another. Allie picks up the first toy and appraises it but likewise decides it's not really that interesting and discards it. Her attention shifts to another toy that the other twin is playing with.

What is my daughter doing? She doesn't appear to be engaging in *pure conformity;* she's not yet self-conscious enough to worry about fitting in. That will probably come later. (If she were, she would have objected strongly to her last Halloween costume.) Further, her behavior does not seem to reflect *instrumental conformity;* she is not old enough to play catch with her friends, or other games in which the

---

[13] Koshar (2004), p. 131.
[14] Ibid., p. 132.

fun grows as more join in. Rather, what she seems to be doing is taking cues from her playmates about what is most fun to play with. She appears to be engaging in the kind of *informational conformity* that we as adults engage in when we ask our colleagues about their new computer software, satellite TV, or 50-in-1 multi-gadget formerly known as the cell phone.

Do we really believe that this kind of behavior vanishes as people enter adulthood? Most psychologists and sociologists do not believe so, and many economists are beginning to agree. Technology adoption by adults is like toy behavior among toddlers. I observe my friend tinkering with his new BlackBerry. He seems to like it. So do several other friends. If they all have a BlackBerry, then it *must* be worth its price. I buy one too.

Economists have begun to capture the dynamics of informational conformity, or *social learning* in technology adoption with simple, yet insightful, economic models.[15] The following captures the basic idea behind this work and is based on Bikhchandani, Hirshleifer, and Welch (1998). Consider a rural agricultural economy that uses a traditional seed variety, whose payoff (after all consumption needs are satisfied) is equal to zero; a farm household neither advances, nor declines using the traditional seed. A new potentially high-yielding seed is introduced to Farmer A in the village. The new seed is either Good or Bad. If it is Good, it gives a payoff of 1 to any farmer who uses it. If it is Bad, it yields -1. Before receiving any private information about the new seed, every farmer believes it is Good with probability $\frac{1}{2}$. But in sequence, each farmer receives a private signal about the new seed which is either *High* or *Low,* a signal that is positively correlated with the true yield of the new seed. In other words, if the new seed is Good, the farmer receives the *High* signal with some probability $p > \frac{1}{2}$. This implies that if the farmer gets the *High* signal, then the probability that the seed is Good is equal to p and the probability that it is Good if he receives the *Low* signal is only $(1-p)$.[16]

Thus if Farmer A receives the *High* signal about the new seed, he will adopt it since his expected payoff with $p > \frac{1}{2}$ is $(1-p)(-1) + 1p > 0$, greater than the zero payoff with the traditional seed. Suppose that Farmer B can observe Farmer A's choice of adoption, but not Farmer A's (or any one else's) private signal. If Farmer A adopts, and Farmer B receives his own *High* signal, Farmer B will adopt the new seed as well. He knows that for Farmer A to have adopted the new seed, he must have seen a *High* signal too. The fact that Farmer B sees his own *High* signal only magnifies the probability that the new seed is Good. If Farmer B receives the *Low* signal, he knows that one *High* signal has occurred and one *Low* signal, making him indifferent to adoption. Assume that he flips a coin, and if it lands on heads, he adopts.

Now it's Farmer C's turn. If he observes both Farmers A and B adopting the new seed, he also adopts no matter what signal he gets. Notice that even if Farmer C gets

---

[15] See, for example, Banerjee (1992); Bikhchandani, Hirsheiffer, and Welch (1992); Ellison and Fundenberg (1993); Gale (1996); and Zhao (2005).

[16] That this is a result of the former can be confirmed by using Bayes' Rule. Suppose that given the event X, two events can occur, either Y_1 or Y_2 Bayes' Rule shows that $p(Y_1|X)$, or the probability of Y_1 being true given that X is true, is $p(Y_1|X) = pY_1 \cdot p(X|Y_1)/[pY_1 \cdot p(X|Y_1) + pY_2 \cdot p(X|Y_2)]$.

the *Low* signal, he will still adopt since he knows that Farmer A received the *High* signal, and that Farmer B is *more likely* to have received the *High* signal than the *Low* signal. As a result, an *information cascade* begins with Farmer C if Farmers A and B undertake the same action. In this case, he disregards his private information and bases his decision solely on the sequential actions of Farmers A and B. After this Farmers D, E, and F, etc. continue to adopt the new seed regardless of their own private signal. The same story could be told about nonadoption if Farmer A received a *Low* signal and Farmer B decided not to adopt based on his own *Low* signal or a random coin toss.

Information cascades have two interesting features that are pertinent to technology adoption. First, it is entirely possible to get an information cascade that moves in the wrong direction. Good technologies may be rejected based on faulty information early on, or just plain bad luck. Bikhchandani et al. consider the case of $p = 0.51$. Suppose that the new seed is truly Good. The probability of an "adoption" cascade is equal to the probability that both Farmers A and B received *High* signals plus the probability that Farmer A received a *High* signal and Farmer B received a *Low* signal and his coin landed on heads, or $0.2601 + 0.12495 = 0.38505$. The probability of a "nonadoption" cascade (when the seed is indeed Good) is equal to the probability that both Farmers A and B received *Low* signals plus the probability that Farmer A received a *Low* signal and Farmer B received a *High* signal but his coin landed on tails, or $0.2401 + 0.12495 = 0.36505$. Thus given the same (Good) underlying value of the new seed, the probability of an incorrect cascade is only slightly lower than of a correct one. Of course as the accuracy of the signal, p, increases, the probability of an incorrect cascade diminishes.

The second interesting feature of information cascades is that the order of signals can matter. Suppose that Farmers A and B receive *High* signals, and Farmers C and D receive *Low* signals. This results in an information cascade to adopt the seed beginning with Farmer C. If Farmers A and B receive *Low* signals and Farmers C and D receive *High* signals, then Farmer C begins a nonadoption cascade. Although both patterns are equally likely, they lead to precisely opposite directions. Thus, the question "How can it be beneficial if so many people have rejected it?" may have a simple answer: Timing.

We can modify the basic game slightly by allowing some players to have better information about the new technology than others. Assume that Farmer C receives a clearer signal about the new seed than each of the others. While everyone else's $p = 0.51$, Farmer C's $p = 0.55$. Moreover, it is common knowledge that Farmer C's p is larger than everyone else's p. Now let's say Farmers A and B receive *Low* signals and Farmer C receives a *High* signal. Unlike the previous case, Farmer C chooses to adopt because the probability of Farmer A and Farmer B collectively making the right call [$0.38505/(0.38505 + 0.36505) = 0.5133$] is lower than the probability that *he* alone would choose correctly if he were to follow his own private signal ($= 0.55$). Seeing Farmer C's action to adopt, Farmer D also chooses to adopt, regardless of his own signal. Even if he receives a *Low* signal, the probability of Farmers A, B, and D being collectively right about the new seed is lower than the probability of Farmer C being right: $(0.51 \times 0.38505)/(0.51 \times 0.38505 + 0.49 \times 0.36505) = 0.5233 < 0.55$. From this flows a clear definition of *leadership:* the power of your actions to influence the actions of others, even when your actions conflict with others' private signals. In this context, leadership is based on one individual's more accurate perception of the truth than is had by others, and the common knowledge of this individual's advantage. And our example shows that a leader doesn't have to be that much smarter than the others to influence the herd.

Jinhua Zhao (2005) modifies the basic game by allowing farmers to choose the time at which they decide to adopt the new technology. In Zhao's framework, each farmer i has a different cost of adoption, C_i. For simplicity, he assumes that a decision to adopt is a permanent one. Each has only imperfect knowledge about other farmers' costs of adoption, but can clearly see others' actions. Each farmer also gets some imperfect, but useful signal about the profitability of the technology from those who have adopted it before him. If a farmer adopts the technology, his payoff is equal to $\frac{V}{1-\delta} - C_i$, where V is the expected value of the new technology based on the information gleaned from the history of other farmers' experiences with it, and δ is our discount factor as before. By adopting the technology, the farmer thus expects to get V forever, after subtracting his sunk cost to adoption. Waiting allows a farmer to get more information from other adopters, but this delays his use of a potentially beneficial technology. As with many things, having it now is better than later. The upshot of Zhao's model is that low-cost farmers will adopt the technology first, even when information about V isn't too clear. This makes sense because the low-cost adopters have less to lose if the technology turns out to be a bust. If and when the remaining farmers observe signals of higher profit, they become more willing to adopt it as well. Others continue to follow (in order of increasing C_i until a point is reached when either all farmers have adopted the technology or when the most recent adopters begin to give signals that show in hindsight that they made a mistake and shouldn't have adopted it.[17]

Empirical Research

How does the technology adoption of real people compare to the predictions of some of these theories? This is the task of econometrics, and the first serious work on this issue was done by the late Zvi Griliches (1957). Griliches, then at the University of Chicago (later at Harvard until his death in 1999), carried out the seminal study in the field studying the adoption of hybrid corn by American farmers. Hybrid corn itself is not an invention per se but rather a method of breeding adaptable hybrid strains of corn that are high yielding and disease resistant in a particular area. Consequently, individual hybrids must be developed for specific regional areas to

---

[17] There is an interesting contrast between Zhao's model and an empirical study on the adoption of new sunflower crop in northern Mozambique. Oriana Bandiera and Imran Rasul (2006) discover a nonlinear (inverse U-shaped) relationship between the probability of adoption and the number of adopters in a farmer's network. The probability of adopting the new crop is higher with more adopters in the network, but having many adopters in the network provides an incentive to delay adoption and learn from the knowledge accumulated by previous adopters.

suit a particular region's climate and soil type, so that farmers in different regions not only face the question of adoption, but also the question of availability. If the right hybrid was available in his study, it was able to increase yields by an average of about 20 percent, with the actual increase varying significantly between regions. Griliches fits the pattern of hybrid corn adoption by farmers in his sample to an S-shaped (logistical) curve: Adoption of hybrids begins slowly, then picks up steam as nearby farmers jump on the hybrid bandwagon, with the pace lagging at the end as the last stragglers embrace the technology before adoption converges to an upper equilibrium point. He finds this pattern of adoption fairly consistent across thirty-one states and 132 crop-reporting districts. Moreover, Griliches finds the pace of technology adoption to be correlated with its benefits: In areas where there were greater differences in the profits between the hybrid corn and the traditional variety, the rate of adoption of the hybrid corn was faster.

In many respects, empirical studies that explore the underlying mechanics of technology adoption or behavioral imitation face significant challenges. One of the most significant of these challenges is the "reflection problem" brought to light by Charles Manski of Northwestern University.[18] Suppose three friends all have bikes, but not cars. Are they friends because all three live in a poor neighborhood in which nobody can afford a car? Does each ride a bike instead of a car because lack of economic opportunity in their neighborhood prevents each from earning enough money to have a car? Or does one friend ride a bike because he wants to imitate the behavior of his friends?

Manski (1995) calls the first of these explanations for behavioral imitation within social networks a *correlated effect*, in which individuals in a group tend to behave similarly because they face similar environments or by their characteristics they self-select into a given social network. The second is an example of a *contextual effect*, in which the propensity for a given type of behavior varies with the background characteristics in a social network. The third is an example of what Manski calls an *endogenous effect*, in which the propensity of an individual to behave in some way varies with the prevalence of that behavior in the group. The first two effects involve no real imitation, in the strictest sense of the word. The third (endogenous) effect, however, may be due to pure conformity, instrumental conformity, or informational conformity. Determining which of these effects is operational in empirical work has caused more than one social scientist to bang his head against a wall. Manski asserts that even some of the most celebrated research in the social sciences, particularly sociology, have confused two or more of these effects in the interpretation of their empirical results.[19]

I will conclude this chapter by briefly reviewing three recent empirical studies in development economics that examine the role of social networks in behavioral and technology adoption. Each of these studies is extraordinary, not only in the questions each addresses, but in the care that the authors take in striving to

[18] Manski (1993, 1995).
[19] Manski (1995), p. 129.

distinguish endogenous from correlated and contextual effects, and even within the scope of endogenous effects identifying social learning (informational conformity) as distinct from pure conformity or instrumental conformity.

Tim Conley and Christopher Udry (2004) study social learning among pineapple farmers in Ghana. Specifically, they examine the optimal application of fertilizer in pineapple plantations near the Ghanaian towns of Nsawam and Aburi. During the time of their survey, pineapple in this region was a new export crop. As a result, many farmers were struggling to learn proper cultivation techniques – creating an excellent time and place for a study focusing on social learning. Conley and Udry collected detailed information on which farmers talked to each other about farming. They categorized any two farmers falling into this category as "informational neighbors." This helps to identify how behavioral imitation occurs because agricultural yields are often spatially as well as temporally correlated, making data especially susceptible to picking up correlated effects rather than social learning. Conley and Udry also use a time dimension to separate learning from other kinds of imitative behavior since it takes an entire growing season for one farmer to learn the resulting crop yield from an information neighbor's fertilizer use.

Conley and Udry find convincing evidence of social learning among their pineapple farmers. In particular, they find that a given farmer is more likely to reduce his fertilizer use after information neighbors using similar amounts of fertilizer had realized lower than expected pineapple profits. If a farmer's information neighbors realized unexpectedly high profits, they find that the farmer adjusts his use of fertilizer toward that of his successful neighbors. Moreover, they find that rookie pineapple farmers rely on the information of their neighbors more than do veteran pineapple farmers. Further, rookies rely on veterans more than they rely on the other rookies. Thus, their results reflect the importance of both social learning in economic behavior, and leadership in the formal sense described previously.

Over 25 percent of the people in the world suffer from intestinal helminthes, that is, worms. The most common are hookworm, roundworm, whipworm, and schistosomiasis. Mild worm infections often go undetected by the host, but severe infections can cause abdominal pain, iron deficiency, stunting (low height for age), and wasting (low weight for height).[20] Michael Kremer and Edward Miguel (2003) employ a randomized implementation of a school-based de-worming program in Kenya to study the impact of social networks on the adoption of worm-treatment drugs. A survey was administered to both children and parents of the children in the program that gathered information on their social networks, especially the five individuals they spoke with most frequently, relatives with whom they had frequent social interaction, and individuals with whom they discussed child health issues.

Like Conley and Udry, they find that informational flows within a social network influence individual choices and that people learn from the bad experiences of others. They found that children with greater exposure to others who had taken the de-worming drugs through their parent's social network were actually *less* likely to

---

[20] Kremer and Miguel (2003, 2004).

take the treatment than children with less exposure to others who had taken the drugs. Specifically, every social link between a child's parent and the parent of a child who received the treatment in the early phases of the program is associated with a 3.1 percentage point *lower* likelihood that that the parent's child received the treatment. Every similar social link between teenagers reduced the probability of receiving the treatment by 2.8 percentage points. Links between small children, not surprisingly, were not statistically significant. The randomized nature of their study helps to isolate informational conformity from other types of imitative behavior.

Kremer and Miguel attribute these results to the fact that reinfection typically occurred in children within a few months after the treatment, as de-worming medicine treats the existing condition but does not prevent reinfection. Moreover, many of the recipients reported the typical side effects associated with worm treatment: stomachache, diarrhea, and vomiting, not to mention the shock and awe when the paralyzed worms are expelled through the anus. As a result, many of those receiving treatment learned through their social network that the personal costs of the treatment outweighed the benefits. As they note, while the benefits to the individual may be less than expected, the de-worming treatments retard the cycle of transmission, and so the greatest benefit may accrue not to the individual, but to the larger community.

Kaivan Munshi and Jacques Myaux (2006) examine neighborhood effects in contraceptive use in Bangladesh. The setting for their data is a time of change in Bangladesh during the late 1970s, when The International Centre for Diarrheal Disease Research launched what they claim was one of the most intensive family planning programs ever implemented. Most villages receiving the program contained both Hindus and Muslims, with the latter comprising a little over 80 percent of the total in the sample. The program provided both free contraceptives and free visits by community health workers to the 144,000 households involved in the program.

Despite being showered with incentives to use birth control, and although neither the Koran nor the Hindu scriptures take an overt stand against contraception, those in the villages were slow to adopt contraceptives. Adoption of contraceptives increased, but slowly considering the highly intensive program effort. In 1983 contraceptive use was about 44 percent among Hindu households and 38 percent among Muslim households. Ten years later, 68 percent of Hindus and 62 percent of Muslims were using contraceptives, the more conservative Muslim households maintaining slightly lower use rates.

But the most striking result of Munshi and Myaux's study is the pattern of contraceptive use within individual villages. Their analysis shows that contraceptive adoption varied considerably within religious groups within the same village. The behavior of individual women was strongly responsive to the prevalence of contraceptive use by other women within their own religious group, but clearly *un*responsive to the prevalence of contraceptive use by others outside of their religious group. Moreover, when they partition their sample of women across other personal characteristics, such as age and education, Munshi and Myaux find considerable influences between groups; for example, illiterate women were influenced not only by other illiterate women but by literate women, and vice versa. The authors conclude that the origin of these patterns in contraception adoption lies in the *purda*, which severely restricts young married women to socializing only among women, and women of the same religious group. Thus, they interpret the results as a desire for social conformity among women within one's local religious group.

Interestingly, Munshi and Myaux appear to uncover a different type of endogenous effect than the research of Conley and Udry and the research of Kremer and Miguel. While the optimal level of fertilizer for each pineapple farmer and the effect of the de-worming treatments were unknown variables, the effect of contraception in Munshi and Myaux's sample of villages was unquestioned – it was the social acceptance of contraception that remained the open question. Thus whereas the studies on pineapples and worms reveal informational conformity, Munshi and Myaux's study on contraception uncovers imitative behavior based primarily on a desire for pure conformity.

Postscript: Does Better Technology Always Make Us Better Off?

It is easy to associate the adoption of new technology with "progress." This need not always be the case, even when the efficiencies rendered by the new technology are unquestioned. Take first an extreme example: the new "performance-enhancing drug" technologies available to athletes. Are baseball players, for example, better off from access to steroids than the baseball players of yesteryear? Of course not. Steroids make cheaters better off only when others refrain from using them. If every player were using steroids, the same players would lead the league in home runs as when everyone was clean. But if taking steroids is necessary to stay on the home-run hitting bandwagon, it makes players all as whole worse off, not better off, because steroids cause cancer, balding, mood swings, and sexual dysfunction. These negative side effects are unappealing to anyone, perhaps especially to ballplayers.

The performance-enhancing drug technology is an extreme example. But are the games underlying the new technologies that have been adopted in the industrialized workplace any different at their root? The last decade or two, white collar workers everywhere have been blitzed with an unprecedented array of new communication technologies including cell-phones, instant messaging, and e-mail, which have dramatically reshaped our everyday lives both at home and at work. At the outset, we might view the adoption of such technologies in the framework of a Coordination game like the game presented in Figure 8.1. If the new technology is more efficient, everyone may be better off if she, along with everyone else, adopts it. And this may be true in the use of such technologies at the *consumer* level.

But examining the communications technology game at the level of the workplace suggests a different kind of game. Cell phones and e-mail make workers more "available" to their bosses. They allow for a more rapid transfer of information and ideas, enabling tech-savvy employees to do more and better work in any given period of time. Increases in productivity ought to drive up wages and benefit workers – but the fact is that everybody has access to more or less the same technology.

Suppose though that internal promotions within firms involve some use of the "rank-order tournaments" proposed by Edward Lazear and Sherwin Rosen (1981). Lazear and Rosen's idea is that people often get promoted to better jobs with higher salaries based on competition with their fellow workers. It is not your productivity that matters for promotion and salary increases; it is how your productivity ranks relative to your colleagues. Here, cell phones and e-mail may turn from being delightful friend to detested foe. Cell phones not only make sycophantic employees on call to slave-driving bosses during evenings, weekends, and vacations, but they encourage workers to squeeze work into every conceivably productive moment in order to (try to) stay ahead of their peers. Anecdotal evidence abounds of employees frantically doing business on their cell phones while driving, shaving, trying to enjoy a meal with friends or family, and even while sitting on the commode in public restrooms. Since everyone has the opportunity for such "productivity gains," failing to adopt the technology to its full capacity means being left behind in the tournament. This kind of phenomenon is not a Coordination game but an ill-fated Prisoners' Dilemma.

Ironically, it is the collective *in*ability of workers to be available for work any time and any place that helps solve the Prisoners' Dilemma in workplace promotion tournaments in favor of workers. In important ways, these natural barriers between work and leisure are analogous to the "sheriff" who places limits on the exploitation of the commons (or on individual production in a cartel) to foster a Pareto-superior outcome for players. Communications technologies such as cell phones have "shot the sheriff" by breaking down these natural barriers between work and leisure, fueling the Prisoners' Dilemma of the white-collar worker's treadmill.

The dilemma continues with e-mail. The facility with which e-mailers can heap addresses onto a recipient list makes e-mail a medium of communication in which it is truly "more blessed to give than to receive." A friend who is a manager in the home products division of Hewlett-Packard tells me he typically receives two hundred work-related e-mails per day. Many of these are bulk e-mails sent as memos to multiple recipients in the division. Nevertheless, it is expected that they are to be read. Adding another recipient to an e-mail is virtually costless to a sender, but costly (in terms of time) for the receiver to have to read. Everyone would be better off if everyone else cooled it with the e-mails, but nobody wants to appear unproductive or out of the loop. It is a dominant strategy to send e-mails.

If the adoption of communications technology in the workplace represents a Prisoners' Dilemma for employees, where do the benefits from such innovations accrue? Nominal wages of workers may increase, but only to the extent that there is some scarcity in the supply of labor that is able to interact with the new technology. Real wages may rise little if the cost of living (principally from high housing costs) is bid up from increases in wages. Rents from such innovations in large part become capitalized in assets associated with production that are *inelastically* supplied, such as in the common stock of firms in which the technology gains are most extensively realized, and local real-estate prices near these firms. Consequently, those who happen to purchase these assets *before* their appreciation ultimately wind up as the ultimate, but rather arbitrary, winners from the new technology.

Shirking usually gets a bad rap from economists, but the truth is that a bit of shirking probably benefits everyone. With e-mail and other instantaneous forms of electronic exchange such as fax machines, and Internet-based work sharing, firms can demand quick turnaround time with projects, even within the same day. Before such technology, firms could work a little slower, able to claim that the papers were "in the mail" (an advantage when the mail takes an unknown amount of time to arrive.) Technologies that purge the work environment of the occasional round of jokes at the watercooler in favor of unmanageable stress are, in the end, not "welfare enhancing." It is not irrational for some white-collar workers visiting developing countries to envy a simpler life.

CHAPTER 9
Property Rights, Governance, and Corruption

The Lord hates dishonest scales, but accurate weights are His delight.
– Proverbs 11:1

ONE OF THE fundamental human dilemmas is that individuals potentially stand to gain from *competition* as well as *cooperation* with one another. Costly mistakes have been made from failing to recognize the two horns of this dilemma and that the tension between these conflicting incentives underlies nearly all social behavior. For example, this failure has led some to overemphasize the competitive nature of market-oriented societies, where social benefits are misperceived to accrue chiefly from the competitive aspects of markets. Economists have more recently come to understand that the cooperative aspects of market-oriented societies are just as important as their competitive aspects. The institutional constraints that check self-interested behavior are instrumental to the freedoms that allow for the pursuit of self-interested gain.

Institutions dictate the rules of the game in any society. They serve as guidelines for human interaction, and they set the limits for human freedoms. In his *Institutions, Institutional Change, and Economic Performance* (1990), Nobel laureate Douglas North defines institutions as "the framework within which human interaction takes place." He draws an analogy between the rules that govern competitive economic activity, and rules that govern competitive sports. In each, the rules of the game create a stable, predictable structure to behavior. Even in a sport as seemingly violent as American football, an elaborate (some would argue *too* elaborate) set of rules carefully governs play. The structure and predictable application of the rules make a better, fairer game for everyone; without a clearly specified set of rules, American football, or virtually any sport, would degenerate into mindless chaos. In the context of a market economy, institutions provide a cooperative framework within which economic competition can safely take place.

Failing to understand the importance of such a framework was responsible for one of the largest economic policy failures of the twentieth century: the initial policy advice given to Russia in the early stages of its transition to a market economy. Russia became an independent country on December 8, 1991, when the former

147

Soviet Union dissolved into the Commonwealth of Independent States. However, as early as October of 1991, Boris Yeltsin had articulated to the Russian parliament his plan for economic reform.[1] Poland had implemented a macroeconomic "shock therapy" plan on New Year's Day of 1990, in which prices in the economy were immediately and comprehensively liberalized. In providing incentives for the production of agricultural and consumer goods, the plan had been generally successful in the Polish transition from a socialist to market-based economy. The Yeltsin plan included a quick mass privatization scheme along with the price liberalization of the Polish model, and it sought to transform the Russian economy rapidly from central planning to one stressing markets and private ownership. The plan became popularly known as the Big Bang. The Big Bang, under the leadership of Acting Prime Minister Yegor Gaidar, was implemented on January 2, 1992. The system of socialist planning was demolished overnight.

However, the Big Bang quickly became the Big Bust. Prices shot up nearly fourfold in January 1992.[2] Part of the problem was clearly macroeconomic: To keep state enterprises afloat, Russia began to print money at a frenzied rate while increasing credits to moribund industries. Surpluses of cash held by consumers, the result of chronic shortages in the old economy, were immediately used to bid up prices. The hope had been that competition would begin to bring down prices, as it had in the Polish experience. However, Russia's state-run firms attracted little competition, and new entrepreneurial activity, especially in the manufacturing sector, was scarce. Although Russian economic ministers (and the western economists who advised them) had emphasized macroeconomic policy, they had bet that privatization would subsequently create a demand for the accompanying institutions that regulate a market economy and allow private enterprise to function. Although prices had indeed been liberalized, the creation of contract law, property rights, civil courts, antitrust law, and other institutions that establish the rules of the game for a market economy were thus downplayed in the earliest stages of reform. But as Karla Hoff and Joseph Stiglitz (2004) point out, privatization in the absence of a strong institutional infrastructure only created an incentive in Russia for enterprise owners to strip their firms of assets rather than build value into them. Thus instead of a sound market economy, Russia witnessed the emergence of a kind of "kleptocracy," a rent-seeking, gangster-plagued free-for-all that concentrated the benefits of reform in the hands of a few opportunistic oligarchs.

Where formal institutions are weak, as was the case early during the Russian reforms, economic activity becomes confined to the kind of trustworthy networks of entrepreneurs described in Chapter Five. One-shot, anonymous transactions in the larger market are risky. As a consequence, economic transactions become limited to those in which trust is established through repeated interaction within a close network of associates, a constraint to broadly based economic growth.

---

[1] Bergson (1994).
[2] Ibid., p. 57.

Legal Institutions, Confidence, and Economic Exchange

Confidence is the glue that holds a market economy together. Most economic transactions are not fully consummated in a simultaneous, face-to-face manner, but instead involve some degree of promise keeping. To provide an incentive for exchange, people have to be confident in the contractual promises of their reciprocating partners, such as payment of an invoice or a specification about the quality of goods. Without such confidence, even a transaction that could significantly benefit both parties may not happen.

Institutions such as contract law, property rights, and civil courts inspire confidence by ensuring that partners on the other side of a transaction keep their promises. Though the institutions that underpin a market economy often lie silently in the background, they serve as guarantors of promises, such that most economic transactions do not need to end up in civil court. But the knowledge that the transacting parties *could* end up in civil court (if one party failed to live up to its promises) creates underlying confidence in the transaction.

In game-theoretic parlance, one would say that with strong institutions, the contracting parties ending up in court would normally lie "off the equilibrium path," or not actually happen. Yet, the latent threat that either of the two parties could haul the other to court to enforce a promise fosters the cooperative Nash equilibrium. Therefore, the better the legal system is at punishing defectors, the less punishment the legal system is likely to have to dole out: Efficient legal institutions are more likely to deter cheaters, charlatans, and quacks from dishonest behavior, and maybe even turn them into reasonably good citizens. Consider the example presented in Figure 9.1. Boris and Vladimir simultaneously execute a transaction in which either can Comply with the terms of the contract or try to Swindle the other. In the case that one party Swindles, the Complying party has the option of taking legal action. In this game, the variable x is related to the *punitive power* of the legal system, its ability to levy damages against a defendant. If x is high, punishments are a credible deterrent to breaking agreements. The variable y is related to the *efficacy* of the legal system, principally the costs incurred by the plaintiff from initiating legal action. If y is low, the legal system is efficient, making it relatively easy to obtain a verdict against a cheater. If either $x < 2$ *or* if $y > 5$, the unique Nash equilibrium to a one-shot play of the game in Figure 9.1 is one in which everybody plays Swindle, and exchange breaks down. But if $x \geq 2$ and $y \leq 5$, a Nash equilibrium exists in a one-shot play of the game in which both parties play Comply, and exchange happens.

If the x condition is unsatisfied, punishments levied against the accused are insufficient to deter him from Swindling. If the y condition is unsatisfied, then the prospect of legal action by the plaintiff is a noncredible threat, whether or not punishments against a defendant are stiff. If, however, both the x and y conditions are satisfied, the threat of legal action is a credible deterrent, and a Nash equilibrium exists in which both parties comply rather than swindle, even in a one-shot game.[3]

---

[3] If the judicial system is so efficient that $y < 3$, then the Nash equilibrium in which both players play Comply is the unique Nash equilibrium to the game. Moreover, when both players can credibly threaten court

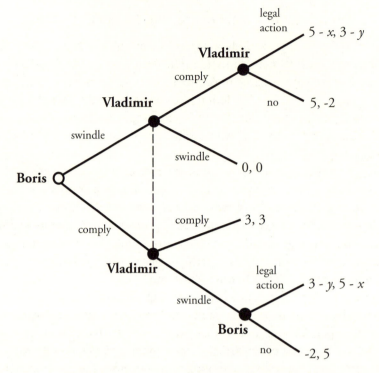

Figure 9.1. Market Exchange Game with Legal Institutions

In this way, formal institutions preclude the need to restrict economic activities to a local network, vastly widening the scope for exchange within the economy, and establishing an important foundation for economic development.

Private Domestic Investment

In *The Economic Institutions of Capitalism* (1985), Berkeley economist Oliver Williamson illuminates the role that institutions play in facilitating exchange in the market economy. He observes how economic incentives and efficiencies are largely shaped by two phenomena: *agency problems* (contracts between a principal, who requires a task to be completed, and an agent, hired to carry out the task) and second, issues of *property rights*. He notes several important aspects of property rights over an asset, specifically the right to *use* the asset, the right to *alter* the asset, and the right to *appropriate returns* from the asset.[4]

Although all three functions of property rights are important to economic development, many researchers, such as Sanford Grossman and Oliver Hart (1986), have emphasized the role of the third function – the right to appropriate returns. They

action, it meets the higher standard of a unique *subgame-perfect* Nash equilibrium, meaning that players' strategies pass an added credibility refinement in that they form a Nash equilibrium in each subgame, the remainder of a game after a single decision node (see the appendix for details).

[4] Williamson (1985), p. 28.

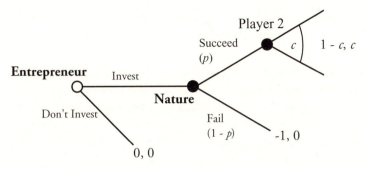

Figure 9.2. Investment and Property Rights Game

point out that when property rights have fuzzy edges, it produces a set of incentives that work against the creation of rents, or added economic surplus. Conversely, when the rights of individuals to residual claims (profit, more or less) over their owned assets are secured, it creates an economic environment in which entrepreneurial risk-taking and creativity become rewarded rather than punished.

In light of Grossman and Hart's observation, consider an Entrepreneur deciding whether to undertake a risky investment with one unit of capital in Figure 9.2. If she decides not to invest, her payoff is zero. If she invests, Nature then determines if the project will succeed with probability p, or fail with probability $1 - p$. If the investment fails, the capital is lost and the Entrepreneur receives a payoff of -1. If the investment succeeds, it yields a 100 percent return for a payoff of 1, but some Player 2 is able to exert some claim over a fraction c of this unit of return.

Who is this Player 2? There are a number of possibilities, of which I will list five: Player 2 could represent (a) a neighbor or friend who is (or feels) socially entitled to the fraction c of the entrepreneur's bounty;[5] (b) a thief who is able to steal c of the entrepreneur's profit; (c) organized criminal elements, who are entitled to the fraction c in exchange for "protection" services rendered to the entrepreneur; (d) government officials who are able to extract c in the form of bribes in exchange for compliance in securing the necessary legal permits for the entrepreneur; or even (e) the state itself, collecting the fraction c as a legal profits tax.

Assuming that a variety of investment projects can be undertaken at varying levels of risk (represented by different levels by p) the Entrepreneur will choose to invest in the project only if $p > \frac{1}{2-c}$. Obviously if Player 2's share $c = 1$, then by using backward induction, we see that no investment will be undertaken. As c gets close to zero, then all investments will be undertaken that have a greater than 0.5 probability of success. Accordingly, the higher the level of c, the lower the level of investment. Because the economic growth process is the culmination of countless such decisions to invest (rather than consume) resources in the present that will yield returns in the future, disincentives for entrepreneurs to invest choke economic development.

[5] For an excellent source on kin systems as a cause of poverty traps, see Hoff and Sen (2006).

How do the different cases (a–e) relate to different classes of ambiguities in property rights? Case (a) is related to social norms of reciprocity in the moral economy common to many traditional societies discussed in Chapter Five. With success comes the burden of responsibility to one's kinsmen, whether it be transfers of income, provision of employment to unproductive relatives, or other responsibilities. Although such generosity to those less fortunate is an admirable aspect of many cultures, the expectation that any successes must always be shared with one's friends may stifle entrepreneurial motivation. Case (b) is symptomatic of a weak state's difficulty in controlling common street crime, as in much of Latin America and Africa. Case (c) also describes a weak state that battles with organized criminal institutions for the fundamental source of power and authority in society, as in Russia and many of the former Soviet Republics. Case (d) is that of the strong, yet corrupt, rent-seeking bureaucracy, often the result of an overregulated economy. Such has been the case historically in countries such as India, where rent seeking has become a way of life for underpaid government bureaucrats. Case (e) represents, for exceedingly high levels of c, the strong and perhaps noncorrupt, but overly intrusive state, in which excessive tax rates may stifle economic growth and development.

An example of case (c), gangsters appropriating profits, appeared in an article in the *Boston Globe*, which featured an interview with "Misha," the owner of a Moscow kiosk, not long after the transition of the Russian economy was under way.[6] "I buy enough goods from the wholesaler to last one to three days," Misha says. "I keep a sheet listing all my merchandise, in case of a surprise visit from the tax inspector. But after I sell everything, I tear up the sheet, as if I had never bought anything and never sold anything. Then I start all over again. . . . I'm ready to pay taxes," says Misha, "but only if the state protects me against the racket."

The "racket," of course, refers to the Russian mafia, to which kiosk owners routinely pay "protection fees," usually about 5 to 10 percent of profits, much of it payable in merchandise. "The mafia also provides a package of services," the kiosk owners explain. "Unlike the state, they will protect you if you get ripped off." Some kiosk owners observe that the gangsters often are better able to monitor profits of the kiosks than the state. At times, a racketeer will sit inside the kiosk for a couple of days, jotting down all transactions, so that the mafia knows how much to demand when it comes to collect the "protection fee." The Russian tax police, in contrast, have fewer human resources and have almost no leverage for enforcing the law. Misha says many believe that a single gangster, an Asiatic Russian referred to as "China Mike," controls the entire racket involving the kiosks in Moscow; yet, others dismiss this, saying control is split up geographically.

The ability of criminal organizations or the government itself to engage in blatant rent-seeking behavior fundamentally alters economic incentives. As Vilfredo Pareto noted in the early twentieth century, "The efforts of men are utilized in two different ways: they are directed to the production or transformation of economic

---

[6] Fred Kaplan, "Dirty Capitalism: The Kiosk Has Become a Symbol of Moscow's Changing Economy," *Boston Globe*, June 25, 1993, p. 61.

goods, or else to the appropriation of goods produced by others."[7] Michael Porter of the Harvard Business School has argued that ill-defined property rights alter the perception of which of these approaches constitutes a "winning" economic strategy in a given economic environment:

> Prevailing beliefs about the basis for prosperity itself are . . . central. The attitudes of individuals and organizations and their economic behavior *are strongly affected by what they perceive to be the way to win.* Perhaps the most basic belief undergirding successful economic development is acceptance that prosperity depends on productivity, not on control of resources, scale, government favors, or military power, and that the productivity paradigm is good for society. Without such beliefs, rent seeking and monopoly seeking will be the dominant behavior, a pathology still afflicting many developing countries. (2000: p. 21 – italics mine)

Given a sufficiently high "tax rate" c in the game in Figure 9.2, cases (a) through (e) above portray weaker property rights environments in which the "winning" economic strategy may shift from entrepreneurialism toward passivity, theft, or bureaucratic rent seeking.

Another note on the importance of property rights: They create incentives in *input* as well *output* markets. As we have seen in output markets, property rights give entrepreneurs and investors the right to appropriate returns over their owned assets. As Hernando de Soto (2000) notes, property rights are critical to input markets as well, most importantly in securing business credit. He claims in *The Mystery of Capital* that the failure in the developing world to secure property rights over land that is de facto owned by the poor may be the greatest single impediment to economic development in the Third World. According to de Soto's calculations, the total value of this real estate held, yet not legally owned, by the poor of the Third World and countries transitioning from socialism is at least *$9.3 trillion.*[8] Consequently, he argues that policies establishing property rights in the developing world, especially in the form of land titles, may be one of the most important conditions for broadly based economic growth.

De Soto argues that establishing property rights allows the poor to harness the power of their existing assets to foster economic development in a number of ways. Property rights for land unleash the economic potential of assets, allowing people to borrow using their land as collateral. The possibility of collateral, he maintains, allows a poor person to go beyond regarding a house as mere shelter to regarding it as an asset that can create new rents. Collateral helps make people accountable to society and society accountable to people: That property can potentially be confiscated from individuals holds them accountable for their economic choices and risks. And because property rights integrate disbursed asset information into a centralized government system, people are no longer reliant on local or personalized relationships to protect their assets or to secure a loan. Finally, de Soto points out that property rights protect transactions. A by-product of property rights has been

---

[7] Pareto (1927, 1971), p. 341.
[8] Figures for the value of untitled landholdings for specific countries are Haiti ($5.7 billion), Peru ($74 billion), the Philippines ($133 billion), and Egypt ($240 billion).

title insurance, which has brought about security of ownership, so that assets can easily and securely be harnessed to generate surplus rents.

Foreign Investment, Property Rights, and Contract Law

In developing and transitional countries, where capital is often scarce, foreign investment frequently offers a substantial boost to economic growth. Because of this, leaders of most developing nations painstakingly court foreign investment. Yet, there is little that can scare away foreign investors more quickly than ambiguous laws concerning property rights and contracts or a lack of a central political will to enforce such laws. An example is the murky set of laws surrounding signatures on Russian business contracts. According to Russian law of the late 1990s, a foreign economic contract of a Russian firm had to be signed by both the head of the company and the deputy head to be considered valid. But there remained considerable debate by foreign investors, as well as Russian firms, over whether this rule remained operative or was supplanted by more recent Russian legislation.[9]

Weakness in property rights and contract law typically affects foreign investors more than domestic investors for at least two reasons: Local citizens learn to adapt to the legal environment through learned experience and their networks of relationships, but foreigners stand at a disadvantage in this regard. Moreover, foreign direct investments tend to involve large fixed costs, such as the construction of a plant or factory, and therefore involve greater risk. Foreign investors have more to lose when the rules are not clear.

As a result, foreign investors can be very skittish. Even a single act by a host government that causes foreign investors to lose confidence in the government's commitment to protecting property rights and contracts can cause huge gyrations in foreign investment. This can happen in foreign direct investment, investment in manufacturing plants (or other types of fixed physical assets), as well as in equity and bond markets.

One instance of this occurred on October 25, 2003, when Russian agents stormed onto the private jet of Mikail Khordorkovsky, chief executive of Russia's Yukos Oil, during a refueling stop in Siberia. Khordorkovsky was immediately arrested on charges of tax evasion and fraud.[10] The arrest was interpreted by foreign investors as a power play by President Vladimir Putin against capitalist oligarchs in particular, and against the institutions safeguarding the free market in general. The result was the biggest one-day drop in the Russian stock market since the crash of 1998; $14.5 billion of market value was lost in less than seven hours of trading, equivalent to a 960-point drop in the Dow Jones average.[11] Subsequent actions taken by the Russian government have included an unexpected threat in 2004 to strip Exxon of

---

[9] Ivanova (1997).

[10] Gregory L. White and Jeanne Whalen in Moscow, Susan Warren in Houston and Anita Raghavan, "Tough Drill: For West's Oil Giants, Vast Fields in Russia Prove Hard to Tap; Exxon Mobil's Awkward Dance with Moscow Shows Perils," *Wall Street Journal*, April 27, 2004, p. A1.

[11] Peter Baker and Susan Glasser, *Washington Post*, October 28, 2003, p. AO1.

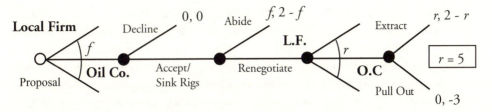

Figure 9.3. Foreign Investment Game

an oil-drilling license for a $12 billion joint venture in the icy but oil-rich waters of the Pacific near Sakhalin Island.[12]

The latter example represents one of the biggest fears of foreign investors: a central government that is unable or unwilling to enforce legal business contracts. Such fears are seen easily in the data: By 2004, these and other actions by the Russian government had led foreign investors to question Russia's commitment to enforce business contracts, leading to a quadrupling of capital flight from Russia from $1.9 billion in 2003 to $9.4 billion in 2004.[13] This kind of reaction by foreign investors may be reasonable, given that potential downside losses in foreign investment can be enormous. The credibility of government promises to enforce contracts through formal legal mechanisms are often the linchpin to foreign investment. The game in Figure 9.3 conveys this idea:[14]

The two players are a Local Firm that contracts with a foreign Oil Company. Both the Local Firm and the foreign Oil Company wish to develop an oilfield from which oil revenues are equal to 7. Fixed costs of sinking the oil rigs make up a majority of the costs and are equal to 3. Variable costs of extracting the oil are equal to 2. This leaves a profit of 2 to be divided between the two players. The Local Firm proposes an initial fee from the Oil Company equal to f, which will lie between 0 and 2. The Oil Company can either decline the proposal, leaving each party with a payoff of zero, or accept the proposal and incur the fixed costs of oil extraction (sink the rigs). The Local Firm can either abide by the contract or renegotiate the contract, potentially increasing the fee from the Oil Company to some amount r. In this second stage, the Oil Company can either continue on and extract the oil or pull out.

It is not hard to see by backward induction that after the Oil Company has accepted the contract, the Local Firm has an incentive to renegotiate. Assume that if the Oil Company is indifferent to two payoffs, then it continues to extract the oil. To maximize its plunder from the foreign Oil Company, in the absence of functional legal institutions, the Local Firm has an incentive to set r equal to 5. Since sinking the rigs is (literally) a sunk cost that the Oil Company can no longer recover, it proceeds with the oil extraction, leaving the Oil Company with -3, the same payoff as pulling out, and leaving the Local Firm with a payoff of 5.

[12] White et al. "Tough Drill," p. A1.
[13] "Oil Booms, but Investors Flee Russia," *Christian Science Monitor*, April 12, 2005, p. 1.
[14] I learned this game from Berkeley political scientist Robert Powell.

Paradoxically, the real problem lies with the Local Firm. Since the foreign Oil Company is not foolish, it can see this whole scenario coming down the road. Therefore in the absence of a credible commitment to contract enforcement, the foreign Oil Company chooses to decline the Local Firm's initial offer.[15] In this way, government neglect to commit to property rights and the enforcement of contract law can deprive developing and transitional countries of foreign investment, a valuable source of capital. Working together, property rights, contract law, and court systems establish a framework for economic growth.

The Emergence of Property Rights

Yet, even as property rights and commercial law have been written into the books in many transitional economies, by and large they have been relatively unenforceable.[16] Even President Vladimir Putin in a 2005 news conference remarked that despite new laws protecting property rights, "Anyone who registers a new firm (in Russia) should be awarded a medal for personal courage." Part of the problem undoubtedly lies in the limited resources of cash-strapped governments to enforce contracts and property rights. But another problem is the need for changes in social norms regarding the behavior of firms and consumers. Virtually no level of government resources is sufficient to enforce laws that have not gained the acquiescence of the general population. How then do property rights emerge as a fundamental building block for economic behavior?

It is nearly impossible to legislate property rights overnight. They grow from a set of conventions that evolve in society over a long period. This is the argument of many evolutionary game theorists such as Ken Binmore in *Game Theory and the Social Contract* (1994, 1998), Peyton Young in *Individual Strategy and Social Structure* (1998), and most originally articulated by Robert Sugden in the *Economics of Rights, Cooperation, and Welfare* (1986, 2004).

Sugden begins his argument assuming a Hobbesian state of nature that pits "every man against every man," as individuals pursue their own interests. The original claim of Thomas Hobbes was that such a state of nature would lead to a perpetual state of violent conflict:

> And therefore if any two men desire the same thing, which nevertheless they cannot both enjoy, they become enemies; and in the way to their end, which is principally their own conservation, and sometimes their delectation only, endeavor to destroy, or subdue one another. (Hobbes, 1651, ch. 13), cited in Sugden (1986).

Sugden argues, in contrast, that even from a Hobbesian state of nature in which individuals brutally act in their own interest, organized codes of social behavior will evolve spontaneously, such as clearly defined property rights. This will occur through a process of "role recognition" in which players begin to mutually recognize

---

[15] Given that the government can make no credible offer to keep to its contract of *r*, the Nash equilibrium in which the Oil company declines the initial offer forms a subgame-perfect Nash equilibrium. (See note 3.)

[16] Shleifer (1994).

that a player in a given "role" will stake claim to a given resource and defend claims against that resource by potentially challenging players in other roles. As in the Hawk-Dove example in Figure 2.3, a player occupying a piece of land, a Possessor, may challenge the claim of a Challenger, such that the convention "if Possessor, play Hawk; if Challenger, play Dove" leads to a Pareto-efficient Nash equilibrium in which property rights begin to evolve as a convention in the game. The game also works the opposite way, of course, but there are better reasons to think that an individual is more likely to be aggressive in fighting for land that he already occupies than land for which he must challenge someone else's possession. Notice that if players in the role of Possessor begin to always (or nearly always) play Hawk and in the role of Challenger play Dove, then a nascent form of property right has spontaneously emerged.[17]

Once the social convention governing land claims has taken root in society, codifying such a norm into law is a rather mundane step in the process; virtually everyone is already following the convention anyway. However, such was not often the case in the transition economies of the former Soviet Union, where private forms of land ownership were virtually nonexistent in many areas, so that social conventions governing property rights had little chance to evolve. This may explain why simply writing property rights into law, no matter how clear or strict, has largely failed.

More generally, Sugden considers the evolution of property rights in a "division game" in which players in two roles, A and B, make respective claims to shares of a divisible resource. If players' claims sum to an amount less than or equal to 1, each player receives his claim. If the players' claims sum to greater than 1, they both get zero. One can usefully think of this as an application of a simplified version of the game presented in Figure 9.2 in which a rent-seeking member of the community is able to make some claim to a portion c of an entrepreneur's surplus. Consider the entrepreneur in Role A and the extended family network, organized crime, or other potential rent-seeker in Role B. Sugden illustrates that the only class of stable equilibrium outcomes are the strategy pairs with claims $1 - c$ and c, respectively, by A and B, where c can take any value between 0 and 1.

What this implies is that if a past convention has dictated a certain share of surplus c for B, and A expects B to follow the convention, A's best response is the claim $1 - c$. Notice that the equilibrium holds no matter how large c might be – and more importantly, perhaps – irrespective of formal laws that dictate otherwise. This again presents an example in which governments in developing and transitional countries may undertake reforms to facilitate property rights, but where these reforms have little effect until the expectations by players about social conventions become congruent with written law.

But how did conventions over property rights and contracts emerge in some areas of the world but not in others? Since property rights and contracts are typically only

---

[17] This brings to mind Hernando de Soto's observation that even in remote areas of developing countries in which formal property rights are absent, de facto property rights are established by the "barking of the dogs," where owners' dogs begin to bark at the point that trespassers cross the informal boundaries to family property.

as strong as the institutions that enforce them, the question is why these institutions emerged so strongly in some countries while so weakly in others. Stanley Engerman of the University of Rochester and the late Kenneth Sokoloff (1994) were among the first to try to answer this question. They argued that the origins of the differences between North American society (the United States and Canada) and most Latin American societies had its roots in the concentration of Native Americans during colonization. In North America, the density of Native Americans was low, making crop labor scarce, thus sowing the seeds for a more egalitarian society built around institutions that favored exchange between settlers rather than the exploitation of cheap labor. In Latin America, a high density of Native Americans fostered labor-intensive crop cultivation and mineral extraction. In this context, a society emerged in which a few European elites were able hold most of the wealth and political power, and were consequently able to shape institutions that perpetuated these inequalities to their benefit.

Daren Acemoglu and Simon Johnson of MIT and James Robinson at Harvard (2001) followed Engerman and Sokoloff's work, contending that differences in institutional quality between former colonies can be traced back through a historical sequence of events that originated at the earliest period of colonization. Their theory is that in colonies where European settler mortality was low, these settlers established institutions early on that laid the foundation for long-term economic growth. Where settler mortality was high, settlers established institutions that favored extraction rather than exchange. Moreover, if the mortality rate of early European colonial settlers is correlated with modern institutional quality but in other ways uncorrelated with current economic performance, one could use settler mortality rates as an instrumental variable to identify the impact of institutions on economic development.

Acemoglu et al. examine data on the mortality rates of early European settlers: soldiers, bishops, and sailors stationed in colonies between the seventh and nineteenth centuries. In countries where these mortality rates were low, European settlers imported European institutions that favored the development of market exchange. This process occurred in lands in which mortality of early settlers was relatively low, such as New Zealand (8.5 per 1,000), Hong Kong (14.9), the United States (15), South Africa (15.5), Canada (16.1), Malaysia (17.7), Chile (68.9), and Costa Rica (78.1).

In other parts of the new world, diseases such as yellow fever and malaria often dissuaded settlers from prolonging their stay or killed them, making European labor scarce relative to native labor. The authors argue that the presence of these diseases indirectly induced settlers to establish institutions that favored the long-term extraction of precious minerals and metals, and the cultivation of cash crops using domestic labor. They argue that this pattern emerged in high settler-mortality-rate countries such as Vietnam (140 per 1,000), Nicaragua (163.3), Angola (280), Guinea (483), Madagascar (536), and Côte d'Ivoire (668).

Acemoglu, Johnson, and Robinson's empirical results appear to confirm their hypothesis, although certain aspects of their methodology have come into question.[18] Nevertheless, from their results they predict improvements in per capita income as a result of having better institutions: For example, they estimate that improving Nigeria's institutional quality to the level of Chile could, over the long run, result in a *sevenfold* increase in per capita GDP of Nigeria – an astounding effect for any single variable on per capita income.[19]

Corruption

Although the state may ultimately emerge as the guardian of property rights, sometimes the problem may be the state itself. For a long time, economists regarded the government rather benignly in their theoretical models. While they treated economic agents as shrewd, utility and profit maximizers, they treated the government and its agents as subservient ministers of the people, happily and passively transforming taxes into public goods. Although economic liberals (conservatives to everyone else) may have argued against high taxes and big government, such admonitions were more often based on the deleterious effects of high taxes on the incentives of private economic agents, rather than on the incentive issues within government itself.

Others argued that, when it existed, a little corruption might even be a good thing. Columbia University's Nathaniel Leff (1964), for example, maintained that corruption circumvents inefficient and cumbersome government regulations and thus permits entrepreneurs to efficiently sidestep arbitrary delays and otherwise grease the wheels of a rusty bureaucracy. Leff's theory viewed bribes as highly incentivized piece-rate wages to government officials.[20] Similarly, Harvard political scientist Samuel Huntington (1968) argued that "the only thing worse than a society with a rigid, overcentralized, *dishonest* bureaucracy is one with a rigid, overcentralized, *honest* bureaucracy."[21]

This view of corruption as an economic lubricant is intuitively appealing, and especially in isolated instances, may convey important aspects of truth. Nevertheless, most research since this time has painted a far less glowing picture of corruption. Although in the 1960s, the jury was, for the most part, still in deliberation over economic development strategies that relied heavily on centralized bureaucratic administration and coordination, since that time the jury has had time to render its unsympathetic verdict.

---

[18] The validity of using settler mortality as an instrumental variable rests on the strength of its correlation with modern institutional quality and its lack of correlation with otherwise unexplainable differences in modern per capita GDP. This assumption has been called into question, especially since settler mortality rates were taken from later periods than when the first settlers indeed arrived. Some such as Bardhan (2005, and forthcoming) dispute the use of early settler mortality as an indentifying instrument because "it is doubtful that this approach captures the major historical forces that affect the social and economic institutional structures of a former colony," further arguing that it may be "improper and too Eurocentric an approach to attribute underdevelopment largely to 'bad' colonial institutions imposed by Europeans" (2005, p. 4). Moreover, if good institutions are more likely to endure in more prosperous countries, then settler mortality may produce bias when used as an instrumental variable.

[19] Acemoglu and Robinson elaborate more broadly on the worldwide emergence (and nonemergence) of democratic systems of government in their *Economic Origins of Dictatorship and Democracy* (2006).

[20] Leff (1964).

[21] Huntington (1968), cited in Bardhan (2005), p. 140.

Experience with the state-led development strategies and the trade barriers enacted by import-substituting countries during the mid-twentieth century illuminated the inconsistency with viewing economic agents as shrewd maximizers while simultaneously viewing bureaucratic agents as benign altruists. In a seminal paper, Anne Krueger (1974) uncovered the extent and consequences of rent-seeking and corruption regarding the issuance of import licenses in India and Turkey, where she calculated the value of these rents to government officials at an astounding 7 percent and 15 percent of GDP, respectively. Krueger argued that the opportunity for government officials to repatriate such shockingly high rents from the private sector redirects labor and resources from entrepreneurial rent-creation to bureaucratic rent-seeking, thereby stifling productive activity in the economy and generating a corruption-induced development trap.[22]

Following Krueger's work, Jagdish Bhagwati (1982) coined the term DUP (Directly Unproductive Profit-seeking; pronounced *dupe*) activities. DUP activities are economic behaviors that represent mere transfers of surplus rather than surplus creation, typically by government officials through bribes.[23] Descriptive accounts of corrupt governments brought additional attention to the existence and consequences of corruption in less-developed countries. Robert Klitgaard's (1990) *Tropical Gangsters*, for example, relays tales from Equatorial Guinea in which "business limps and government crawls" within the shackles of a predatory bureaucracy rife with corruption.[24]

How much does corruption affect economic development? The most well-known empirical study of the effects of corruption was carried out by the International Monetary Fund's Paolo Mauro (1995), then a doctoral student at Harvard. Mauro's study was the first to use a now well-known data set compiled by *Business International*, which measures corruption, red tape, and the efficacy of the judicial system based on reports from its correspondents in seventy countries. Mauro's study covers the years 1980–1983.

Research that purports to analyze the impact of corruption on economic variables runs into a problem, however: Corruption may retard economic development, but economic development may also retard corruption. The problem is not unlike that faced by Acemoglu et al. in which good institutions seem to bring prosperity, but also vice versa. Causality in both cases could theoretically run either direction (which is one of the fundamental characteristics of any development trap). To address this problem, Mauro uses an index of "ethno-linguistic fractionalization" for each country, a variable that is conveniently correlated with corruption, but not directly with his economic variables.[25] This allows the index to be used as an instrumental variable in order to obtain a measure of corruption solely associated with

---

[22] Krueger (1974).

[23] Bhagwati (1982).

[24] Klitgaard (1990).

[25] The index measures the probability that two randomly drawn persons from a country's population will not belong to the same linguistic group. Exactly why ethno-linguistic fractionalization is positively related corruption is uncertain, though it is likely related to internal systems of patronage within ethnic groups.

ethno-linguistic fractionalization, which Mauro then employs to isolate corruption's effect on investment and GDP growth. Mauro finds corruption to exhibit significantly negative impacts on both investment and GDP growth. Specifically, if a (very) corrupt country such as Bangladesh were to reduce its level of corruption to that of an (only moderately) corrupt country such as Uruguay, the investment rate of Bangladesh would increase by five percentage points and its annual GDP growth rate would increase by over half a percentage point. Indeed, corruption appears to matter.

Governance, Bureaucrats, and Incentives

A rather complex set of relationships influences the performance of public officials. Viewed in the principal-agent framework of Chapter Six, "the people" (joint principals) in a democratic polity elect a government (an agent) to create and uphold laws, levy taxes, and provide public goods. The government (then reversing its role now to a principal) hires officials (agents) to carry out these tasks, who may in turn hire other agents under them. Consequently, public officials, as agents, are at least two steps removed from the original principals ("the people") that need them to carry out a particular task. It is no wonder then that moral hazard problems arise. An insight of Leff, Huntington, and others who take a more rosy view of corruption is that bribes to public officials, even for carrying out honest work (like delivering the mail), represent direct incentive mechanisms that circumvent a system in which incentives from principal to agent to agent to agent . . . have become too diluted to matter.

Andrei Shleifer and Robert Vishny (1993) discuss the impact that different types of corruption have on economies. They distinguish between two different types of corruption: (a) "Corruption without theft," in which the corrupt official accepts a bribe to provide whatever service (such as issuance of a permit, inspection, or repair) he is supposed to carry out anyway, but then turns over the legal price of the service to the government and (b) "Corruption with theft," in which the corrupt official accepts the bribe, but then doesn't turn over anything to the government at all. In the latter case, the actual cost of the service to the member of the public could even be less than the official price.

Corruption with theft is more likely to occur when the job of the government official is to regulate individual behavior, such as when a police officer issues a speeding ticket. Bribery of this kind is rampant and hard to stop. This is because, for example, when a police officer accepts a bribe (to keep for himself) that is less than the official fine, the bribe is in the joint interest of both the briber and the bribee. Moreover, neither has an incentive to report it.

Shleifer and Vishny's work is novel because they develop a framework for thinking about the behavior of public officials if they acted as genuine profit-maximizing agents, given their control over the service they have been charged to provide to the public. If the corrupt official has "monopoly" power over his service, he may be able to price discriminate (by charging less to people who he knows are willing to pay less and more to people who he knows are willing to pay more). If so, then by virtue of his position, the corrupt official is able to capture virtually all of the rents created by private economic agents that require his particular service. If he cannot price discriminate, then via his bribes he charges essentially what amounts to the standard monopoly markup.

Shleifer and Vishny note the grave consequences to the economy when there is competition within a particular private industry, but noncompetition between government service providers. Consider corruption with theft in the context of a perfectly competitive industry, and its impact on the spread of corruption. Since long-run economic profits are equal to zero in perfect competition, any firm that fails to pay a bribe is put out of business. Firms are thus forced into paying bribes just to stay on the competitive treadmill, spreading corruption like a virulent cancer across the industry. This creates an adverse selection problem as competitive pressures drive honest firms out of the market in favor of dishonest ones. It also generates moral hazard: Borderline firms turn from honesty to dishonesty.

The worst of all corruption scenarios occurs when firms require a sequence of government services provided by a series of monopolistic bureaucrats.[26] An entrepreneur establishing a restaurant, for example, may require a building permit, business license, and approval from a government health inspector. The problem is exacerbated when, just as he thinks that everyone has been properly paid off, corrupt officials keep coming back for more. Pranab Bardhan (1997) relays the example of General Manuel Noriega who bragged only half-jokingly that he could not be "bought"; he could only be "rented."[27]

Multiple roadblocks manned by bureaucrats with insatiable appetites may have perverse effects not only for the private sector, but for the bureaucrats themselves. It may lead to a kind of "overfishing of the commons" by corrupt public officials. Too many rent-seekers able to line their pockets at the expense of rent-creators will induce the rent creators stop creating rents, or go somewhere else.[28] This historically has been the case in many parts of Africa in places where the institutions needed to check corruption are weak, and in Russia and other parts of the former Soviet Union. As in the games presented in Figures 9.2 and 9.3, if all rents will be captured by others, why bother creating them in the first place? It is here that the strongest negative effects of corruption on economic activity as seen in empirical studies such as Mauro's are likely to be manifest.

More centralized forms of corruption, for better or worse, appear to be more sustainable. Corrupt leaders such as Indonesia's Suharto family, Ferdinand Marcos of the Philippines, or even the former Soviet government have no interest in slaying the goose that lays the golden eggs. Instead, they insist on a form of restrained collusion over corruption within the bureaucracy, in which there is an agreed-upon level of bribe-taking by different arms of the bureaucracy.

While economic competition and bureaucratic monopoly can increase the spread of corruption, Shleifer and Vishny note that competition within the bureaucracy

---

[26] Shleifer and Vishny (1993).
[27] Bardhan (2005), p. 143 (original article, 1997).
[28] Shleifer and Vishny (1993), p. 605.

should decrease it. If there is competition between public officials in the provision of a given service, then bribes should be rare and small if they exist at all. For example, if there are at least two officials to whom a builder can visit to obtain an electrical permit, builders will frequent the official charging the lowest bribe for the permit. Because each official has an incentive to offer a slightly lower bribe than the other, the competitive process should take the Nash equilibrium bribe down toward zero. This has important implications for the institutional structure of a bureaucracy: The establishment of multiple offices for similar permits and multiple officials within each office may significantly reduce both the breadth and depth of corruption.

In recent years, the World Bank and other policy makers have encouraged governmental *decentralization* as a means of controlling corruption. Even in democracies, elections constitute an extremely blunt instrument for holding government officials accountable for their actions. A decentralization process relocates most government functions from the capital to provincial and local levels, where ostensibly the instrument is somewhat less blunt, therefore bringing more direct accountability between the citizenry, politicians, and bureaucracy. Decentralization policies, and their potentially positive effect on both political and economic incentives, have been identified as a major cause of the economic growth in both China and India (Bardhan 2005).

Bardhan notes, however, that decentralization may have both positive and negative effects. Decentralization of the bureaucratic machine can foster better accountability between government and the citizenry, since local governments may have better information about local issues and are also more directly accountable to local voters.[29] However, decentralized governments and their agents may also be more susceptible to capture (in the form of bribes or favoritism) by local elites.[30] Bardhan and Dilip Mookherjee of Boston University carry out an empirical study to test the effects of bureaucratic decentralization on the targeting of credit and minikits to the poor in 80 *panchayats* (village municipalities) in West Bengal.[31] What they discover is that decentralization does not seem to result in the capture of resources by local elites in their sample; targeting of the poor does not seem to vary with variables measuring the political power of the poor. Unfortunately, what they do find is that *intervillage* (as opposed to *intravillage*) allocation of resources were biased against villages with greater levels of inequality and against those containing a disproportionate share of low-caste members. This may have happened, they note, because the *Left Front* state government in Bengal at the time tended to favor middle-income villages at the expense of the very rich as well as the very poor.

In this and other related work, Bardhan and Mookherjee conclude that decentralization may be more effective if (a) it is implemented in areas that are more egalitarian, where the risk of elite capture is minimized (such as has been successful in rural China); (b) village funding is allocated by a formula structured around the needs of the poor rather than by political decision; and (c) governments

---

[29] Bardhan (2005), p. 114.
[30] See Drèze and Sen (1989) and Bardhan and Mookherjee (2006a).
[31] Bardhan and Mookherjee (2006b).

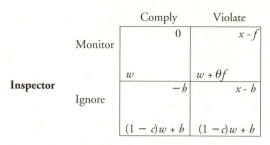

Figure 9.4. Inspector-Builder Corruption Game

consider, instead of inter-governmental fiscal grants, the implementation of use fees, which allow for greater levels of feedback and accountability between provider and user of services.[32] In summary, decentralization may not be a silver bullet for mitigating bureaucratic corruption, but if it is implemented with an eye toward the incentives of both users and providers of services, it may offer distinct advantages over centralized governance.

Another approach toward fighting corruption has been to address it at the level of the individual incentives given to public officials. There is general agreement, for example, that higher wages for public officials are associated with less corruption.[33] Some countries, such as Singapore and Hong Kong, have intentionally raised wages of public officials to discourage corruption based on efficiency wage theory: Higher wages make the prospects of an official being caught and fired less appealing. The challenge with offering efficiency wages to public officials, however, is that the job security often accompanying public-sector positions may make officials frustratingly hard to fire (even corrupt ones). Thus exceedingly high wages may be required to induce honesty.[34] Moreover, anger over governmental corruption is often manifest in cries for reductions in government spending; that is, if the government is perceived to be bad, then less of it ought to be better than more. But combined with the difficulties of laying off public employees, moves to downsize government (budgets) may simply mean lower salaries for existing public workers, thus fueling more corruption rather than reducing it.

Another approach is to provide public officials with direct incentive mechanisms in their contracts, for example, rewards for apprehending violators of pollution, drug, health, or labor laws, and other codes and regulations. The Corruption/Compliance game in Figure 9.4 is an extension of the corruption game presented in Figure 2.1 and captures some of the issues involved with incentives for public officials and those with whom they interact in the private sector.[35]

[32] See Bardhan (2005) and Bardhan and Mookherjee (2006b).
[33] See, for example, Van Rijckeghem and Weder (2001).
[34] Bardhan (2005).
[35] The game incorporates ideas from various work such as Becker and Stigler (1974) and Mookherjee and Png (1995).

The game is motivated by the Kocaeli earthquake in Turkey on August 17, 1999, which killed approximately 14,000 people and the Kashmir earthquake on October 8, 2005, which killed over 90,000 in Pakistan and India. Many of the deaths in both earthquakes were blamed on the corruption and oversight of building code inspectors in the years prior to the quakes.[36] It is after such tragedies that the real costs of corruption can become disturbingly clear.

The two players in the game are an Inspector and a Builder. Suppose that the Inspector is paid a wage w and is charged with monitoring the work of the Builder. The Builder can comply with the building code, for example, by using the amount of rebar required by code to enforce concrete walls, or can violate the code by skimping on rebar, through which he saves money and earns a payoff of x. If the Inspector monitors the Builder and the Builder violates the code, the Builder receives a fine equal to f. The Inspector can ignore the project in exchange for a bribe equal to b, but if the Inspector is caught taking the bribe he loses his wage w with probability c. Aside from this stick, the Inspector also is given a carrot: If he catches the Builder violating the code, he collects some fraction θ of the Builder's fine, f.

We can presume that $f > x$, or that the fine is high enough that the Builder has an incentive to Comply provided that the Inspector is monitoring. Likewise, we can presume that $b < x$, since it wouldn't make sense for the Builder to offer a bribe that is greater than his benefit from skimping on rebar.

There are a number of insights from this Corruption/Compliance game that rely on the relationship of w to b/c. In the case where $w > b/c$, it is a dominant strategy for the Inspector to Monitor, and the unique Nash equilibrium to the game is (Monitor; Comply). This makes sense. If wages are high, bribes are low, and the Inspector's probability of getting caught with a bribe is high, the Inspector Monitors, which forces the Builder to Comply to avoid the fine.

In the other extreme case, in which $w < (b - \theta f)/c$, then it is a dominant strategy for the Inspector to Ignore, and the game yields a unique Nash equilibrium of (Ignore; Violate). Here the wage is so low that even when the Builder violates, the bonus incentive θ in the contract doesn't induce the Inspector to Monitor. Either the Inspector himself is not monitored adequately, his wage is too low, or his incentives to catch a violating Builder are too weak. This is the case of ubiquitous corruption.

Finally, there is the interesting intermediate case in which $b/c > w > (b - \theta f)/c$. In the intermediate case there is no pure strategy Nash equilibrium. If the Inspector Monitors, the Builder Complies. But if the Builder Complies, the Inspector Ignores (since there are weaker incentives to monitor a Builder who is complying with the code). Yet, when the Inspector Ignores, the Builder wants to Violate. Because it is only a violating Builder that the Inspector wants to Monitor, this causes the Builder again to Comply, the dynamics of the game becoming like a cat chasing his tail in a circle. The game in this intermediate case yields a *mixed strategy* Nash equilibrium, in which the Inspector monitors part of the time and the Builder complies part of the

---

[36] "Poverty, Code Issues Contribute to Extensive Earthquake Damage in Turkey," *Multidisciplinary Center for Earthquake Engineering Research*, MCEER Archives, August 19, 1999.

time.[37] Specifically, this Nash equilibrium occurs with the Inspector monitoring the Builder with probability $p_I = x/f$, and with the Builder complying with the building code with probability $p_B = (\theta f + wc - b)/\theta f$. (Notice that the latter probability always lies between zero and one since in the intermediate case, $wc < b$.) In this mixed-strategy equilibrium, the nice (Monitor; Comply) outcome occurs $p_I \cdot p_B$ of the time or (through substituting in the values of p_I and p_B), a fraction $x(\theta f + wc - b)/\theta f^2$ of the time.

This fraction yields some interesting insights into the effect of different incentives that can be given to the Inspector to increase the likelihood of the good outcome. From it, we can see that higher wages, a stronger bonus incentive θ, and the monitoring of the Inspector himself are all good things, increasing the probability of the time when there is compliance and no corruption. So is reducing the size of the bribe that the Builder is willing to pay the Inspector, which is a function of what he perceives as his benefit from violating. But contrary to intuition, increasing f, the fine on violators, is not always a good thing. It is not obvious from visual examination of the fraction, but elementary calculus shows that when f is larger than $2(b - wc)/\theta$, raising the fine has the perverse effect of actually *reducing* the likelihood of (Monitor; Comply). The intuition is that increasing the fine against violators may make the option of a bribe more attractive, thus inducing more corruption.

Public Servants and Absenteeism

Good governance not only involves establishing property rights and regulating the behavior of citizens; it also involves providing citizens with vital public goods and services. Related to the problem of corruption among public officials is a general motivation problem among public servants. With public servants, such as teachers and public health workers, the problem is not so much one of graft as of diligence.

Comedian Woody Allen remarked once that "80 percent of life is just showing up." By this measure, public servants in developing countries are not fairing well. Nazmul Chaudhury et al. (2006) present data from a major study on absenteeism based on spot checks on the work attendance of 35,000 public teachers and health care workers in six developing countries on three continents.[38] Their data indicate that, relative to private sector peers in their home countries as well as their public sector counterparts in developed countries, public servants in LDCs seem to find it remarkably difficult to show up for work. According to their data, 19 percent of teachers and 35 percent of primary health workers, who were supposed to be on duty, were absent when researchers carried out random spot checks in classrooms and clinics. This includes absentee rates of 25 and 40 percent, respectively, in the largest country in the sample, India. Furthermore, they note that such rates of absenteeism for teachers are four to five times the typical rates reported in industrialized

---

[37] The appendix explains the technical details of solving for a mixed-strategy equilibrium.
[38] Countries included in the study are Bangladesh, Ecuador, India, Indonesia, Peru, and Uganda. See Chaudhury et al. (2006).

countries, while the absentee rates among health workers in India are about four times higher than the rate among Indian factory workers.

Chaudhury et al. try to uncover the factors responsible for these strikingly high rates of absenteeism. First, they note that the problem is not just concentrated among a relatively few undependable slackers. On the contrary, they observe high rates of absenteeism across a large majority of public servants in most LDCs in the study. Second, they find that absenteeism, among public school teachers in particular, is strongly correlated with regional per capita income, but strangely unrelated to a teacher's salary. Moreover, their evidence suggests that, relative to other teachers, those with more power and status are absent more often: men, head teachers, more educated teachers, more experienced teachers, and older teachers. Third, both teachers and health workers who work in the district in which they were born are absent less. It appears that serving in one's home community promotes work attendance, or at least provides a stronger framework for accountability.

They posit that the reason for such dramatically high rates of absenteeism is related to the consequences for being absent: In most cases, there are none. In India, for example, despite a 25 percent absenteeism rate among teachers, they were able to uncover only one reported instance of a teacher being fired for repeated absences. In fact, as the researchers remark about these public sector workers, "The mystery for economists may not be why absence from work is so high, but why anyone shows up at all."

Esther Duflo at MIT and Remma Hanna at NYU (2005) test a creative incentive device to mitigate teacher absenteeism implemented by a local NGO within the rural Udaipur school district in the state of Rajasthan, India.[39] Rural Udaipur is a sparsely populated mountainous area in which it is hard to monitor teachers. As a result, public school teacher absenteeism during a baseline study carried out in 2003 was 44 percent. Adding to the tragedy of teacher absence is the fact that most of the schools are "one teacher" schools. This means that if the teacher fails to show up, children are forced to return home without any instruction for the day.

To address the problem, the program distributed cameras to teachers in sixty schools, while another sixty schools were used as a control group. The cameras came equipped with a tamper-proof date and time feature, which in every picture displays the date and time the picture was taken in the lower right-hand corner. The teachers in the test group were instructed to take pictures of themselves at the beginning and end of a day with their students. Based on photos of the teachers and their students printed from their cameras, the teachers in this group were paid 1,000 rupees a month if he or she was present at least twenty-one days during that month. A bonus of 50 rupees was added to their pay for every day of attendance over twenty-one days, and an equal amount was subtracted for every missed day under twenty-one days.[40] In the control group of sixty schools, teachers were given the routine warning that they could be dismissed for poor performance.

---

[39] See Duflo and Hanna (2005) and Banerjee and Duflo (2006).

[40] The exchange rate between the rupee and the dollar at the time of the experiment was approximately 50 rupees/US$.

The impact of the camera self-monitoring system was stunning. The rate of absenteeism in the camera schools plummeted to 18 percent, to half the rate of the control schools, in which absenteeism remained high at 36 percent. The number of child days of teaching in the former was one-third higher per month than the latter. Moreover, the incentives created by the cameras affected teachers across the attendance distribution: It virtually eradicated hard-core absenteeism (defined as showing up to work less than half the time) as well as dramatically increased the number of teachers with a perfect or almost perfect attendance record. A final remark concerns the cost of the system as reported by the researchers: only $6 per child per year, buying more than a 30 percent increase in the number of days per year a child receives instruction.

Duflo and Banerjee (2006) compare these results with a different randomized field experiment designed to reduce absenteeism of teachers developed by Harvard's Michael Kremer and the University of Chicago's Daniel Chen (2001).[41] In this experiment, headmasters in a western Kenyan district were given the task of monitoring the attendance of kindergarten teachers. If the teacher had a "good" attendance record, he or she was to be given a bicycle at the end of the term. If not, then the headmaster could use the money for other school needs. What Kremer and Chen discovered was that in all of the schools in which the system was implemented, the headmaster became rather soft in his standards for teacher attendance, lowering them to such an extent that all of the teachers ended up receiving the bicycle. But when the researchers compared the attendance of the teachers at the bicycle-prize schools with the control schools, the attendance figures were statistically identical.

Duflo and Banerjee conclude that it may be critical to remove the element of subjective human judgment in monitoring schemes. Headmasters, for example, may be hesitant to confront teachers, with whom they must work on a day-to-day basis, favoring a positive working relationship with them over parents, with whom they interact far less frequently. Using the camera as an accountability mechanism may add the objectivity necessary to avoid problems associated with personal judgments, which are more open to accusations of bias.

Though proper incentives matter, ultimately social norms may exhibit one of the most powerful influences over societal ills such as corruption and absenteeism. Here we clearly have a game with multiple equilibria, where one equilibrium exists in which corruption and/or absenteeism are rare, and the relatively few violators are frequently identified and punished. But another equilibrium exists in which so many public workers violate the standard that it is impossible to punish everybody, making it difficult to punish anybody. As in the example given in Chapter One, such equilibria can be further locked in by expectations: Once the deviant behavior becomes the expected behavior, others adjust their own behavior to accommodate it. (Entrepreneurs are quick to offer bribes, and bureaucrats begin to expect such offers. Parents don't send their children to school if the teacher rarely shows, and given that few children attend, then why should the teacher?) Which equilibrium

---

[41] Kremer and Chen (2001).

exists in a particular context is probably determined by the kind of historical process described by Acemoglu and Robinson, where seemingly innocuous events in the past may set the trajectory of society on the wrong path. Here economic, political, cultural, social, and religious factors work together over time to produce the *social capital* that characterizes a society, a concept whose influence on economic development we will pursue more deeply in Chapter Eleven.

CHAPTER 10
Conflict, Violence, and Development

And knowing their thoughts Jesus said to them, "A kingdom divided against itself is laid waste; and any city or house divided against itself will not stand."
– Matthew 12:25

JOSEPH KONY IS not an ordinary guerrilla leader. A former priest and witch doctor, he heads the Lord's Resistance Army (LRA), an insurgent movement that roams the jungle areas of northern Uganda and southern Sudan. Regarded as one of the world's most brutal revolutionary movements, the LRA's stated purpose is to overthrow the Ugandan government, replacing it with one that rules the country by the Ten Commandments. Ironically, it is difficult to think of an insurgency that violates the Ten Commandments more thoroughly than the LRA. The modus operandi of the LRA has been to conduct nightly raids on the houses of rural homesteaders, pillaging food and supplies, raping women and young girls, and abducting young boys to flesh out its ranks. The number of its victims is staggering. According to the United Nations, in the two decades since its foundation in the mid-1980s, members of the LRA have abducted more than 20,000 boys and driven more than 2 million people from their homes.[1] When abducted, the boys are regularly forced to kill or maim members of their own families in the hope that they will be ashamed to return home. The LRA then assimilates the abducted boys into its company as guerilla soldiers by brainwashing them with its quasi-religious doctrine. This doctrine hails Joseph Kony as a divine prophet sent to bring peace, prosperity, and freedom to all Ugandans, making the LRA something of a hybrid between a guerrilla movement and a cult.

Sam Childers is not an ordinary missionary. An ex-gang member and drug dealer, his new mission is to rescue boys who have been abducted by the LRA. Childers does not believe Kony to be a divine prophet. Instead, like most Ugandans, he views the LRA as a cancer to central Africa. Like many missionaries, Childers carries a Bible. Unlike most missionaries, he also carries an assault rifle. Childers is the only white commander in the Sudan People's Liberation Army (SPLA), an armed group of pastors and other concerned individuals who have had enough of the

---

[1] Jess Bravin, "For Global Court, Ugandan Rebels Prove Tough Test," *Wall Street Journal,* , June 8, 2006, p. 1.

LRA's child development program. Childers prays with other SPLA warriors before battle and pledges to use his weapon only in self-defense while re-capturing boy-soldiers to return them to their homes. For boys unable to return home, Childers built an orphanage to provide them with food, shelter, and education. LRA leaders have become concerned about Sam Childers. For one man, he has been remarkably successful at depleting their ranks.[2]

While the LRA is admittedly more bizarre than the average insurgent group, the LRA conflict in northern Uganda and southern Sudan shares an important charac-teristic with most other wars in the world today: It is a civil war.[3] As wars between nations have become rarer in recent decades, wars within nations have sadly pro-liferated. At the turn of the twentieth century, most wars were international wars, but by the turn of the twenty-first century, all but one were civil wars.[4] The rela-tive absence of civil conflict in LDCs before World War II may have been an ironic by-product of the heavy hand of colonialism. Because colonial powers were often ruthlessly efficient at squashing the movements of agitators within their colonies, peace commonly prevailed. Since that time, as countries have gained their indepen-dence and foreign troops have left, weak governmental institutions have created a vacuum that has too often led to civil wars. Unfortunately, civil wars tend to drag on longer than international wars. While the average international war lasts only six months, the average modern civil war lasts about seven years.[5]

The Effects of Civil War

The World Bank (2003) describes civil war as "development in reverse." In many ways, this is literally true. As mentioned in the beginning of Chapter One, economies develop when they began to acquire increasingly greater levels of capital, technol-ogy, and education. Civil war wreaks havoc on all of these.

Civil war destroys the physical capital of a country in myriad ways. One is sim-ply through the increase in state resources that must be devoted to "guns rather than butter," or military versus nonmilitary expenditures. All governments face this trade-off. But with the onset of civil war, the average share of a poor country's budget allocated to military expenditures increases from 2.8 percent to 5.0 percent.[6] So even before considering the destructive effects of war, the considerable increase in what is earmarked for guns and bullets (and paying people to shoot them) cannot be spent on transportation, communications infrastructure, and other useful public capital.

Civil war also reduces a country's capital accumulation through private capital flight. International investors are skittish, and the instability of war scares them. At

---

[2] Sliwa (2006), pp. 22–5.

[3] Civil wars have become formally defined as military conflicts in which an identifiable rebel group chal-lenges a central government militarily, with the result that there are more than 1000 combat-related deaths, with at least 5 percent on each side (World Bank, 2003).

[4] World Bank (2003), p. 93. For an excellent review of the causes of modern civil wars, see Kalyvas et al. (2006).

[5] World Bank (2003), p. 78.

[6] Ibid., p. 14.

the onset of war, or even the *rumor* of war, international investors often liquidate portfolio investment in the country and curtail flows of foreign direct investment (which is harder to liquidate). This happened even in a country as relatively stable as Mexico during the 1994 uprising of the small Chiapas guerilla movement (EZLN), under the direction of the mysterious Subcomandante Marcos. Foreign portfolio liquidation, a result of the unexpected instability, caused the peso to dive to only half its previous value against the dollar (3.46 pesos/$ to 6.26 pesos/$) in only six weeks. Domestic investors are also likely to move portfolio capital abroad during unstable times. Collier, Hoeffler, and Pattillo (2004) find that before a typical civil war, citizens of a country held an average of 9 percent of their wealth in overseas assets. By the end of a war, this average had risen to 20 percent, implying that a tenth of all private assets had been moved abroad.[7] Moreover, the high interest rates required to attract and maintain investors and bondholders in risky war environments lure investors away from other potentially productive opportunities in the economy.

The third cause of capital loss in civil war is simply through sheer destruction. It is impossible to guard all public and private assets, making unguarded assets juicy targets for rebel armies whose objective is to grind normal life to a halt. During the civil war in Mozambique in the 1980s, for example, warring armies destroyed about 40 percent of the immovable capital stock.[8] Transportation infrastructure, critical to foreign exchange earnings though agricultural exports, was almost totally destroyed. Moreover, less than one-fifth of the cattle stock that had existed in 1980 remained in 1992.[9] Similar destruction and pillaging by rebel armies have crippled infrastructure in El Salvador (by the FMLN), in Nepal (by Maoist guerillas), in Colombia (by the FARC rebel movement), in Sri Lanka (by the Liberation Tigers of Tamil Eelam), and in Iraq (by Al-Qaeda and Sunni militias).

Most important, of course, are the human costs of civil war. Combatant deaths are easiest to measure, but these have come to represent a smaller and smaller fraction of the total loss of life in war. At the beginning of the twentieth century, approximately 90 percent of war casualties were soldiers and only 10 percent were civilians. But by the end of the twentieth century, the figures were reversed: 10 percent are soldiers and 90 percent are civilians.[10] Research has shown that mortality rates continue to climb among the general population years after hostilities have ended, principally from disease, injury, and loss of economic opportunity.[11] Infant mortality rates have been shown to increase an average of 13 percent during a typical civil war, but remain 11 percent higher than normal even up to five years after conflicts have ceased.[12]

Aside from war's tragic cost in fatalities, the effects of civil war on both soldiers and civilians are also devastating to education, health, and other aspects of human capital. War directly disrupts education and other vocational development for

[7] Collier, Hoeffler, and Pattillo (2004), pp. 15–54.
[8] Bruck (2001).
[9] World Bank (2003) p. 15.
[10] Cairns (1997).
[11] World Bank (2003), p. 25.
[12] Hoeffler and Reynal-Querol (2003).

soldiers. War also causes cognitive and psychosocial development problems in children affected by the war that impair their ability to learn and function in society. School-age children in war-torn areas are rarely able to attend school. Children who are forced into refugee camps and settlements may fare little better.[13] Diseases are also more likely to spread during wartime as infrastructure for water and electricity is destroyed. Disease spreads not only because war creates rotten living conditions but because war robs the government of the resources needed to maintain an adequate public health system.[14]

Arguably as devastating to society is the damage to institutions and social capital. Institutions create the rules of the game within which social, political, and economic activity takes place. Institutions that establish rights to resources and delineate a society's rules are stressed in civil war. Resources are stretched for law enforcement, lawlessness is widespread, and social norms of behavior are capriciously violated. Social capital is, generally speaking, the trust within a society that facilitates social, political, and economic activity (more on this in Chapter Eleven). Civil war destroys trust. In desperate times, the expectation that strangers will behave with integrity is likely to decline. Moreover, those that are most socially connected may be seen as the greatest threats to those seeking power, causing such people to turn inward for their own safety.

The following is but one example of the breakdown of social capital from civil war: During my field survey work as a graduate student near the end of the civil war in Guatemala in the early 1990s, I was stunned when people in rural villages did not know the names of some of their nearest neighbors. It was explained to me that during the war, rural Mayans pulled back from networks of relationships, as they did not want to be accused of being a friend to a foe of the next death squad to enter the village. People learned to trust only within the family and a few close friends. The motives of others were open to suspicion.

What Causes Civil Wars?

Civil wars, like corruption, can be viewed abstractly in a principal-agent framework. If an objective of society is that its citizens should be peacefully engaged in production and exchange, corruption can be viewed as a breach of the incentive constraint: Citizens participate in the system, but the incentives of the system induce a disproportionate number to prey on the surplus created by others. In contrast, civil war can be viewed as a radical breach of the participation constraint: A sub-group within society chooses not to participate at all, and seeks to either separate itself, or subvert the institutions of society through force.

Economists and political scientists have had divergent views of what causes people to break away from the system in this way and begin civil wars. Political scientists have most often attributed the causes of civil war to *grievances* that drive people to

[13] Sommers (2002).
[14] World Bank (2003), p. 26.

violence, usually following the direction of a charismatic leader.[15] Economists, on the other hand, have traced the causes of civil war to *greed*, the monetary costs and benefits of war.[16] Paul Collier and Anke Hoeffler (2004) present empirical work that tries to ascertain the relative importance of grievance versus greed in the emergence of seventy-nine civil conflicts occurring in different parts of the world between 1960 and 1999.

Collier and Hoeffler find little evidence for grievance and much evidence for greed. First, they find that a major factor increasing the probability of civil war is the means to finance a breakaway movement. They find two leading sources of insurgency finance to be revenue from primary-commodity exports and remittances from diasporas living abroad. Revenues from commodities, such as diamonds or oil, provide both a reason to extort the central government and a reward for victory. Collier and Hoeffler also find male secondary school attainment, the higher wages from which they take as a higher opportunity cost of fighting, to be negatively correlated with the outbreak of civil war. Thus in counting the costs of war, potential guerilla fighters appear to follow a kind of economic calculus. But upon examining potential measures of political grievance, Collier and Hoeffler find factors that should be associated with grievance to be insignificantly related to the outbreak of civil war: inequality, political rights, religious fractionalization, and even ethnic fractionalization.

The relationship between civil war and poverty is complicated. Most countries that experience civil war are poor countries. But does low income cause civil war, or does the instability brought by civil war cause low income? Furthermore, third factors such as bad governance could cause both. Edward Miguel, Shankar Satyanath, and Ernest Sergenti (2004) employ a creative strategy to determine what causes what. In their analysis, they use rainfall as an instrumental variable to identify the extent to which poor economic conditions cause civil war in sub-Saharan Africa. Their strategy to identify the relationship exploits the fact that rainfall substantially affects economic output in regions like sub-Saharan Africa that rely heavily on rainfed agriculture. There is no direct relationship, however, between rainfall and civil conflict. By identifying the variability in economic conditions caused only by rainfall, they are then able to isolate the component of civil war caused only by rainfall and then determine how the rainfall-based changes in economic conditions affect the probability of a country falling victim to a civil war. What they find is that a 5-percentage-point drop in annual economic growth is associated with an increase in the probability of civil war by more than one-half. Furthermore, they find that their result holds in both rich countries and poor countries in the region, and in democracies and dictatorships alike. In large measure, their results are consistent with Collier and Hoeffler – that economic variables are key causes of civil wars.

The fact that so many civil conflicts appear to occur between ethnic or religious groups would suggest that heterogeneities within countries are a source of civil war.

---

[15] Collier and Hoeffler (2004).
[16] See for example, Grossman (1999).

Yet researchers have been unable to identify a clear empirical relationship between ethnic and religious *fractionalization* – roughly the number of similar-sized groups within a country – and civil conflict.[17] Jose Montalvo and Marta Reynal-Querol (2005), however, address this paradox by demonstrating that although ethnic and religious *fractionalization* does not appear to be related to civil conflict, ethnic and religious *polarization* indeed appears to be.

The difference may appear to be a quibble over mere technical semantics, but Montalvo and Reynal-Querol show the difference to be critical. Whereas *fractionalization* reaches its maximum as the number of equally sized (ethnic or religious) groups increase, *polarization* reaches its maximum with two large ethnic groups, each comprising half the population. The authors offer an example: Sierra Leone, with 47 percent from the Mande and 48 percent from the Bantoid ethno-linguistic families, is not highly fractionalized ethnically but *is* highly polarized. Similarly ethnically polarized is Guatemala, with a 55 percent Latino and 42 percent Mayan population. It also has a high degree of religious polarization at roughly 55 percent Catholic and 45 percent Evangelical Protestant. Religious polarization is also high in countries such as Nigeria (45 percent Christian and 50 percent Muslim) and Bosnia-Herzegovina (50 percent Christian and 40 percent Muslim). During the sample period of their study from 1960 to 1995, 7 out of 10 of the countries with the highest level of religious polarization suffered civil wars, whereas this was true in only 3 out of the 10 most religiously fractionalized countries. Their econometric results on the entire sample of countries during this time period show both ethnic and religious polarization (but not fractionalization) to be associated with a significantly higher probability of civil war.

Whatever the motives for a particular conflict may be, conflict is more of a general facet of economics than most economists would like to admit. Alfred Marshall, the great British economist of the early twentieth century, helped solidify an approach in which economists have traditionally studied the "allocation of resources among competing wants" within a clean, institutional framework, such as exchange in the context of markets or the government provision of public goods. This makes for tidy analysis. But when the state is weak, as in many developing countries, aggression and defense play much more central roles in the allocation of resources. As the late Jack Hirshleifer writes,

> Recognizing the force of self-interest, the mainline Marshallian tradition has nevertheless almost entirely overlooked what I will call the *dark side of the force* – to wit: crime, war, and politics . . . You can produce goods for the purpose of mutually beneficial exchange with other parties – OK, that's Marshall's "ordinary business." But there's another way to get rich: you can grab goods that someone else has produced. *Appropriating, grabbing, confiscating* what you want – and the flip side, *defending, protecting, sequestering* what you have – that is economic activity too. (Hirshleifer, 2001: p. 9)

---

[17] Collier and Hoeffler (2004).

The analytical tools of traditional economics (in large part developed by Marshall himself) are ill-suited for analyzing and understanding conflict. But economists have acquired a new set of analytical tools that yield substantial insight into understanding conflict between both individuals and groups. Borrowed from biologists in the early 1980s these tools taken together have come to be known as *evolutionary game theory*.

Violence: The Basics

Originally developed by biologist John Maynard Smith in the early 1980s to study changes in animal behavior, evolutionary game theory is now regularly used by social scientists to study a range of issues, including institutional structures, social norms, and civil conflict. Here I will present some of the basic tools of evolutionary game theory in order to explain how – absent properly functioning institutional structures – interpersonal and intergroup conflict may emerge as the norm rather than the exception. This framework makes it easier to understand the genesis of many of the conflicts we see in the developing world today. Moreover, some of the insights even yield hints toward possible solutions.

There is one main difference between classical game theory and evolutionary game theory, aside from the fact that the former was originally developed to study human behavior, and the latter to study guppies, bears, and bugs. In the former, players actively strategize, whereas in the latter, a complex of genes (genotype) determines player behavior (or phenotype). In evolutionary game theory, players don't *think*, they just *do*. Payoffs in evolutionary game theory are typically interpreted as representing reproductive fitness, but this concept has been easily translated into the standard economic notion of welfare.

The first concept in evolutionary game theory that is helpful in understanding conflict is *risk dominance*. The idea was developed by Nobel Prize–winning game theorists John Harsanyi and Reinhardt Selten (1988) as they searched for a method for selecting between multiple Nash equilibria that co-exist in a single game. We say that a particular Nash equilibrium *A risk dominates B* if *A* shows a greater "resistance" to behaviors by the other player that deviate from its equilibrium than does Nash equilibrium *B*. This means that *A* enjoys a greater threshold against "mutants" playing the *B* strategy without inducing movement to *B* than vice versa.

In any symmetric 2 × 2 Coordination game (where the payoffs are the same between players), the risk-dominant strategy also happens to yield the highest payoff when each player believes that the strategies of the other player are equally likely.[18] The underlying assumption is that, under a veil of ignorance about which strategy will be played by the other player, a player should assume each strategy to be equally likely. Within this veil of ignorance, the risk-dominant strategy gives a player his highest expected payoff.

---

[18] For a more general definition, see Young (1998), p. 67.

Shiite

Aggressive   Passive

	Aggressive	Aggressive	Passive
		5	0
Sunni Aggressive	5		7
Passive		7	8
	0		8

Figure 10.1. Sunni-Shiite Conflict/Risk Dominance

Figure 10.1 presents a Stag Hunt game that illustrates the tension between the risks and rewards of social cooperation. In the game players choose between "Aggressive" and "Passive" behaviors. Observe that for both Shiite and Sunni the (Passive; Passive) equilibrium is Pareto superior to the (Aggressive; Aggressive) equilibrium. By acting pacifically toward one another, each is spared the costs of violence. Yet under a veil of ignorance, Aggressive is preferred: If Sunni believes Shiite to be Aggressive or Passive with equal probability, the payoff to playing Aggressive is 6, while the payoff to Passive is 4. Being Passive is risky because it yields a particularly low payoff when facing aggression.

Stag Hunt games such as the game in Figure 10.1 also illustrate that a peaceful equilibrium is more fragile than a violent equilibrium. If m is the probability that a member of the rival group plays the "mutant" nonequilibrium strategy, the (Passive; Passive) equilibrium is resistant to mutant Aggression only when $5m + 7(1 - m) \leq 8(1 - m)$, or when $m \leq 1/6$. Similar calculations show the (Aggressive; Aggressive) equilibrium to be resistant to mutant Passivity when $5(1 - m) + 7m \leq 8m$, or $m \leq 5/6$, a much higher threshold. This implies again that the (Aggressive; Aggressive) equilibrium is risk-dominant.

In general, a conflict equilibrium is more likely when the payoff to aggression is high, the payoff to a cooperator from meeting an aggressor is low, and when the payoff from cooperation is not particularly high. Hirshleifer (2001) argues that this may explain why trading partners seldom go to war with one another, and why violence between women and men is rarer than violence between men. In such relationships, payoffs from cooperation are high.

A second fundamental solution concept in evolutionary game theory is the *evolutionary stable strategy*, or ESS. An ESS is an equilibrium that is resistant to a small fraction of "invading mutants" that play a different behavior. Any incumbent behavior A played within a population is an ESS if (1) the payoff to the mutant behavior B against A offers no higher payoff than when A is played against itself; and (2) where the payoff for playing B against A happens to be *equal* to the payoff of A against A, the payoff to behavior B when played against B must be lower than when A is played against B. Every ESS must be a Nash equilibrium since, taking the previous example, no individual player benefits from deviating from the (A; A) behavior if it is an ESS.

Role 2:

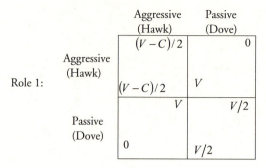

Figure 10.2. Hawk-Dove Game, General Form

Consider a large population of individuals who all desire a scarce resource in the Hawk-Dove game, now presented in its general form, in Figure 10.2. Examples of a scarce resource could be land, food, or an attractive mate. Each individual enters the game with a preprogrammed behavior (called a *phenotype*). Two individuals, randomly selected from the larger population, are chosen to play each game. In the next round, other pairs are randomly matched, and the game is played in this way repeatedly by randomly matched pairs.

The value of the resource is equal to V, which is obtained by playing Hawk against Dove, who acquiesces to the aggressive behavior. If the players both play Hawk, they fight. Each player wins the fight with equal probability, the winner obtaining V, but each also incurs a fighting cost $C/2$.[19] If $V > C$, then playing Hawk is a dominant strategy and the game really is not a Hawk-Dove game at all; it is a Prisoners' Dilemma, and the only Nash equilibrium and ESS is characterized by everyone playing Hawk. If $0 < V < C$, the game is a classic Hawk-Dove game, and there are three Nash equilibria. Two occur when one player plays Hawk and obtains the resource and the other plays Dove and doesn't. In both of these Nash equilibria, there is no fighting; the Dove acquiesces to the Hawk. In the third Nash equilibrium, a mixed strategy, each plays Hawk with probability $p^* = V/C$.

Consider the case of a society in which no convention has developed that prescribes the play of individuals in either Role 1 or Role 2. This means that players must interact blindly; they lack an "identity" that gives them a prescription for play. As the homogeneous players within the larger population are randomly matched over plays of the game, the mixed strategy emerges as the only ESS to the Hawk-Dove game.

Here is why: Suppose all players play Dove. In this case, a mutant player who is a little Hawkish some fraction p of the time does better than the incumbent Doves. The "hawkish mutant" receives a payoff of $pV + (1 - p)V/2$, which is greater than

---

[19] Some versions of the game assume that only one player (the loser) incurs a fighting cost equal to C with $p = \frac{1}{2}$.

the Dove payoff, $V/2$. The Dove strategy fails to satisfy condition (1) of an ESS. A Hawk among Doves prospers.

Similarly, if all players are playing Hawk, then a player who plays Dove some fraction, $1 - p$, of the time does better than a pure Hawk, since the pure Hawk player gets $(V - C)/2 < 0$, while the at least slightly more Dovish player receives a payoff of $(1 - p)(V - C)/2$, less negative than the former. Consequently, condition (1) of an ESS is again not satisfied. A layman biologist's explanation for this is that because the more Dovish player doesn't fight as frequently, he doesn't get beat up as frequently as a Hawk who fights all the time with other Hawks, and as a result enjoys a higher level of reproductive fitness.

The mixed-strategy $p^* = V/C$, however, is an ESS. As shown in the appendix, playing Hawk exactly p^* of the time yields a payoff that satisfies condition (1) of an ESS. It yields a payoff equal to any mutant strategy $p^* + \varepsilon$ when each is played against the incumbent strategy p^*, regardless of whether ε is positive or negative; that is, whether the mutant is a little more hawkish or a little more dovish. Because condition (1) holds with equality, it must also satisfy condition (2), and it does. When played against itself, the mutant strategy $p^* + \varepsilon$ does worse against itself than p^* does against $p^* + \varepsilon$. Thus, the "occasional fighter" is able to repel mutants in a homogeneous population who either fight too much or fight too little.

Similar to the *risk-dominant* equilibrium in the Stag Hunt, conflict emerges in the anarchic world of a Hawk-Dove game as kind of "fact of life," an optimal strategy in the absence of institutions to check and guide behavior. In fact, the factors that create more conflict in the ESS in Hawk-Dove are comparable to those in the risk-dominant equilibrium of the Stag Hunt. The probability that a player fights in the ESS of the Hawk-Dove game, V/C, is positively related to the "spoils of war," V, and negatively related to its cost, C.

However, in a game of conflict involving property rights over scarce resources, such as land, food, or mates, certain recognizable asymmetries typically emerge in the roles of players. We will see that as asymmetries become recognized over roles of players, conventions evolve that may thwart conflict, producing equilibria in which a player in one role will tend to play Hawk and the other, Dove. Take, as an example, conflicts over land. Asymmetries may evolve in which, for instance, one player may have made improvements to the land, while another has made no improvements to it. A second asymmetry might be that a specific piece of land may lie directly adjacent to one player's land, while far away from that of a rival claimant. Third, one player may already have lots of land, and the other may have little and need it more. Each of these asymmetries may provoke a more "hawkish" posture by one player while fostering a more "dovish" behavior by the rival.

The most obvious asymmetry often occurs over the roles of "Possessor" and "Challenger" (Sugden 1986). When facing a Possessor, a Challenger knows that playing Hawk brings a high probability of some kind of fight. How often will someone grab food off another person's plate? Will not even the most indiscriminant swinger hesitate before making a pass at another man's wife? The leader of any armed movement understands that those who have occupied land for generations will be difficult to displace without some kind of resistance. The general recognition of asymmetries, their gradual evolution into conventions, and then later perhaps into formal law is an under-appreciated precondition to a functional society. Manners, marriage, and property rights create prescriptions for behavior that thwart conflict and are precursors to both societal harmony and economic prosperity.

The game in Figure 10.2 refers to these asymmetries as Role 1 and Role 2. In the land example, I will assume the former to be "Challenger," and the later the "Possessor," where a Challenger covets land that a Possessor has occupied first. (I will refer to players as individuals, but they can just as easily represent people groups, or even nations.) If both Challengers and Possessors play Hawk V/C of the time and Dove $1 - (V/C)$ of the time, the mixed strategy by both players is a Nash equilibrium, but it is unstable; any slight change in the population of players in either role A or B will cause players to change their strategies. However, if for some reason "possession" (or any other of the above asymmetries) makes players in the Possessor role slightly more prone to playing Hawk (more than V/C of the time), then the best strategy for players in Challenger role becomes Dove.

We can see the evolution of this kind of conflict-mitigating convention by examining the evolutionary dynamics of the asymmetric Hawk-Dove game. The study of evolutionary dynamics is another key concept in evolutionary game theory, similar to the dynamics that governed *fictitious play* in Chapter Eight. Evolutionary dynamics assume that players obtaining relatively higher payoffs prosper and increase within the population through their higher "fitness level," while those obtaining relatively lower payoffs will wither and decline as a fraction of the population. The dynamics of the land-conflict game with the asymmetric roles of Possessor and Challenger can be seen in Figure 10.3.

Let x be the fraction of Possessors playing Hawk, those willing to fight for the land they currently possess, while $1 - x$ play Dove, the accommodating strategy. Similarly, let y be the fraction of Challengers playing Hawk, those willing to fight to obtain land

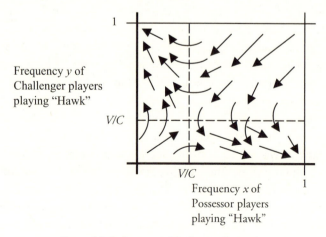

Frequency y of Challenger players playing "Hawk"

V/C

V/C

Frequency x of Possessor players playing "Hawk"

Figure 10.3. Possessor/Challenger Dynamics

that they do not yet possess, while $1 - y$ play Dove, those willing to acquiesce. When will fighting result in "increased fitness" to Possessors? When $y\frac{V-C}{2} + (1-y)\,V > y\,(0) + (1-y)\,\frac{V}{2}$, meaning that given a current fraction y of Challengers playing Hawk, the payoff to a Possessor from playing Hawk is higher than from playing Dove. Not surprisingly, this inequality holds when Hawk-playing Challengers are relatively rare, for $y < V/C$. As a result, when $y < V/C$, the higher payoff for Hawk-playing Possessors leads to an evolutionary dynamic in which Hawk-playing among the population of Possessors increases. This is illustrated by the arrows moving to the right in the area in Figure 10.3 below the V/C line along the vertical (Challenger) axis. Above this line the arrows move to the left, because when $y > V/C$, the payoff is higher for Possessors playing Dove.

In the same way, playing Hawk will lead to "increased fitness" of a Challenger when $x\frac{V-C}{2} + (1-x)\,V > x\,(0) + (1-x)\,\frac{V}{2}$. As with the Possessor, this will occur only when $x < V/C$. Yet when $x > V/C$, Dove leads to a higher payoff. Thus, the arrows in Figure 10.3 move the evolutionary dynamics upward to the left of the horizontal V/C line and downward to the right of it.

There are two "dynamically stable" equilibria to the game in Figure 10.3, the convention "if Possessor, play Hawk; if Challenger, play Dove" as well as the convention "if Possessor, play Dove; if Challenger, play Hawk." The southeast quadrant and nearby areas to the north and west form a "basin of attraction" for the former convention. The northwest quadrant in Figure 10.3 and nearby areas to the east and south form a basin of attraction for the latter. From states that lie within these basins of attraction, the population will inexorably move toward the respective convention, like an ant being sucked into a bathtub drain. Both dynamically stable equilibria in this game are an ESS. Any fraction of mutants is repelled by the equilibrium strategy of players in the opposing role. The movement toward these conventions is healthy, in the sense that increasing role recognition reduces conflict.

Note that the "if Possessor, play Hawk; if Challenger, play Dove" equilibrium will not necessarily evolve in all situations. For example, consider individuals in line at a public water pump or public latrine. A convention may have emerged that if the individual in the role of Possessor is taking too long, the next in line should have a turn. (Particularly in the latrine example, Challengers are prone to becoming unusually *hawkish*.) Thus, while "time of possession" may solidify Hawk play by a Possessor in one instance, it may solidify Hawk play by Challengers in another. It is entirely likely that a convention may emerge "if Possessor, play Dove; if Challenger, play Hawk" that is equally adept at resolving conflicts over resources. Such conventions are more likely to emerge when it is most efficient for resources to be shared and when "fairness" operates within a population.

Conflict is likely to occur when parties recognize different conventions or when common conventions have multiple interpretations. I will mention two well-known examples of such conflicts.

In the infamous conflict between India and Pakistan over the Kashmir area, India appeals to a convention of first possession, pointing to the signed agreement in 1948 between Maharaja Hari Singh and Prime Minister Sheikh Abdullah that assigned the

Jammu and Kashmir region to India after British decolonization. (This reluctant deal was made in exchange for military aid against invading Pakistani tribal militants.) Pakistan, in contrast, appeals to a convention of self-determination, repeatedly calling for a plebiscite among the Kashmiri population to ultimately decide the allegiance of Kashmir (a plebiscite to which India had agreed in a 1951 accord). Given the Muslim majority in the province, it is likely that a plebiscite would favor union with Pakistan.

Similarly, the Israeli-Palestinian conflict has legendarily crippled both political and economic development in the region. Yet in this example, both parties appear to recognize the convention "if Possessor, play Hawk; if Challenger, play Dove." But the core question remains to which side belongs the legitimate role of Possessor. Many Israelis trace their legitimate role as Possessor back to God's covenant with Abraham (Genesis 15:7), while Palestinians claim their role as Possessor based on their widespread occupation of the land in more modern times, in the centuries before the return of the Jewish diaspora after the Second World War. Of course, sometimes a party may justify violent behavior by appealing to one convention or another, but even honest differences in the perception of roles may lead to conflict.

Categorizing Conflict

Conflict typically arises out of an aggressive response to aggression. I would like to distinguish two types of aggression from a second player in response to aggression from a first player. I will classify these into *resistance* and *revenge*. Consider the game in Figure 10.4a, in which a Challenger initiates with either Passive or Aggressive behavior toward a Possessor. If the Challenger is Aggressive, the Possessor can then respond in kind by playing Aggressive, or by playing Passive. (I will use these terms to avoid confusion with the traditional 2×2 Hawk-Dove game, though the ideas are similar.)

If the Challenger is Aggressive and the Possessor is Passive, the Challenger wins something from the Possessor with value V. I will assume that if the Challenger is Aggressive, the Possessor, by resisting the Challenger, can win back what was his own with certainty, but at a cost of C_2 to himself and C_1 to the Challenger. If $C_2 < V$, then violence by the Possessor is "rational" in the traditional sense. Thus by

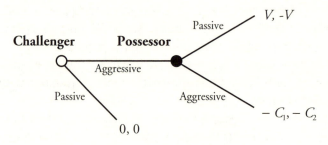

Figure 10.4a. Resistance Game

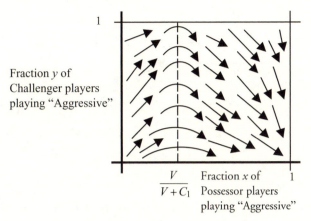

Fraction y of
Challenger players
playing "Aggressive"

$\dfrac{V}{V + C_1}$ Fraction x of
Possessor players
playing "Aggressive"

Figure 10.4b. Resistance Game Dynamics

backward induction, the credible threat of Aggressive by the Possessor at the second node induces the Challenger to play Passive in the first node of the game, assuming $C_1 > 0$. The special characteristic of the Possessor's aggressive response here is that his violence serves a practical end. This is the type of violence I will call *resistance*. As a form of violence, *resistance* is easy to understand. It is in a player's own interest, it may serve as a credible deterrent to violence by others, and it elicits the sympathy of third parties.

The evolutionary dynamics of the resistance game in Figure 10.4a are shown in Figure 10.4b. Let x and y be the fraction of Possessors and Challengers playing Aggressive, respectively. Assuming $C_2 < V$, the payoff to Aggressive Possessors is always higher than it is to Passive Possessors. This means that in every state with $x < 1$ within Figure 10.4b, the fraction x of Possessors who "resist" is increasing; as seen by the consistent left-to-right movement of the evolutionary dynamics in Figure 10.4b. The fraction y of Challengers who are Aggressive, however, is increasing only if the fraction x of Possessors who "resist" is low. Specifically, y will be increasing only when $x(-C_1) + (1 - x)V > 0$, that is when $x < V/(V + C_1)$. When $x > V/(V + C_1)$, y is decreasing because the expected cost of initiating conflict is too great. The Nash equilibrium "if Challenger, play Passive; if Possessor, play Aggressive" is dynamically stable; any small perturbations will lead the dynamics right back to the equilibrium point. The equilibrium is also an ESS; any mutant Possessors who play Aggressive or mutant Challengers who play Passive less than 100 percent of the time will immediately fare worse against the opponent's incumbent equilibrium strategy than incumbents in their same role.

Two comments about "resistance": First, if $C_2 < V$, then resistance should lie off the equilibrium path; the Challenger should never challenge. Yet "resistance happens." Why? One reason may be that the Challenger misjudges the payoffs. The Challenger may either overestimate C_2 (which represents the cost of victory to the Possessor) or underestimate V. Would the United States have gone to war in Viet

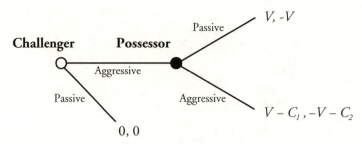

Figure 10.5a. Revenge Game

Nam had it know that the Viet Cong were willing to sustain 1,100,000 military and 2,000,000 civilian casualties[20] to achieve victory in the war?

Second, resistance itself is a morally neutral term. The judgment we make about the legitimacy of an act of resistance stems from rights that we assign to Challenger and Possessor in a particular context. The activity of Sam Childers and the SPLA in central Africa is an act of violent resistance. In this particular case, most would agree that a Challenger who abducts someone else's child is violating the rights of both the child and his parents. Thus the "resistance" of the SPLA, acting on behalf of victimized households as Possessors, may be widely recognized as legitimate. But many cases are less straightforward. For example, the actions of the Sandinistas and the Contras in Nicaragua during the 1980s could both be classified as "resistance," the Sandinistas resisting the dictatorship of the Somoza regime, and the Contras resisting the quasi-Marxist dictatorship of the Sandinistas. Both armed movements sought legitimacy by claiming to recover rights confiscated by a Challenger. Consequently, rhetoric plays an important role in conflict. Rhetoric seeks to justify one party's violence by mobilizing popular opinion behind that party's claims as legitimate resister. One person's "terrorist" may be another person's "freedom fighter."

In contrast, consider the game in Figure 10.5a. In this game, the violence by the Challenger causes some kind of damage that cannot be rectified. For example, the Challenger may have detonated a bomb killing innocent people from the Possessor's group. If the Challenger is rational, we must assume that committing such an act gives the Challenger some positive payoff V. However, the people killed in the violence cannot be revived. Unlike the previous case, aggression by the Possessor cannot redeem the act of violence. Responding in kind with aggression only augments the loss realized by the Possessor to a payoff of $-V-C_2$. But if $V-C_1 < 0$, and the Possessor does respond, then despite the additional damage to the Possessor, the Challenger will regret initiating the violence in the first place. In fact, this may be one objective of the Possessor. In the literature, this type of reciprocating violence is sometimes labeled *negative reciprocity*. I will call it *revenge*.

---

[20] Agence France Presse (French Press Agency, April 4, 2006) news release concerning the Vietnamese government's release of official figures of North Vietnamese who died during the Vietnam war. According to the Vietnamese government, the North Vietnamese deliberately falsified the figures during the war to avoid demoralizing the population.

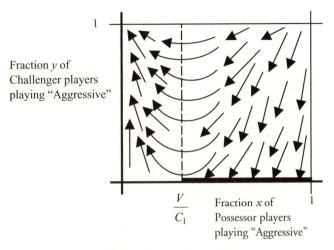

Fraction y of
Challenger players
playing "Aggressive"

$\dfrac{V}{C_1}$

Fraction x of
Possessor players
playing "Aggressive"

Figure 10.5b. Revenge Game Dynamics

In contrast with resistance, *revenge* is not easily explainable from a game-theoretic standpoint. It is not *rational* as the term is commonly used in economics and game theory. For example, revenge is not the Nash equilibrium in the game obtained by backward induction. As seen in Figure 10.5a, once the Possessor has been the victim of a one-shot incidence of violence, he should let bygones be bygones. Yet in such instances, Possessors routinely carry out what is often called *second*-party revenge, when the offended takes justice into his own hands.

This is obvious from most people's life experience, but also in laboratory experiments of what is called the Ultimatum game. In the Ultimatum game, Player A receives a lump of currency, say 100 units, and offers a fraction of it, f, to Player B. If Player B accepts the allocation, players receive $100(1 - f)$ and $100f$, respectively. If Player B rejects A's offer, then both players receive zero. While a "rational" Player B should accept any f greater than zero, laboratory evidence consistently reveals Player B rejections of f between zero and one-half. Player B's rejections of $f > 0$ are a form of revenge; the Player Bs are essentially paying to "get even" with a cheapskate Player A. Moreover, Player As *expect* revenge in response to a lowball offer, making the most common offer by Player A one-half.[21]

Revenge is more likely to occur when the cost inflicted on the Challenger is large relative to its cost to the Possessor so that (C_1/C_2) is high, and revenge yields a bigger bang for the buck. Individual examples of revenge abound in civil conflict between Israeli and Palestinian, Muslim and Christian Nigerian, Serb and Kosovar, Shiite and Sunni Iraqi, Crip and Blood in the American inner city. Feelings of revenge come naturally to human beings; even a subtly aggressive act by a rival provokes creative fantasies of revenge, even though we know revenge would "drag us down."

The evolutionary dynamics of revenge are shown in Figure 10.5b. In this game, evolutionary dynamics leads to two places. The first is the backward induction Nash

---

[21] Guth and Tietz (1990).

equilibrium, with an Aggressive Challenger and a Passive Possessor. The fraction of Aggressive Challengers, y, increases when the payoff to an Aggressive Challenger exceeds that of a Passive one, that is, $x(V - C_1) + (1 - x)V > 0$, or when $x < V/C_1$; it decreases when $x > V/C_1$. When x is small, Aggressive Challengers do better, because their acts are seldom avenged. The basin of attraction for this equilibrium lies in the space to the left of the $x = V/C_1$ line and in a northwest area of the rectangular space to its right.

The second place the dynamics lead is a dynamically stable area along the horizontal axis to the right of the $x = V/C_1$ line (shown in bold in Figure 10.5b). Its basin of attraction is a set of states in the southeast region of the rectangular space to the right of the $x = V/C_1$ line. In this equilibrium, if there is a high fraction of revenging Possessors (for whatever reason), it deters aggression by Challengers. The dynamically stable area along the bold line is a Nash equilibrium, though it relies on an "irrational" threat of revenge that lowers the payoff to the Possessor. The equilibrium is *not* an ESS. A significant invasion of mutant Challengers who play Aggressive means that the payoff of Possessors playing Passive will exceed that of those playing Aggressive. This is able to move the system away from the bold-line equilibrium toward the equilibrium in the northwest corner. The equilibrium along the bold line is dynamically stable (except for its most leftward point at $x = V/C_1$, meaning a *small* movement away from the equilibrium causes the dynamics to revert back to it.

So although the "revenge equilibrium" falls short by some evolutionary game theory criteria, it satisfies others. Moreover, the equilibrium is intriguing because (1) in everyday life, potential Challengers in many instances will recognize revenge as a credible threat; and (2) the equilibrium is characterized by a notion of deterrence that yields a relatively high payoff to Possessors. All of this, however, begs the question about why the urge for "revenge" plays such a large role in human conflict while the act itself, when taken at face value, is irrational.

One explanation is that some people derive a hidden benefit from violence, and revenge provides that opportunity. Social psychologists claim that approximately 3 percent of all people have psychopathic tendencies, people who actually receive a positive payoff from inflicting violence on other people.[22] But even at this (surprisingly high) 3 percent level, sadism is happily the exception rather than the norm. A second explanation may be that revenge acts as a signal to dissuade future attacks. Revenge could be a strategy that establishes a reputation for retaliation against a perennial foe in a repeated game context. But while this may apply in many cases, in practice revenge is often carried out in response to a solitary act of aggression, not just in repeated games. Third, it is also possible that unprovoked attacks may trigger some internal impulse for justice or fairness in human beings that overrides individual "rationality."

But what appears most likely is that revenge, as a "fitness mechanism," operates at the group level. In other words, as social beings, we are sometimes called to "take one for the team." Individually, sacrificial behavior is prevalent in the animal

---

[22] See both Pinker (2002) and Magid and McKelvey (1988), pp. 4–7.

kingdom when it benefits the group. For example, schools of guppies send small teams ahead for the dangerous job of scouting potential predators. Occasionally, a scout is gobbled up in the line of duty, but surviving scouts live to report the danger back to the school.[23] When honeybees sting an intruder, the barbed stinger attaches in the victim. As the bee flies away, the stinger remains, pulling out the venom gland along with many of the other vital insides of the bee. This kills the bee within minutes, but the venom gland continues to pump poison into the victim, more effectively protecting hive and queen.[24] An even more intriguing example is that of the African termite *Globitermes sulfureus*.[25] When faced with an ant invasion, the soldier termites of this species literally convert themselves into miniature suicide bombers. Equipped with massive glands full of deadly yellow fluid, the termites boldly march into the midst of their enemy. When they become surrounded by ants, they explode their glands and themselves, spraying the deadly fluid in all directions, leaving this world for their reward in the next, but also leaving behind a battlefield full of enemy casualties.

Biologists refer to schools of fish, hives, and colonies as *superorganisms*. Within a superorganism, individual organisms are prepared to sacrifice for the security of the larger group (especially if they share a high percentage of genes with the other members).[26] In this way, a group of individuals behaviorally wired for sacrificial altruism is more apt to repel a potentially Aggressive Challenger than a group in which individuals fight solely based on their individual payoffs. A payoff structure that resembles revenge at the individual level may represent resistance at the group level.

In the game in Figure 10.5a, populations that contain a critical mass of revenge-takers enjoy a higher fitness level than those that do not. They are more able to deter aggression from both without and within. Moreover, the "wear-and-tear" on revenge-takers, which could conceivably threaten their fitness, may be compensated by the esteem and rewards bestowed by other group members on those who are able to enforce justice within a social network (e.g., the good guy who kills the bad guy gets the girl). Similarly, groups may deny resources of one kind or another to those who do not adhere to the revenge norm, placing them at a reproductive disadvantage.[27] Within an environment lacking institutions of justice, probably the historical norm, the "revenge gene" may have thus played an important role in the security and survival of social groups.

---

[23] Pool (1995).

[24] Wilson (1978/2004), p. 152.

[25] Ibid.

[26] Dugatkin (1999), pp. 149–50.

[27] This theory has been fleshed out in fascinating papers by Dan Friedman and Nirvikar Singh (1999, 2004). That revenge appears to play a greater role in some groups than others is supported by research such as Richard Nisbett and Dov Cohen (1996), who describe the "culture of honor" within some social groups. The latter carry out an experiment among male students at the University of Michigan who grew up in either the North or the South. In their experiment, a stranger bumps into one of the subjects while simultaneously insulting him with an expletive. Relative to Northerners, who were relatively unaffected by the insult, Southerners showed a greater propensity to become upset and retaliate with their own aggressive behavior.

Swiss economists Helen Bernhard, Ernst Fehr, and Urs Fischbacher (2006) carried out an experiment to ascertain the existence of *third*-party revenge among two indigenous tribal groups in the Western Highlands of Papua New Guinea. The subjects of their experiment, the Ngenika and the Wolimbka, were grouped into games consisting of three players. The players played a "dictator game" in which player A (the dictator) was given 10 *kina*, roughly equal to a day's wage. Player A then dictated that any fraction of this amount (from zero to 10) to be allocated to Player B. After observing the contribution (if any) from A to B, Player C, to whom the researchers had given 5 *kina*, could then "invest" zero, one, or two *kina* to punish A, ostensibly for being greedy toward B. For every *kina* invested by Player C in punishing A, three of A's remaining coins were taken away.

The researchers found that dictators who transferred half their coins or more were rarely punished by Player C. But when Player A transferred less than half of his or her coins, C punished A substantially, and the smaller the fraction transferred by A, the more he or she was punished. When two or fewer coins were transferred, player C's average punishment was about 1.5 *kina* (reducing A's income by about 4.5 *kina*). According to their expectations, the punishments varied based on tribal membership among the players. In games where A and C (as well as A and B) were from a different tribe than the other player, punishments for greedy Player A behavior were more gentle. When B and C were from a different tribe than A, punishments were more savage.

The existence of institutions that effectively mediate justice between individuals and groups clearly lessen the need for revenge (though such feelings may naturally persist). But where there is a perception that such institutions are absent, acts of revenge proliferate. This seems to explain much of the violence we observe in developing countries. Note how the following acts of violent revenge (one of Muslims against Christians, the other of Christians against Muslims) appear to stem from a perception of extreme group insecurity:

NIGERIA: Death Toll Rises to 30 in Revenge Slayings Muslim mobs brandishing machetes and clubs attacked Christians in the streets of Kano and burned houses as Nigerian security forces struggled to quell a two-day rampage that erupted to avenge a massacre of hundreds of Muslims last week in the town of Yelwa. Police confirmed at least 30 killed in Kano, where thousands, mostly minority Christians, cowered in army barracks and police stations as mobs attacked people outside. (*Los Angeles Times*, May 13, 2004)

KOSOVO: Stubborn Ethnic Strife Shatters Kosovo's Fragile Peace As the region knows too well, violence begets violence. In Serbia itself, drunken football fans and others vowing revenge on "Albanian terrorists" torched two mosques, including one from the 17th century that had miraculously survived the Bosnian war. Crowds moved on to smash the front windows at a local McDonald's. About 1,000 Kosovo Serbs have been evacuated to NATO bases inside Kosovo and another 2,600 driven from their homes. (*Time International*, March 29, 2004)

Theologians, such as Berkeley's Ted Peters in *Sin: Radical Evil in Soul and Society* have explained sin, especially in its most egregious forms, as a response to the temptations wrought by anxiety.[28] He uses the example of the 1968 My Lai massacre, in which a unit of American GIs known as Charlie Company willingly carried out orders to slaughter 450–500 villagers in the Quang Ngai province of South Vietnam, mostly women, children, and elderly grandparents. Peters and others have traced the massacre to the extreme anxiety and insecurity experienced by the American soldiers during chaos of the Vietnam War. As Peters explains, killing any Vietnamese became a way to indirectly revenge the horror of seeing their own buddies killed, and a way to exert some kind of control over the chaos that constantly threatened their own lives. A similar set of circumstances may have prompted the Haditha Massacre of twenty-four Iraqi civilians by U.S. Marines on November 19, 2005, after the detonation of a roadside bomb that killed one marine and injured several others.

The apparent irrationality of human suicide bombing may likewise be understood as a desperate act in the context of extreme group insecurity. Suicide bombing has become a lamentable hallmark of Middle East conflict in the twenty-first century. From 2001 to 2006, there were 148 suicide attacks by Palestinian militants against Israelis, where in the vast majority of cases, an individual with explosives strapped around his or her body, detonated the bomb in a crowd.[29] During 2005 in the war in Iraq, an average month saw seventy-five suicide attacks by individuals strapped with explosives or by individuals driving explosive-laden cars into a target.[30] Such acts may occur in the context of both resistance and revenge, as a means to achieve a concrete objective, or as retaliatory punishment. Either way, suicide bombing represents the definitive expression of "taking one for the team."

Complicating our understanding of the problem is that while suicide bombers are often accused of being insane, driven by dire poverty, undereducated, and gullible, research evidence points to the reverse: Middle Eastern suicide bombers and others who have engaged in suicide attacks in the past, such as Japanese kamikaze pilots in World War II, are typically more educated than their peers, are almost never living in desperate poverty, and display little other evidence of psychological dysfunction.[31] Instead, suicide bombing appears to be an act with its roots in a perception by a Possessor that (a) justice is not available for addressing aggression by a Challenger; and (b) conventional methods of fighting will prove ineffective for a weaker foe against a stronger one. Suicide attacks by individual members of a weaker group against a stronger one may be a primary behavioral mechanism that has emerged to force a stronger group to think twice before challenging a weaker group.[32] It also represents the comprehensive submission of the individual to the superorganism of a larger group that effectively taps into and exploits the human instinct for revenge. Promises of honor to one's family and rewards in the afterlife heighten an individual's willingness to carry out such an act. In short, though many view suicide attacks as

[28] Peters (1994), p. 40.

[29] Ken Ellingwood, "Israel Court Bars Residency for Palestinians," *Los Angeles Times*, May 15, 2006, p. A9.

[30] Rick Jervis, "Car Bombings Down, Military Says," *USA Today*, May 9, 2006, p. A4.

[31] See Silke (2004); Berrebi (2004); and Alan Krueger, "Poverty Doesn't Create Terrorists," *New York Times*," Section C, p. 2, November 29, 2003.

[32] Attran (2003).

irrational, it may be helpful to understand them as a desperate form of group survival mechanism in the context of extreme group insecurity.

Ethnic Conflict

Pranab Bardhan (2005) points to two views about the origins of ethnic conflict.[33] The first view is that animosity between groups is ingrained as a primordial condition, a view held by many anthropologists and sociologists, who tend to view human behavior within the constraints of social structures. The second view is that underlying the passion of ethnic rivalries, groups interact with some degree of interest and calculation, and that group boundaries are to some degree malleable. Economists, of course, favor the latter view. In this view, class warfare and economic battles over resources underpin many ethnic clashes. This viewpoint is certainly consistent with empirical findings that civil conflict is more likely in countries that are rich in natural resources.[34]

Francesco Caselli of the London School of Economics and Wilbur Coleman at Duke University (2005) develop a theory along these lines.[35] The basis of their theory is that every society is endowed with a set of wealth-generating assets, such as natural resources or lucrative state enterprises. Political coalitions will naturally arise that seek to capture these assets for themselves to the exclusion of other citizens. The challenge for these coalitions is that exclusion is difficult, as others may want to infiltrate the coalition by applying for government positions, and in other ways trying to infiltrate the inside group. In order to prevent infiltrators from diluting the coalition's political dividend, they argue that coalitions have an incentive to form along ethnic lines. Because ethnicity is readily identifiable, it makes it easier to spot infiltrators from the losing coalition. Tension arises in their model between large ethnic groups, who have greater resources to achieve victory both democratically and by force, and smaller ethnic groups, with lesser means, but who would enjoy greater dividends per capita if they held power. The minority group's stronger incentive to rule creates a need for ethnic repression by the majority group, even when they would prefer a peaceful coexistence (as the governing majority, of course).

A model that shares some of these characteristics is developed by Stanford political scientist Barry Weingast, which I will present in more detail. His model has two ethnic groups playing a repeated "reciprocal vulnerability game" in which alternating groups choose between what I will call Trust and Oppression strategies. He assumes that each group is large, but not large enough to dominate society (recalling Montalvo and Reynal-Querol's emphasis on ethnic *polarization* as an underlying factor in conflict). The game emphasizes the importance of reciprocating cooperation among groups in divided heterogeneous societies. Group 1, currently holding power, makes the first move, deciding whether to take advantage of Group 2. If Group 1 plays Trust, Group 2 has the opportunity to reciprocate, or it can Oppress

---

[33] Bardhan (2005).
[34] Collier and Hoeffler (2004).
[35] Caselli and Coleman (2005).

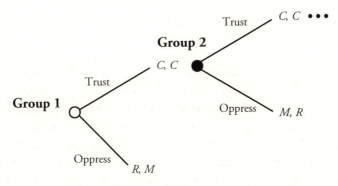

Figure 10.6. Weingast's Ethnic Conflict Game

Group 1. If a group chooses to Oppress in any period, it derives some long-run benefit R, while the victim receives the lower long-run payoff M. Cooperation yields C in each period. If two groups cooperate for consecutive plays, the model assumes they cooperate forever.

How the groups behave depends largely on their view of one another. Weingast assumes that groups can be inherently either Benevolent or Hostile. Nature chooses a group's type at the onset of the game (not illustrated in the diagram). The difference between the groups is that a Benevolent group prefers to Trust; that is, for such a group, $C/(1 - \delta) \geq R$, whereas the Hostile group prefers to Oppress the other, *i.e.* $C/(1 - \delta) < R$, where δ is the discount factor. A group believes another group to be Benevolent with probability p and Hostile with probability $(1 - p)$. This belief, by one group about another, substantially governs group interaction. Weingast considers three scenarios:

Scenario 1 occurs when each group is certain that the other is Benevolent ($p = 1$). In this scenario, Group 1 trusts Group 2, but Group 1 also believes Group 2 will trust it, and vice versa. The Nash equilibrium here is long-run cooperation. This is the happy scenario.

Scenario 2 occurs when a Benevolent Group 1 is certain that it is facing an aggressive Group 2 ($p = 0$). While Group 1 would like to Trust, it is certain that cooperation is not possible given the Hostile nature of Group 2. Provided that $R > C + \delta M$, Group 1 must play Oppress to prevent itself from being a victim.

In Scenario 3, each group is uncertain about the other's type. There is a lack of trust, but not complete mistrust. Assume that Group 1 is Benevolent, but it believes Group 2 is Benevolent only with probability p. Group 1 will Trust if $C + p\delta C/(1 - \delta) + (1 - p)\delta M \geq R$. Let p^* be the critical level of p that is just sufficient for Group 1 to play Trust. This required threshold p^* will be lower if the consequences of victimization are not too severe, if the payoffs from cooperation are high, and if the gains from oppressing are *not* too high. For levels of trust p at or above p^*, Group 1 will Trust. For p below p^*, Group 1, although Benevolent, will Oppress regardless of Group 2's true type. Scenario 3 is particularly tragic if the payoff to being a victim is perceived as particularly harsh. In this case, Group 1 may Oppress in the first move even if Trust about Group 2 is relatively high.

Weingast's theory helps explain why violence can blow up so quickly between ethnic groups. Suppose p is only marginally above p^* and a relatively minor incident of ethnic violence occurs, slightly increasing the perception that one of the groups is Hostile. Even a seemingly minor event can push the groups over the edge into violence and oppression. Two clear examples of this kind of explosive violence are the Rwandan genocide, in which approximately 800,000 Tutsis and moderate Hutus were massacred by radical Hutus from April to July in 1994, and the war erupting in June 1991 between Serbs and the Croats in the former Yugoslavia. In both instances, during the months before both of these clashes, distrust grew as a result of ethnically charged radio broadcasts. In the Rwanda case, distrust grew though the broadcast of propaganda against Tutsis by government-operated *Radio Télévision Libre des Mille Collines*. In the Yugoslav case, President Slobodan Milosevic broadcast a speech declaring the primacy of Serbs in the new Yugoslavia over other ethnic groups.[36] In both instances, relative peace had prevailed before the ethnic eruption.

Other intriguing theories have been presented that help to explain sudden flare-ups in ethnic violence. Pranab Bardhan (2005) applies the information cascade model of Bikhchandani, Hirshleifer, and Welch (1992) discussed in Chapter Eight to ethnic violence. Here the pronouncements made by only a few initial actors against a particular ethnicity can determine the subsequent behavior of the masses who operate under imperfect information. Each believes a rumor about a group to be true, simply because so many others believe it. In a bad information cascade, false rumors about threats from a rival ethnic group may incite unfounded mass violence against them.

Kaushik Basu (2007) develops a model in which two rival ethnic groups that randomly interact with one another contain populations that can be internally ranked in terms of each member's innate hostility toward the other group. In his model, aggressive behavior by only a few hard-core racists within a group can provoke an aggressive response by their counterparts in the other group, who want to avoid being victimized. Because members of each group are unable to distinguish between those in the opposing group who harbor varying degrees of hostility toward them, this sequentially causes the slightly more moderate members of both groups to adopt the aggressive posture, ultimately leading to a domino effect in which all members of both groups adopt the aggressive behavior toward each another. The tragic outcome in Basu's model can be violence even though the fraction of true racists in each group may be quite small, and the cooperative outcome is both Pareto efficient and risk dominant.

Building Trust

Although the most deeply rooted changes in ethnic relations occur at a personal level, institutions can be constructed that can build trust between groups. What specific roles can institutions play in establishing this trust? One key role is to

---

[36] Weingast (1998), p. 177.

guarantee the fundamental rights of groups that do not hold primary political power, whether they be in the minority or the majority. A rational fear held by a group such as Iraq's Sunnis, is that by yielding to the Shiite majority, they lose economic power (because they release control of the country's oil reserves), and they lose access to bureaucratic positions, public services, political power, and other government functions such as internal security.

To address the issue of rights over resources, some have advocated a straightforward division of permanent control over resources between groups or provincially based control that is based on ethnic concentrations.[37] A credible, permanent division of natural resources (e.g., oilfields, fisheries, or diamond mines) that is not subject to political whim may alleviate the anxiety faced by ethnic groups over potential loss of political power.

Game theorists, such as Stephen Brams at New York University, have developed ways of thinking about this process called "fair division mechanisms."[38] One such mechanism is an *envy-free* division, in which no party prefers another party's allocation of the resource to his own. The famous cookie-division problem, in which a parent assigns one child to divide the cookie and the other to choose her preferred piece, is a mechanism that yields both a Pareto-efficient Nash equilibrium as well as an envy-free solution. The mechanism maintains these properties even with a heterogeneous resource, when the chips and nuts (read oilfields and diamond mines) are concentrated in different parts of the cookie.

When indivisibilities exist, such as in the case of a holy shrine, cooperation can be fostered by mechanisms such as the following: Suppose that in the course of peace negotiations it becomes clear that in place of holding the land on which the holy shrine exists, the minimum that Israel would accept in outside development assistance (plus the right to United Nations-guaranteed access to the shrine) is X_1, while the minimum that Palestine would accept is X_2. Suppose that $X_1 > X_2$, and consider a division in which (1) the land where the shrine rests is given to Israel; and (2) along with access to the shrine, an amount X of development assistance is granted to Palestine, (where $X_1 \geq X \geq X_2$). This division yields a Pareto efficient, envy-free solution. We should thus view "envy-freeness" as at least a necessary (if not sufficient) condition for a peaceful settlement.

Both developing and developed countries have also used race-based preferential policies to help address ethnic tensions, which give preferences to underrepresented ethnic minorities in government hiring and admissions to public colleges and universities. The most well-known policies of this kind are the "affirmative action" policies that have existed in the United States since the Kennedy administration. But more recently such policies have been adopted in countries as diverse as Brazil, India, Malaysia, and South Africa. The idea is that the preferences are temporary, put in place to rectify past imbalances and the advantages enjoyed by privileged groups in schooling and economic networks. If overt discrimination is

---

[37] See, for example, Lijphart (1984).
[38] See Brams and Taylor (1996), Brams and Kilgour (2001), and Su (1999).

widespread, or even if it isn't but mentoring and imitation are important processes in upward economic mobility, then preferential hiring and admissions policies can foster more broadly based economic opportunity.

Nevertheless, there are important caveats to consider with such programs. Affirmative action in university admissions is likely to induce labor market discrimination, lowering the wages of graduates purportedly benefiting from such programs unless adequate resources are devoted to academic preparation across ethnic groups (Wydick 2002). Moreover, with affirmative action in the labor market, Stephen Coate and Glenn Loury (1993) demonstrate that if preferences for the under-represented group are too strong, employers have to hire less-qualified members from the preferred group. Understanding this, members of the group will have an incentive to underinvest in their own training, creating entrenched differences in productivity between ethnic groups in what Coate and Loury call a "patronizing equilibrium." If preferential policies are enacted to ease ethnic tension, they must be implemented in a way that minimizes their negative side effects.

A third mechanism for building trust over ethnic divisions involves the creation of either explicit or implicit veto power for large minority groups. Let's return to Weingast's model to examine this approach. What causes the Oppressive behavior by Group 1 in Scenarios 2 and 3? The motive is fear. Group 1 acts in a hostile manner, although it is not a Hostile type, because it fears being taken advantage of by Group 2. The basis for this fear is the inability of Group 2 to commit to Trust in the second move of the game. If Group 2 could credibly commit to Trust, Group 1 would rather play Trust over Oppress. Thus what is needed is a mechanism that allows Group 2 to credibly promise not to Oppress when it has power. Weingast proposes a dual-veto mechanism as illustrated in Figure 10.7.

Here Group 1 is free to Trust when it holds power, knowing that it can Veto an attempt by Group 2 to use the apparatus of the state to Oppress it. Notice that veto power is in the interest of a majority group as well as a minority group. By allowing both groups to enjoy veto power, the majority group takes away the uncertainty that could cause explosive violence to erupt against it from the minority group under

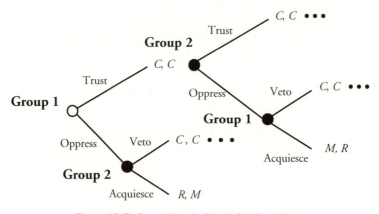

Figure 10.7. Group Veto in Ethnic Conflict Game

Scenario 3. While granting veto power may constrain it politically from undertaking certain actions in its interest, instituting mutual veto power protects both groups from victimization and violence. One advantage of minority veto power is that it is a self-enforcing constraint: Veto power itself should be able to block any proposed attempts to take the veto away, making it a credible commitment device.

There has arguably been no stronger attempt to incorporate checks and balances between groups than in the design and ratification of the Iraqi constitution of 2005. Political architects made an over-arching attempt to incorporate an implicit veto for Sunni and Kurdish groups to protect them from Shiite political domination. In the October 2005 ratification process, a two-thirds "No" vote within three or more of Iraq's eighteen provinces would have sent the drafters of the new constitution back to the drawing board. The voting mechanism was designed in particular to try to protect the rights of Sunnis, who make up a majority in four of the eighteen provinces. In the constitution itself, implicit veto power is given to Sunnis by requiring a two-thirds vote in the Council of Representatives over key decisions, such as the election of the President.[39] A vote to dissolve the Council can be undertaken by request of only one-third of its members.[40] Moreover, the constitution gives political power to provinces to form "regions" made up of multiple provinces (e.g., Iraqi Kurdistan) in the attempt to give various ethnic groups a large measure of self-determination and to prevent oppression of one group by another.[41] The constitution also states, at least in principle, that each region is entitled to an equitable share of oil revenues.[42]

Nevertheless, group veto power is not a panacea for quelling ethnic discord, and the disadvantage of extreme checks and balances is that it can become politically difficult for a society to move forward with one gas pedal and twenty-five brakes. Ultimately, an institutional balance must be achieved that protects the rights of individual groups, but also allows for political decision making.

While in some instances the checks and balances of democracy can thwart conflict through protection of minorities, in other instances democracy emerges as an alternative to violent repression by a minority elite. In their theory of the origins of democracy, Daron Acemoglu and James Robinson (2006) argue that democracy emerges at certain times and places in history because it begins to lie in the best interest of an elite minority to establish a credible commitment to shift political power to the less-privileged majority. This transition to democracy, they contend, is most likely to occur when minority elites face an increasingly strong revolutionary threat by the rest of society. They write,

> The first option for the elite is to give them what they want today: redistribute income and more generally adopt policies favorable to the majority. But, suppose that concessions today are not sufficient to dissuade the citizens from revolution . . . these promises may not be *credible* . . . If it wants to save its skin, the elite has to make a credible promise to set policies that the majority prefer; in particular, it must make

---

[39] Iraqi Constitution, Article 67, paragraph one.
[40] Iraqi Constitution, Article 61, paragraph one.
[41] Iraqi Constitution, Article 114.
[42] Iraqi Constitution, Article 109, paragraph one.

a credible commitment to future pro-majority policies . . . it has to transfer political power to the citizens. (2006, p. 26, italics in original)

Elites view democracy as a better alternative than conflict and repression because repression is costly for them, involving the risk of destruction of wealth and assets, loss of life, and international condemnation. They point to concrete examples of this pattern in the histories of Britain, France, Germany, Sweden, Colombia, and Venezuela. They proceed to ask

> Why does the creation of democracy act as a commitment when we know that democracy often collapses once created? This is because although coups sometimes occur, it is costly to overthrow democracy, and institutions, once created, have a tendency to persist. This is mostly because people make specific investments in them. For instance, once democracy has been created, political parties form and many organizations, such as trade unions, arise to take advantage of the new political circumstances. The investments of all these organizations will be lost if democracy is overthrown, giving citizens an incentive to struggle to maintain democracy. (2006, p. 28)

Thus in Acemoglu and Robinson's framework, civil conflict, or at least the potential for civil conflict, can become a seedbed for the growth of democratic institutions. Democracy is then consolidated as the institutions that support it endure over time. This consolidation process is more likely to happen, they argue, when the incentives for a coup are smaller, which depends on the extent to which democracy, and its effect on economic reform and redistribution in a particular context, threatens the interests of the minority elite.

The establishment of democratic institutions can establish systems of checks and balances that mitigate conflict and create a propitious environment for economic development. But an equally essential ingredient for economic development is a widespread level of trust in society, both within and across groups. The two do not necessarily march hand-in-hand. A widespread level of trust within society can, however, aid in the construction of civic institutions and also in economic exchange, thus benefiting economic development both indirectly and directly. This widespread trust, the *social capital* that exists in a society, is the topic that we will pursue in the next chapter.

CHAPTER 11
Social Capital

A generous man will prosper, and he who refreshes others will himself be refreshed.
Whoever trusts in his riches will fall, but the righteous will thrive like a green leaf.
– Proverbs 11:25, 27

IN *CHEATING MONKEYS and Citizen Bees*, biologist Lee Dugatkin describes the grooming behavior of the impala.[1] (For Americans who think of an impala as gas-guzzling Chevy, the impala, closely related to the gazelle, inhabits the savannah of Kenya and other parts of southern and eastern Africa.) Impala face a problem unfamiliar to humans: They are unable to clean important parts of their body, especially their backs, since they have no arms, and their legs are facing the wrong way. This is a problem particularly with ticks, which are itchy and carry nasty impala diseases. Whereas the rhinoceros solves this problem though his symbiotic friendship with the oxpecker (tick bird), who stands on his back feasting on his ticks, impala are too jumpy for a piggybacking mate. As a result, they usually ask another impala for help. But there are costs in grooming: lapses in vigilance for lions and wild dogs, hairballs, loss of saliva, and so forth. The substantial health benefits of grooming would justify these costs if another impala would reciprocate. Yet what is to keep a "groomee" from bounding off on his own business after the groomer does his work? Here, impala play a Trust game, with a guarantee of reciprocity hard to secure.

Researchers have found that impala have found creative ways to check free-riders in their midst.[2] First, impala turn a one-shot Trust game into a repeated Trust game by breaking up grooming into smaller bits. Instead of finishing the job in one go, the groomer engages in one episode of grooming, by running his or her tongue about six to twelve times across a grooming partner's back and neck. The groomee then reciprocates with a similar six to twelve licks. The whole process usually consists of more than a half-dozen reciprocating rounds.

The repeated structure of the interaction helps to thwart cheaters. Moreover, there is a backup mechanism: A herd forms a tight social network within which impala are astonishingly accurate scorekeepers of grooming. Researchers have found that impala are the beneficiary of about the same number of grooming sessions that

---

[1] Dugatkin (1999).
[2] Hart and Hart (1992).

they administer to others.[3] In short, the size of herds, the information flows within a herd, and the mechanisms of reciprocity that emerge, foster a kind of *social capital* among the impala.

Humans, of course, have plenty of their own unreachable ticks. But the itch that we long to scratch is usually for something that we can't produce ourselves – either it would cost us too much time, or we don't know how. We need partners who do have the time and do know how. Most of what human beings have, even in the least developed economies, is obtained through exchange with others. Exchange, how-ever, often involves a Trust game. We exchange money for a service to be rendered later, or for a good whose true quality will be ascertained only over time. We sell a good to someone on credit who may or may not repay. Like the problem faced by the impala, what encourages us to hold up to our side of the bargain in the course of exchange?

The *social capital* within a society helps establish the trust that facilitates exchange and, in time, economic development. As Nobel Laureate Kenneth Arrow noted long before the study of social capital became fashionable:

> I have remarked about the responsibility for truthfulness in economic life, but the issue goes even further. Virtually every commercial transaction has within itself an element of trust, certainly any transaction conducted over a period of time. It can be plausibly argued that much of the economic backwardness in the world can be explained by a lack of mutual confidence. (1972, p. 357)

Cambridge University's Partha Dasgupta (2000) gives three reasons why parties to an agreement are likely to trust that other individuals will behave honestly in the course of exchange: (1) The formal institutions discussed in Chapter Nine enforce the agreement. (2) A larger social network externally enforces the agreement through a system of rewards and penalties within the network, penalties that may be either social, pecuniary, or both. (3) Agreements are internally enforced because people are honorable; religious beliefs, moral upbringing, identity, and conscience play the leading roles here. *Social capital*, broadly defined, relates to the second and third of these mechanisms, which facilitate trust and, its counterpart, trustworthi-ness. Some have even defined the third category more precisely as *spiritual capital*, implying that individuals may behave altruistically not as a result of earthly rewards and punishments, but because they believe some actions are good and some are bad, and may have spiritual as opposed to mere social implications. Societies rich in social capital are less dependent on formal institutions to check malfeasance and opportunism in their midst. In developing countries, formal institutions are often too weak to establish and enforce the rules of the economic game, so the role of social capital becomes magnified.

The influence of social capital, its measurement, and even its very definition, have emerged as a vibrant area of cross-disciplinary research within economics, sociology, and political science. Social capital is a term whose burgeoning academic popularity has long since outstripped its precision, though a number of leading

---

[3] Dugatkin (1990), p. 96.

social scientists have pioneered the idea and helped shaped its meaning. I will briefly describe the work of several of these.

Stanford sociologist Mark Granovetter was the first of these early pioneers. Granovetter (1973) attributed successful employment searches, for example, to the "strength of weak ties" of a job-seeker. He argued that is it is not a person's "strong ties" (family members and close friends) that are critical to success, as these networks are generally too small, and the information within them too similar to one's own, to be helpful. Rather, he maintained that it is *friends of friends* that are most valuable because they foster exchange *between* local networks and connect people to the outside world.

Granovetter's subsequent (1985) work built in this idea to challenge the early economic theories of institutions by Oliver Williamson (1975) and others, arguing that such theories postulated an "under-socialized concept of man." Granovetter's thesis, that we can only fully understand economic activity in relation to its "embeddedness" within social structures, of course challenged the traditional economic view, which he argued placed economic behavior in too "atomistic" a framework. Thus, the starting point of the social capital literature is the premise that economic activity takes place within the context of a social network, which may facilitate economic exchange when formal institutions can't fully enforce agreements.

Another early pioneer in the study of social capital was the late sociologist James Coleman of the University of Chicago. Coleman famously, but rather amorphously, defined social capital as "social structure that facilitates certain actions of actors within the structure," yet he aptly saw social capital as better understood in terms of examples.[4] Coleman provides one example of social capital operating among retail traders in the Kahn El Khalili market in Cairo: A leather merchant, asked by a customer where one can buy jewelry, will immediately escort the customer to a nearby associate dealing in jewelry. Similarly, a moneychanger will lead customers to a rug dealer, and a jeweler will direct his foreign customer to the moneychanger. Coleman points out that some of these referrals earn commissions, while others merely create obligations that are repaid later.

A third social capital pioneer, Johns Hopkins political scientist Francis Fukuyama, expanded on Coleman's ideas by defining *social capital* in terms of *trust* that exists more broadly within a given society:

> *Trust* is the expectation that arises within a community of regular, honest, and cooperative behavior, based on commonly shared norms, on the part of other members of that community. . . . *Social capital* is a capability that arises from the prevalence of trust in a society, or in certain parts of it. It can be embodied in the smallest and most basic social group, the family, as well is the largest of all groups, the nation, and in all the other groups in between. . . . Widespread distrust in a society . . . imposes a kind of tax on all forms of economic activity that high-trust societies do not have to pay. Social capital is not distributed uniformly across societies. [5] (Italics mine.)

---

[4] Coleman (1988).
[5] Fukuyama (1996), pp. 26–8.

In other words, Fukuyama views trust as a necessary condition for the development of social capital, and social capital as a necessary condition for prosperity. He identifies social capital at the intermediate institutional-level as especially critical, between the level of the family and the state. He argues that some countries such as France, Spain, China, and the Latin American countries enjoy strong families and a strong state, but have relatively little in between, therefore have low social capital.[6] A much stronger set of intermediate-level social capital exists, Fukuyama argues, in countries such as the United States, Germany, and Japan, which has helped these countries develop strong entrepreneurial cultures.

Some have set out to try to measure empirically the importance of trust-based social capital to development. The most well-known effort in this area is by Harvard political scientist Robert Putnam (1993), *Making Democracy Work: Civic Traditions in Modern Italy*. Putnam examines historical differences in social capital between Northern and Southern Italy, as measured by civic participation in sports clubs, choral groups, literary guilds, and other associations. He finds civic participation by these measures to be widespread in the North back to the turn of the twentieth century. In contrast, he uncovers a remarkable dearth of social capital in the South, which he traces back to the social and political havoc wreaked by Norman invaders of the eleventh century. The historical differences in social capital turn out to be powerful econometric predictors of the resulting quality of governance in the two regions as well as differences in economic growth.[7]

Other researchers, such as Yale University's Dean Karlan, have employed experimental methods to measure the effect of social capital at the micro-level. Karlan (2005) looks at the importance of trust and trustworthiness on microfinance loan repayment in Peru. Karlan and his team had microfinance participants play a Trust game before they began borrowing. Subjects were randomly divided into pairs with different roles. A subject in Role A (the Truster) was given three coins (*nuevos soles*) and could pass any number of these coins (including zero) to his partner assigned to Role B (the Receiver). Any amount passed to the Receiver was doubled by the experimenter. The Receiver then had the opportunity to pass any number of coins back to the Truster. The number of coins passed by the Truster was therefore taken to be a measure of *trust*, and the percentage of coins passed back by the Receiver a measure of *trustworthiness*. The outcomes of the experiment were recorded, and for 12 months Karlan waited patiently as the borrowers repaid their loans. What he found was that trustworthiness, the number of coins passed back by a Receiver, was significantly and positively related to how well the person repaid his loans as a real-life borrower.[8]

---

[6] Ibid., p. 55.

[7] Putnam followed his work on Italy with *Bowling Alone: America's Declining Social Capital* (1995), which laments the declining level of civic participation and social capital in the United States, forewarning of an impending American political and economic malaise if such concerns are not addressed.

[8] Interestingly, Karlan finds that the number of coins originally passed by the Truster in the game to be related to be associated with *problematic* borrower behavior. This he attributes to poor judgment and risk-taking behavior by Trusters, as on average Trusters only received 85 cents back for every dollar passed to a Receiver. In Karlan's game, trusting a Receiver with coins was a bad investment.

Such studies indicate that trust and trustworthiness matter to economic behavior within a particular context but does this relationship generalize across countries? Apparently, the answer is yes. Stephen Knack and Philip Keefer (1997) obtain data on responses to the World Values Survey, which asks a set of the same questions across countries that are intended to measure differences in social capital. This survey includes the question: "Generally speaking, would you say that most people can be trusted, or that you can't be too careful in dealing with people?" Knack and Keefer's measure of trust for each of the 29 countries in their survey is the percentage of people who answered "most people can be trusted" in each country, the overall average being 35.8 percent, with a standard deviation of 14 percent. What they find is that an increase of 10 percentage points in this measure of trust is associated with a little less than a 1 percent increase in a country's average annual growth rate from 1980 to 1992. Moreover, their results hold even when they correct for possible reverse causality by using the number of lawyers in a country as an instrumental variable for trust. (Apparently, there is a negative correlation between trust and lawyers, and an increase in the number of lawyers contributes approximately zero to national income.) Even after checking the robustness of their results by this technique, by alternative sets of control variables, and by eliminating outliers such as Brazil (very low trust, very low growth) and South Korea (very high trust, very high growth), the relationship between societal trust and economic growth continues to hold. Trust matters.

The remainder of this chapter will focus on three of what I believe are the most important facets of the study of social capital on economic development: (1) the role of *social networks* as external (but informal) enforcement mechanisms (I will also mention work on the role of human emotion in the context of social inter-action as well.); (2) the potential role of *religion* as a trust builder and catalyst for economic development, *i.e. spiritual capital*; and (3) the growing importance that social scientists have begun to place on *identity* in economic and social behavior, and its implications for creating and escaping poverty traps. Identity represents something of a hybrid between internal and external motivations. I will illustrate important concepts in each with simple models.

Trust and Social Networks

What allows people to trust? What causes people to be trustworthy? It is unlikely that any inherent differences in human beings across countries account for differences in trust and trustworthiness. Human beings are quick to judge, often attributing dif-ferences in patterns of behavior to innate differences between groups of people. But human nature being what it is, people tend to behave in similarly commendable or contemptible ways as influenced by their expectations of others. These expectations are influenced by relational experience within one's sphere of social interaction: People that appear open and trusting have likely become so from repeated inter-action with trustworthy people. Similarly, cold or "suspicious" behavior among a particular group may be confused as an innate trait. But this behavior has likely emerged as a response from repeated interaction with untrustworthy people that has concluded "trust doesn't pay."

Psychologists Ken Magid and Carole McKelvey (1988) claim that human beings learn a basic level of trust in the first two years of life when infants learn to trust their mothers for basic needs.[9] An infant gradually learns that cries of hunger are met with food; cries of fright are met with comfort. Through thousands of such cycles, an infant learns to trust the outside world. Magid and McKelvey argue that what infants learn about trust from these experiences in the first two years of life largely determines their lifelong responses to others. Orphans who lie alone in a crib and are not held regularly in the first months of their life often develop Antisocial Personality Disorder (APD), a disorder that renders people virtually incapable of trust and trustworthiness.[10] Magid and McKelvey find that even if the external "trust conditions" after these first two years become relatively normalized by the time the children are toddlers, the damage from infancy is likely to be permanent. It is as if the brains of infants in a loveless environment get permanently programmed on "distrust."

Magid and McKelvey's toddlers may yield some insight into the emergence of trust and social capital within societies and nations. In many places wars, genocides, and other historical calamities have provoked widespread distrust in the distant past. Calamitous events may make widespread trust a disadvantageous behavior. People who naively trust the outsider in the milieu of chaos and violence often end up exploited or dead. Those who find the outside world to be an untrustworthy place withdraw into smaller trust networks, where trust happens only at the *intra*group level. The behavior is reinforcing. Once *inter*group contact has been broken, the lack of contact with other groups affords little opportunity for more widespread trust to be reestablished. Mechanisms evolve that informally enforce trust at the intragroup level, principally via repeated interaction and intragroup information flows, which subsequently establish a pattern of interaction in social life, politics, and economic exchange. Once this pattern of limited, intragroup exchange has been solidified, there is little desire to invest in the development of formal institutions if there is a common mistrust of those "outside the clan."

In many areas of the world, mistrust of outsiders is the norm. For example, Francis Fukuyama observes that throughout most of their history, people in many areas of Latin America and the former Soviet Union who have been victims of numerous historical wars and revolutions are noted for exceptionally trusting behavior within their close social network, but for being exceptionally suspicious of those outside of their network.[11]

Such limited networks of exchange stifle economic development. As Adam Smith famously pointed out, the division of labor is limited by the scope of the market. Entrenched mistrust affects economic development because it limits the scope for

[9] Magid and McKelvey (1988), p. 3.
[10] Ibid., p. 4.
[11] Fukuyama (1996), ch. 6.

exchange to a small network. Entrepreneurial risk taking outside the network is thwarted, and enterprises are unable to specialize, expand, and prosper.

But for many who interact within high social-capital communities, trust is not a rational, strategic decision, but operates as a social norm, like a rule of thumb. A rule of thumb in a high-trust context says, "Trust others, unless there is explicit evidence of untrustworthiness." In a low-trust context, the rule of thumb may be "Don't Trust." Moreover, people themselves may not even understand why they are trusting and trustworthy (or distrusting and untrustworthy). They learn the behavior because, in their context, "that's just how people are." This does not contradict the rationality of trusting or trustworthy behavior. It is simply that the mechanisms have been in place for so long that the particular behavior has become a habit, an artifact of culture.

Evolutionary game theory helps us to see, in a more formal framework, how historical events can form these habits, or social rules of thumb (like trust or mistrust) ultimately become self-enforcing behaviors. If these "incumbent" behaviors can repel "mutant" behaviors that challenge them within the social network, they form evolutionary stable strategies, and can persist indefinitely.

This idea is illustrated in the following game: Suppose a group of buyers and sellers interact randomly on market day every week within a network of size S.[12] On every market day half are buyers and half are sellers (but individuals may change roles over different weeks). Let's say that the buyers and sellers exchange goods whose quality is hidden at the time of the transaction. An example would be milk, bread, or meat, whose true quality is only ascertained after it is taken home and consumed. Moreover, suppose that buyers always buy on credit, a short-term loan that they promise to repay within a few days after the transaction (before next week's market day.)

The buyers and sellers are playing a Prisoners' Dilemma, in which both have the chance to take advantage of each other. Buyers can Cooperate by following through and paying for the good, or can Defect, by not paying. Similarly, sellers can Cooperate by, say, providing good-tasting meat, or Defect by selling foul-tasting meat. Let's say that Buyers and sellers exchange weekly – 51 times a year (allowing for a week of vacation).

The average number of times a given pair of individuals will exchange in the market over any year is inversely related to the size of the network. For example, if size of the network S is equal to 10, after an initial exchange, a member of the network can expect to exchange with that same member of the network an average of five more times, for an expected total within that year of six times. If S is equal to 25, the average number of total exchanges in that year with that member will be three; and if S is equal to 50, the average expected number of exchanges with that member will be two, and so forth. To keep things simple, let's ignore discounting, assuming all transactions in the year are weighted equally. Using our payoff notation

---

[12] This game is an extension of an example given by Dixit and Skeath (2004).

$S = \infty$
(average $n = 1$)

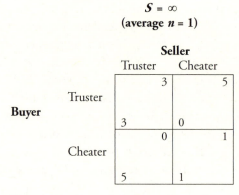

Figure 11.1a. Network Exchange Game, $S = \infty$

$S = 50$
(average $n = 2$)

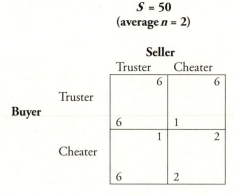

Figure 11.1b. Network Exchange Game, $S = 50$

for Prisoners' Dilemma games from Chapter Four, let's assume that $r = 5$, $s = 3$, $t = 1$, and $v = 0$, so that we have the payoff matrices in Figure 11.1a–d.

Suppose that market participants in our networks can operate under two cultural "rules of thumb." The first rule of thumb is trusting: "Trust, unless there is explicit evidence of untrustworthiness." In this strategy, an individual plays Cooperate initially, and continues to do so, unless she is defected on by another, and then she retaliates by playing Defect against the offender for *exactly one year after the defection* if they should meet again. I will call such an individual a "Truster." In short, the Truster trusts, retaliates against a defection for a time (one year), but then forgives and forgets. The second rule of thumb is "Don't Trust," a strategy that amounts, through its own suspicious sense of self-preservation, to playing Defect in every exchange. I will call this kind of market participant a Cheater. It is important to remember that in an evolutionary framework, our market participants are not strategic actors as such. Cheaters are truly cheaters to the core, and Trusters really do trust. The question is which imbedded behavior can survive and establish an evolutionary stable strategy in a given context.

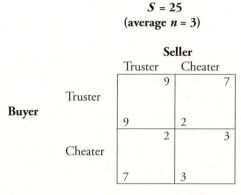

$S = 25$
(average $n = 3$)

Figure 11.1c. Network Exchange Game, $S = 25$

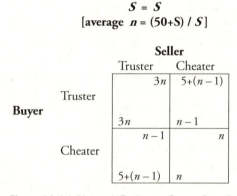

$S = S$
[average $n = (50+S) / S$]

Figure 11.1d. Network Exchange Game, $S = S$

Consider first the example in Figure 11.1a in which there is a very big network, that is, where S is so large it might as well be infinity. Here market participants know that after they exchange with someone they have virtually no chance of dealing with the individual again within the next year. In this case (Defect; Defect) is the unique Nash equilibrium in the stage game, and the unique evolutionary stable strategy (ESS) is a market full of Cheaters, who each receive a payoff of 1. Any mutant Trusters will have a lower level of fitness than the Cheaters. Moreover, a population of Trusters is susceptible to an invasion of mutant Cheaters, who receive an average payoff of 5, greater than the 3 garnered by the incumbent Trusters.

In Figure 11.1b, there are fifty market participants in the network. A pair of market participants who interact as buyer and seller can expect to meet one additional time within a year ($n = 2$). A Truster who meets a Truster receives a payoff of 3 in the initial exchange, and a 3 in an expected second exchange for an expected payoff of 6. A Cheater also gets an expected payoff of 6 from interacting with a Truster: 5 in the initial exchange and 1 in the second. The Truster receives 0 and then 1. Two Cheaters each get 1 in two exchanges for an expected total of 2. It would seem that in this case with $S = 50$, a market full of Trusters could be an ESS since Trusters do as well as Cheaters against other Trusters. However, a market full of Trusters can be invaded by a group of mutant Cheaters: Granted, the payoffs of Cheaters and Trusters are equal against the incumbent Trusters. But in the *secondary* criterion for an ESS, when both types happen to exchange with one of the handful of mutant Cheaters, the Cheaters do better (obtaining 2 versus 1). Hence, with $S = 50$, a market full of Cheaters remains the only ESS.

As the size of the network falls, interaction becomes more frequent. Figure 11.1c gives the case of $S = 25$. Here, $n = 3$ and Cheaters become more accountable for their sins. Informal sanctions begin to bite, and it becomes *possible* for a market of Trusters to form an ESS. Such a market is able to repel a small group of mutant cheaters since a Cheater's payoff would be 7, while the payoff to the incumbent Truster would be 9. Notice, however, that a market full of Cheaters can also form an ESS. A mutant Truster receives a payoff of 2 against an incumbent Cheater, while a Cheater receives a 3 against a Cheater. Thus with $S = 25$, the game has two ESSs.

We can see from the general case in Figure 11.1d the criteria for an ESS to form around a market full of Trusters within a network of size S. Let x be the fraction of Trusters in the market and $(1 - x)$ the fraction of Cheaters. This makes the payoff to a Truster in the market equal to $3nx + (n - 1)(1 - x)$ and the Cheater payoff equal to $(5 + n - 1)x + n(1 - x)$. A little algebra shows that this condition will hold for $x > 1/(2n - 3)$. Substituting $(50 + S)/S$ for n, gives a relationship between the size of a network and the fraction of Trusters in the network required to drive the game to a Trusting ESS. The criterion is that $x > S/(100 - S)$ or that $S < 100x/(1 + x)$.

The relationship between S and x is important. What it establishes is the relationship between the size of a network and the "critical mass" of Trusters needed to drive the system to a Trusting ESS, a "high social capital" environment. In this example if S is 50, then x must be greater than one, which is impossible. But if S is 40, then x must be greater than $2/3$. If S is 25, then x must be greater than $1/3$.

I would like to point out three implications of the model that are illustrated by existing empirical work. First, as the model demonstrates, smaller, informal networks offer some advantages that are not characteristic of more formal economies where interaction is more anonymous. In many parts of the developing world, economies continue to function primarily though such networks. Marcel Fafchamps and Bart Minten (1999, 2002), for example, study networks of agricultural traders in Madagascar, finding that these networks lower transaction costs in a number of ways. Trust within a smaller network allows their traders to grant credit easily without costly screening and repayment enforcement mechanisms. Moreover, exchange within the network allows traders to receive product without engaging in time-consuming inspections.

Another example of economic efficiencies within networks is Christopher Udry's (1994) work on credit contracts in Nigeria as well as his (2004) work with Tim Conley on pineapple farmers in Ghana. Both pieces of research, discussed in more detail in Chapters Seven and Eight, illustrate how social networks in developing countries can facilitate credit contracts and the adoption and efficient use of new technology. In particular, the shock-contingent credit contracts Udry describes in

Nigeria have been viewed as more efficient, from a welfare standpoint, than the impersonal, anonymous credit contracts found in more economically "advanced" countries.

A second implication from the network model is that as networks grow in size, there will come a point at which they are unable to sustain trust based on informal punishment mechanisms, and formal institutions must emerge to curtail opportunism. In tightly knit networks, whether they are a tightly knit group of traders or a small herd of impala, Cheaters find that soon enough, no one wants to lick their ticks. But while Cheaters can be appropriately punished in a small network, they can disguise themselves in a large crowd. At some critical level (in this example with $S > 50$), it becomes impossible to curtail opportunism via informal mechanisms. Thus as markets expand, societies tend to develop a set of institutional mechanisms that curtail opportunism more broadly.[13] The development of these institutions, such as contract law, civil courts, and credit bureaus, then becomes a problem of collective action. The development of such formal mechanisms, however, is ultimately more conducive to long-term economic development.

Stanford economic historian Avner Greif (1994) illustrates this idea in his study of two groups of Mediterranean traders from eleventh and twelfth century, Genoese merchants from the Italian city-state of Genoa, and the Maghribis, Jewish traders from the Muslim world. Both groups of merchants typically found it cost effective to contract overseas shipping agents to transport their merchandise, but developed very distinct mechanisms to prevent the overseas agents from embezzling their goods. The Maghribis's culturally collectivist beliefs led them to develop mechanisms to thwart opportunism based on a set of internal punishments within smaller social networks of traders, via the threat of damaging an agent's reputation within the network. Such a threat was credible given the high level of communication between Maghribi merchants. The kind of social capital that existed in Maghribi networks was thus similar to that observed in developing countries today, for example, by Fafchamps and Minten in Madagascar.

In contrast, the more individualistic nature of Genoese society allowed individuals more independence from any specific social network, making an individual act of malfeasance less subject to damaging gossip. As a result, the Genoese developed formal institutions early in their history to thwart marine-based opportunism. While the informal collectivist enforcement mechanism was arguably more efficient within its own social network, the formal institutional mechanisms were more efficient *across* networks, allowing the Genoese to develop partnerships across a wide range of agents. Greif conjectures that the more broadly applicable enforcement mechanisms contributed to the subsequent domination of the Mediterranean by the Genoese merchants.[14]

---

[13] See Kranton (1996).

[14] Sobel (2006) demonstrates in a model of bilateral contracting that economic relationships in which contracts are enforced by informal mechanisms tend to "last too long," in that while entering into a relationship with a new partner would yield a greater return, the old relationship is maintained because of its greater enforceability. Formal mechanisms, he shows, allow for such transitions.

A third insight of the network model is that wars and other historical calamities of the past can affect social capital in the present. Suppose that a Trust equilibrium exists in which exchange occurs in networks of forty, which can support a Trusting ESS for any $x > 2/3$. Then a civil war erupts that causes widespread mistrust and suspicion, so that the fraction of Trusters x plummets to $1/4$ of the population. One of two things must happen for society to adjust to the calamity: The first may be that, to maintain a Trust equilibrium, networks downsize by falling to less than half their previous scope (*i.e.*, $S < 100 \cdot 0.25/(1 + 0.25) = 20$), as individuals cope with uncertainty by withdrawing into smaller networks. The second possibility is that the calamity moves society away from the Trusting ESS to one in which everyone is a Cheater. This new equilibrium characterizes the anarchy that is pervasive during and in the aftermath of many conflicts, when social capital disintegrates. Eventually, however, small-sized networks may form in which Trust begins to reemerge. If x continues to increase, Trust can be supported in increasingly larger networks, but this may be difficult if low levels of Trust result in little intergroup exchange.

Douglas North's (1990) historical analysis of the development paths of England and Spain illustrates this point. During the relatively stable and tranquil period of the late middle ages in England, a set of formal and informal rules emerged in day-to-day commerce that became antecedents to more sophisticated forms of contract law and other means of enforcing commercial agreements. Spain, in contrast enjoyed no such period of tranquility. In the centuries before the renaissance, Spanish villages suffered under the constant peril of the Moorish wars, sometimes finding themselves on the same side and other times on opposite sides of a particular conflict. As a result, broadly based trust and codes of commerce across family and village networks failed to materialize. Personal relationships, local social networks, and paternalism came to constitute the key to survival and occasional economic success. These early differences in the English and Spanish peasantries may have shaped the course of history in profound ways: North contends that early patterns of behavior in England and Spain, establishing themselves during their divergent experiences in the late middle ages, were spread to their colonies in North America and Latin America.[15]

As a result, events in the distant past may have a powerful effect on the present through their effect on social capital. This makes the unfolding of history a *non-ergodic* process, in which historical events can dramatically influence the nature of the present, as opposed to an *ergodic* process, in which the effects of past events dissipate with time. In a non-ergodic historical process, once the genie of intergroup distrust has escaped from the bottle, it may be hard to put him back in. Mistrust breeds mistrust, spreading across networks and becoming further entrenched based on expectations, persisting through generations and spreading across civilizations, perhaps affecting economic development for centuries.

Social networks not only can be an important source of reward and punishment, but they can also be important conduits for the flow of information (Granovetter,

---

[15] North (1990), pp. 113–7.

2005). People typically regard personal sources of information received through their network to be more reliable than impersonal sources. As a result, information received through one's network yields opportunities for some and serves as a screening function for others. A potential slacker may exert extra effort for an employer within his social network, the employee fearing that laziness might not only result in termination, but in damage to his reputation in the minds of those closest to him. In this context, *reputation* within networks can be an underlying motive for trusting and trustworthy behavior. Although some models, such as in our network example so far, assume that market participants maintain information about Cheaters as a closely guarded secret, models that incorporate reputation allow for *gossip*.

Gossip makes matters worse for a Cheater. With gossip, any instance of cheating not only triggers the wrath of the offended Truster, but other Trusters as well, who likewise don't want to be burned. Let's create g, a "gossip parameter," which describes the speed with which information travels within a network about the actions of a Cheater. Assume Trusters are gossips, but *honest* gossips, so that we can ignore the complications involved with false rumors. With $g = 1/4$, for example, then a quarter of uninformed market participants learn of the cheating behavior each round after it occurs. In this case, after seventeen rounds (weeks) of exchange, over 99 percent of market participants will have identified a Cheater. In a slightly more gossipy network with $g = 1/3$, this identification process only takes twelve rounds. When $g = 1/2$, it takes only seven.

After this point, the Cheater might as well enter the market with a big "C" tattooed on his forehead. Virtually nobody trusts the Cheater, except for a very few Trusters who by chance end up "out of the loop," but even this number steadily declines with each subsequent round. A destroyed reputation lowers the Cheater's payoff to 1 in each of the subsequent rounds, while increasing the Truster's payoff to $3x + (1 - x)$, higher than the Cheater's for any $x > 0$. Thus, gossip and reputation within social networks makes it more likely for Trust to exist as an ESS.

Still, this kind of framework sees trust and trustworthiness generated within a network based on rational, self-interested behavior. Can trust emerge for other reasons? Borrowing from important ideas in psychology, Cornell economist Robert Frank (1988) provides another rationale for trust and trustworthiness that relies less on the hardheaded rationality of economics. He argues that trustworthiness in society may emerge as a set of subtle, but perceptible behavioral traits that allow trustworthy individuals to communicate their trustworthiness to others, allowing the possessor of these traits a higher level of "fitness" than those who do not possess them. These behavioral traits, which are observed as communication before exchange (in which opportunism is possible), allow players to establish emotional commitments to honesty.

Suppose we consider only one-shot games of exchange in which market participants never expect to meet again, as in Figure 11.1a, where $S = \infty$. Trusters, who in this framework are also trustworthy, are people who would genuinely feel bad about cheating. Their inherent honesty may have been acquired through good parenting, religious commitment, or cultural influences. Trusters are people, as Frank says, who have a conscience. Cheaters, for one reason or another, do not.

If Trusters and Cheaters look identical, then in the struggle for survival with one-shot play and no reputation effects, Trusters are doomed, receiving a payoff of $3x + 0(1 - x)$, which is always less than the $5x + 1(1 - x)$ received by Cheaters (remembering that x is the fraction of Trusters within the population).

But what if Trusters, through their inherent genuineness, are able to communicate their trustworthiness to another market participant? Frank argues that a person's trustworthiness may be communicated in a very subjective manner, through a choice of words, tone of voice, or facial expressions. Research has shown that much of the decoding of human facial expressions that convey trustworthiness occurs at the subconscious level, and that it tends to be powerfully accurate in humans.[16] The subjective and subtle nature of this communication does not belie its importance. What is critical is that through these emotional signals, the possibility exists that a *Truster can identify another Truster*. If so, then Trusters will only exchange with Trusters, and Cheaters are left to exchange only with other Cheaters. Here Trusters earn a payoff of 3 and the Cheaters a payoff of only 1.[17]

The implication of Frank's idea is profound for economic development. The ability of individuals within a culture to communicate genuine trustworthiness may play an important role in establishing the framework for trust in human interaction. If Trusters are able to communicate their trust, then they can survive and even multiply in a dog-eat-dog world full of Cheaters. In such a world, Cheaters can only survive by then trying to imitate the preexchange behavior of Trusters. But if Trusters are able to effectively differentiate themselves, then *the trusting behavior wins out*. If it is as Arrow, Granovetter, Fukuyama, and others argue, that widespread trust is foundational to economic development, then one of the key components of prosperity may lie in the ability of trustworthy individuals to communicate their trustworthiness.

Religion

The study of religion and its impact on economic development originated with Adam Smith and was developed more fully in Max Weber's *Protestant Ethic and the Spirit of Capitalism*. However, until recently the subject was downplayed by mainstream social scientists, perhaps due to fears over subjectivity or controversy in treating religious topics. Others (myself included) are apprehensive about analyzing religious faith as if it were a *means* toward a social end rather than something of substance in itself. Nevertheless, this discomfort has begun to abate. The idea of *spiritual capital* has captured the attention and research agendas of leading social scientists, including well-known economists such as Gary Becker, Robert Barro, and

---

[16] Malcolm Gladwell (2005) describes research illuminating the subtleties in interpreting human facial expressions in his popular book *Blink: The Power of Thinking without Thinking*.

[17] What if Cheaters try to imitate the behavior of Trusters? I will consider this problem in exploring the presence of hypocrisy in the context of religious faith, and its implications for social capital.

Michel Kremer. A 2005 Templeton Foundation request for grant proposals involving research on spiritual capital attracted 560 applicants, with $150,000 awarded to ten recipients from major research institutions, half of whom held positions at Harvard, Cambridge, and Notre Dame. Most topics were related in some fashion to the subject of economic development.[18] The study of religion and economic development has reentered the mainstream of social science.

The most important historical work on religion and economic development was Max Weber's (1905) *Protestant Ethnic*. Weber traced the origins of capitalism and much of the economic development realized in Europe to Protestant Christianity, and in particular to Calvinist strains of Protestantism existing in the sixteenth, seventeenth, and eighteenth centuries. Weber identified the Calvinist doctrine of predestination as central to character changes in Western Europe leading to capitalist development. This is ironic: An emphasis on predestination could have easily fostered a fatalistic society, in which actions were irrelevant because one's eternal fate had long ago been sealed. But while predestination asserted that individual salvation or perdition is predetermined, as it was practiced some uncertainty remained – even to the individual in question – regarding the camp to which one belonged. As a result, what became important to the Western European Protestants of this time was outward *evidence* of salvation, a display of character consistent with true redemption: honesty, hard work, humility, and an efficient use of money and time. Moreover, ostentatious living was distained; what we would now call brazen consumerism was viewed as a clear outward sign of inward spiritual decay. On top of these values, early Protestantism promoted literacy: Since everyone had direct access to the Scriptures, everyone was expected to read them. As a result, mothers taught children how to read, resulting in a culture that was highly literate, as well as frugal and hardworking. A combination of increased productivity and tastefully restrained consumption meant that investment flourished and economies grew.

Many twentieth-century scholars mistakenly identified religion as a cultural relic, dying with the intellectual advancement of humankind, as if intellect and spirituality were somehow substitutes. Yet, with the paradoxical exception of the Western Europe (the very subject of Weber's study), religious belief is clearly on the rise rather than on the decline worldwide. Ronald Inglehart at the University of Michigan chairs the World Values Survey, which collects religious data from eighty countries representing 85 percent of the world's population. Inglehart commented in an address at the Pew Forum for Religion in Public Life:

> There are more people alive today with traditional religious beliefs than ever before in history, and they're a larger percentage of the world's population than they were 20 years ago. The World Values Survey data make that unequivocal. When I was a grad student, I was not at all interested in religion because it was so obvious – all the major intellectuals knew – it was dropping off the map . . . That was colossally wrong, as we all now know. (Remarks, May 8, 2006)

---

[18] "Research on 'Spiritual' Capital," *PR Newswire*, Philadelphia, February 21, 2006.

The two largest religions in the world are Christianity and Islam, with approximately 2.1 billion and 1.3 billion adherents respectively.[19] Christianity and Islam are not only the largest religions, they are by far the fastest growing, with the vast majority of this growth occurring in developing countries. Most scholars trace the growth in Islam to population increases in Muslim countries, where infant mortality is relatively low, birthrates remain high, and life expectancy has increased. Islam has also rapidly grown in Western Europe, mainly from the inflow of migrants from North Africa, Turkey, and Pakistan. Combined with these demographic changes, Islam has strengthened (and sometimes become radicalized) in countries where its appeal has been to provide a structure of spiritually based ethics in an uncertain and often threatening time of rapid globalization and confrontation with the West.

Growth in Christianity has come primarily from two sources: high birth rates in Catholic countries in the developing world, and the growth of evangelical Christianity, particularly among Pentecostals, in Latin America and Africa. [20] Paul Freston (2001) describes the rapid growth of evangelical Christianity in many areas of the developing world and its effects on social and political structures. He shows that while the makeup of all Protestants in most Latin American countries was less than a few percent only forty years ago, most today have a substantial and growing minority of Protestant evangelicals, including Brazil (15 percent), Nicaragua (15 percent), Chile (16 percent), with estimates being as high as 40–50 percent in Guatemala.[21]

In Africa, ranks of evangelicals have also swollen, through the growth of Pentecostal churches, but also within traditional mainline denominations. Growth has been rapid: In 1931 Nigeria, Africa's most populous country, was 6 percent Christian and 45 percent Muslim; today it is about 45 percent Christian and 50 percent Muslim.[22] Much of the growth in Nigeria has been within the Anglican Church, which now boasts 18 million Nigerian members, a church whose evangelical theology often conflicts sharply with the church's more liberal teaching in Britain and the United States.[23] Other Anglophone countries such as Ghana, Kenya, and Uganda display similar patterns of religious change.

In Asia, the strongest growth in evangelical Protestantism has been in South Korea and China. The Protestant evangelical population in South Korea (mostly conservative Presbyterian) has grown so rapidly that the fraction of evangelical Protestants in South Korea is now similar to that of the United States, somewhere between 20 to 25 percent. Protestants have become disproportionately influential at the national level in politics; in the 1992 election, for example, they comprised 90 out of

---

[19] British Broadcasting Company World Service, http://www.bbc.co.uk/religion/religions/statistics. Following in order of world adherents are Atheistic/Agnostic/Nonreligious (1.1 billion), Hinduism (900 million), Chinese Traditional (394 million), Buddhism (373 million), and Primal/Indigenous (300 million).

[20] Daniel Pipes, "Surge in Christianity Worth Watching," *The Jewish Advocate*, December 12, 2002, p. A21. Pentecostals, a subset of the larger evangelical movement, emphasize the use of supernatural gifts such as healing, speaking in tongues, and prophecy.

[21] Freston (2001). Guatemala estimate is from U.S. Department of State, International Religious Freedom Project, Bureau of Democracy, Human Rights, and Labor.

[22] Freston (2001), p. 181.

[23] *Christianity Today*, July 2005.

299 members of congress.[24] In China, while all agree that there has been tremendous growth among Protestant evangelicals, precise estimates are difficult since most Chinese Christians congregate in secret house churches that remain unregistered with the government. Most estimate the number to be between 25–50 million though some sources have placed the number as high as 100 million.[25]

What influence can we expect this increasing religious belief in the developing world to have on social capital and economic development? Theological details aside, belief in an omniscient God of justice is a powerful tonic for problems of moral hazard, if such a belief promises that every act of cheating will be ultimately castigated and every act of kindness will be ultimately rewarded. Belief in an omniscient God of justice may induce someone to be trustworthy who otherwise might not, and may inspire someone to trust who might otherwise prefer not to.[26] (Given a sufficiently high utility weight on the future, of course.) Such belief lays a foundation for a moral conscience that in turn creates a basis for societal trust and trustworthiness, especially when it is common knowledge that others share the same belief. Benefits mushroom when the shared beliefs are widespread, for example in Weber's *Protestant Ethic*, where trust-based exchange in Europe flourished outside the scope of local networks.

Despite the difficulties with establishing a clear relationship between religiosity and economic outcomes (which I will illustrate later), the notion that religion affects behavior and economic performance has empirical support. Harvard's Rachel McCleary and Robert Barro (2006) carry out empirical estimations on cross-country data, seeking to ascertain the relationship between religious beliefs, behavioral traits (such as the prevalence of work ethic, thrift, and honesty in a society), and economic growth. They find that monthly religious attendance appears to be insignificantly, or even sometimes negatively, correlated with positive behavioral traits and growth. However, they find belief in heaven to have a moderately positive influence on these variables and belief in hell to have a strong influence, particularly on increased work ethic and economic growth. McCleary and Barro conclude that "beliefs related to an afterlife appear to be crucial as economic influences" (p. 66). They interpret their findings to imply that the direct effect of religious beliefs on the economy outweighs the potential advantages of the social networking associated with religious attendance.[27]

Jean-Philippe Platteau lists five effects of moral formation that help facilitate cooperation when there is scope for opportunism:

> The effect of moral upbringing is (1) to inculcate in people preferences of the reciprocity type by leading them to adopt the other's viewpoint in situations where their

---

[24] Freston (2001), p. 68.

[25] Freston (2001), p. 102.

[26] For an example of an admonition for trustworthiness in Judeo-Christianity see Leviticus 19:36, "Use honest scales and honest weights. . . . I am the LORD your God who brought you out of Egypt"; for trust, see Proverbs 11:25, "A generous man will prosper; he who refreshes others will himself be refreshed."

[27] McCleary and Barro's findings are consistent with other research such as Gerhard Lenski's (1963) work, which suggests that religious belief and commitment are linked to a spirit of capitalism and a humanitarian outlook, whereas mere membership in a religious subculture promotes behavior less auspicious to growth.

own acts are susceptible of causing harm to others; (2) to instill an optimistic rather than a cynical perception of other individuals, thereby contributing to establish trust in the other's predisposition to abide by the same ethical code; (3) to make external monitoring and punishment of dishonest behavior less necessary owing to the desire to avoid guilt feelings and enjoy the pleasure of self-satisfaction; (4) to drive people to resist the temptation to give in too easily to dishonest behavior after they have had unpleasant experiences in which they were the victims of fraud and malpractices; and (5) and to arouse feelings of moral outrage so that they are willing to detect and punish dishonest behavior even at a personal cost and even when they have not been themselves harmed by this behavior. (2000, p. 300)

There is a remarkable correspondence between Plateau's effects of moral formation and scriptural admonitions underlying the *Protestant Ethic*. Regarding Platteau's (number 1) consider "We must help the weak, remembering the words the Lord Jesus himself said, 'It is more blessed to give than to receive.'" (Paul in Acts of the Apostles, 20:35); regarding (2) "Accept one another, just as Christ accepted you, in order to bring praise to God." (Paul, in Romans 15:7); regarding (3) "(Let) your giving be in secret. Then your Father who sees what is done in secret will reward you." (Christ, in the Gospel of Matthew 6:4); regarding (4) "If you forgive people when they sin against you, your Father will also forgive you." (Christ, in the Gospel of Matthew 6:14); and regarding (5) "Speak up and judge fairly: Defend the rights of the poor and the needy." (Solomon, in Proverbs 31:9).

These kinds of prescriptions for social behavior help to facilitate the development of social capital on a number of levels: Internalizing the consequences of negative behavior toward others reduces defections in Prisoners' Dilemma and Trust games. This inspires confidence that an initiating player, such as a lender in a Trust game, is less likely to get burned. Continuing with the lending example, if there is a critical mass of borrowers for whom defaulting has moral (and even spiritual) implications, lending becomes safer and costly screening procedures less necessary.

A rather comical anecdote from Guatemala illustrates this point. Approximately a dozen borrowing groups had formed in a small Mayan village in western Guatemala, and had been receiving loans from a microfinance institution with which I was carrying out a research project. A loan officer from the institution told me that several months previously, a borrowing group made up of young men had decided that they didn't need to repay their group loan. The loan officer had informed them that if they didn't repay, their group wouldn't receive another loan. This threat, however, didn't seem to disturb the young men. The lending institution then upped the ante, announcing that if young men didn't repay, then credit would be denied to the rest of the groups in the village as well. Complaints and coercion from other borrowing groups neither moved nor swayed the mutinous group. Finally, the Pentecostal pastor of the village approached the young men, apparently informing them that the temperature of their afterlives would be heavily influenced by whether or not they repaid their group loan. The loan was repaid. (Given the level of deprivation in the village and the dire need for credit, the pastor was probably right.)

Another positive effect of religion is that faith may trump past negative experiences, providing a means for escaping dysfunctional behavioral patterns. Suppose a given individual from network A believes people from network B to be less trustworthy than those from her own network, perhaps via rumor, or even from limited experience. A may not see it in her immediate interest to enter a Trust game with a person from network B (e.g., extending credit, renting out a draft animal, paying upfront for a good or service), but feel that as an act of faith she will choose to trust the person from network B regardless. Why does she do it? Because based on her faith she may believe that *ultimately* she is better off (safer, more fulfilled, happier, and closer to God) by doing so. In this way, faith can augment any existing potential for trust-based exchange.

Additionally, religious faith that simultaneously prescribes forgiveness and accountability is likely to achieve a balance between the extremes of Grim Trigger strategies, which can degenerate into a trap of perpetual noncooperation, and a "door-mat" equilibrium, in which defectors are able to prey upon the naïve. When religious teaching clearly defines moral boundaries, outrage by third parties at a perpetrator over the victimization of another is likely to be rewarded by other members of the community. This deters cheating. Individual A knows if he cheats B, then C, D, and E will chastise A for doing so, and that F, G, and H will commend C, D, and E for their chastisement of him, and what is more, sympathize with the plight of B. In a society in which moral standards are less objective and defined by a vaguer sense of moral and spiritual truth, such unanimity against a perpetrator is less probable, making defections more likely.

But there is a problem with attempting to establish an empirical relationship between social capital and the prevalence of religion. The problem is that if religious people are perceived as more honest than the average citizen, then people have an incentive to be perceived as religious. Many developing countries with stunningly high rates of nominal religious adherence, for example, also suffer stunningly high rates of corruption. A casual investigation into the matter might suggest that religion at best doesn't make any difference. The phenomenon occurs notably in relatively free societies, where "signals" of religiosity are reasonably inexpensive to send (semiregular attendance at religious meetings, occasional public prayer, and so forth), creating a situation in which at least nominal affiliation to the dominant religion becomes synonymous with being "decent people." Each individual, regardless of her true belief, dares not fail to send the religious signal, lest she be thought of poorly. Game theorists call this a "pooling" equilibrium to a signaling game, in which the cost of a potentially advantageous signal is so low that virtually everyone sends it, making it impossible to separate the mice from the cheese. As a result, claims to religion in many societies are often viewed as "cheap talk."

The frequent result is an equilibrium characterized by a religious culture that is a mixture of genuine faith, nominal faith, and hypocrisy. The exceptions to this rule are societies in which a particular religion, or religion in general, is persecuted, such as currently in China, and formerly in the officially atheistic nations of the old Soviet bloc. In such contexts, the signal of religiosity is too costly for the nonbeliever to send, and only the truly faithful dare to claim the faith. Thus, in the context of persecution, the religious signal is costly, and more likely to indicate genuine trustworthiness. Persecution is unpleasant, but it purifies a church.

However, the norm in most societies is widespread nominal adherence to the dominant religion, often for social, economic, or political reasons. Notable examples have occurred in the politics of developing countries, where leading politicians have used conversion in the context of strong evangelical movements to gain political advantage. Examples flow from a wide array of countries: the regimes of Presidents Efain Rios Montt (1982–83) and Jorge Serano (1991–93) in Guatemala, Kim Young-Sam (1993–98) in South Korea, Hastings Kamuzu Banda (1966–94) in Malawi, and Daniel arap Moi (1978–2002) in Kenya. Subsequent to their terms, each was implicated in scandal and abuse of power.

I will use the game in Figure 11.2 to demonstrate the complications with establishing a clear relationship between religion, trust, and social capital. Figure 11.2 describes a one-shot Trust game, which here I will apply to lending and borrowing. Like the lending games in Figures 2.5a and 7.3, this game sets aside concerns of misfortune with investment, simply addressing the issue of whether or not a borrower chooses to repay. Payoffs are ordered $r > s > t > v > 0$. There are two main types of borrowers: The first type are Believers, who believe in Ultimate Justice, and represent a fraction x of the population. Believers believe that they will ultimately be held accountable for all of their actions. This includes fulfilling a promise to a lender, since willful nonrepayment in this model essentially amounts to theft. For the purposes of the model, it is beside the point whether cheaters believe that they will pay for their misdeeds by additional suffering in this life, hell, or reincarnation as a toad – the key issue is belief in ultimate accountability. Suppose that this means for Believers that the payoff to *non*repayment is zero, so as a result they always repay, giving them a default rate of zero. The second main type is a Nonbeliever; they make

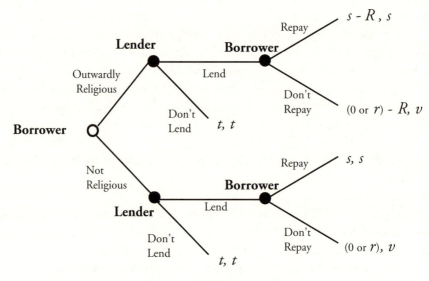

Figure 11.2. Religion as a Signal

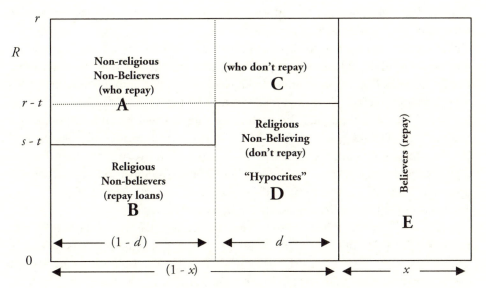

Figure 11.3. Map of Religion and Moral Hazard in Exchange

up $1 - x$ of a population that is morally mixed: For a fraction $1 - d$ of Nonbelievers the payoff to nonrepayment is also zero because their conscience tells them it is wrong not to repay. But for the other fraction d the payoff to nonrepayment is r so that, as seen in Figure 11.3, they never repay. Upon initial request for a loan, the Lender can't tell the difference between any of these types.

A borrower begins by choosing to identify himself as religious or nonreligious, irrespective of whether he is a Believer. Sending the religious signal costs R. It is best to think of R as the cost of "going through the (religious) motions." Signals of religiosity – church, synagogue, mosque, or temple attendance, corporate prayer, tithing of income – are costless to Believers (so for them $R = 0$). However, they are costly to Nonbelievers, and are more costly to some than others. Let's assume that this cost R varies uniformly across all Nonbelievers, lying between zero and the highest payoff, r.

Let's also suppose that there is a fixed number of individuals N in the market who desire loans, but not enough loanable funds to meet everyone's needs, so that credit is rationed.[28] As a result, some people will get loans, and some won't. Because everyone knows that only Believers have a 100 percent repayment rate, a Lender would like to fill his portfolio with as many Believers as possible. This creates an incentive for people to falsely claim religious faith.

So what kinds of people will claim they are religious? For Believers, being religious is essentially a sunk cost, because the actions of faith are something they choose regardless. An *honest* Nonbeliever (honest except for the fact that he says he is a Believer, but isn't) chooses to signal outward religiosity if $R < s - t$. A *dishonest*

---

[28] Credit rationing is now seen as an important feature of credit markets. Stiglitz and Weiss (1981) is the seminal article. (See Chapter Seven.)

Nonbeliever will choose to be outwardly religious if $R < r - t$, a less restrictive condition. The condition is less restrictive, because by defaulting on his loan, he makes out with more than the honest one who repays. Those with R greater than the critical level do not send the signal and are nonreligious, nonbelievers, some honest, some not. For these people, "doing" religion is particularly difficult.

With payoffs weighted by the areas given in Figure 11.3, if $\frac{(B+E)s+Dv}{B+D+E} > t$, then lending to people identifying themselves as religious will be advantageous to a Lender. This will hold provided that x, s, and v are relatively large and d and t are relatively small. Among this group claiming religion are three types: (1) Believers (area **E**); (2) Nonbelievers who have a low cost of displaying religiosity but are otherwise honest and repay loans (Area **B**), and (3) Nonbelievers who display religiosity, but are dishonest and do not repay loans, *i.e.*, hypocrites (Area **D**).

Now if $\frac{As+Cv}{A+C} > t$, then it will also pay for the Lender to lend to the nonreligious. But when the quotient of the areas $(B + E)/D > A/C$, the Lender prefers to lend to people who send the religious signal. Thus there will be an inflow of Nonbelievers (for whom religious signaling costs are relatively low) into "religiosity," until a Nash equilibrium is reached where the expected probability and benefits of receiving a loan come to be outweighed for some Nonbelievers by the cost of sending the signal. Thus as part of this equilibrium, the existence of a group of true Believers generates both a class of nominal believers as well as a class of religious hypocrites, who both benefit from identifying themselves with religion.

There are three implications for the relationship between religion and social capital from this model. First, there is a greater economic incentive for the dishonest than the honest to falsely claim religion. A greater fraction of *dishonest* Nonbelievers will identify themselves as religious than honest ones, simply because the former gain $r - t$ from falsely claiming belief, while the latter gain only $s - t$. This is because the payoff from cheating in the one-shot game is greater than the payoff from honesty. Thus, when true religious belief is strong in a society, hypocrisy will always attract the dishonest for whom "religiosity" comes easily. As a result, it is unsurprising that studies such as McCleary and Barro's find little positive correlation between variables such as religious attendance and economic and social behavior, and that questions based on actual beliefs do somewhat better as predictors of behavior.

Second, especially in a society where religious signaling costs are low, in a Nash equilibrium rates of dishonesty may be similar among people claiming to be religious as they are among the nonreligious. Seen in the current example, the ratio of $(B + E)/D$ may be uncomfortably close to A/C, making it appear that religion has no effect on people's behavior. Because claims of religiosity are often "cheap talk," it becomes impossible to separate the motives and behaviors of the different groups who will claim religion, making it difficult to measure the contribution of genuine religious belief to social capital. It is this dynamic, especially in "open" societies, that confounds the relationship between religious prevalence, trust, trustworthiness, and social capital: It is only when religious signaling costs are high due to state or social persecution that we should expect the correlation between the religious signal and moral behavior to be strong.

Lastly, many point to the pervasiveness of religious hypocrisy as evidence against the authenticity of religion. Yet as has been shown, the truth is precisely the opposite: Religious hypocrisy makes sense only in the presence of authentic belief. The very existence of religious hypocrisy is evidence that popular opinion associates religious belief with a greater propensity for trustworthy behavior. It indeed suggests that a critical mass of those who claim religious faith put their belief into practice. (No one hopes to induce trust by claiming to be a swindler, crank, or pirate.) Only genuine faith will attract hypocrisy. That hypocrisy perpetually resides in the shadow of faith is evidence *for* the existence of sincere of religious belief rather than against it. It is twenty-dollar bills that are counterfeited, not pennies.

Identity and Economic Development

Academic researchers in psychology, sociology, anthropology, and political science have long identified the need for *identity* as an important determinant of human behavior. Economists are now just catching up. Recent work by George Akerlof and Rachel Kranton (2000, 2002, 2005) has applied game-theoretic models to develop a clearer conceptual understanding of identity and its contribution to poverty traps and underdevelopment. Their work on identity has been able to explain an array of seemingly self-defeating behaviors that had been unexplainable by previous approaches.

Identity is formed by the set of personal or behavioral characteristics by which an individual is recognized as a member of a group. It also establishes an individual's sense of *self*. Because the survival of human beings is usually a corporate rather than an individual effort, most of us deeply desire to be accepted as a valuable contributor to a group. It is likely that the longing for identity stems from this basic desire.

In Akerlof and Kranton's model, identity is based on a set of social categories that exist in a particular context. Examples in an American high school might be nerd, jock, burnout, cowboy, grease monkey, or drama queen. Examples in a Latin American context might be *campesino*, *patrón*, rural *madré* of a big family, indigenous teenage male, wealthy Latino businessman, or urban Latina professional. To some extent, people may choose their social category, but their basic model takes a person's social category as given. A set of prescriptions indicates behavior appropriate for the different social categories in different situations. As in standard game theory models, people derive utility from their own actions and the actions of others, but they also derive utility from identity, which depends on (1) a person's assigned social category; (2) the extent to which one's personal characteristics match the prescription for that category (e.g., gender, age, ethnicity); as well as (3) how closely one's own actions and the actions of others in a peer group match the prescription.

Akerlof and Kranton demonstrate the conditions under which the quest for identity can perpetuate behaviors that promote prosperity or perpetuate poverty. The collective behavior of individual efforts to preserve identity comprises a key component of a group's social capital. For example, Brazil displays tremendous ethnic, economic, and social diversity. Consider the social category "Brazilian University Student." Perhaps from an upper-middle class well-educated family, the student is enrolled at *Universidade de Sao Pāulo*, arguably the top-ranked university in the developing world.[29] The prescription for behavior: outstanding academic achievement – a behavior reinforced within the student's social group, a by-product of which will tend to be prosperity. In this context, the student derives utility not only from the direct reward of good grades, but from the development of an identity that comes from filling the prescription for that particular social category. The actions of individuals also affect the identity of others, so that the identity of the upper-middle-class family in this example – where the prescription may be to have academically successful children – may be threatened by an underachieving child.

Now consider the social category of a teen-age orphan of indigenous or African blood living on the streets of Rio de Janeiro. The powerful film by Fernando Meirelles, *City of God*, depicts the heartbreak of Rio's slums. In the film, a young boy cutely nicknamed "Steak and Fries" tries to convince gang leaders of his worthiness for membership: "I smoke, I snort, I've killed, and I've robbed," he boasts convincingly. "I am a man." The prescription for behavior in the gangs of Rio, of course, contrasts with the previous example. Horrifically violent acts against rival gang members are rewarded by the group. Any "weaker" member of the group unwilling to fulfill this prescription threatens the identity of the other members, making part of the prescription for being an upstanding gang member to physically punish weaker members of the group. Academic excellence is not stressed.

Although both of these examples contain strong (and even rigid) prescriptions for behavior, identity in the first case fosters social capital and prosperity, while in the latter it degrades social capital and undermines the foundations of prosperity. Figure 11.4 presents Akerlof and Kranton's model, which yields insight into this dynamic.

There are two individuals who choose between two activities: Activity 1 and Activity 2. If a player chooses her preferred activity she receives a payoff of V; otherwise she gets a payoff of zero. Both players belong to one of two social categories, Red or Green; let's say that they are both Greens. Suppose that the behavioral prescription for a Green is Activity 1 and for a Red is Activity 2. If a Green were to engage in Activity 2 it would mean a loss of her Green identity equal to I_S, where the "s" stands for self. Moreover, if a player chooses an activity that is contrary to the prescription of the social category, it results in a loss of identity to the other player as well.[30] (For example, a marine wearing leotards while fighting in combat might threaten the "tough as nails" identity of a platoon.) In the present game, this constitutes a loss of identity to the other player of I_O, where "o" stands for other. This is important

---

[29] Other highly ranked universities in developing countries include Universdad Autonoma de Mexico, Bejing University, Universidad de Chile, Indian Institute of Science, University of Cape Town, and Seoul National University. (Source: Institute of Higher Education of the Shanghai Jiao Tong University and Rankings of World Universities, www.webometrics.info. Both rankings are based on quantity and quality of research publications.)

[30] Psychologists describe this loss of identity as occurring through anxiety over a loss of internalized rules or order; Akerlof and Kranton (2000), p. 728.

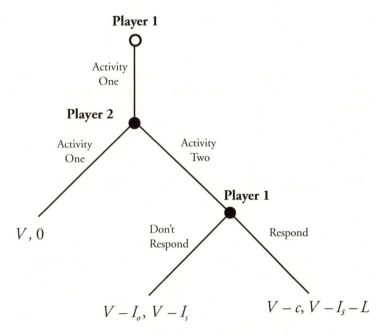

Player 1

Activity
One

Player 2

Activity
One

Activity
Two

Player 1

$V, 0$

Don't
Respond

Respond

$V - I_o, V - I_s$

$V - c, V - I_s - L$

Figure 11.4. Akerlof and Kranton's Identity Game

because a player's own tastes do not necessarily coincide with the prescription for her social category. The game in Figure 11.4 shows that Player 1 (illustrated by the first move) indeed prefers Activity 1, but Player 2, though also a Green, prefers Activity Two. If Player 2 chooses Activity 2, then Player 1 has the opportunity to respond. If Player 1 responds, she inflicts a loss on Player 1 equal to L, but can restore her own identity at a cost, c. An example might be a gang member striking another member who he feels is acting like a wimp, the act punishing the offending member while enhancing his own identity as a sadist.

Akerlof and Kranton identify four interesting Nash equilibria to the game that can be found by backward induction, based on different values of the parameters. In describing the equilibria, I will move away from the general form of the game, postulating Activity Two as one strongly linked to economic development such as "obtaining an education," while Activity 1 is a less favorable activity, *e.g.* "dropping out." The Nash equilibria are as follows:

(1) Player 2 deters Player 1 from education if $c < I_O$ and $V - I_S - L < 0$. This equilibrium occurs when the loss in identity to Player 1 from Player 2 "breaking the code" is high, and when both the loss in identity to Player 2 and the punishment inflicted by Player 1 are severe. This equilibrium characterizes a socially based development trap.

(2) Player 1 responds against Player 2, but does not deter her from obtaining education, when $c < I_O$ but $V - I_S - L > 0$. In this equilibrium, transition out

of the anti-development behavior is costly, but possible if Player 2's value of education is high.

(3) Player 2 chooses education and Player 1 does not respond. This is a Nash equilibrium when $c > I_O$ and $V - I_S > 0$, and represents the equilibrium in which transition to the positive educational behavior is easiest, although if $I_S > 0$, it remains costly.

(4) Player 2 "drops out" no matter what Player 1 would do in response to her education, a Nash equilibrium when $V < I_S$. Here, the loss in identity is so great from "breaking the code" that any threatened punishment from Player 1 is irrelevant. This scenario constitutes another socially based development trap.

The Akerlof and Kranton model is general and powerful, using key ideas in social and behavioral psychology to explain a wide array of behaviors that may appear to be dysfunctional, if not entirely self-defeating, to one outside a particular social category. The influence of identity in human behavior gives insight into numerous decisions that affect economic development and societal welfare: education, fertility decisions, choice of diet, consumer behavior, whether to take drugs, one's general propensity for risk taking, and a willingness to experiment with new ideas or technologies.

Because the prescription of an identity shapes behavior, and most decisions affecting economic development are at some level behavioral choices, traditional economic thinking underestimates the costs of undertaking many "pro-development" decisions if they could be accompanied by a loss in identity. For example, a large family may fulfill the prescription for a Central American *campesino*, although large families tend to perpetuate poverty. And if *campesino* culture prescribes participation in rural agricultural tasks (collecting wood, planting maize, etc.), then choosing schooling past the sixth grade may result in too great a sacrifice in the activities that shape the rural identity of teenagers and their households.

Identity plays a particularly strong role in educational choice in a variety of contexts. Harvard University's Roland Fryer has studied the perception of "acting White" in the African American community.[31] This work demonstrates how in the absence of peer effects, different individuals of different abilities will naturally choose different levels of education. But if achievement is low among peers and ethnicity based solidarity is important, the economic need for education conflicts with the social need for peer group acceptance. This conflict between social and economic motivations within individuals, Fryer argues, helps explain the ongoing puzzle of black underachievement in education. As a result, the anxiety faced by an African American who seeks to "break the code" by overachieving in school relative to his peers may be no less than the anxiety of an Asian American who fears "breaking the code" of high academic expectations by underachieving relative to his peers.

---

[31] See, for example, Fryer (2006) and Austen-Smith and Fryer (2005).

One lesson from Akerlof and Kranton's work is that to the extent that identity can be chosen, it is arguably the most important choice one makes. A young person may consider his family's economic status, his academic prowess, and his skin color in deciding whether to be a mediocre student or a proficient gang member. Based on his personal characteristics, he might, quite rationally, choose to be a proficient gang member. Once the identity decision is made, his optimal behavior is then governed by how to best fill the prescription for that role. Some of his subsequent behavior may appear totally irrational, even self-defeating and pathological, to someone fulfilling the prescription for a more favored social role.

In the past, social science tried to separate the economic and social motivations of human beings. Economists emphasized the freedom of choice of an individualistically optimizing "economic man." Sociologists, in contrast, studied a "social man," constrained by the directives of ethnicity, gender, and class. The two caricatures are equally misleading. Lawrence Blume remarks in *The Social Economics of Poverty*:

> *Homo economicus* and *homo sociologus* are the two straw men of social science. For *homo economicus*, each social act is a considered choice, an exercise in naked self-interest. For *homo sociologus*, there is no choice. Man is a boat without rudder, drifting at the mercy of the powerful tide of social forces. (2005, p. 106)

There is irony in the belief that embeddedness in social structure constrains human behavior, for it is the same embeddedness in social structure that, by restricting opportunism, often provides the freedom for exchange. These external controls imposed from a social network that check opportunism are no less important, however, than the internal controls established by moral and religious beliefs. And in the best scenario, social networks coupled with moral and religious beliefs foster identities that facilitate trust and trustworthiness. In light of this, it is paradoxical that the conditions fostering economic development are probably weakest when individuals act out of a purely autonomous self-interest. In truth, the evidence appears to show that when individuals develop an identity within a social network with a healthy moral and spiritual foundation, that the trust, trustworthiness, and other behavioral patterns conducive to economic development become most clearly manifest.

CHAPTER 12

The Political Economy of Trade and Development

The notion that globalization needs a human face . . . is wrong. Globalization has a human face, but we can make that face yet more agreeable.
– Jagdish Bhagwati (2004)

THE DOHA ROUND of world trade negotiations began in November 2001 in an atmosphere of heightened anticipation. The 148 members of the World Trade Organization began the round of talks (named after the capital of Qatar where the kickoff meeting was hosted) with an objective that was both lofty and noble: The Doha round was to incorporate the poorest countries of the world into a free and fair global trade system. The talks sought to rectify a long-identified bias against the poor countries in international trade – the forbidding shield of protection erected by the rich countries to defend domestic farmers against foreign agriculture. The sheer size of agricultural protection in the OECD[1] countries is staggering. Recently calculated at $279 billion, it equals 30 percent of total agricultural receipts, and six times the amount spent on foreign aid to the developing countries.[2]

Serious reductions in agricultural protection in the Doha round would have momentous implications for economic growth in the developing world. Indeed, as the Doha round began, the World Bank had estimated that better poor-country access to rich-country markets would increase world income by $520 billion, and would lift 144 million people out of poverty by 2015.[3]

Benefiting most directly by a Doha trade agreement would be the rural poor in the less-developed countries (LDCs). As the United States, the European Union, and Japan slashed tariffs, quotas, and export subsidies on agricultural products, it would create, finally, a level-playing field in world agricultural trade. It would be a world in which the small producer in Africa or Latin America could finally compete with the North American farmer riding atop his thirty-foot harvester, no longer benefiting from the added protection of Uncle Sam's thick wallet. But after almost two years of negotiations, it appeared that this was a world not to be.

---

[1] Organization of Economic Cooperation and Development, a group of thirty rich industrial nations.
[2] *The Economist*, June 21, 2005; April 11, 2003.
[3] Elizabeth Becker, "Poorer Countries Pull out of Talks over World Trade," *New York Times*, September 15, 2005, p. A1.

As the Doha talks dragged on, trade negotiators from the developing countries grew increasingly frustrated over the recalcitrance of the rich countries. The developing countries found the rich countries lacking the domestic political resolve needed to end the agricultural trade wars between themselves, in which the developing countries often wound up as the primary casualties. The developing countries' exasperation with the Doha round reached a boiling point at the now-infamous September 2003 meetings in Cancún, Mexico. During the Cancún talks, a group of twenty-one developing countries known as the G-21, headed by China, India, and Brazil, united in responding to what they viewed as hypocritical trade policy by the rich countries.

The G-21 directed much of its venom at the European Union's CAP or "Common Agricultural Policy." Much anger was aimed specifically at the intransigence of France, where farmers have a habit of turning the Parisian streets into vegetable salad at the very mention of EU tariff reductions on agricultural products. Japan and its pampered rice farmers, protected by an import-killing 490 percent rice tariff, also received much of the blame for the stalled talks. Not to be outdone by its major trading partners, the United States had recently passed the enormous 2002 Farm Bill, which allocated $248 billion of U.S. taxpayer money over ten years to subsidize and protect U.S. agricultural products such as barley, corn, cotton, rice, and wheat. The bill represented an 80 percent increase in agricultural spending over the Clinton administration's Freedom to Farm Act of 1996.[4] The G-21 repeatedly singled out one of the most egregious clauses in the Farm Bill, a $3 billion agricultural subsidy bestowed on 25,000 U.S. cotton farmers. This single item was believed to have caused world cotton prices to drop so substantially that it has rendered the cotton crops of extremely poor West African nations such as Guinea and Mali noncompetitive in world markets. The perspective of the developing countries was well summarized by the representative from Bangladesh: "We are told that this is a development round. We are yet to see concrete manifestation of the desire of the Membership to meaningfully help the LDCs."[5] Amazed at their unwillingness to seriously consider tariff reductions in agriculture, World Bank President James Wolfensohn labeled the dialogue of the rich countries in the Doha round as "the dialogue of the deaf."[6]

The G-21 began to collapse when American lawmakers such as U.S. Senator Charles Grassley, chairman of the Senate Finance Committee, insinuated that no country in the G-21 would be able to negotiate a bilateral trade deal with the United States.[7] Shortly after, Costa Rica, Guatemala, Peru, Colombia, and Ecuador, eager to implement the Central American Free Trade Agreement (CAFTA) and other accords with the United States, sheepishly withdrew from the G-21. Though some progress has since been made between the European Union and the United States in attempting to end their agricultural subsidy war, it appears unlikely that agricultural

---

[4] Mittal (2002).
[5] Fatoumata and Kwa (2004).
[6] *The Economist*, April 11, 2003.
[7] *The Economist*, October 18, 2003.

protectionism in the rich countries will end anytime soon. Protection is likely to continue in some form through the Doha round and beyond.

Is a world of unfettered free trade really worth all of this fuss? Most economists believe so, as the underlying arguments for trade are powerful, simple, and convincing. Indeed, they form the basis for economic exchange in general, not merely international trade. While trade negotiations are messy, trade theory is wonderfully elegant. And its fundamental insights are something on which the vast majority of economists are willing to bet the house. Moreover, trade theory predicts that the most substantial gains may be realized among trading countries that are most different from one another, such as developed and developing countries.

Why Trade?

The brilliant mathematician Stanislaw Ulam, famous for his work with Edward Teller on the hydrogen bomb, once challenged economist Paul Samuelson: "Name me one proposition in all of the social sciences which is both true and non-trivial." Samuelson responded to Ulam by explaining David Ricardo's theory of comparative advantage: "That it is logically true need not be argued before a mathematician; that it is not trivial is attested by the thousands of important and intelligent men who have never been able to grasp the doctrine for themselves or to believe it even after it was explained to them."[8]

As a backdrop for exploring the political economy of international trade between developed and developing nations, it is worth reviewing Ricardo's luminous insight. Suppose that the number of labor hours required to produce an automobile in one country (call this country North) is ℓ_{NA}, and in another country (South) it is ℓ_{SA}, and the number of labor hours required to produce a bushel of beans in North is ℓ_{NB} and in South, ℓ_{SB}. Here the opportunity cost of automobile production (in terms of beans) in each country is given by ℓ_{NA}/ℓ_{NB} and ℓ_{SA}/ℓ_{SB}, respectively. Without trade, these opportunity costs represent the true "prices" of automobiles in each country, while the inverse of these fractions represents the nontrade price of beans. Suppose that $\ell_{NA}/\ell_{NB} > \ell_{SA}/\ell_{SB}$, or that the nontrade price of automobiles is higher in North than South. In that case, North can gain from trade by specializing in beans and South by specializing in automobiles, trading with one another at a price ratio for automobiles and beans, p_A/p_B, that lies between the internal nontrade prices in the respective countries. Notice that before trade, North was forced to give up ℓ_{NA}/ℓ_{NB} bushels of beans in order to "purchase" one automobile; after trade, a single automobile costs only p_A/p_B. Similarly, before trade South was able to obtain only ℓ_{SA}/ℓ_{SB} bushels of beans for a single automobile; after trade, South is able to obtain p_A/p_B bushels of beans. Both countries win. Furthermore, the result holds even when the labor requirements of one country are higher, even multiple times higher, for *both* goods than in the other country. As Ricardo himself pointed out,

[8] Samuelson (1969).

this insight is particularly helpful for thinking about trade between developed and developing countries, where opportunity costs differ most substantially.

But how can any economically developed country participate in a world of free trade with the rock-bottom wages given to workers in many developing countries? To address this important question clearly, we can extend Ricardo's basic model to incorporate wages and exchange rates by including three additional relationships into the model. The first is that the inverse of a labor-hours requirement is simply the marginal product of labor, or $mp_\ell = 1/\ell$. The second is that, in labor market equilibrium, the wage paid to a worker in any industry is equal to the value of the marginal product of that worker, that is, the price of a good multiplied by what a worker adds to the total production in one hour, $w = p \cdot mp_\ell$. Finally, we can compare prices between one country and another by converting the prices in North to the currency of South through an exchange rate, such that $e \cdot p_N = p_S$. By substituting $1/mp_\ell$ for the labor requirement ℓ for beans in each country in Ricardo's basic model, and multiplying each side by the price of automobiles (adjusted for the exchange rate) we see that, for example, North will export beans to South if the opportunity cost of producing beans in North is lower, or $\ell_{NB} \cdot w_N \cdot e < \ell_{SB} \cdot w_S$.[9] This is often called the Monetized Ricardian model, the basis of a well-known framework for understanding trade developed by Rudiger Dornbusch, Stanley Fischer, and Samuelson at MIT.[10]

Some have come to describe global trade as a "Race to the Bottom," where countries with the lowest wages win all the exports. But what the Monetized Ricardian model implies is that the exports of a country are determined by a confluence of factors: labor productivity across different industries, domestic wages, and the strength of a country's currency. Even though developing countries generally have lower wages, developed countries will be exporters in industries where worker productivity outweighs the disadvantage of higher wages. It is impossible for, say, South to export everything; if it did, North's currency would depreciate (e would fall), allowing more of North's goods to satisfy the export condition. As the number of goods North exports begins to grow, it will put upward pressure on e, which then begins to choke off North's exports, bringing trade back into balance.[11]

Research by Stephen Golub of Swarthmore College and others has illustrated the strong correlation between wages and worker productivity across countries, such that a higher average wage in a country nearly always implies higher average productivity, and vice versa.[12] This makes sense, because wages in a given country are directly tied to the marginal productivity of labor. The higher wages in the industrialized countries stem from the greater accumulation of capital, education, and technology in these economies. Although higher wages imply greater worker

[9] Appleyard, Field, and Cobb (2006).

[10] Dornbusch, Fischer, and Samuelson (1977).

[11] Of course under a fixed exchange-rate regime, a positive trade balance will lead to the accumulation of foreign reserves, unless it is counterbalanced by a corresponding deficit in the exchange of assets between countries. This analysis assumes a balance in the "capital account," the trade in *assets* as opposed to goods and services. Growing foreign reserves, nevertheless, will also lead to pressure for a revaluation (strengthening) of the domestic currency.

[12] Golub (1998).

productivity, which boosts exports, they also imply higher production costs, which reduce exports. The playing field of world trade levels itself more naturally than most people think.

Diminishing Terms of Trade for Developing Countries

What is clear from Ricardo's basic theory is that two nations will simultaneously benefit from trade when the terms of trade, the prices at which goods are exchanged, lies between their respective opportunity costs of producing the two goods. Yet the closer these terms of trade lie to a country's own internal opportunity costs of production, the less a country benefits from trade. Thus it is possible that a country may continue to trade while facing terms of trade, determined in world markets, that leave it only marginally better off than it would be under autarky, while trade partners benefit substantially.

Historically, the exports of many developing countries followed the pattern of comparative advantage established during the era of colonization, producing and exporting basic commodities such as fruits, tea, coffee, sugar, rubber, and minerals. In many countries, exports of a single commodity often comprised an enormous percentage of annual export earnings, for example in Ghana (cocoa 50–60 percent), Venezuela (petroleum 90–95 percent), Bolivia (tin 45–55 percent), and the Ivory Coast (coffee 40–60 percent).[13] Developing countries exported such commodities in world markets in exchange for manufactured goods produced in the industrialized countries.

But by the middle of the twentieth century, developing countries became increasingly concerned that the terms of trade were turning against them. The catalyst for this growing commodity export pessimism was influential papers by Raul Prebisch and Hans Singer, which attempted to demonstrate empirically declining terms of trade for LDCs, and to explain the causes for this decline.[14] They viewed the main causes to be (a) increasing world income, which increased the demand for manufactured goods relatively more than the demand for food commodities, and (b) the introduction of synthetic substitutes for nonfood commodities such as rubber and tin.[15]

Meanwhile, the Green Revolution of the 1960s had brought about higher agricultural output in developing countries by introducing new high-yield-variety strains, fertilizers, and intensive cultivation techniques to the LDCs. Many developing nations eagerly adopted the new agro-technologies in hopes of meeting domestic consumption needs as well as boosting commodity exports. But in some respects the Green Revolution actually worked against commodity-exporting LDCs: Higher worldwide agricultural output led to lower commodity prices, further deteriorating

[13] LeClair (2000).

[14] See Prebisch (1950) and Singer (1950). The empirical research has been criticized by some such as Robert Baldwin (1955) and others who argue that declining transportation costs could have accounted for apparently declining terms of trade from the perspective of the LDCs.

[15] Singer (1987).

terms of trade against the developing countries, a phenomenon labeled by Jagdish Bhagwati as "immiserizing growth."[16] In the end, the agricultural technologies introduced in the LDCs by the industrialized nations may have principally benefited the industrialized nations.

Especially by the 1960s, calls began to arise in the developing world to reverse the downward trend in commodity terms-of-trade and its associated economic malaise. In 1964, a group of seventy-seven developing countries established the United Nations Conference on Trade and Development (UNCTAD). By 1974, UNCTAD had led the General Assembly of the United Nations to declare a "New Economic Order." Part of this New Economic Order would include a concentrated effort by the commodity-exporting LDCs to shift terms-of-trade toward developing countries through the creation of cartels for a number of basic commodities including rubber, sugar, cocoa, and coffee.

There was good reason to believe such a strategy might work. Only recently before, the Organization of Petroleum Exporting Countries (OPEC) had succeeded in quadrupling the price of oil from about $3/barrel in 1972 to about $12/barrel in 1974, creating a class of high-income Arab countries virtually overnight. This was the first time that a group of low-income countries had effectively stared down the industrialized world, dramatically shifting the terms of trade in its favor. Gasoline prices skyrocketed in the United States and Western Europe, and OPEC had become an inspiration. The commodity-cartel strategy glittered with promise.

The cartel strategy seemed appealing because commodities such as coffee are similar in important respects to gasoline (my own home brew, in particular). More generally, however, for caffeine addicts and gas-guzzling automobiles alike, there are no good substitutes for the real thing, whether it be a hot cup of java or petroleum-based fuel. The lack of substitutes for such commodities renders their consumers vulnerable to cartel-type behavior.[17]

But the problem with cartels is that the more successful they are at jacking up prices (and profits to their members), the more apt they are to implode. The reason is that cartels function by encouraging members to abide by quotas that restrict output on world markets, causing a commodity price to skyrocket if demand is sufficiently inelastic. (Demand is liable to be inelastic if there are few available substitutes for the commodity, as in the case of coffee or gasoline.) This allows cutbacks in production to exhibit their maximum leverage on prices. But the problem is that when prices are higher, it creates an added incentive for a single producer to cheat by producing more than it is supposed to.

The following example illustrates this dilemma. As the market for oil is dominated by a handful of large oil-producing countries, the world market for coffee is

---

[16] Bhagwati (1958).

[17] Debora Spar (1994) lists four other important structural factors that favor cartelization of commodities include (1) concentration of production (few producers), (2) high barriers to entry in the market, (3) only a small number of fringe producers who could bypass the cartel, and (4) nondifferentiation in the commodity, so that producers will not engage in nonprice competition while simultaneously trying to maintain above-market prices.

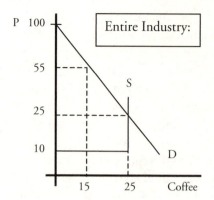

Figure 12.1a. Supply and Demand for Coffee, Industry

dominated by a handful of large *processors*. This group of large multinational companies includes Kraft, Nestlé, Procter & Gamble, Sara Lee, and a European firm, Tchibo.[18] Let's construct an example in which the world price of processed coffee is equal to US$100 per sack minus three dollars for every million sacks processed and released on the world market, or $P = 100 - 3S$. Suppose that there are ten coffee processors, each with constant average costs of $10/sack with a capacity of processing up to 2.5 million sacks. With each firm processing and marketing at full capacity, the world price of coffee would then be equal to $P = 100 - 3(10 \cdot 2.5) = \$25$/sack.

This would leave each processor with $37.5 million in net revenues. But could the processors do better? Yes, because fortunately for people marketing coffee, a large number of the world's coffee drinkers are willing to pay whatever it takes to get their coffee fix. Imagine that each of these ten coffee processors agreed to form a cartel by cutting the amount of coffee on the market by a million sacks to only 1.5 million each. Reducing the world coffee supply to 15 million sacks would cause coffee prices to zoom from $25/sack to $55/sack. The cartel action would increase total net revenues from $375 million to $675 million, as seen in Figure 12.1a, and to each of the ten coffee processors from $37.5 million to $67.5 million.

Unfortunately for the cartel, the higher cartel price of $55/sack creates a strong incentive for each member to cheat. Although Figure 12.1a shows the total coffee industry demand, Figure 12.1b shows the *individual* demand faced by each processor if the others happen to abide by the quota. Again, it shows net revenues to any individual firm abiding by the quota to be ($45 × 1.5 million) = $67.5 million. But even this looks diminutive in comparison to the $105 million windfall that can be obtained through cheating by increasing one's own output to capacity, since the world price falls only by $3/sack when just a single processor cheats ($42 × 2.5 million = $105 million). Since each individual firm faces the same incentives, the whole scheme is likely to unravel, bringing the world coffee supply back to

---

[18] Oxfam (2002).

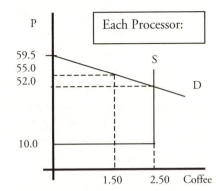

Figure 12.1b. Supply and Demand for Coffee, Processor

25 million sacks. The incentive structure behind cartels contains all the pitfalls of the classic Prisoners' Dilemma.

As a result, cartels are effective only if they can establish discipline within their organization, that is, catch and punish cheaters. Because cheating causes the world price to fall, knowing that *someone* is cheating is easy. Identifying the culprit is usually more difficult. To identify cheaters, cartel members must acquiesce to some level of monitoring. Moreover, once a cheater has been identified, punishments must be clear and certain. In the context of a repeated game, this would ostensibly involve other members retaliating by flooding the market with the commodity in question. But such threats hurt not just the cheating member but *all* members, and thus it may be more convenient to avoid actually carrying out such punishments, making them less than credible. Cartels are inherently unstable.

In practice, the most effective commodity cartels maintain discipline through an "enforcer," a big and powerful member who assumes the responsibility and costs of punishing cheaters. Typically, the "enforcer" role is assumed by the player who has the most to lose if the cartel falls apart. There is some evidence, for example, that Saudi Arabia plays such a role in OPEC. Empirical studies present evidence that Saudi Arabia has periodically engaged in tit-for-tat retaliation with other members of the oil cartel if cheating exceeds a given threshold.[19] This was particularly evident during the mid-1980s when high oil prices in the 1970s had encouraged new oil exploration, and cheating in the cartel became particularly egregious. Rejoicing in their gushers, the new oil-rich countries flooded the world market with oil. The resulting oil glut, of course, caused world prices to plummet. In response, the data seems to indicate that during 1983–86 Saudi Arabia actually carried out threats to temporarily exceed their own normal production levels in order to punish other OPEC members for refusing to cap some of their wells.

Like Saudi Arabia in the world of oil, DeBeers, leader of the diamond cartel, has been remarkably successful on a number of fronts. On the demand side, it has so effectively convinced prospective grooms-to-be that "diamonds are forever,"

---

[19] See Yang (2004) and Griffin and Nielsen (1994).

that most now shudder at risking a proposal with a diamond-less engagement ring. Meanwhile, on the supply side, DeBeers has become the definitive example of a ruthless cartel "enforcer." The cartel operates through the Diamond Trading Company (formerly called the Central Selling Organization), through which DeBeers purchases stones from the cartel's members and resells them on the world market.[20] Few in the diamond market have risked approaching other potential buyers. One brave exception was President Mobutu of Zaire, who in 1981 proclaimed brashly that his country would begin to sell its industrial-grade diamonds outside DeBeers to Belgian and British diamond brokers. As economist Debora Spar relates:

> Just two months after Zaire's diamonds entered the market independently, about one million carats of industrial diamonds from undisclosed sources suddenly flooded the market, causing the price of Zairian diamonds to drop from $3 per carat to less than $1.80 . . . (DeBeers) was accepting this financial burden to punish a supplier whose production had accounted for only about 3% of its total receipts. For DeBeers, though, stable long-term profits were more important than short-term losses, and the principle of unity had to be maintained. The cartel would be preserved, and defectors would be punished. (1994, pp. 62, 63)

To relate the cartel enforcer idea to our present example, suppose that there are only seven coffee processors, one considerably bigger than the other six (call it Big Coffee). Big Coffee differs from the smaller processors in two respects: First, it is bigger, with the capacity to place 12 million sacks on the market in any season. Moreover, like many cartel leaders it holds much of its marketable commodity in reserves. Suppose that half of Big Coffee's 12 million sack capacity is harbored as Everest-sized mountains of beans in its warehouses. As the cartel leader, suppose that Big Coffee allocates the same annual quota to each smaller member of 1.5 million sacks, with 6 million sacks per year for itself. By the Folk Theorem, a myriad of Nash equilibrium threats, strategies, and outcomes can occur in the repeated game, and the following is but one interesting possibility.

Suppose that the small processors agree to abide by their quota as long as Big Coffee keeps its reserves in its warehouse; if it puts its reserves on the market without cause, the cartel agreement is over and each processes at capacity. Big Coffee, meanwhile, conveys to the other members that if even one small member were to cheat and cause the world price to dip below $55/sack, it will immediately dump its reserves onto the world market for a season. In this way, Big Coffee removes the incentive for a small firm to cheat. Monitoring in the scheme is relatively easy: Big Coffee monitors the world price; the small processors keep an eye on Big Coffee's warehouse.

Notice that, absent a rare degree of myopia, Big Coffee itself has little incentive to cheat on the scheme. Its optimal cheating strategy would be to place 10.5 million sacks on the market if the small processors abide by their quota of 9 million sacks; this would increase its net revenues from $270 million to $330.75 for one season. (Placing any more than 10.5 million sacks would lower the world price to

---

[20] An excellent history of the DeBeers cartel is given in Spar (2006).

such an extent that Big Coffee's own profits would fall.) With cartel breakdown, however, the small members of the cartel would process at their collective 15-million-sack capacity. Big Coffee's optimal response would be to place only 9 million sacks on the market, in which case the world price falls to $28, yielding it only ($18 × 9 million =) $162 million in net revenues thereafter. Little enforcement is required for the enforcer, since the enforcer has little to gain from cheating and much to lose. With the Grim Trigger strategy, Big Coffee will stick to its quota of 6 million sacks if $330.75 + \delta 162/(1 - \delta) < 270/(1-\delta)$, or $\delta > 0.355$. This kind of behavior is consistent with what we observe in commodity cartel leaders; because they have so much at stake in keeping prices high, it is more often the smaller suppliers that are the cause of cartel instability. Experience has shown that when cartels lack a central enforcer like a Saudi Arabia or DeBeers, they tend to have little success in boosting prices.

This, ironically, has been the case for the most part when coffee *growers* have tried to engage in cartel behavior, principally through the International Coffee Organization (ICO). Despite a series of agreements since its foundation in 1962, the cartel has had only sporadic success in elevating coffee prices at the grower level. For the most part, except for some successes at raising prices in the 1970s, the ICO's foremost achievement has been to reduce price volatility to its growers in member countries (LeClair 2000). The main reasons for the inability of coffee producers to exhibit strong cartel behavior on raising prices at the grower level are the large number of disparate producers with different incentives, and the inability of a cartel to control the entry of new producers, such as Vietnam, now the number two coffee producer in the world.

As a result, prices at the grower level have continued to plummet. Nevertheless, multinational processors have maintained high margins in the face of declining world coffee prices, largely through their ability to dominate the value-added supply chains that bring coffee to the consumer and new technology that has allowed them to remove the bitter flavor and aroma of lower-quality Robusta beans (grown largely in Vietnam) and substitute them for the more traditional and aromatic Arabica beans. The result has been increasing poverty among coffee growers of Arabica beans in Latin America and Africa, and increasing profits among the large coffee processors. A 2002 Oxfam study found the following:

> At the beginning of 2002, a Ugandan farmer received 14 cents (US) for 1 kg of beans. The local middleman who transported it to the mill took 5 cents profit as did the miller, and the cost of transport to Kampala added a further 2 cents, making the cost of the coffee when it arrived at the exporter's warehouse 26 cents. The exporter, operating on a tiny margin, added 19 cents to the kilo, taking the total value of a kilo up to 45 cents. Freight, and the importer's cost and margins took the price to $1.64 by the time it reached the factory of one of the giant roasting companies. But by the time the same kilo was sold in the shops in the form of instant coffee it was worth $26.40, 7,000% more than the farmer got for it.[21]

---

[21] Data from Oxfam (2002). Text cited in "What Do Ecuadorean Bananas, Ugandan Coffee and English Apples, Have in Common? No Power," *UK Guardian*, May 17, 2003.

Tariffs and Quotas

The first section highlighted the immense amount of resources, $279 billion, devoted to protecting domestic producers of agricultural products in the OECD countries. The irony of such a figure is magnified in light of even the most fundamental economic models, which show that social welfare increases in both import and export markets with free trade. Figure 12.2a portrays a potential import market, in which the world price is lower than a country's domestic price. In contrast, Figure 12.2b shows a potential export market in which the world price is higher than a country's domestic price. If the economy moves to free trade in which commodities are exchanged at world prices instead of domestic prices, total social welfare (consisting of consumer surplus and producer surplus) increases in both import and export markets.

In the import market in Figure 12.2a we see that producer surplus, the difference between the price producers receive and the minimum price they would accept (reflected by the supply curve) shrinks from **C + B** to **C**. However, consumer surplus, the difference between the willingness to pay (reflected by the demand curve) and the market price, increases by the areas **B + D**. Cheaper imports, given by $Q_D - Q_S$, increase consumption from the original domestic equilibrium, but reduce both prices and domestic production. As a result, total social welfare increases by **D**. In

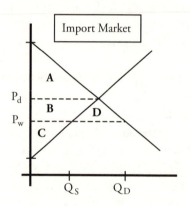

Figure 12.2a. Supply and Demand, Import Market

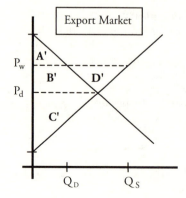

Figure 12.2b. Supply and Demand, Export Market

the export market of Figure 12.2b, prices rise as production increases to fuel exports, $Q_S - Q_D$, but the producer surplus increase of $\mathbf{B'} + \mathbf{D'}$, outweighs the loss in consumer surplus equal to $\mathbf{B'}$.

All of this raises the following question: If we believe that society is better off as a whole without trade protection, then why, perhaps especially in democracies, is there so much protectionism? What we will see is that although a strong case can be made against protectionism from an economic point of view, trade protectionism is primarily a political animal, and that instruments of trade protectionism, such as tariffs and quotas, often have their origins in the democratic political apparatus. In the end, trade policy is made not by economic theorists, but by politicians.

So what process shapes the political views of politicians, and thus a country's trade policy? The following example is inspired by Wolfgang Mayer's (1984) seminal paper on the political economy of international trade.[22] Consider a political campaign where, locked in hand-to-hand combat for a senatorial seat, are the incumbent, Paddington Porkmire, and his challenger, Soloman Swineheart. The central campaign issue is the import tariff on textiles.

The preferred textile tariff of the voters spans the political spectrum uniformly between zero and 50 percent.[23] On one end of the spectrum are voters whose relationship to the textile industry is such that they are likely to be hurt by free trade. This would include, of course, textile workers, many of whom would lose their jobs under free trade; they favor a job-saving 50 percent tariff. On the opposite end of the spectrum are consumers who enjoy wearing cheap T-shirts; they favor no tariff at all. Lying in between are people who feel the negative effects of the tariff only indirectly: a cheap-T-shirt-wearing voter with an aunt who is a textile worker, or the owner of the local mini-mart in a textile town. Figure 12.3a portrays the spectrum of voters ordered by their preferred tariff.

Swineheart, a (more or less) ideological free-trader by nature, begins the campaign by advocating a low 8 percent tariff. Porkmire plays to his base, staking out a position heavily in favor of local textile producers, and is quoted as supporting a 40 percent tariff. The two political positions are seen in Figure 12.3a.

Upon consultation with his political advisor, Swineheart begins to re-consider his position. By taking a stand for a higher tariff, Swineheart can capture all of the voters he had before, plus those that favor a higher tariff. Shortly thereafter, he is heard in speeches advocating a 35 percent tariff, and in the polls garners the votes of a whopping 75 percent of the voters (37.5/50), as shown in Figure 12.3b.

The experienced career politician Senator Porkmire, understanding that two can play at the tariff game, immediately responds by insisting that he was previously misquoted by reporters. He goes on record as supporting a 30 percent tariff, and basks in the glow of a dramatic pendulum swing in the polls, returning to his favor.

---

[22] Mayer (1984).

[23] Using the well-known Hecksher-Ohlin framework, Mayer demonstrates that each voter in his model has an optimal tariff rate that is influenced by his relationship to the factors used in production of tradable goods.

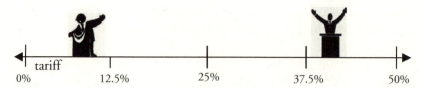

Figure 12.3a. Tariff Game, Stage 1

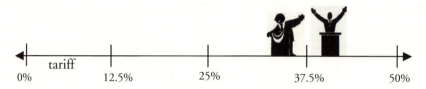

Figure 12.3b. Tariff Game, Stage 2

Figure 12.3c. Tariff Game, Stage 3

Figure 12.3d. Political Equilibrium in Tariff Game

They show his position on the textile tariff now to be closest to the views of 65 percent (32.5/50) of all voters as seen in Figure 12.3c.

What is the result of all this political maneuvering? Clearly, each candidate has an incentive to leapfrog over the other's position until the Nash equilibrium has been reached that is portrayed in Figure 12.3d, in which each candidate takes the middle ground of the 25 percent tariff.

Suppose that in a deadlocked contest, the political tiebreaker becomes which candidate's toupee appears more "natural" on television. Swineheart thus emerges victoriously, and carries to the Senate a platform for a 25 percent textile tariff. In like fashion, each of the 100 victorious U.S. senators brings a preferred tariff to office derived from the preference of the median voter in his or her state.

In the final establishment of tariff policy, the game has a second level. Rank each of the 100 senators in order of their preferred tariff from lowest to highest. As various proposals are considered for textile tariffs, each proposal will compete for the senator's vote with the median tariff preference. As it happens, we find that Senator no. 51 is Wyoming's Senator Harry Hogsnout, who comes from a small state, but suddenly is a man with profound powers. For a trade agreement to pass, it must capture the vote of Hogsnout. Being the senator with the median tariff preference itself made up of median tariff preferences, it is extremely unlikely that Senator Harry Hogsnout's preferred tariff is zero.

This game of political maneuvering is a variant of Harold Hotelling's famous location game.[24] In the commercial version of Hotelling's game, two stores competing with one another over proximity to consumers end up locating adjacently in a city-center Nash equilibrium. In the political version of the game, the Nash equilibrium is characterized by politicians catering to the wishes of the median voter on political issues.

As a result, the social welfare-maximizing zero-percent tariff (free trade) is rarely the political Nash equilibrium. Though economic theory gives us good reason to believe that society as a whole will benefit from free trade, it also tells us that there are clear winners and losers within the process.[25] Though according to theory the winners from trade should be more than able to compensate the losers through monetary compensation or worker retraining, compensation to the losers is never perfect. Given that the political system insufficiently compensates the losers enough to attract their votes for free trade, the resulting political Nash equilibrium is likely to involve some level of protectionism, since winners and losers are equally allotted one vote.

There are other important factors that help us understand why the import-competing sector receives additional political weight in the creation of trade policy. A highly influential paper by 2002 Nobel Prize–winner Daniel Kahneman and Amos Tversky (1979) demonstrates, in a challenge to neoclassical consumer theory, that people place a greater weight on economic losses than they do on gains of equal magnitude around a reference point, such that most of us are characterized by some degree of "loss aversion." In other words, people appear to become more upset if something is taken away from them than they become happy if that same thing is given to them.

The "loss aversion" phenomenon is confirmed by some creative experimental studies. Kahneman, Knetsch, and Thaler (1990), for example, randomly handed out souvenir Cornell University coffee mugs that sold for $6 at the bookstore to half the subjects in a large room; the lucky recipients were allowed to keep their mugs or sell them to those who weren't given one. What they found was that the median

---

[24] Hotelling (1929).
[25] The seminal paper illustrating this point is Stolper and Samuelson (1941).

asking prices among those who had been given a mug were *more than twice* the median offering prices of the (mug-less) mug buyers. As a result, the volume of trade in mugs was only one-fifth as large as what would be predicted in the absence of loss aversion. The "loss aversion" phenomenon has important implications for international trade. If jobs lost via trade receive a disproportional weight in people's minds than jobs gained via trade, it will lead to a systematic political bias against the implementation of free-trade agreements.

Returning to the political process, we can uncover a further source of antitrade bias. Senators are not only influenced by the popular opinion of their constituents, but also by political lobbying. Suppose the fixed cost of political organization and lobbying by any individual affected by trade is equal to c. In most industries, the number of consumers of a product, let's call this number n, far exceeds the number of producers, m. This may seem like good news for tariff-free imports. But despite the overall welfare increases from international trade, the *gain* is markedly less concentrated than the *pain*. Since the benefits of free trade to consumers ($\mathbf{B} + \mathbf{D}$ in Figure 12.2a) are spread over such a large number of individuals, n, it will not be worth the effort for the average consumer to lobby for lower tariffs if $c > (\mathbf{B} + \mathbf{D})/n$. Although the loss to producers is only equal to $\mathbf{B}$, the loss is felt more sharply because it is concentrated among fewer individuals, making it more likely that $c < \mathbf{B}/m$, where lobbying by producers is worthwhile. This explains why relatively concentrated groups of producers such as in sugar and cotton wield a disproportionate influence on U.S. trade policy, and why protection in these industries continues to remain astonishingly high to the detriment of consumers. Concentrated pain is simply more noticeable, and it is usually the squeaky wheel that gets the political grease. A political campaign may be run on a platform of saving textile jobs (e.g., John Edwards's presidential bid of 2004), but no politician will run on a platform of reducing the price of T–shirts by a dollar.

Trade economist Robert Baldwin of the University of Wisconsin (1989) clarifies this general idea, noting that from the perspective of consumers, free trade is like a public good: Its benefits (in the form of lower prices) are both nonexcludable and nonrival. Consequently, the decision for consumers to contribute to a campaign favoring free trade has the structure of a Prisoners' Dilemma: Each consumer would benefit if import protection were eliminated, but would like to free-ride on the efforts of others to achieve such results.

Free-Trade Agreements

Suppose a U.S. President wants to negotiate a free-trade agreement with one or more developing countries, like the CAFTA reached in 2005 between the United States and the Central American nations plus the Dominican Republic. Even if a President's preference were to maximize social welfare by implementing a trade agreement with tariffs as low as possible, such tariffs are subject to the political constraint that the agreement must pass a representative Senate.

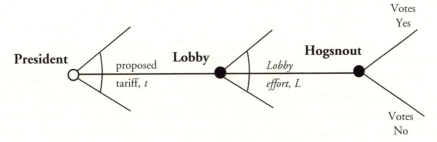

Figure 12.4. Political Effects of Lobbying

Let us assume that the total number of votes cast against the trade agreement is an increasing function of the resources used in lobbying against it, or $V(L)$. After incurring fixed costs of organization equal to mc, textile producers are willing to spend up to $(\mathbf{B} - mc)$ in political contributions to defeat the agreement. The most efficient lobbying tactic is to employ a kind of "triage" strategy: Senators on the high end of the preferred tariff spectrum, such as those from heavy textile producing states, need no further encouragement to vote against the trade agreement. Senators with a very low preferred tariff are too expensive to convince. The textile producer lobby thus begins by targeting a middle group, starting with the senator with the *highest* preferred textile tariff who initially would *favor* the agreement, then continuing down the spectrum until (it hopes) fifty-one senators are opposed to the trade agreement ratification.

If $V(\mathbf{B} - mc) \geq 51$, then the President knows that a zero-tariff agreement will not fly in the Senate, and so he must seek a compromise in his first-stage negotiations.[26] Using backward induction, our economic-welfare-maximizing President will negotiate a trade agreement in an import-competing area, such as textiles, only if he knows that the agreement will be able to satisfy our median Senator Hogsnout, as seen in Figure 12.4.

The President can do this by negotiating some positive level of U.S. textile tariff that reduces the domestic price after the agreement merely to $P_w + t$, higher than the free-trade world price of P_w. This reduces the height of area $\mathbf{B}$ in Figure 12.2a from $P_d - P_w$ to $P_d - P_w - t$, and reduces its area and hence the total amount of resources textile producers are willing to spend in a lobbying effort against the agreement. Using backward induction, see that the optimal tariff level t^* chosen by the President in the first play of the game in Figure 12.4 forms a Nash equilibrium that shrinks the producer loss $\mathbf{B}$ to the point that $V(\mathbf{B} - mc) = 49$.

---

[26] Why wouldn't producers in the export market offer a competing lobby to counteract that of producers in the import sector? One reason, perhaps, is that expansion in the export sector would incorporate resources that are not fully identified. For example, there is likely to be uncertainty over which workers will be hired in as yet unbuilt manufacturing plants, or which workers will be hired to build the plants themselves. Such uncertainty reduces incentives for positive lobbying. In contrast, import competition directly impacts an identifiable group of existing producers.

The equilibrium in the game can help us understand why even a social-welfare maximizing, tariff-minimizing President may have an incentive to bring a watered-down agreement before the Senate if it must be ratified by a majority vote. For example, to gain passage of CAFTA, trade negotiators made major concessions to the textile industry, maintaining nearly all of the 1983 Caribbean Basin Trade Partnership Act that requires U.S. textile imports to be produced from U.S. fabrics and yarn. Completely scrapping these requirements would have added another $9–$14 billion per year to U.S. consumer surplus.[27] In addition, though the U.S. sugar lobby did concede to 107,000 new tons of Central American sugar imports, the figure represented only 1.7 percent of total U.S. consumption and maintained a 100 percent U.S. tariff on sugar.[28] Although U.S. consumers ingest sugar at one of the highest rates in the world, the U.S. sugar-producer lobby is concentrated and powerful; after the agreement the United States will still pay more than twice the world price for sugar.

In light of the game in Figure 12.4, it is interesting that trade agreements so often barely slip by the ratification process. Once a Nash equilibrium tariff has been negotiated that can pass the Senate, the lobby no longer has an incentive to waste its resources trying to defeat it. If a trade agreement will be watered down sufficiently to gain a majority in the Senate, why bother to lobby against it?

The truth is that in tallying the final votes in Congress, even victorious trade deals often prove to be squeakers. In July 2005, for example, CAFTA was passed in the Senate by a vote of 54 to 45, and by the slimmest possible majority in the U.S. House of Representatives, on a vote of 217 to 215. One reason for this could be that many senators have already committed themselves to a "no" vote based on prior lobbying. Second, it could represent a (lost) gamble or a miscalculation by the producer-lobbyers, believing that they had swayed more lawmakers than was actually true. Third, it may be that politicians must commit themselves to interest groups in order to receive the necessary support for re-election; a "flip-flop" on an issue may not wear well with key constituents.

The World Trade Organization

When the Uruguay round of the GATT (General Agreement on Tariffs and Trade) concluded in 1994, it had reached substantive agreements on a number of issues: It achieved a more than one-third reduction in worldwide tariffs, made some progress in lowering agricultural subsidies in the developed countries, and wove the Multifiber Agreement (which had consisted largely of quotas) into an economically preferable tariff system. Remarkably, Japan and South Korea even promised to lower some barriers to rice imports. But the most enduring legacy of the Uruguay round was the metamorphosis of the GATT itself into the World Trade Organization (WTO), on January 1, 1995.

---

[27] Rotsko and Powell (2005).
[28] Ibid.

The WTO is a global institution that helps create, implement, and enforce trade agreements among its members.[29] Five guiding principles define its mission: (1) countries should engage in trade without *discrimination* either between their trade partners or between domestic and foreign-produced products; (2) *freer* trade is ultimately better for the world than restricted trade; (3) trade should be *predictable* and not subject to arbitrary barriers; (4) for the benefit of consumers, trade should operate in line with principles that foster *economic competition*; and (5) the priorities of *developing countries* allow them some special privileges in the formation of rules governing international trade. In shaping these principles into policy, the WTO operates through the consensus of its 148 members. Unlike other global institutions such as the United Nations and the World Bank, no major decisions are made without the collective agreement of all of the member countries. As a result, the WTO effectively operates with one gas pedal and 148 brakes. Considering its institutional design, it is impressive that WTO members have reached agreements on such a wide array of issues.

Another salient feature of the WTO is its dispute settlement mechanism. Under the old GATT system, rulings against a country could be implemented by consensus only, which theoretically made it possible for even the offending country to veto a ruling against it. Now within the WTO, dispute rulings can only be *blocked* by consensus, giving them much more force and making them harder to overturn.[30] Moreover, the entire dispute process is quicker, designed to take less than a year. Any WTO member country can take its trade grievance with another member country before a panel of experts appointed by the Dispute Settlement Body. After reviewing the issues involved in the dispute, the panel submits a ruling that recommends what actions, if any, should be taken by the offending nation. The priority is for the offending country to bring its policy in line with the recommendations made by the WTO panel. If it does not state in writing that it will do so within 30 days, it must open negotiations with the complaining country to find some means of compensating it for losses. If the two countries cannot reach such a settlement, the WTO ultimately grants the complaining country the right to impose limited trade sanctions against the offending country.[31] Ideally, these sanctions, which usually come in the form of retaliatory tariffs, should be imposed in the same sector as the dispute, but this is not always the case. Legal retribution for violation of a trade agreement in petrochemicals may sometimes result in retaliatory tariffs against underwear.

Thus while serving as a forum for new negotiations, the WTO also acts as a "sheriff" to enforce previous agreements, similar to the sheriff over the Commons described in Chapter Four. Real-life sheriffs are not always popular, and it is no different with the WTO. Indeed, partially through a general misunderstanding of the institution,

---

[29] World Trade Organization (2005). www.wto.org. (Accessed 7/31/07)

[30] World Trade Organization (2005b). http://www.wto.org/english/thewto/e/whatis/e/tif_e/org1_e.htm#council (Accessed 7/31/07)

[31] World Trade Organization (2005a). "Understanding the WTO." http://www.wto.org/english/thewto/e/whatis_e/tif_e/disp1_e.htm (Accessed 7/31/07)

United States

		Imports: Open	Imports: Closed
China	Imports: Open	A+B+C+D+ A'+B'+C'+D' A+B+C+D+ A'+B'+C'+D'	A+ω_uB+C+ A'+B'+C'+D' A+B+C+D+ A'+B'+C'
	Imports: Closed	A+B+C+D+ A'+B'+C' A+ω_cB+C+ A'+B'+C'+D'	A+ω_uB+C+ A'+B'+C' A+ω_cB+C+ A'+B'+C'

Figure 12.5. Trade Negotiation Game, U.S. vs. China

the WTO has become a favorite whipping boy of the antiglobalization movement. On the basis of some of its rulings, critics accuse the WTO of striving to create a world full of sweatshops and air pollution. Ostensibly, however, the WTO's purpose is not to promote poor working conditions or environmental degradation, but to hold countries to their trade agreements.

Governments have two main motives for establishing trade protection. The first is economic: If an import market is large enough, trade protection lowers world prices for the imported good, shifting the terms of trade in favor of the importing country. The second is political: As seen in our previous example, governments face heavy lobbying pressure from domestic producers forced to compete with imports, and therefore place a greater weight on these interests in calculating their own gains and losses in trade negotiations. But as Dani Rodrik (1995) and others have noted, trade is actually one of the most blunt and inefficient instruments for compensating domestic producers hurt by imports.[32] Why it is routinely used in favor of other far more efficient mechanisms of redress, such as lump-sum cash payments to affected workers, has long been a source of torment and sleepless nights for economists. Nevertheless, in practice the political motive for trade protection is by far the more dominant of the two, and so we examine it here.

To explore the incentives involved in trade relationships, consider the following example, which uses the basic game-theoretic framework employed by Kyle Bagwell of Columbia University and Robert Staiger of the University of Wisconsin.[33] In the following framework, the payoff to the respective governments is the politically weighted social welfare created in the markets for the two goods.

Consider a pair of WTO countries in a trade relationship, say, the United States and China. Suppose that each of the two countries has a strategy that is either "open" or "closed" to a particular category of foreign imports. The payoffs in Figure 12.5

---

[32] Rodrik (1995).
[33] See Staiger and Bagwell (1999), Staiger (1995), and Staiger and Bagwell (1990).

are given in terms of social welfare (consumer and producer surplus) as shown in Figure 12.2a and 12.2b.

As in Staiger (1995), assume that the government places a special weight $\omega > 1$ on producer surplus in the import-competing sector, *e.g.* petrochemicals in China, underwear in the United States. Focusing on cases in which ω is symmetric ($\omega = \omega_c = \omega_u$ in Figure 12.5), if $\omega B < D + B$, then each country has a dominant strategy to maintain open import markets, and there is no need for a WTO. The opposite extreme is when producer surplus in the import-competing sector carries extremely heavy political weight such that $\omega B > D' + D + B$. In this extreme case, the government payoff is higher if both countries are closed to imports than if both are open to each others' imports. Few examples of such hermit-like countries exist (perhaps one example might be North Korea). There is little scope for trade negotiations in this case.

What appears in practice to be the most likely case is that ω is of some intermediate value so that $D + B < \omega B < D + D' + B$, that is, that $(D/B) + 1 < \omega < [(D + D')/B] + 1$. In this intermediate case, the game in Figure 12.5 has the structure of a Prisoners' Dilemma. Although politicians may have a dominant strategy to maintain barriers against imports, politicians are happier (and social welfare is higher) if both countries lower barriers to imports than if they maintain trade barriers. It is in this final case where a global institution that fosters trade agreements and punishes violations of these agreements is important.

The institutional role of the WTO can thus be seen in light of a repeated version of game in Figure 12.5. Through rounds of trade negotiations, member countries come to essentially agree on (Open; Open) strategies. In the event that one country cheats on the agreement by playing "Closed" when the other plays "Open," as a last resort the Dispute Settlement Body of the WTO allows the cheated country to play "Closed" for T periods of the repeated game. Observe that, politically speaking, the threat to play "Closed" as a retaliatory mechanism constitutes a credible threat by a government since it represents a dominant strategy independent of the action taken by the partner country. Staiger (1995) notes that such strategies could be part of a "natural" trigger mechanism that would deter defections in a bilateral trade relationship. But retaliatory measures as approved and codified by the WTO's Dispute Settlement Body can be popularly viewed as legal, legitimate actions. This renders any retaliation as part of a legal framework, and thus less susceptible to an endless series of counter-retaliations, making trade relationships in the end more predictable.

An interesting case in Figure 12.5 is when one country, say China, is characterized by $(D/B) + 1 < \omega_C < [(D + D')/B] + 1$, but the other country, say the United States, is characterized by $\omega_U < (D/B) + 1$. In this case, China as a producer-oriented society, has a dominant strategy to maintain closed import markets, while the United States, as a consumer-oriented society, has a dominant strategy to maintain open import markets. This produces a Nash equilibrium (in the one-shot game) with the United States maintaining open import markets while China maintains closed import markets. Indeed it also makes the threat of retaliatory tariffs by the United States, even in response to a ruling of the Dispute Settlement Body of the WTO, less credible; the proposed threat is not a Nash equilibrium. The consequence of this asymmetry is that it makes threats of trade barrier retaliation in the United States less credible than in countries when the political weight assigned to domestic producer surplus is higher. Such a case indeed does resemble the relationship between United States and China (as well as the United States and Japan), where the domestic producers receive greater political weight in the latter countries. An implication is that the consumer-oriented nature of the United States results in putting its producers in a worse bargaining position with respect to trade disputes. Nevertheless, a ruling against a foreign producer by the WTO may be beneficial in creating a domestic political environment in which tariff retaliation by a consumer-oriented country like the United States becomes more credible.

Some such as Thomas Hungerford (1991) have noted a further role played by dispute settlement procedures. Suppose that there is imperfect information in ascertaining whether a country has indeed cheated on a trade agreement (perhaps by enacting some less easily observable nontariff barrier) and that a drop in exports could have been caused by either. He argues that if retaliatory tariffs must be conditioned on an informative investigation to determine whether the drop in exports was unavoidable or a deliberate act of cheating, an important role of an institution such as the WTO is *information-gathering* as well as coordinating punishment strategies. Under these conditions, the dispute settlement process is able to avert trade wars that could have been ignited by unavoidable mishap rather than by deliberate cheating.

The "Race to the Bottom" in Environmental and Labor Standards

One of the greatest nightmares of those who fear increasing globalization is of a "Race to the Bottom" in worldwide environmental and labor standards. The basis for this fear is the assumption that footloose multinational corporations have an incentive to locate offshore plants wherever environmental standards are weakest (or least enforced) and where labor commands the lowest wages, and shows the least potential for organization. According to the Race to the Bottom, it is the country with the dirtiest environment and the most slave-like labor conditions that wins the foreign investment prize.

Figure 12.6 illustrates the plight of a small manufacturing-export country with the potential to enter the Race to the Bottom. Take the example of El Salvador, which exports around US$100 million annually in paper and cardboard products, potentially a very dirty industry. The country starts operating at supply curve S_1 which equals the marginal cost, MC_1, of the domestic industry. Because of the air, land, and water pollution associated with cardboard production, however, the *marginal social cost*, MSC, is greater than the simple marginal cost of production realized by producers. The difference between the bold MSC line and the $S_1 = MC_1$ line represents the total cost of the pollution at any given level of cardboard production, Q.

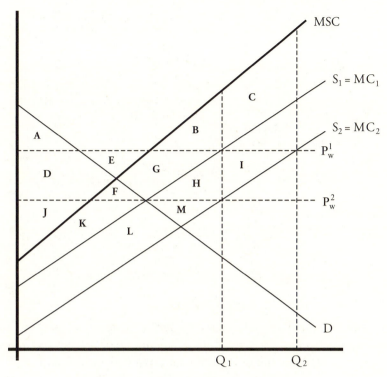

Figure 12.6. Environmental Externalities in Trade

Suppose that environmental standards for cardboard production can be either "high" or "low," and that El Salvador wants to gain an edge in attracting foreign investment by shifting its environmental standards to the latter. (We could tell virtually the same story if the country weakened its labor laws.) As the government relaxes pollution abatement requirements for cardboard producers, it transfers pollution costs from Salvadorian producers to Salvadorian society. Lower marginal costs shift the supply curve downward to the parallel line, $S_2 = MC_2$, but society now must endure more pollution per unit of cardboard output. (For ease of graphical exposition, Figure 12.6 assumes that marginal social costs, private costs plus pollution costs, remain constant.) This increases producer surplus from the area $D + E + F + G + J + K$ to the larger area $D + E + F + G + H + I + J + K + L + M$, assuming El Salvador is a sufficiently small exporter that its increase in exports does not significantly reduce the world price. However, facing the same incentives, if every other exporter does the same, the increased supply lowers the world price of cardboard from P_w^1 to P_w^2. This reduces producer surplus back to $J + K + L + M$, which is equivalent to the original producer surplus area $D + E + F + G + J + K$.

Consider the extreme example in which El Salvador engages in a mercantilist economic policy where producer surplus receives the entire political weight in formulating environmental and trade policies. In this case, we can represent the "Race to the Bottom" game by Figure 12.7 in which the strategic interdependence between

Other Cardboard Exporters

		High Environmental Standards	Low Environmental Standards
El Salvador	High Environmental Standards	D+E+F+ G+J+K (2) D+E+F+ G+J+K (2)	D+E+F+G+H+ I+J+K+L+M (3) J+K (1)
	Low Environmental Standards	J+K (1) D+E+F+G+H+ I+J+K+L+M (3)	J+K+L+M (2) J+K+L+M (2)

Figure 12.7. The "Race to the Bottom" Game

the environmental standards set by all cardboard exporters constitutes a Prisoners' Dilemma. Levels of producer surplus are ranked in the payoff matrix from highest ($=3$) to lowest ($=1$). Whether or not other cardboard exporters institute "high" or "low" environmental standards, each has an incentive to implement the low standards. Low environmental standards are a dominant strategy and form the Nash equilibrium, hence the Race to the Bottom.

It is important to see where the breakdown occurs for a Race to the Bottom to exist. In this example, the real breakdown has occurred in the failure of domestic governments to formulate policy based on general social welfare rather than based on producer surplus. In the game in Figure 12.7, producer surplus is the same whether high or low environmental standards are maintained by each country. The level of pollution in each cardboard-producing country and total social welfare, however, is not. Under high environmental standards the cost of total pollution in each country in Figure 12.6 is equal to $K + F + G + B$; in the Race to the Bottom Nash equilibrium it is $K + F + G + B + L + M + H$. While consumer surplus increases from A to $A + D + F$ from lower prices, total social welfare (the sum of consumer and producer surplus less pollution costs) falls from $A + D + E + J - B$ to $A + D + J - G - H - B$, a net change of $- E - G - H$.[34]

Consequently, it is when governments pursue a mercantilist economic policy that a Race to the Bottom may result, which has a negative environmental impact and lowers total social welfare for host countries of foreign direct investment. Thus when a Race to the Bottom seems to exist in a certain industry, we can trace the roots in part to domestic political failure. What is less clear is whether the role of the

---

[34] It can furthermore be seen in Figure 12.6 that even if all other producers engage in a "Race to the Bottom" it is still best from the standpoint of social welfare in an individual country for it not to lower environmental standards.

WTO should be to extend itself into domestic environmental policies, or whether in accordance with the principles of its charter it should limit itself to resolving trade disputes between its members.

The WTO and Labor/Environment Issues

Why is a supposedly fair-minded institution like the WTO the target of so much ill will from the political left in areas such as protection of the environment? The answer is illustrated by a couple of well-known trade disputes that have emerged in the WTO's Dispute Settlement Body and its predecessor in the GATT.

In the Pacific Ocean, dolphins and yellowfin tuna often swim near one another. Being mammals and not fish, schools of dolphins tend to swim near the surface, with the tuna below them. As a result, dolphins often lie between tuna fishermen and their prey, and they are frequently killed as they are unintentionally trapped in tuna nets. Years before the dispute, the U.S. Marine Mammal Protection Act established a policy that imposed a tuna embargo on any country not able to prove that it abided by dolphin protection standards. Mexico, a leading exporter of tuna to the United States, brought the case before a GATT trade dispute panel in 1991. The panel ruled against the United States, arguing that "GATT rules do not allow one country to take trade action for the purpose of attempting to enforce its own domestic laws in another country, even to protect animal health or exhaustible natural resources."[35]

A second dispute came about in 1995 as the United States implemented tighter environmental regulations over gasoline. It set higher standards regulating the chemical content of gasoline, but allowed domestic producers to regulate their content using a 1990 baseline level of chemical content. Venezuela and Brazil accused the United States of applying stricter rules to the chemical content of their gasoline than were applied to U.S. domestic producers. The Dispute Settlement Body of the WTO ruled against the United States, and forced the United States to negotiate a new set of import standards with gasoline-exporting countries.[36] Both of these rulings enraged environmentalists, who argued that the WTO was creating policies that were both anti-dolphin and pro-toxic gasoline fumes. But on closer examination, the root of the dispute with the WTO and the political left ironically lies in the WTO's policies (a) not to interfere in the domestic policies of sovereign nations; and (b) not to let differences in environmental and labor standards between countries be used as a basis for de facto protectionism. In the latter case, it is clear that if the United States had formulated a clean-air policy that did not discriminate between sources of fuel, the WTO would have had no basis for its ruling.

The position of the WTO is that environmental policy should be established by member countries themselves, but that these environmental policies should not favor domestic goods over imports. Most economists feel that it is not best to deal with labor and environmental issues via trade policy, but rather by policies focused

[35] World Trade Organization (2005b).
[36] Krugman and Obstfeld (2006).

on labor and environmental issues directly. This point can be illustrated easily in the diagram of Figure 12.6. If there are negative spillover effects from cardboard production, the government should levy taxes on cardboard production such that the initial marginal cost ($MC_1 = S_1$) curve in Figure 12.6 increases until it reaches the MSC curve. In this way, the pollution tax "internalizes" the negative cardboard production externality. This yields a total social welfare equal to $A + D + J + E$, certainly greater than social welfare in the Race to the Bottom, $A + D + J - G - H - B$, and even greater than social welfare under "high" environmental standards in the game, $A + D + E + J - B$.

Kyle Bagwell and Robert Staiger (2001) have proposed a creative mechanism by which policies can be specifically targeted to directly address labor and environmental issues in international trade. Their intention is that it may help countries to implement stronger labor and environmental policies without jeopardizing export markets, and furthermore may help to ensure that environmental standards are not used as a guise for protectionism.

The essential feature of their idea is that under WTO rules, countries should be forced to neutralize the effect of any changes in environmental laws on domestic market access by their trading partners. In practice this would mean that if, for example, a developing country decided to relax its own environmental or labor standards in a way that would benefit domestic producers over foreign producers, it must make tariff concessions to those foreign producers in some other area that guarantees them the same market access as they enjoyed previously. Bagwell and Staiger also argue that if a country chooses to *raise* its environmental or labor standards, it should be entitled to raise tariffs in some other area that guarantees that foreign producers on the whole will not be able to take advantage of the policy change to the detriment of domestic producers. Such a mechanism has the potential to allow trade talks to continue to foster global economic openness, while simultaneously giving individual countries the opportunity to enact appropriate labor and environmental standards that take into account their level of economic development and their specific circumstances. This kind of creative mechanism is one more example of the potential for institutions to shape the incentives in a game for the benefit of the common good.

Appendix

THIS APPENDIX IS here to give you a little more background on the basic solution concepts and techniques used in game theory. A warning: This is only a brief overview, and it is somewhat terse. To delve into these concepts at a more satisfying level, I recommend several books that can serve as excellent introductions to game theory at the end of this section.

A game consists of two or more players, and often we index the players by a number or letter (e.g., 1, 2, 3, . . ., n), where n represents the number of players in a game. Each player in a game has a set of strategies. For example, in a game of peasant farmers we might represent the set of strategies available to Player 1 and Player 2 as $S_1 = S_2 = \{$Beans; Coffee$\}$ in a two-player, two-strategy game where the players have the same strategies. Any combination of strategies, one by each player in the game is called a "strategy profile." Here, each player i chooses one of the strategies in her strategy set, or chooses one particular strategy s_i that is part of S_i. Thus a strategy profile for n players is a combination of strategies, one by each player, $(s_1; s_2; s_3; \ldots s_n)$. The strategy profiles in our two-player, two-strategy game would be (Beans; Beans), (Beans; Coffee), (Coffee; Beans) or (Coffee; Coffee).

Each strategy profile yields a payoff to each of the players in the game. The payoff to a player is therefore determined by the strategy chosen by the player himself, and by the strategies chosen by the other players. If U_i represents the utility of player i, then U_i is a function of the strategy chosen by all players in the game, or $U_i(s_1; s_2; s_3; \ldots; s_n)$. To continue with our previous example, the payoff to Player 1 from growing Coffee when Player 2 grows Coffee, or U_1(Coffee; Coffee) might be 5, while the payoff U_1(Coffee; Beans) might be 4. The difference in payoffs might exist because there are economies of scale in coffee growing; perhaps wholesale buyers pay a higher price if they can collect more beans in one trip to a village. However, different phenomena might be operational here that determine the payoffs. Maybe with fewer coffee producers, the price of coffee is higher. In this case, the payoff U_1(Coffee; Coffee) could be 3 instead of 5. What matters in many cases is simply the ordinality, or rankings, of payoffs rather than the precise numerical values. The rankings of payoffs tell a story that captures the essence of the strategic interdependence in the particular game. If players can rank payoffs from the different strategy profiles, then it becomes possible to find a solution to the game.

Nash Equilibrium

The most fundamental solution concept in game theory is the Nash equilibrium. If a strategy profile to a game is a Nash equilibrium, then no player in the game wishes to deviate from his strategy given the strategies of the other players. We can represent the idea of a strategy profile from which no player wishes to deviate by $(s_1^*, s_2^* \ldots s_n^*)$. Using our notation, this means we can describe a Nash equilibrium as a strategy profile in which for every player i among the n players, $U_i\left(s_1^*, s_{i-1}^*, s_i^*, s_{i+1}^* \ldots s_n^*\right) \geq U_i\left(s_1^*, s_{i-1}^*, s_i, s_{i+1}^* \ldots s_n^*\right)$. This means that every player i can do no better playing some other s_i in his own strategy set than by playing s_i^* given the strategies that are being played by the others.

Let's first examine the Nash equilibrium concept in the context of games in which players make their decisions simultaneously, or at least under a veil of ignorance regarding the strategies of other players. It is only after players' strategies are revealed that we can ascertain whether a player would deviate from the given strategy profile. In Game A, you can verify through cell-by cell inspection that there are two pure-strategy Nash equilibria, (Beans; Beans) and (Coffee; Coffee). (A pure strategy is simply when a player employs a single strategy rather than randomly mixing over multiple strategies.) Game A forms a particular type of Coordination game called a Stag Hunt. Notice the game has one Nash equilibrium that is *Pareto superior* to another. A Pareto superior outcome is an outcome in which at least one player is better off than the alternative outcome(s), while others are no worse off. An outcome that has no others that are Pareto superior to it is *Pareto efficient*. In the case of Game A, both players happened to be better off in the (Coffee; Coffee) Nash equilibrium than in the (Beans; Beans) Nash equilibrium. However, when either the Coffee or Beans equilibrium is reached, neither player wishes to deviate from his strategy given the strategy of the other player.

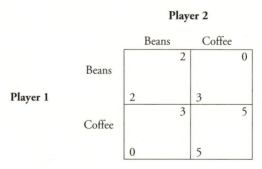

Game A: Coffee/Beans Game 1

Player 2

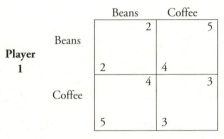

Game B: Coffee/Beans Game 2

Player 2

	Beans	Coffee
Beans	4 / 4	5 / 2
Coffee	2 / 5	3 / 3

Game C: Coffee/Beans Game 3

The payoffs for different strategy profiles can portray different phenomena that influence the Nash equilibria in the game. Game A could represent an instance in which strong external economies of scale for coffee; coffee is only best if everyone grows it. Game B , in contrast, could represent a situation in which demand is very inelastic for each crop, meaning that prices fall substantially with increased production of any single crop. In this case, there are also two pure-strategy Nash equilibria, (Beans; Coffee) and (Coffee; Beans), but in these equilibria players choose opposite strategies – one cultivates beans and the other will grow coffee. Instances in which players choose contrarian strategies are a defining characteristic of Hawk-Dove games. Here it is preferable to grow coffee, but in the equilibrium, there will only be one coffee grower

Game C represents a Prisoners' Dilemma in which there is only one Nash equilibrium, (Coffee; Coffee). A scenario that might generate such an outcome might be, for example, if coffee had a higher market price, but inflicted negative externalities on the environment from pesticides. Everyone would be collectively better off growing beans, but there is an individual financial incentive to grow coffee; a farmer receives all the cash from his coffee crop, but only bears a fraction of the pollution costs. In Game C, both players would receive higher payoffs in the (Beans; Beans) strategy profile, but they get stuck in the (Coffee; Coffee) equilibrium.

Let's expand this game to allow for three strategies on the part of both players. Suppose that S_1 = {Beans; Coffee; Maize} and S_2 = {Beans; Coffee; Tea}. The

Player 2

	Beans	Coffee	Tea
Beans	3 \ 3	2 \ 4	2 \ 6
Coffee	4 \ 2	5 \ 5	4 \ 3
Maize	4 \ 5	2 \ 5	2 \ 5

(Player 1: Beans, Coffee, Maize)

Game D: Coffee/Beans/Tea Game 1

Player 2

	Beans	Coffee	Tea
Beans	4 \ 4	3 \ 4	3 \ 4
Coffee	4 \ 3	6 \ 6	6 \ 5
Maize	4 \ 4	3 \ 4	3 \ 4

(Player 1: Beans, Coffee, Maize)

Game E: Coffee/Beans/Tea Game 2

strategies of the players are now not only larger, they are asymmetric. There are now nine possible strategy profiles: (Beans; Beans), (Beans; Coffee), (Beans; Tea), (Coffee; Beans), (Coffee; Coffee), (Coffee; Tea), (Maize; Beans), (Maize; Coffee), (Maize; Tea). Before reading on, as an exercise try to find the Nash equilibria that exist in Game D and Game E.

In Game D, the two pure-strategy Nash equilibria are (Maize; Beans) and (Coffee; Coffee). A plausible story we could tell that might generate these two strategy profiles as Nash equilibria to the game are that there are local strong price inelasticities in maize and beans, the local consumption crops, fostering an equilibrium with only one local producer in each. At the same time an equilibrium is possible for the village if both growers make use of economies of scale through coordinating on coffee production. Two equilibria are possible: one in which a diversity of local consumption crops are grown, and one in which a single export crop is grown (coffee). It is the latter Nash equilibrium in Game D that represents the Pareto efficient outcome.

In Game E, there are four pure-strategy Nash equilibria, (Beans; Beans), (Maize; Beans), (Coffee; Coffee), and (Coffee; Tea). The Pareto superior outcome among these is (Coffee; Coffee). Here, payoffs could be largely determined by wholesale buyers dealing in the village who purchase *both* coffee and tea, allowing for economies of scale even when peasants produce the two different export crops. (Beans; Beans) and (Maize; Beans) remain possible (but Pareto-inferior) Nash equilibria; unless both peasants produce export crops, they cannot attract whole-sale buyers to the village and peasants cultivate the consumption crops.

Classification of 2 × 2 Games

Some of the most insightful games are those involving only two-players and two-strategies, it is possible to classify these into three fundamental types of games.[1] This is true for all symmetric games in which no two payoffs to any player are equal. Consider Game F-1, a symmetric game in which payoffs are such that $a_{11} = b_{11}$, $a_{12} = b_{12}$, etc.

Player 2

	Strategy 1	Strategy 2
Strategy 1	b_{11} / a_{11}	b_{21} / a_{12}
Strategy 2	b_{12} / a_{21}	b_{22} / a_{22}

Player 1

Game F1: Two Players and Two Strategies

We can "normalize" the game by letting $X = a_{11} - a_{21} = b_{11} - b_{21}$ and $Y = a_{22} - a_{12} = b_{22} - b_{12}$ so that the payoffs appear as the following in Game F-2:

Player 2

	Strategy 1	Strategy 2
Strategy 1	X / X	0 / 0
Strategy 2	0 / 0	Y / Y

Player 1

Game F2: Two Players and Two Strategies, Normalized

[1] See Weibull (1995).

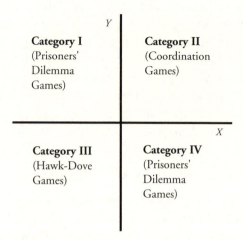

Figure A-1 Categorization of Canonical Games

From this payoff matrix, there arise four categories of games as seen in Figure A-1, of which two are identical:

Category I: Games in which $X < 0$ and $Y > 0$. All of the games in this category contain one Nash equilibrium in which both players play Strategy 2. All Prisoners' Dilemma games fall into this category, although it also includes other games with a single Nash equilibrium. For example with the Prisoners' Dilemma game in Figure 2.4, we have $X = 3 - 4 = -1$ and $Y = 0 - (-1) = 1$, yielding a Nash equilibrium on Strategy 2 (Maximum; Maximum).

Category II: Games in which $X > 0$ and $Y > 0$. Every game in this category contains two pure-strategy Nash equilibria in which both players play either Strategy 1 or both play Strategy 2. In every game of this type there also exists one mixed-strategy Nash equilibrium. All Category II games fall under the general heading of Coordination games. For example with the Stag Hunt game in Figure 2.2 we have $X = 3 - 1 = 2$ and $Y = 1 - (-2) = 3$, yielding pure-strategy Nash equilibria on Strategy 1 (Go; Go) and Strategy 2 (Stay; Stay).

Category III: Games in which $X < 0$ and $Y < 0$. Every game in this category also contains two pure-strategy Nash equilibria, but in this case players choose opposite strategies in equilibrium. There also exists one mixed-strategy Nash equilibrium. This category contains all Hawk-Dove games. For instance, with the Hawk-Dove game in Figure 2.3 , we have $X = -10 - (-5) = -5$ and $Y = 0 - 5 = -5$, yielding pure strategy Nash equilibria on (Strategy 1; Strategy 2) and (Strategy 2; Strategy 1), that is (On Land; Elsewhere) and (Elsewhere; On Land).

Category IV: Games in which $X > 0$ and $Y < 0$. This category is a mirror image of Category I, and contains all Prisoners' Dilemma games.

All types of Coordination games, including Stag Hunt, Battle of the Sexes, and games of pure coordination all lie within Category II. Trust games contain two payoffs that are equal for each player, and therefore cannot be categorized in this framework.

Mixed Strategies

Every game with a finite number of strategies for each player contains a Nash equilibrium, but some of the Nash equilibria may be in *mixed* strategies. Again, a mixed strategy occurs when a player randomizes between strategies with some fixed probability. Many applications of mixed strategies occur in two-player, two-strategy games such as Game G, which have only a single, mixed-strategy Nash equilibrium.

In Game G verify that there is no pure-strategy equilibrium. This is because predictable behavior by either player can be exploited to the advantage of the other: If the Shady Character "Abides" within the law, the Policeman will Refrain from action against him. However, if the Policeman always Refrains, the Shady Character will Violate. But in this case, the Policeman wants to Arrest, which makes the Shady Character want to Abide.

Game G:

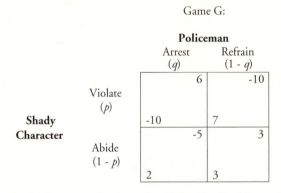

Game G: Game with One Nash Equilibrium in Mixed Strategies

There is, however, an equilibrium in mixed strategies in which the Shady Character Violates some of the time and the Policeman Arrests some of the time. How does one find this equilibrium? It is obtainable by finding the randomized (mixed) strategy by a player that neutralizes the other player through making her indifferent between strategies. This way predictable behavior by a player cannot be exploited by the other. To find the mixed-strategy equilibrium in Game G, let the Shady Character choose p to make the Policeman indifferent between Arrest and Refrain by setting $6p + (-5)(1-p) = -10p + 3(1-p)$ and solving for p. This exercise yields $p = 1/3$. Now do the same for the Police officer, choosing q to make the Shady Character indifferent between Violating and Abiding: $-10q + 7(1-q) = 2q + 3(1-q)$. This gives us $q = 1/4$. As a result, the mixed-strategy Nash equilibrium in the game occurs when the Shady Character Violates one-third of the time, and when the Policeman Arrests one-fourth of the time. This creates a Nash equilibrium because given the strategy of the other, neither has an incentive to change his own strategy.

Dynamic Games and Backward Induction

There are many cases in which players make decisions in sequence rather than simultaneously. It is possible to model such games in the *normal form*, as in Games A through G. If we do this, it is important to remember that a strategy constitutes a plan of action for the entire game, since in dynamic games players may be called upon to take actions at multiple points in a game. But it is most convenient to model dynamic games in what most game theorists call the *extensive form*. An example of the extensive form is given in Game H.

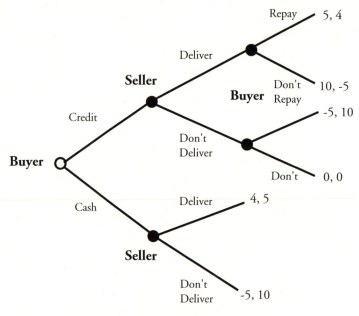

Game H1: Extensive Form

To find a Nash equilibrium in a dynamic, extensive-form game, we start from the end of the game, working our way back to the beginning, noting the choices players make at their respective decision nodes. We can use *backward induction* easily in this way when we have a game of perfect information, or when there is no uncertainty of players past moves. Game H is such a game.

We can see in this game between a Buyer and a Seller the decisions that each will make at their respective nodes, starting at the end of the game. The game as an illustration of the problems with market exchange in the absence of legal institutions when one-shot transactions must be carried out in sequence. If a Buyer offers credit, whether or not the Seller Delivers or Doesn't Deliver the goods, the Buyer's best response is Don't Repay (as indicated by the arrows in the diagram). If the Buyer pays in Cash, the best response of the Seller is Don't Deliver. Given this sequence of best responses, the best response of the Buyer at the initial node is to offer Credit. This equilibrium path is shown by the bold arrows. On the equilibrium path, the Buyer doesn't pay the seller and the Seller doesn't deliver the goods anyway,

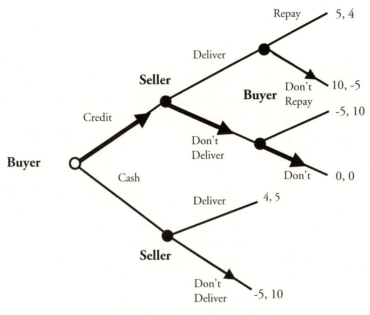

Game H2: Extensive Form

the transaction essentially amounting to a market failure. The backward induction solution to this game is thus the strategy profile (Credit, Don't Repay, Don't Repay; Don't Deliver, Don't Deliver), noting that the Buyer's and Seller's strategies always constitute a plan of action for the entire game.

A solution by backward induction always gives a Nash equilibrium. Backward induction yields a nice prediction for dynamic games because a solution (if obtainable) is always "subgame-perfect," or constitutes a Nash equilibrium in every subgame. Subgame perfection is a concept developed by German game theorist Reinhardt Selten. A subgame is a part of an extensive-form game that starts at a player's solitary decision node in the game and continues along the subsequent branches until the remainder of the game. Game H has five subgames, including the game as a whole that begins with the initial node. Game H theorists like subgame-perfect Nash equilibria because they are outcomes to a game that rely only on "credible" statements – things players really *would* do if they got to that point in the game. Other Nash equilibria in dynamic games sometimes rely on "idle threats," that are off the equilibrium path, statements players make as part of their strategies that they wouldn't really carry out if they arrived at that decision node in the game.

Repeated Games

Some dynamic games consist of a repeated one-shot game. These games are called "repeated games" and the one-shot game that is repeated over and over is called the "stage game." At least in theory, to obtain a cooperative outcome to many such games, it is critical that the stage game be infinitely rather than finitely repeated.

An illustration with the repeated Prisoners' Dilemma illustrates why: Since (Defect; Defect) is the only strategy profile that forms a Nash equilibrium in the final stage game of a finitely repeated Prisoners' Dilemma, promises of future cooperation in the penultimate stage are noncredible statements. This spreads the end-game defection to the penultimate stage game, the "pre-penultimate" stage game, the "pre-pre-penultimate" stage game, and so forth, so that defection spreads like a contagion all the way back to the beginning of the game. In practice, provided that the number of repetitions games is sufficiently large, researchers have found in experimental work that cooperation often can exist, especially in early rounds of the game.[2]

If, however, the game is infinitely repeated or at least has some probability after every stage game of continuation, then by the Folk Theorem, virtually any average payoff over the course of the game is possible, given a sufficiently high discount factor, δ. Cooperation may be possible under different types of punishment strategies. Two of the most common punishment strategies are "Grim Trigger" (perpetual defection in retribution for defection by another player) and "Tit-For-Tat" (a one-period defection in retribution for defection by another player.) With payoffs ordered $r > s > t > v$, cooperation may be possible in a Prisoners' Dilemma under Grim Trigger, for example, if $s + \delta s + \delta^2 s + \cdots + \delta^\infty s > r + \delta t + \delta^2 t + \cdots + \delta^\infty t$.

We can simplify this cumbersome-looking sequence into a tidy formula by using a very simple mathematics trick. Suppose a player is to receive a sequence of s's forever. Let Z represent the value of this sequence so that $Z = s + \delta s + \delta^2 s + \cdots + \delta^\infty s$. We can find a more concise expression for Z by multiplying both sides of this expression by δ to obtain $\delta Z = \delta s + \delta^2 s + \delta^3 s \cdots \delta^{\infty+1} s$. Subtracting both sides of this from the original expression yields $Z(1 - \delta) = s$, and thus $Z = s/(1 - \delta)$. Using this result, Grim Trigger can sustain cooperation in the Prisoners' Dilemma if $\frac{s}{1-\delta} > r + \frac{\delta t}{1-\delta}$. Under mutual "Tit-For-Tat" strategies by the players cooperation is possible if $\frac{s}{1-\delta} > r + \delta v + \frac{\delta^2 s}{1-\delta}$ (if a defecting player does not punish the punishing player for punishing him.) Intermediate threats of punishment between Tit-for-Tat and Grim Trigger of length T can sustain cooperation provided that $s + \delta s + \delta^2 s + \cdots + \delta^\infty s > r + \delta v + \delta^2 v + \cdots + \delta^T v + \delta^{T+1} s + \cdots + \delta^\infty s$.

Credibility is an issue with punishment strategies in repeated games. Certain punishments may be able to deter defections by another player in an infinitely repeated game, but they may not be credible (subgame-perfect). An example of this credibility problem may occur even in relatively mild punishments such as Tit-for-Tat if, for example, part of the defecting player's strategy is to counter-retaliate against the punishing player with his own subsequent one-period defection. In this case, if a player chooses to carry out the Tit-for-Tat strategy in response to another player's one-time defection, he receives $r + \frac{\delta(v+r)}{2(1-\delta)}$, whereas if he abstains from carrying out the punishment he receives $\frac{s}{1-\delta}$. Choosing to "renegotiate" to avoid carrying out the punishment will be advantageous in this case if, say, s is sufficiently large. But if one player knows that the other has an incentive not to carry

---

[2] For example, see Abbink et al. (2006).

out a punishment, that is, has an incentive to "renegotiate" his punishment strategy, this may invite defections in the repeated game, making cooperation difficult.

Evolutionary Games

This section of the appendix may be of greater interest to readers who have been more broadly exposed to the analytical foundations of game theory. Here I will discuss three concepts in evolutionary game theory in more detail that are applied to economic development issues in the main section of the book. The first of these is *risk dominance*, a concept developed by Nobel Prize co-winners (with John Nash) John Harsanyi and Reinhardt Selten (1988). Consider Rousseau's Stag Hunt in Game below in which two hunters decide whether to individually pursue the Hare or together pursue the Stag (a male deer). There are two Nash equilibria to the game, (Hare; Hare) and (Stag; Stag). Suppose that a large population of players plays the game in randomly matched pairs. In selecting between the two equilibria it is tempting to choose the Pareto-superior (Stag; Stag). However, suppose that a mutant behavior appears in the population with some probability m. Harsanyi and Selten's criterion for choosing between the equilibria is to select the equilibrium that offers the greatest resistance barrier m to a mutant infiltration. We say that equilibrium C *risk dominates* another equilibrium D in a game if C's resistance against D exceeds D's resistance against C.

Player 2

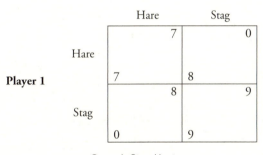

Game I: Stag Hunt

We can calculate the resistance of the Stag equilibrium in Game I, by solving for the level of m at which the Stag equilibrium remains optimal over the Hare equilibrium. This is true when $9(1 - m) + 0m > 8(1 - m) + 7m$, or when $m < 1/8$. The resistance of the Hare equilibrium is calculated by setting $7(1 - m) + 8m > 0(1 - m) + 9m$, which yields a resistance level of $m < 7/8$. Thus the (Hare; Hare) equilibrium is risk-dominant, but the (Stag; Stag) equilibrium is Pareto efficient. Here we observe a class of Coordination games in which we observe a trade-off between Pareto-efficiency and risk, and a tension between social cooperation and individual safety.

The evolutionary stable strategy (ESS) developed by biologist John Maynard Smith is the most widely used solution concept in evolutionary games. An incumbent strategy x is played within a population that is susceptible to invasion by a mutant strategy *y*. Individuals within a large population are paired randomly to play the game. Payoffs are given in terms of reproductive fitness. The mutant strategy, played by some small fraction *m* of the population, will die out within the population if it has a lower level of reproductive fitness than the incumbent strategy. This occurs when $U_i [x; my + (1 - m) x] > U_i [y; my + (1 - m) x]$, where U is a payoff function and the term before the semi-colon represents the strategy played by the individual and the term after the semi-colon is the weighted set of strategies played within the population. A more common way of expressing this criterion for evolutionary stability is examining whether the incumbent strategy satisfies the following two conditions:

ESS Condition 1: $U_i (y; x) \leq U_i (x; x)$, and only if this condition holds with strict equality,

ESS Condition 2: $U_i (y; y) < U_i (x; y)$.

What this means is that the incumbent strategy *x* is an ESS if the mutant strategy *y* has a strictly lower payoff against the incumbent strategy than the incumbent strategy has against itself. But in case where the mutant strategy does equally well against the incumbent strategy, the mutant strategy must earn a worse payoff in the event that it is played against itself than when the incumbent strategy is played against it.

Game J: Hawk-Dove Game

To explore the ESS concept, let's first take a simple example of herders who would like to graze their animals on a given area of land. Assume there are many herders who meet randomly at different grazing sites with their animals. Each herder can play a hawkish strategy by immediately setting their animals out onto the land, or they can play a dovish strategy by moving their animals on to another area, as seen in Game J.

There are three Nash equilibria to the game: (Graze; Move On), (Move On; Graze), and a mixed strategy in which each Grazes with probability 2/3 and Moves On with probability 1/3. What behavior could be an ESS in a single homogeneous population playing the game against one another?

Let's first consider a behavior in which all herders Move On. Notice here that some group of mutant herders playing Graze with probability = 1/2 could successfully invade this population, receiving an expected payoff of $0.5(4) + 0.5(2) = 3$, which would exceed the incumbent population payoff of 2. Therefore, the incumbent strategy would fail to meet ESS Condition 1, and it would die out; the strategy is not an ESS.

Now let's check the behavior in which all herders Graze. Again, see in this case that the group of mutant herders with a strategy of Grazing with probability $= 1/2$ could also successfully invade a population of Grazers, receiving an expected payoff of $0.5(-1) + 0.5(0) = -0.5$, which would exceed the incumbent population payoff of -1, a low payoff from always conflicting over grazing land. Therefore, the strategy would again fail to meet ESS Condition 1, and the incumbent strategy would die out; the strategy is not an ESS.

Finally, let's check the mixed strategy, in which herders play Graze with probability $2/3$ and Move On with probability $1/3$. First we check ESS Condition 1, where we must have $U_i(y; x) \leq U_i(x; x)$ or, in this example, $U_i\left(p_G = \frac{1}{2}; p_G = \frac{2}{3}\right) \leq U_i\left(p_G = \frac{2}{3}; p_G = \frac{2}{3}\right).U_i\left(p_G = \frac{1}{2}; p_G = \frac{2}{3}\right) = \frac{1}{2}\left[\frac{2}{3}(-1) + \frac{1}{3}(4)\right] + \frac{1}{2}\left[\frac{2}{3}(0) + \frac{1}{3}(2)\right] = \frac{1}{2}\left(\frac{2}{3}\right) + \frac{1}{2}\left(\frac{2}{3}\right) = \frac{2}{3} \leq U_i\left(p_G = \frac{2}{3}; p_G = \frac{2}{3}\right) = \frac{2}{3}\left[\frac{2}{3}(-1) + \frac{1}{3}(4)\right] + \frac{1}{3}\left[\frac{2}{3}(0) + \frac{1}{3}(2)\right] = \frac{2}{3}\left(\frac{2}{3}\right) + \frac{1}{3}\left(\frac{2}{3}\right) = \frac{2}{3}$. So the first condition holds with equality. Let's check the second condition: $U_i\left(p_G = \frac{1}{2}; p_G = \frac{1}{2}\right) = \frac{1}{2}\left[\frac{1}{2}(-1) + \frac{1}{2}(4)\right] + \frac{1}{2}\left[\frac{1}{2}(0) + \frac{1}{2}(2)\right] = \frac{1}{2}\left(\frac{3}{2}\right) + \frac{1}{2}(1) = \frac{5}{4} < U_i\left(p_G = \frac{1}{2}; p_G = \frac{2}{3}\right) = \frac{2}{3}\left[\frac{1}{2}(-1) + \frac{1}{2}(4)\right] + \frac{1}{3}\left[\frac{1}{2}(0) + \frac{1}{2}(2)\right] = \frac{2}{3}\left(\frac{3}{2}\right) + \frac{1}{3}(1) = \frac{4}{3}$. So we see that the second condition holds. In this case, when faced by an invasion of mutants who are slightly less hawkish than the incumbent population, the number of mutants declines over time. Indeed, the mixed-strategy Nash equilibrium in which a herders play Graze with probability $2/3$ and Move On with probability $1/3$ can repel not only the incumbent strategy we propose here, but any other mutant strategy. (You can experiment with this.) But what is required is a general test for an ESS against *any* other mutant strategy entering the population.

To do this, let's consider the example of the Hawk-Dove game in Figure 10.2, where we can verify that the incumbent strategy where individuals play Hawk with probability $p^* = V/C$, the mixed strategy Nash equilibrium, is an ESS. We test it against any mutant strategy $p = V/C + \varepsilon$, where ε can be either positive or negative. Here we see ESS Condition 1 holds with equality, $\left(\frac{V}{C} + \varepsilon\right) \left[\frac{V}{C}\left(\frac{V-C}{2}\right) + \frac{C-V}{C}(V)\right] + \left(\frac{C-V}{C} - \varepsilon\right)\left[\frac{V}{C}(0) + \frac{C-V}{C}\left(\frac{V}{2}\right)\right] = \frac{V}{C}\left[\frac{V}{C}\left(\frac{V-C}{2}\right) + \frac{C-V}{C}(V)\right] + \frac{C-V}{C}\left[\frac{V}{C}(0) + \frac{C-V}{C}\left(\frac{V}{2}\right)\right]$ which after some algebra yields $0 = \varepsilon V\left(\frac{V}{2C}\right) + \varepsilon V\left(\frac{C-V}{C}\right) + \varepsilon V\left(\frac{V-C}{2C}\right) = 0$. Because Condition 1 only holds with equality, ESS Condition 2 must also hold for the incumbent strategy $p^* = V/C$ to be an ESS: $\left(\frac{V}{C} + \varepsilon\right)\left[\left(\frac{V}{C} + \varepsilon\right)\left(\frac{V-C}{2}\right) + \left(\frac{C-V}{C} - \varepsilon\right)(V)\right] + \left(\frac{C-V}{C} - \varepsilon\right)\left[\left(\frac{V}{C} + \varepsilon\right)(0) + \left(\frac{C-V}{C} - \varepsilon\right)\left(\frac{V}{2}\right)\right] < \left(\frac{V}{C}\right)\left[\left(\frac{V}{C} + \varepsilon\right)\left(\frac{V-C}{2}\right) + \left(\frac{C-V}{C} - \varepsilon\right)(V)\right] + \left(\frac{C-V}{C}\right)\left[\left(\frac{V}{C} + \varepsilon\right)(0) + \left(\frac{C-V}{C} - \varepsilon\right)\left(\frac{V}{2}\right)\right]$, which becomes $\varepsilon\left[\left(\frac{V}{C} + \varepsilon\right)\left(\frac{V-C}{2}\right) + \left(\frac{C-V}{C} - \varepsilon\right)V - \left(\frac{C-V}{C} - \varepsilon\right)\left(\frac{V}{2}\right)\right] < 0$ and in turn simplifies to $-\frac{1}{2}\varepsilon^2 C < 0$. As a result, we have verified that $p^* = V/C$ is an ESS.

Although evolutionary stability is the best known concept in evolutionary game theory, it is a static concept that is unable to describe the dynamics of behavioral systems. Studying the *replicator dynamics* of a system is an increasingly utilized tool for understanding the evolution of institutions and social norms, providing many applications in development economics. Analyzing the replicator dynamics of a system allows one to understand the increasing and decreasing propensity of different behaviors as they meet within a population.

Suppose x_i is now the fraction of the population playing one particular pure strategy i within a population of players. Conversely, we can denote by x the probability weighting across all strategies that is being played at any time by the population as a whole. The growth in x_i is given by $\dot{x}_i = x_i [U_i (x_i; x) - U_i (x; x)]$, where $\dot{x}_i$ is just the growth of x_i over time.[3] What this means is that the fraction of the population x_i will increase if the payoff to playing strategy i against the combination of strategies employed within the general population fairs better than the general population does when it plays against itself, and decrease if i does worse.

The equilibrium concept used in the replicator dynamics framework is loosely called *dynamic stability*, often referred to more specifically as *asymptotic* stability.[4] Intuitively, the state of a population playing a given mixed or pure strategy x is dynamically stable if any small change in the strategy mix does not lead the dynamics away from returning back to x. The following relationships between dynamic stability, evolutionary stable strategies, and Nash equilibria hold for a general class of games: Every dynamically stable point is a Nash equilibrium, but not every Nash equilibrium is dynamically stable. Moreover, every ESS is dynamically stable, but not all dynamically stable population states are ESSs (as seen in Figure 10.5b).[5] Thus the ESS is the most stringent of the three concepts, dynamic stability second, and the Nash equilibrium third.

Dynamically stable points are either unique or form part of "absorbing sets" that are surrounded by *basins of attraction*. The basin of attraction is the set of states from which the selection mechanism moves the system to the absorbing set in a finite number of time periods (in the absence of mutations).[6] A few examples illustrate these concepts.

Let's consider the aforementioned Category I games, which include the Prisoners' Dilemma, taking the case of $X < 0$ and $Y > 0$. Here, if x_1 represents the fraction of the population playing Strategy 1, and x_2 the fraction of the population playing Strategy 2, the replicator dynamic is equal to $\dot{x}_1 = x_1 (x_1 X - (x_1^2 X + x_2^2 Y))$, which after some algebra (and recalling that $x_2 = 1 - x_1$) becomes $\dot{x}_1 = x_1 x_2 (x_1 X - x_2 Y)$. It is clear from this expression of the replicator dynamic that x_1 is a doomed strategy within the population since the sign of the expression is always negative. (An example might be if x_1 represents cooperative behavior in an anarchic society characterized by one-shot interaction.) Since $x_2 = 1 - x_1$, we know that $\dot{x}_2 = -\dot{x}_1$, and the dynamics of the system move toward a population of defectors. The basin of attraction for the equilibrium consists of all population states where $0 < x_1 < 1$.

---

[3] See Weibull (1995), p. 72 and Samuelson (1998), p. 143.

[4] Some evolutionary game theorists favor the notion of Lyapunov stability. The difference is that a state x is Lyapunov stable if no small perturbation in the strategy composition of the population can lead it away from x. It is *asymptotically stable* if (moreover) any sufficiently small such change results in a movement back *toward* x. (Weibull, 1995, p. 75).

[5] For details, see Samuelson (1998), p. 68–71.

[6] Ibid., p. 213.

Consider a second example from Category II games, in which $X > 0$ and $Y > 0$. Here the replicator dynamic is again equal to $\dot{x}_1 = (x_1 X - x_2 Y) x_1 x_2$, yet the sign of the expression is indeterminate. If $x_1 X > x_2 Y$, then $\dot{x}_1 > 0$ (and $\dot{x}_2 < 0$). If $x_1 X < x_2 Y$, then $\dot{x}_1 < 0$ (and $\dot{x}_2 > 0$). The basin of attraction for the Strategy 1 equilibrium lies between the mixed-strategy Nash equilibrium and the equilibrium itself, that is, $Y/(X + Y) > x_1 > 1$. Conversely, the basin of attraction for the Strategy 2 equilibrium lies between the Strategy 2 equilibrium ($x_1 = 0$) and the mixed-strategy Nash equilibrium, that is, $0 < x_1 < Y/(X + Y)$.

Player B

		Accept $(1 - x_2)$	Reject (x_2)
Fair (x_1)		2 2	2 2
Greedy $(1 - x_1)$		1 3	0 0

Player A

Game K: Ultimatum Game

We can also obtain the replicator dynamics from an asymmetric game, such as a simplification of the Ultimatum game in Chapter Ten, in which Player A can offer a "Fair" 50-50 split of a lump sum of 4 to Player B, or can be "Greedy" and only offer only 1.[7] Here x_1 will stand for the fraction of Player As playing the Fair strategy while $1 - x_1$ play the Greedy strategy, and x_2 the fraction of Player Bs playing the Reject strategy while $1 - x_2$ play the Accept strategy. If Player A is Fair, it is assumed that the players keep the 50-50 split. If Player A is Greedy, then Player B has the opportunity to Reject. The normal-form of the game is in Game K.

The replicator dynamic for $\dot{x}_1 = x_1[U_i(x_1, x) - U_i(x, x)]$, noting that $U_i(x_1, x) = 2(1 - x_2) + 2x_2 = 2$ and $U_i(x, x) = 2x_1(1 - x_2) + 2x_1 x_2 + 3(1 - x_1)(1 - x_2) + 0(1 - x_1)x_2$. Thus $\dot{x}_1 = x_1 [U_i(x_1, x) - U_i(x, x)] = 3x_2 + x_1 - 3x_1 x_2 - 1 = (1 - x_1)(3x_2 - 1)$. The first expression in the parentheses is always positive when x_1 is a fraction less than one, and the second term is negative for $x_2 < 1/3$ and positive for $x_2 > 1/3$. Found in a similar fashion, the replicator dynamic for $\dot{x}_2 = x_2[U_i(x_2, x) - U_i(x, x)]$, where $U_i(x_2, x) = 2x_1 + 0(1 - x_1) = 2x_1$ and $U_i(x, x) = 2x_1(1 - x_2) + 2x_1 x_2 + (1 - x_1)(1 - x_2) + 0(1 - x_1)x_2$ yielding $\dot{x}_2 = x_2 [U_i(x_2, x) - U_i(x, x)] = x_1 - 1 + x_2 - x_1 x_2 = (x_1 - 1)(1 - x_2)$. Notice that because the fractions x_1 and x_2 can never be greater than zero, $\dot{x}_2$ is never increasing. The replicator dynamics of this simplified Ultimatum game are thus as seen in Figure A-2.

[7] Ibid., p. 142.

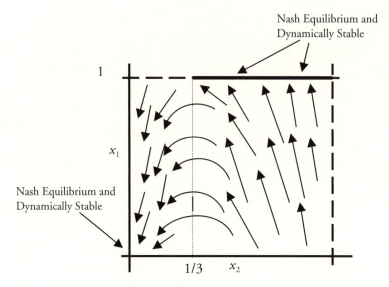

Figure A-2 Replicator Dynamics

Further Reading in Game Theory

For a fuller treatment of the basic concepts in game theory, I would like to recommend three books. The first is the introductory game theory book I use in my
undergraduate game theory class, *Games of Strategy*, by Avinash Dixit and Susan
Skeath (2nd ed., 2004, W. W. Norton). The book is entertaining (especially for a text-
book), with a clear presentation style and interesting examples and applications
across economics and the social sciences. I recommend this book for people with
little background in formal mathematics and game theory. For people with a slightly
more advanced background in mathematics, I recommend *Game Theory for Applied
Economists* by Robert Gibbons (1992, Princeton University Press) and *Game Theory
for Political Scientists* by James Morrow (1994, Princeton University Press). Those
with more mathematical training who would like an excellent introduction to evolutionary game theory should read *Evolutionary Games and Equilibrium Selection*
by Larry Samuelson (1997, MIT Press).

Exercises for Interested Readers

Chapter Two

1. Consider a game in which there are two peasant farmers. One has land on which it is slightly better to grow corn, and the other has a land on which it is slightly better to grow wheat. They want to buy a simple harvesting machine together that can be used only for corn or for wheat. What kind of coordination game is this? Is it a Stag Hunt, Battle of the Sexes, or a Pure Coordination game? Explain.

2. Suppose that one player abides by one convention over the use of a resource, while a second player abides by another. Show in the context of a Hawk-Dove game how this can produce conflict.

3. Consider an application of the Prisoners' Dilemma to cooperatives. Suppose that a development institution establishes an agricultural cooperative. There are n people in each cooperative, who equally share all of the output. Each person in the cooperative can produce 100 pesos/day, and the effort for each person to produce this amount is given by e. What is the threshold number of people in the cooperative below which people will still choose to Work rather than Shirk?

4. Is it possible to turn a Prisoners' Dilemma game into a coordination game by changing only one player's payoffs? If so, which payoff? If not, what kind of game results when only one payoff is changed?

Chapter Three

1. Simultaneous investments in steel, coal, and railroad industries were instrumental in the development of the U.S. economy. Can you provide examples of similar phenomena that initiated a period of development in other countries?

2. Suppose a college education costs 30 and the payoff to a college education is equal to $0.5n$, where n is the number of college educated people and the population. If there are 100 individuals in the economy, what are the Nash equilibria to the game? Which of these are stable Nash equilibria?

3. Search the Web to research the kinds of firms that have located in Bangalore, India. (Suggestion: Using search engines such as ProQuest, Lexis/Nexis, and Google, search under "Bangalore" and "technology industries." What do you notice about these firms? What kinds of complementarities exist between them?

4. What kinds of policies implemented by the developing countries could mitigate the brain drain?

Chapter Four

1. What kinds of institutional arrangements to cover the commons might have prevented the demise of the Rapanui civilization on Easter Island?
2. What factors will keep e sufficiently small to foster a "self-governing commons" in the model of Elinor Ostrom?
3. Consider the Prisoners' Dilemma game in Figure 4.2a in which players can either Conserve or Plunder. To deter "Plundering" of the commons, how large must the payoff s be in terms of r and v? Assume that players use a Tit-for-Tat strategy in which they do not retaliate for being punished and that the discount factor $\delta = 0.9$.
4. A government official must monitor a large number of rural farmers and is only able to catch someone who is illegally de-foresting a neighboring protected area with probability 0.10. Suppose that $r = 10$, $s = 8$, $t = 6$, and $v = 3$. How strong must be a fine F to deter deforestation?
5. Using search engines such as ProQuest, Lexis/Nexis, and Google, search the Web under "common pool resources developing countries." What examples do you find of indigenous management of the commons?
6. Considered the game presented in Figure 4.6. Suppose that $k_1 = 10$ and $k_2 = 4$. What will be the Nash equilibrium to the game if there is no "assignment rule" for the two fishing spots? What kind of game would this be? How many fish would be caught each day by the two fishermen? Now assume that $k_2 = 6$. How do your answers change?

Chapter Five

1. Suppose the utility of income to a peasant household is equal to $\sqrt{Y}$, and the probability of a flood (which ruins all of the household's crops) is equal to p. This would yield an income of zero. If there is no flood, the household earns $\overline{Y}$. The head of the household is considering either working as a day laborer for a fixed wage w, which he earns whether it floods or not, or farming his own plot. How big must be the yield of his crop (when there is no flood) for him to prefer the risk of having his own plot to the fixed wage? How does your answer depend on w and p?
2. What kinds of qualities is a peasant likely to have that would give him a high Shapley value in a solidarity network? What does this imply about what he should receive for being part of the network?
3. Two peasants receive a payoff of s if they cooperate in a given stage game of a solidarity agreement. A peasant receives $r > s$ if he defects and doesn't help his partner in any given period, giving the defectee a payoff of zero. If they both defect, they get t, which is less than s but greater than zero. Assume both peasants

play a Grim Trigger strategy. What is the minimum discount rate for the peasants in terms of the payoffs that allows them to sustain a solidarity network?

4. Consider again the three peasants Ravi, Ashok, and Quezar who maintain a solidarity network via a Grim Trigger strategy as discussed in Chapter Five. Each receives a payoff of 9 when the state of nature is favorable to his economic activity (probability = 1/3), but zero otherwise. Suppose now when Ravi becomes sick, he is able to harvest his rice with some probability $0 < p < 1$. (The sicker Ravi is, the lower is p.) At what point in Ravi's sickness (level of p) will the network coalition of the three peasants together no longer lie in the *core*?

Chapter Six

1. In general terms, when are fixed-rent contracts preferable to fixed-wage contracts? If you are carrying out a field study on agricultural land/labor contracts, when would you expect to find the former rather than the latter?

2. A contract is proposed between a risk-neutral landlord (whose utility equals his expected income) and a risk-averse tiller, whose expected utility is equal to $p\sqrt{(25 - r)} + (1 - p) \sqrt{(18 - r)} - e$, where e is equal to 1 if he toils and 0 if he shirks, and p is equal to 0.5 if he toils and 0.2 if he shirks. The Tiller's reservation utility is $\overline{U}_T = 2.5$. Will a tiller accept a fixed-rent contract with rent equal to 15? 12? 9? (He accepts if it gives him at least his reservation utility.) Assume that the hard work effort can be enforced.

3. Consider the fixed-rent contract in Problem 2 that barely satisfies the participation constraint of the Tiller. What is the Pareto-efficient *share* contract, θ^*, that will make the Landlord *no worse off* than with this fixed-rent contract and make the Tiller *better off*? Again assume that the Landlord can enforce a high work effort. Show that this share contract, θ^*, you solved for will make the Tiller marginally better off than the fixed-rent contract with rent equal to r^*.

4. Suppose that the Landlord cannot enforce the high work effort in Problem 3. Does this share contract satisfy the incentive constraint for the Tiller?

5. Give the intuition for Hallagan's screening model in agricultural contracts in rural peasant economies.

Chapter Seven

1. Consider the institutional role that deposit insurance plays in a banking industry. How does deposit insurance foster a Nash equilibrium without bank runs? In the example given in Figure 7.1, is it necessary to insure 100 percent of a depositor's account? What percent must be insured to prevent a bank run?

2. A borrower is considering investing his 10 units of borrowed capital in a safe project, which will yield 12 for sure by the time the loan comes due, and a risky project that will either yield 25 or zero, each with probability one-half. The lender's cost of capital is zero, and she charges an interest rate of 10 percent. The borrower has no collateral, and both borrower and lender are "risk neutral." Show it is in

the borrower's interest to undertake the risky project, and in the lender's interest that the safe project be undertaken.

3. Moneylenders are a defining feature of credit markets in developing countries. Describe the process by which "credit islands" develop, in which borrowers continue to borrow from a single moneylender. Suppose that p is the probability of lending to a repaying borrower, and $(1 - p)$ is the probability of lending to a non-repaying borrower. Assuming a zero cost of capital to the moneylender, why must the equilibrium interest rate in a repeated transaction between borrower and moneylender fall between zero and $(1 - p)/p$?

4. Group lending is a common credit delivery mechanism used by microfinance institutions in developing countries. Some theories about group lending posit that the potential for social sanctions between group members augment repayment rates under group lending. In the game presented in Figure 7.5 , a what is the requirement for s, the loss in social standing from defaulting on alone if $\delta = 0.45, \delta = 0.55? \delta = 0.65$?

Chapter Eight

1. Describe the different motives for imitative behavior: pure conformity, instrumental conformity, and informational conformity. How are they different from one another, and what are the implications of each for technology adoption in developing countries?

2. In the gas/woodstove technology adoption game in Figures 8.2a–d, suppose that a household's expected payoff to using the gas stove technology is 1 if 50 percent or more of the adjacent households use gas, but -1 if less than 50 percent of the adjacent households have adopted it. As in the original game, an adjacent household is a household to the left, right, above, or below (but not diagonal). Let's say that all households used gas stoves except all of the households in Rows 1 and 6, who still use wood stoves. Is this a Nash equilibrium? What if all of the households except those in Columns 3 and 4 used gas? Is this a Nash equilibrium?

3. In a developing country where the postal system is poor, people can communicate by sending handwritten letters, or via e-mail. If the Sender uses a handwritten letter to send a message and the Receiver does not use e-mail (and can receive only letters), the payoff is 2 to both. If the Sender uses e-mail to send a message and the Receiver *does* use e-mail, the payoff is 5 to both. If the Sender of a message uses a different means of communication, then he and the Receiver both receive zero. Set up this technology adoption problem in a 2 × 2 normal-form game, and as in the currency game in Figure 8.3 and 8.4, plot the dynamics of technology adoption of e-mail versus handwritten letters.

4. Amelie, a Nigerian mother of four, is deciding whether to vaccinate her children. She receives a private signal about whether or not the vaccine is good that is correct with probability equal to 0.70. Her friend Beatrix with several children

of her own receives her own private signal about the vaccine that is correct with probability 0.60 and also observes Amelie's decision about whether to vaccinate her children. Cecile receives her own private signal that is correct with probability 0.50 and also observes the decisions of Amelie and Beatrix. Each knows the accuracy of everybody's signal. What is the probability that Beatrix will make the wrong decision about the vaccine?

5. Discuss the problems with empirically identifying whether imitative behavior exists and if it does, identifying what specific type of behavior is occurring.

Chapter Nine

1. Why is it necessary in a legal system for both punitive power to be strong and legal systems to be efficient? Answer your question in the context of the game presented in Figure 9.1. What are the Nash equilibria you obtain in the game when punitive power is *weak*, but courts are efficient (say in the case where $x = y = 0$)? What are the Nash equilibria you obtain in the game in the opposite case, when punitive power is *strong*, but courts are *in*efficient (say $x = y = 12$)?

2. Consider an entrepreneur in a developing country such as portrayed in a game in Figure 9.2. Use backward induction to determine which of the following investments will be undertaken: (a) An investment that has a probability of success equal to 0.50 if friends and relatives are able to claim half of the entrepreneur's profit. (b) An investment that has a probability of success equal to 0.75 if the entrepreneur expects thieves to steal one-third of the entrepreneur's profit. (c) An investment that has a probability of success equal to 0.60 if government officials are able to claim half of the entrepreneur's profit in bribes.

3. Why are enforceable contracts so essential to foreign investment? In the game in Figure 9.3, for how much must the Foreign Oil Company be able to sue the Local Firm in order to induce the Foreign Oil Company to sink its oil rigs?

4. What are the potential problems with trying to ascertain the impact of corruption on economic development? How does Pablo Mauro use instrumental variables to disentangle the effect corruption on economic growth rates and investment? Describe instrumental variables techniques generally, and discuss its usefulness to development economics.

5. Using the Appendix to review how to solve for a mixed strategy equilibrium, show that the mixed strategy Nash equilibrium to the game in Figure 9.4 occurs with the Inspector monitoring the Builder with probability $p_B = x/f$, and with the Builder complying with the building code $p_I = (\theta f + wc - b)/\theta f$ when $(b - \theta f)/c < w < b/c$.

Chapter Ten

1. What are some of the main characteristics of developing countries that seem to be correlated with civil wars? What are the common effects of these wars?

2. Consider a game between people from two rival ethnic groups in which the payoff to mutual aggression is 4 and mutual passivity is 6. If a passive player meets an aggressive player, the payoff is −1 to the former and 5 to the latter. What are the Nash equilibria to the game? Which of these is Pareto efficient? Which is risk-dominant?

3. Discuss how asymmetries in "roles" can lead to conventions (and perhaps ultimately the development of formal institutions) which prevent conflict over rights to resources such as water and land. How is the development of these conventions related to the notion of an evolutionary stable strategy (ESS)?

4. Two indigenous tribal groups in an area are often in conflict with one another over local resources. Let's model this conflict as a Hawk-Dove game. Suppose that $V = 2$ and $C = 4$. Prove that the solution to this game of conflict is an evolutionary stable strategy in which each tribal group fights exactly half of the time.

5. Let's examine Scenario 3 of Barry Weingast's model of ethnic conflict, the scenario in which each group is uncertain about the others type. Assume $\delta = 0.9$. Solve for the critical level of trust p^* that is just sufficient for Group 1 to trust Group 2 when Group 1 holds political power. Show from your result how p^* changes as C, M, and R change. What are some solutions that Weingast proposes in order to "construct trust" between rival groups and how can you directly relate these to your derivation?

Chapter Eleven

1. Briefly discuss the work of one or two of the early pioneers of social capital theory. What were their major contributions and how do they help us understand the role of social capital to economic development.

2. Show that in the market interaction game presented in Figures 11a–d, in a network with size $S = 40$, a market full of Trusters is an ESS.

3. In the social network game in Chapter Eleven, consider Robert Frank's framework in which trust can be communicated through emotions. What if when confronted with a Cheater in a one-shot game, a Truster is only able to identify a Cheater *one-third* of the time. (Assume that a Truster never mistakes another Truster.) In this case, can a network full of Trusters exist as an evolutionary stable strategy? With what probability must a Truster be able to identify a Cheater for a network of Trusters to be an evolutionary stable strategy?

4. Why is it difficult to establish empirically a relationship between the prevalence of religion, honesty, and economic development? Under what conditions would we expect people who claim to be religious to exhibit behavior different from the general population?

5. What are the conditions in George Akerlof and Rachel Kranton's model of *identity* that could have the most powerful effect on behavioral choices that are related to economic development? Can you provide one illustration each, outside of the reading, how the importance of identity has both fostered prosperity and perpetuated poverty?

Chapter Twelve

1. The number of labor hours it takes to place a barrel of oil and a case of frozen orange juice on the market in Venezuela is equal to x_V and y_V. In Brazil, it is x_B and y_B. Suppose that $3x_V = y_V = x_B = y_B$. What will be the resulting trade pattern between the two countries? Now suppose wages in Venezuela are twice as high as in Brazil. What must be the range of the exchange rate between the Brazilian *real* and the Venezuelan *bolivar* in order to facilitate two-way trade between the two nations?

2. Under what conditions would you expect that there would be a "Race to the Bottom" in which developing countries with low environmental and labor standards attract dirty industries? In your answer incorporate both the monetized Ricardian model as well as the game in Figures 12.6 and 12.7.

3. Suppose there are two coffee producers, Kenya and Colombia, who control their production at the national level and are considering the formation of a cartel at the producer level. Suppose that each sack of coffee costs 5 to produce, and each has a capacity of 30 sacks. World demand for coffee is $P = 105 - Q$, where P is the price and Q is the total number of sacks on the world market. To maximize their surplus from coffee sales, each agrees to produce only 25 sacks. Suppose that the two countries can either Abide by the agreement or Cheat by producing all 30 sacks. Create a payoff matrix showing the payoffs from their respective strategies and determine the Nash equilibrium of a one-shot trade game. Is cooperation possible if the game is repeated, say, under a Grim-Trigger strategy?

4. Why are votes on free-trade agreements among elected officials often so close? Provide intuition for this based on the "free-trade agreement" game in Figure 12.4.

5. Describe the role of the WTO in light of the game presented in Figure 12.5. Describe the three cases of the parameter ω in this game. In which of the three cases does the WTO serve a useful role to arbitrate trade between nations? Why?

References

Abbink, Klaus, Bernd Irlenbusch, and Elke Renner. (2006). "Group Size and Social Ties in Micro-finance Institutions." *Economic Inquiry* 44(4):614–628.

Acemoglu, Daron, Simon Johnson, and James Robinson. (2001). "The Colonial Origins of Comparative Development: An Empirical Review." *American Economic Review*, 91(5):1360–1401.

Acemoglu, Daron, and James Robinson. (2006). *Economic Origins of Dictatorship and Democracy*. New York: Cambridge University Press.

Acharya, Ram, and R. B. Ekelund. (1998). "Mixed and Pure Sharecropping in Nepal: Evidence Supporting the Traditional Hypothesis." *Applied Economics*, 30:37–50.

Adams, Dale, and Norman, Rask. (1968). "Economics of Cost-sharing in Less-Developed Countries." *American Journal of Agricultural Economics*, 50:935–45.

Agarwal, Arun. (2002). "Common Resources and Institutional Sustainability." In *The Drama of the Commons*, ed. Elinor Ostrom, Thomas Dietz, Nives Dolsak, Paul Stern, Susan Stonich, and Elke Weber. Washington, DC: National Academy Press.

Agarwal, Pradeep. (2002). "Incentives Risk and Agency Costs in the Choice of Contractual Arrangements in Agriculture." *Review of Development Economics*, 6(3):460–77.

Akerlof, George, and Rachel Kranton. (2000). "Economics and Identity." *Quarterly Journal of Economics*, 105(3):715–53.

Akerlof, George, and Rachel Kranton. (2002). "Identity and Schooling: Some Lessons for the Economics of Education." *Journal of Economic Literature*, 40:1167–1201.

Akerlof, George, and Rachel Kranton. (2005). "Social Divisions within Schools." In *The Social Economics of Poverty*, ed. Christopher Barrett. New York: Routledge.

Aleem, Irfan. (1990). "Imperfect Information, Screening, and the Costs of Informal Lending: A Study of a Rural Credit Market in Pakistan." *World Bank Economic Review*, 3(4):329–49.

Amsden, Alice. (1989). *Asia's Next Giant: South Korea and Late Industrialization*. New York: Oxford University Press.

Armendáriz de Aghion, Beatriz, and Jonathon Morduch. (2005). *The Economics of Microfinance*. Cambridge, MA: MIT Press.

Appleyard, Dennis, Alfred Field, and Steven Cobb. (2006). *International Economics*. 5th ed. New York: McGraw-Hill/Irwin, pp. 41–5.

Arrow, Kenneth. (1972). "Gifts and Exchanges." *Philosophy and Public Affairs*, 1(4):343–62.

Attran, Scott. (2003). "Genesis and the Future of Suicide Terrorism." Interdisciplines/Interdisciplinary Paper Archive. www.interdisciplines.org.

Aubert, Cecile, Alain de Janvry, and Elizabeth Sadoulet. (2004). "Creating Incentives for Micro-credit Agents to Lend to the Poor." CUDARE Working Paper, University of California at Berkeley, Department of Agricultural and Resource Economics.

Austen-Smith, David, and Roland Fryer. (2005). "An Economic Analysis of 'Acting White'." *Quarterly Journal of Economics*, 120(2):551–83.

Axelrod, Robert. (1984). *The Evolution of Cooperation*. New York: Basic Books.

Bagwell, Kyle, and Robert Staiger. (2001). "Domestic Policies, National Sovereignty, and International Economic Institutions," *Quarterly Journal of Economics*, 116(2):519–62.

Baland, Jean-Marie, and Patrick Francois. (2005). "Commons as Insurance Provision and the Impact of Privatization." *Journal of Public Economics*, 89:211–33.

Baland, Jean-Marie, and Jean-Philippe Platteau. (1997). *Halting Degradation of Natural Resources: Is There a Rule for Rural Communities?* Oxford: Clarendon Press.

Baldwin, Robert. (1955). "Secular Movements in the Terms of Trade." *American Economic Review*, 45(2):259–69.

Bandiera, Oriana, and Imran Rasul. (2006). "Social Networks and Technology Adoption in Northern Mozambique." *Economic Journal*, 116:869–902.

Banerjee, Abhijit. (1992). "A Simple Model of Herd Behavior." *Quarterly Journal of Economics*, 107(3):797–817.

Banerjee, Abhijit, and Esther Duflo. (2006). "Addressing Absence." *Journal of Economic Perspectives*, 20(1):117–32.

Banerjee, Abhijit, Paul Gertler, and Maitreesh Ghatak. (2002). "Empowerment and Efficiency: Tenancy Reform in West Bengal." *Journal of Political Economy*, 10(2):239–80.

Bardhan, Pranab, and Ashok Rudra (1980). "Terms and Conditions of Sharecropping Contracts: an Analysis of Village Survey Data in India." *Journal of Development Studies* 16:287–302.

Bardhan, Pranab. (1984). *Land, Labor, and Rural Poverty: Essays in Development Economics*. New York: Columbia University Press.

Bardhan, Pranab. (1989). "Alternative Approaches to Development Economics." In *Handbook of Development Economics*, ed. Hollis Chenery and T. N. Srinivasan. Vol. 1. London: Elsevier Science.

Bardhan, Pranab. (1997). "Corruption and Development: A Review of Issues." *Journal of Economic Literature*, 35:1320–46.

Bardhan, Pranab. (2000). "Irrigation and Cooperation: and Empirical Analysis of 48 Irrigation Communities in South India." *Economic Development and Cultural Change*, 48(4):847–65.

Bardhan, Pranab. (2005). *Scarcity, Conflicts, and Cooperation: Essays in the Political and Institutional Economics of Development*. Cambridge, MA: MIT Press.

Bardhan, Pranab. (Forthcoming). "The Institutional Economics of Development." In *The Microeconomics of Institutions*, ed. Timothy Besley and Raji Jayaraman. Cambridge, MA: MIT Press.

Bardhan, Pranab, and Jeff Dayton-Johnson. (2002). "Unequal Irrigators: Heterogeneity and Commons Management in Large-Scale Multivariate Research." In *The Drama of the Commons*, ed. Elinor Ostrom, Thomas Dietz, Nives Dolsak, Paul Stern, Susan Stonich, and Elke Weber. Washington, DC: National Academy Press.

Bardhan, Pranab, and Ashok Rudra. (2003). "Terms and Conditions of Sharecropping Contracts: An Analysis of Village Survey Data in India." In *International Trade, Growth, and Development: Essays by Pranab Bardhan*. Oxford: Blackwell; originally published in the *Journal of Development Studies*, April 1980.

Bardhan, Pranab, and Dilip Mookherjee. (2007). "Land Reform and Farm Productivity in West Bengal." University of California at Berkeley Working Paper.

Bardhan, Pranab, and Dilip Mookherjee. (2006a). "Pro-poor Targeting and Accountability of Local Governments in West Bengal." *Journal of Development Economics*, 79:303–27.

Bardhan, Pranab, and Dilip Mookherjee. (2006b). "Decentralization and Accountability in Infrastructure Delivery in Developing Countries." *Economic Journal*, 116:101–6.

Basu, Kaushik. (2007). "Racial Conflict and the Malignancy of Identity." *Journal of Economic Inequality*, forthcoming.

Basu, Kaushik, and Pham Hoang Van. (1998). "The Economics of Child labor." *American Economic Review*, 88(3):412–27.

Becker, Gary. (1975). *Human Capital*. New York: National Bureau of Economic Research.

Becker, Gary, and George Stigler. (1974). "Law Enforcement, Malfeasance, and Compensation of Enforcers." *Journal of Legal Studies*, 3:1–18.

Beine, Michael, Frederic Docquier, and Hillel Rapoport. (2003). "The Brain Drain and LDC Growth: Winners and Losers." IZA Discussion Paper Series No. 819.

Bell, Clive. (1977). "Alternative Theories of Sharecropping: Some Tests Using Evidence from Northeast India." *Journal of Development Studies*, 13(4):317–46.

Bergson, Abram. (1994). "Russia's Economic Reform Muddle." *Challenge*, 37(5):56–60.

Berrnhard, Helen, Ernst Fehr, and Urs Fischbacher. (2006). "Group Affiliation and Altruistic Norm Enforcement." *American Economic Review Papers and Proceedings*, 96(2):217–21.

Berkes, Fikret. (1986). "Marine Inshore Fishery Management in Turkey." In *Proceedings of the Conference on Common Property Resource Management, National Research Council*. Washington, DC: National Academy Press, pp. 68–83.

Berrebi, Claude. (2004). "Evidence about the Link Between Education, Poverty and Terrorism Among Palestinians." Ph.D. dissertation. Princeton University.

Besley, Timothy, and Stephen Coate. (1995). "Group Lending, Repayment Incentives and Social Collateral." *Journal of Development Economics*. 46:1–18.

Besley, Timothy, Stephen Coate, and Glenn Loury. (1993). "The Economics of Rotating Savings and Credit Associations." *American Economic Review*, 83:792–810.

Bevan, David, Paul Collier, and Jan Willem Gunning, with Arne Bigstein and Paul Horsnell. (1990). *Peasants and Governments: An Economic Analysis*. Oxford: Oxford University Press.

Bhagwati, Jagdish. (1958). "Immiserizing Growth: A Geometrical Note." *Review of Economic Studies*, 25:201–5.

Bhagwati, Jagdish. (1982). "Directly Unproductive Profit-Seeking (DUP) Activities." *Journal of Political Economy*, 90:988–1002.

Bhagwati, Jagdish. (2003). *Free Trade Today*. Princeton, NJ: Princeton University Press.

Bhagwati, Jagdish. (2004). *In Defense of Globalization*. Oxford: Oxford University Press.

Bikhchandani, Sushil, David Hirshleifer, and Ivo Welch. (1992). "A Theory of Fads, Fashion, Custom, and Cultural Change as Information Cascades." *Journal of Political Economy*, 100(5):992–1026.

Binmore, Kenneth. (1994). *Game Theory and the Social Contract: Volume I: Playing Fair*. Cambridge, MA: MIT Press.

Binmore, Kenneth. (1998). *Game Theory and the Social Contract: Volume II: Just Playing*. Cambridge, MA: MIT Press.

Bliss, Christopher, and N. Stern. (1982). *Palanpur: The Economy of an Indian Village*. New York: Clarendon Press.

Blume, Lawrence. (2005). "Evolutionary Equilibrium with Forward-Looking Players." In *The Social Economics of Poverty*, ed. Christopher Barrett. New York: Routledge.

Bob's Brain. (2004). Blog Entry June 8, 2004, www.Yexley.net/blogs/bob/archive/2004/06/08/KirbySucks.aspx.

Boserup, Ester. (1965). *The Conditions of Agricultural Growth: The Economics of Agrarian Change Under Population Pressure*. London: Allen and Unwin.

Braido, Luis. (2005). "Evidence on the Incentive Properties of Share Contracts." Ph.D. diss., University of Chicago.

Brams, Steven, and Marc Kilgour. (2001). "Competitive Fair Division." *Journal of Political Economy*, 109(2):418–43.

Brams, Steven, and Alan Taylor. (1996). *Fair Division: From Cake-Cutting to Dispute Resolution*. New York: Cambridge University Press.

Braverman, Avishay, and Joseph Stiglitz. (1986). "Cost-Sharing Arrangements under Sharecropping: Moral Hazard, Incentive Flexibility, and Risk." *American Journal of Agricultural Economics*, 68:642–52.

Bruck, Tillman. (2001). "Mozambique: The Economic Effects of War." In Country Experiences: *War and Underdevelopment*, Vol. 2. Francis Stewart and Valpy Fitzgerald, eds. Oxford: Oxford University Press.

Cairns, Edmund. (1997). *A Safer Future: Reducing the Human Cost of War*. Oxford: Oxfam Publications.

Camara, Pica. (2004). "Access to Land through Rental Markets: A Counter-evolution in the World Bank's Land Policy?" Food and Agricultural Organization Working Paper.

Cardenas, Juan-Camilo. (2003). "Real Wealth and Experimental Cooperation: Evidence from the Fields." *Journal of Development Economics*, 70:263–89.

Carrington, William, and Enrica Detragiache. (1999). "How Extensive Is the Brain Drain?" *Finance and Development*, 36, no. 2 (June).

Caselli, Francesco, and Wilbur Coleman. (2005). "On the Theory of Ethnic Conflict." London School of Economics Working Paper.

Cassar, Alessandra, and Bruce Wydick. (2008). "Does Social Capital Matter? Evidence from a Five-Country Group Lending Experiment." University of San Francisco Working Paper.

Cassar, Alessandra, Luke Crowley, and Bruce Wydick. (2007). "The Effect of Social Capital on Group Loan Repayment: Evidence from Field Experiments." *Economic Journal*, 117:F85–106.

Cassidy, Mike, "Yellow Cab 4 Show Courage But Lose Jobs," *San Jose Mercury News*, September 6, 2005. Article available online at www.mywire.com/pubs/MercuryNews/2005/09/06/992231?extID= 10037&oliID=229

Chaudhury, Nazmul, Jeffrey Hammer, Michael Kremer, Karthik Muralidharan, and Halsey Rogers. (2006). "Missing in Action: Teacher and Health Worker Absence in Developing Countries." *Journal of Economic Perspectives*, 20(1):91–116.

Chayanov. A. V. (1926). *The Theory of Peasant Economy*, ed. Danial Thorner, Basile Kerblay, and R. E. F. Smith (Homewood), Illinois. Subsequently published by Richard D. Irwin for the American Economic Association in 1966.

Coady, David, and Susan W. Parker. (2004). "Cost-Effectiveness Analysis of Demand- and Supply-side Education Interventions: The Case of PROGRESA in Mexico." *Review of Development Economics*, 8(3):331–50.

Coase, Ronald H. (1960). "The Problem of Social Cost." *Journal of Law and Economics*, 3:1–44.

Coate, Stephen, and Glenn Loury. (1993). "Will Affirmative-Action Policies Eliminate Negative Stereotypes?" *American Economic Review*, 83(5):1220–40.

Coate, Stephen, and Martin Ravallion. (1993). "Reciprocity without Commitment: Characterization and Performance of Informal Insurance Arrangements." *Journal of Development Economics*, 40:1–24.

Coleman, Brett. (1999). "The Impact of Group Lending in Northeast Thailand." *Journal of Development Economics*. 60:105–142.

Coleman, James. (1988). "Social Capital in the creation of Human Capital." Reprinted in *Social Capital: A Multi-faceted Perspective*, ed. Partha Dasgupta and Ismail Serageldin. Washington, DC: World Bank.

Collier, Paul. (1988). "Women in Developing Countries." *World Bank Policy Research Working Paper*, 129:3–11.

Collier, Paul, and Anke Hoeffler. (2004). "Greed and Grievance in Civil War." *Oxford Economic Papers*, 56:563–95.

Collier, Paul, Anke Hoeffler, and Cathy Pattillo. (2004). "Africa's Exodus: Capital Flight and Brain Drain as Portfolio Decisions." *Journal of African Economies*, 13(2):15–54.

Conley, Tim, and Christopher Udry. (2005). "Learning about a New Technology: Pineapple in Ghana." Yale Economic Growth Center Working Paper No. 817.

Cooper, Russell, and Andrew John. (1988). "Coordinating Coordination Failures in Keynesian Models." *Quarterly Journal of Economics*, 103(3):441–463.

Dalton, George. (1965). "Primitive Money." *American Anthropologist*, 67(1):44–65.

Dasgupta, Partha. (2000). "Economic Progress and the Idea of Social Capital." In *Social Capital: A Multi-faceted Perspective*, ed. Partha Dasgupta and Ismail Serageldin. Washington, DC: World Bank.

David, Paul. (1975). *Technical Choice, Innovation, and Economic Growth: Essays on the American and British Experience in the Nineteenth Century*. Cambridge: Cambridge University Press.

David, Paul. (1985). "Clio and the Economics of QWERTY." *American Economic Review*, 75(2):332–7.

Davies, Glyn. (1994). *A History of Money: From Ancient Times to Today*. London: University of Wales Press.

Dayton-Johnson, Jeff. (2000). "The Determinants of Collective Action on the Local Commons: a Model with Evidence from Mexico." *Journal of Development Economics*, 62:181–208.

de Janvry, Alain. (1981). *The Agrarian Question and Reformism in Latin America*. Baltimore: Johns Hopkins University Press.

de Janvry, Alain, Craig McIntosh, and Elizabeth Sadoulet. (2006). "The Supply and Demand Side Impact of Credit Market Information." U.C. Berkeley and U.C. San Diego Working Paper.

de Soto, Hernando. (2000). *The Mystery of Capital: Why Capitalism Triumphs in the West and Fails Everywhere Else*. New York: Basic Books.

Deininger, Klaus, and Pedro Olinto. (2000). "Asset Distribution Inequality and Growth." Working Paper No. 2375, World Bank Development Research Group.

Diamond, Jared. (2005). *Collapse: How Societies Choose to Fail or Succeed*. New York: Viking Press.

Dixit, Avinash, and Susan Skeath. (2004). *Games of Strategy*. New York: Norton, pp. 430–7.

Dolinskaya, Irina. (2002). "Explaining Russia's Output Collapse." *IMF Staff Papers*, 49(2): 155–74.

Dornbusch, Rudiger, Stanley Fischer, and Paul Samuelson. (1977). "Comparative Advantage, Trade, and Payments in a Ricardian Model with a Continuum of Goods." *American Economic Review*, 67(5):823–39.

Drèze, Jean, and Amartya Sen. (1989). *Hunger and Public Action*. New Delhi: Oxford University Press.

Duflo, Esther, and Abhijit Banerjee. (2006). "Addressing Absence." *Journal of Economic Perspectives*, 20(1):117–32.

Duflo, Esther, and Remma Hanna. (2005). "Monitoring Works: Getting Teachers to Come to School." MIT Working Paper.

Dugatkin, Lee. (1999). *Cheating Monkeys and Citizen Bees: The Nature of Cooperation in Animals and Humans*. New York: Free Press.

Easterly, William. (2006). *The White Man's Burden: Why the West's Efforts to Aid the Rest Have Done So Much Ill and So Little Good*. New York: Penguin Press.

Easterly, William. (2001). *The Elusive Quest for Growth: Economists' Adventures and Misadventures in the Tropics*. Cambridge, MA: MIT Press.

Ellison, Glenn, and Drew Fundenberg. (1993). "Rules of Thumb for Social Learning." *Journal of Political Economy*, 101(4):612–43.

Engerman, Stanley, and Kenneth Sokoloff. (1994). "Factor Endowments: Institutions, and Differential Paths of Growth Among New World Economies: A View from Economic Historians of the United States." *National Bureau of Economic Research Working Paper*. Number 066, 1994.

Fafchamps, Marcel. (1992). "Solidarity Networks in Preindustrial Societies: Rational Peasants with a Moral Economy." *Economic Development and Cultural Change*, 41(1):147–74.

Fafchamps, Marcel, and Bart Minten. (1999). "Relationships and Traders in Madagascar." *Journal of Development Studies*, 35(6):1–35.

Fafchamps, Marcel, and Bart Minten. (2002). "Returns to Social Network Capital Among Traders." *Oxford Economic Papers*, 54:173–206.

Fatoumata, Jawara, and Aileen Kwa. (2004). *Behind the Scenes at the WTO*. London: Zed Books, pp. 16–17.

Fishlow, Albert. (1965). *American Railroads and the Transformation of the Antebellum Economy*. Cambridge, MA: Harvard University Press.

Floro, Maria, and Debraj Ray. (1997). "Vertical Links between Formal and Informal Financial Institutions." *Review of Development Economics*, 1(1):43–56.

Fogel, Robert. (1964). *Railroads and American Economic Growth: Essays in Econometric History*. Baltimore: Johns Hopkins University Press.

Frank, Robert. (1988). *Passions within Reason: The Strategic Role of Emotions*. New York: W. W. Norton.

Freston, Paul. (2001). *Evangelicals and Politics in Asia, Africa, and Latin America*. Cambridge: Cambridge University Press.

Friedman, Daniel, and Nirvikar Singh. (1999). "The Viability of Vengeance." University of California at Santa Cruz Working Paper.

Friedman, Daniel, and Nirvikar Singh. (2004). "Negative Reciprocity: The Coevolution of Memes and Genes." *Evolution and Human Behavior*, 25(3):155–73.

Fryer, Roland. (2006). "Acting White." *Education Next*, Winter, 53–59.

Fuller, Alfred. (2005). The Original Fuller Brush Man, company website www.myfullerbrush.com/history.htm. (Accessed 10/15/2005.)

Fukuyama, Francis. (1996). *Trust: The Social Virtues and the Creation of Prosperity*. New York: Free Press.

Gale, Douglas. (1996). "What Have We Learned from Social Learning?" *European Economic Review*, 40:617–28.

Ghatak, Maitreesh. (1995). "Group Lending, Local Information and Peer Selection." *Journal of Development Economics*, 60(1):1–18.

Giné, Xavier., Pamela Jakiela, Dean Karlan, and Jonathan Morduch. (2005). "Microfinance games," Unpublished manuscript.

Gladwell, Malcolm. (1997). "Annals of Style: 'The Coolhunt'." *The New Yorker*, March 17.

Gladwell, Malcolm. (2000). *The Tipping Point: How Little Things Can Make a Big Difference*. New York: Little Brown.

Gladwell, Malcolm. (2005). *Blink: The Power of Thinking without Thinking*. New York: Little, Brown.

Golub, Stephen. (1998). "Does Trade with Low-Wage Countries Hurt American Workers?" *Business Review*, March/April, 3–15.

Granovetter, Mark. (1973). "The Strength of Weak Ties." *American Journal of Sociology*, 78(6):1360–80.

Granovetter, Mark. (1985). "Economic Action and Social Structure: The Problem of Embeddedness." *American Journal of Sociology*, 91(3):481–510.

Granovetter, Mark. (2005). "The Impact of Social Structure on Economic Outcomes." *Journal of Economic Perspectives*, 19(1):33–50.

Greif, Avner. (1994). "Cultural Beliefs and the Organization of Society: A Historical and Theoretical Reflection on Collectivist and Individualist Societies." *Journal of Political Economy*, 102(5):912–50.

Griffin, James, and William Nielsen. (1994). "The 1985–86 Oil Price Collapse and Afterwards: What Does Game Theory Add?" *Economic Inquiry*, 17:543–61.

Griliches, Zvi. (1957). "Hybrid Corn: An Exploration in the Economics of Technological Change." *Econometrica*, 25(4):501–22.

Grossman, Herschel. (1999). "Kleptocracy and Revolutions." *Oxford Economic Papers*, 51:267–83.

Guth, Werner, and Reinhard Tietz. (1990). "Ultimatum Bargaining Behavior: A Survey and Comparison of Experimental Results." *Journal of Economic Psychology*, 11:417–49.

Hallagan, William. (1978). "Self-Selection by Contractual Choice and the Theory of Sharecropping." *Bell Journal of Economics*, 9(2):344–54.

Hardin, Garret. (1968). *The Tragedy of the Commons*, 162:1243–8.

Harsanyi, John, and Reinhardt Selten. (1988). *A General Theory of Equilibrium Selection*. Cambridge, MA: MIT Press.

Hart, Benjamin, and Lynnette Hart. (1992). "Reciprocal Allogrooming in Impala, *Aepyceros melampus*." *Animal Behavior*, 44:1073–83.

Hayami, Yuhiro, and Keijiro Otsuka. (1993). *The Economics of Contract Choice: An Agrarian Perspective*. New York: Clarendon Press.

Helfer, Ricki Trigel. (1999). "What Deposit Insurance Can and Cannot Do." *Finance and Development*, 36(1):22–33.

Hildreth, Richard. (2001). *A History of Banks*. Kitchener: Batoche Books.

Hirshleifer, Jack. (2001). *The Dark Side of the Force: Economic Foundations of Conflict Theory.* Cambridge: Cambridge University Press.

Hirshman, Albert. (1958). *The Strategy of Economic Development.* New Haven, CT: Yale University Press.

Hoeffler, Anke, and Marta Reynal-Querol. (2003). "Measuring the Cost of Conflict." Centre for the Study of African Economies, Centre for the Study of African Economies, Oxford University. Unpublished Manuscript.

Hoff, Karla, and Arijit Sen. (2006). "The Kin System as a Poverty Trap?" in *Poverty Traps.* ed. Samuel Bowles, Steven Durlauf, and Karla Hoff. New York: Russell Sage Foundation; Princeton, NJ: Princeton University Press.

Hoff, Karla, and Joseph Stiglitz. (1990). "Imperfect Information and Rural Credit Markets: Puzzles and Policy Perspectives." *World Bank Economic Review,* 3(4):235–50.

Hotelling, Harold. (1929). "Stability and Competition." *Economic Journal,* 39(1):41–57.

Hungerford, Thomas. (1991). "GATT: a Cooperative Equilibrium in a Non-cooperative Trading Regime?" *Journal of International Economics,* 31:357–69.

Huntington, Samuel. (1968). *Political Order in Changing Societies.* New Haven, CT: Yale University Press.

Hviding, Edvard, and Graham Baines. (1994). "Community-Based Fisheries Management, Tradition and the Challenges of Development in Marovo, Solomon Islands." *Development and Change,* 25(1):13–39.

International Labor Organization. (2003). International Program on the Elimination of Child Labor (Bulletin), March.

Ivanova, Liza. (1997). "Russian Contracts: What's in a Signature?" *East European Business Law, London,* no. 97–8.

Jacoby, Hanan, and Ghazala Mansuri. (2003). "Incomplete Contracts and Investment: A Study of Land Tenancy in Pakistan." World Bank Development Research Group, Working Paper.

Kahneman, Daniel, and Amos Tversky. (1979). "Prospect Theory: An Analysis of Decision-making under Risk." *Econometrica,* 47(2):263–292.

Kahneman, Daniel, Jack Knetsch, and Richard Thaler. (1990). "Empirical Effects of the Endowment Effect and the Coase Theorem." *Journal of Political Economy,* 98(6):1325–48.

Kalyvas, Stathis, Peter Lange, Robert Bates, and Ellen Comisso. (2006). *The Logic of Violence in Civil War.* Cambridge: Cambridge University Press.

Karlan, Dean. (2005). "Using Experimental Methods to Measure Social Capital and Predict Real Financial Decisions." *American Economic Review,* 94(5):1688–99.

Kessey, Charles. (2005). "Empowering Muslim Women through Microcredit Scheme: The Case of the Sunyani Gonja Muslim Women's Group." WOPAG—Working Papers on Ghana: Historical and Contemporary Studies No. 7, October.

Khandker, Shahidur. (1998). *Fighting Poverty with Microcredit.* Oxford: Oxford University Press.

Khandker, Shahidur. (2003). "Microfinance and Poverty: Evidence Using Panel Data from Bangladesh." World Bank Policy Research Working Paper No. 2945.

Khwaja, Asim Ijaz. (2000). "Leadership, Rights, and Project Complexity: Determinants of Collective Action in the Maintenance of Infrastructural Projects in the Himalayas." John F. Kennedy School of Government Faculty Research Working Papers Series.

Kidwell, David, Richard Peterson, and David Blackwell. (1993). *Financial Institutions, Markets, and Money.* Fort Worth, TX: Dryden Press.

Klitgaard, Robert. (1990). *Tropical Gangsters.* New York: Basic Books.

Knack, Stephen, and Philip Keefer. (1997). "Does Social Capital Have an Economic Payoff? A Cross-Country Regression." *Quarterly Journal of Economics,* 112:1251–58.

Koshar, Rudy. (2004). "Cars and Nations." *Theory, Culture, and Society,* 21(4):121–44.

Kranton, Rachel. (1996). "Reciprocal Exchange: A Self-Sustaining System." *American Economic Review,* 86(4):830–51.

Krauss, Clifford. (1991). *Inside Central America: People, Politics, and History.* New York: Summit Books.

Kremer, Michael. (1993). "The O-Ring Theory of Economic Development." *Quarterly Journal of Economics*, 108(3):551–75.

Kremer, Michael, and Daniel Chen. (2001). "An Interim Report on a Teacher Incentive Program in Kenya." Harvard University Working Paper.

Kremer, Michael, and Edward Miguel. (2003). "Networks, Social Learning, and Technology Adoption: The Case of Deworming Drugs in Kenya." Working Paper, Harvard University and the University of California at Berkeley.

Kremer, Michael, and Edward Miguel. (2004). "Worms: Identifying Impacts on Education and Health in the Presence of Treatment Externalities." *Econometrica*, 72(1):159–217.

Kreps, David. (1990). "Corporate Culture and Economic Theory." In *Perspectives on Positive Political Economy*, ed. James Alt and Kenneth Shepsle. Cambridge: Cambridge University Press, pp. 90–143.

Krueger, Anne. (1974). "The Political Economy of the Rent-Seeking Society." *American Economic Review*, 64(3):291–303.

Krueger, Anne, and Chinoy. (2002). "The Indian Economy in a Global Context." In *Economic Policy Reforms and the Indian Economy*, ed. Anne O. Kruger. Chicago: University of Chicago Press.

Krugman, Paul, and Maurice Obstfeld. (2006). *International Economics: Theory and Policy.* 7th ed. Boston: Addison-Wesley.

Kuznets, Simon. (1955). "Economic Growth and Income Inequality." *American Economic Review*, 45(1):1–28.

Laffont, Jean-Jacques, and Mohamed Matoussi. (1995). "Moral Hazard, Financial Constraints and Sharecropping in El Oulja." *Review of Economic Studies*, 62(3):381–99.

Lastarria-Cornhiel, Susanna, and Jolyne Melmed-Sanjak. (1999). "Land Tenancy in Asia, Africa, and Latin America: A Look to the Past a View to the Future." Prepared for the Food and Agriculture Organization of the United Nations, Land Tenure Center, University of Wisconsin.

Lazear, Edward, and Sherwin Rosen. (1981). "Rank-Order Tournaments as Optimum Labor Contracts." *Journal of Political Economy*, 90(3):241–76.

Leblanc, Douglas. (2005). "Out of Africa: The Leader of Nearly 18 million Nigerian Anglicans Challenges the West's Theology and Control." *Christianity Today*, July.

LeClair, Mark. (2000). *International Commodity Markets and the Role of Cartels.* New York: M. E. Sharpe.

Leff, Nathaniel. (1964). "Economic Development through Bureaucratic Corruption." *American Behavioral Scientist*, 8(2):8–14.

Lenski, Gerhard. (1963). *The Religious Factor a Sociological Study of Religion's Impact on Politics, Economics and Family Life.* New York: Doubleday.

Leontief, Wassily. (1966). *Input-Output Economics.* New York: Oxford University Press.

Lictheim, Miriam. (1973). *Ancient Egyptian Literature.* Vol. 1. *The Old and Middle Kingdoms.* Berkeley: University of California Press.

Liebowitz, Stan, and Stephen Margolis. (1990). "The Fable of the Keys" *Journal of Law and Economics*, 33(1):1–25.

Lijphart, Arend. (1984). *Democracies.* Hew Haven, CT: Yale University Press.

Luoto, Jill, Craig McIntosh, and Bruce Wydick. (2007). "Credit Information Systems in Less-Developed Countries: A Test with Microfinance in Guatemala." *Economic Development and Cultural Change*, 55(2):313–34.

Madison, Angus. (2001). *The World Economy: A Millennial Perspective.* Paris: Development Centre of the Organization for Economic Co-operation and Development.

Magid, Ken, and Carol McKelvey. (1988). *High Risk: Children without a Conscience.* New York: Bantam.

Manski, Charles. (1993). "Identification of Endogenous Social Effects: The Reflection Problem." *Review of Economic Studies*, 60:531–42.

Manski, Charles. (1995). *Identification Problems in the Social Sciences.* Cambridge, MA: Harvard University Press.

Marshall, Alfred. (1890). *Principles of Economics*. ed. C. W. Guillebaud. London: Macmillan, 1961 ed.

Mas, Ignacio, and Samuel Tally. (1990). "Deposit Insurance in Developing Countries." *Finance and Development*, 27(4).

Mauro, Pablo. (1995). "Corruption and Growth." *Quarterly Journal of Economics*, 110(4):681–99.

Mayer, Wolfgang. (1984). "Endogenous Tariff Formation." *American Economic Review*, 74(5): 970–85.

McCleary, Rachel, and Robert Barro. (2006). "Religion and Economy." *Journal of Economic Perspectives*, 20(2):49–72.

McIntosh, Craig, and Bruce Wydick. (2005). "Competition and Microfinance." *Journal of Development Economics*, 78:271–98.

McIntosh, Craig, and Bruce Wydick. (2007). "Adverse Selection, Moral Hazard, and Credit Information Systems: Theory and Experimental Evidence." University of California at San Diego/University of San Francisco Working Paper.

McMillan, John. (2002). *Reinventing the Bazaar: A Natural History of Markets*. New York: W. W. Norton.

McMillan, John, and Chris Woodruff. (2002). "The Central Role of Entrepreneurs in Transition Economies." *Journal of Economic Perspectives*, 16:153–70.

Miguel, Edward, Shankar Satyanath, and Ernest Sergenti. (2004). "Economic Shocks and Civil Conflict: An Instrumental Variables Approach." *Journal of Political Economy*, 112(4): 725–53.

Miller, William Ian. (2006). *Eye for an Eye*. Cambridge: Cambridge University Press.

Millett, Paul. (1991). *Lending and Borrowing in Ancient Athens*. Cambridge: Cambridge University Press.

Mittal, Anuradha. (2002). "Giving Away the Farm: The 2002 Farm Bill." *Food First*, 8(3).

Montgomery, Tommy Sue. (2000). "El Salvador." In *Latin American Politics and Development*. 5th ed., ed. Howard Wiarda and Harvey F. Kline. Boulder, CO: Westview Press.

Montalvo, Jose, and Marta Reynal-Querol. (2005). "Ethnic Polarization, Potential Conflict,and Civil Wars." World Bank Working Paper.

Mookherjee Dilip, and I. P. L. Png. (1995). "Corruptible Law Enforcers: How Should They Be Compensated?" *Economic Journal*, 105:145–59.

Murphy, Kevin, Andrei Shelifer, and Robert Vishny. (1989). "Industrialization and the Big Push." *Journal of Political Economy* 97(5):1003–1026.

Munshi, Kaivan, and Jacques Myaux. (2006). "Social Norms and the Fertility Transition." *Journal of Development Economics*. 80(1):1–38.

Myerson, Roger. (1991). *Game Theory: Analysis of Conflict*. Cambridge, MA: Harvard University Press.

Nash, John F. (1950). "Equilibrium Points in *N*-Person Games." *Proceedings of the National Academy of Sciences*, 36:48–49.

Nash, John F. (1951). "Non-Cooperative Games." *Annals of Mathematics*, 2(54):286–95.

Nassar, Sylvia. (1998). *A Beautiful Mind*. New York: Simon and Schuster.

Newbery, David. (1977). "Risk-Sharing, Sharecropping, and Uncertain Labor Markets." *Review of Economic Studies*, 44:585–94.

Newbery, David, and Joseph Stiglitz. (1979). "Sharecropping, Risk-Sharing, and the Importance of Imperfect Information." In *Risk, Uncertainty, and Agricultural Development*, ed James Roumasset, Jean-Mark Boussard, and Inderjit Singh. New York: Agricultural Development Council, ch. 17.

Nisbett, Richard, and Dov Cohen. (1996). *Culture of Honor: The Psychology of Violence in the South*. Boulder, CO: Westview Press.

North, Douglas. (1990). *Institutions, Institutional Change and Economic Performance*. New York: Cambridge University Press.

Olson, Mancur. (1965). *The Logic of Collective Action: Public Goods and the Theory of Groups*. Cambridge: Cambridge University Press.

Ostrom, Elinor. (1990). *Governing the Commons: The Evolution of Institutions for Collective Action*. Cambridge: Cambridge University Press.

Ostrom, Elinor, Roy Gardner, and James Walker. (1994). *Rules, Games, and Common-Pool Resources*. Ann Arbor: University of Michigan Press.

Otsuka, Keijiro, Hiroyuki Chuma, and Yuhiro Hayami. (1992). "Land and Labor Contracts in Agrarian Economies." *Journal of Economic Literature*, 30(4):1965–2018.

Oxfam. (2002). "The Coffee Report: Mugged–Poverty in Your Coffee Cup." Oxfam Report, September 2002.

Paige, Jeffery. (1997). *Coffee and Power: Revolution and the Rise of Democracy in Central America*. Cambridge, MA: Harvard University Press.

Pareto, Vilfredo. (1902/1966). "Les Systèmes d'Economie Politique." In *Vilfredo Pareto: Sociological Writings*, ed. S. E. Finer. New York: Praeger.

Pareto, Vilfredo. (1927/1971). *Manual of Political Economy*. New York: A. M. Kelley.

Peters, Ted. (1994). *Sin: Radical Evil in Soul and Society*. Grand Rapids, MI: Eerdmans Press.

Pinker, Scott. (2002). *The Blank Slate: The Modern Denial of Human Nature*. New York: Viking Press.

Platteau, Jean-Philippe. (2000). *Institutions, Social Norms, and Economic Development*. Amsterdam: Harwood Academic.

Pool, Robert. (1995). "Putting Game Theory to the Test." *Science*, 267:1591–93.

Popkin, Samuel. (1979). *The Rational Peasant: The Political Economy of Rural Society in Vietnam*. Berkeley: University of California Press.

Posner, Richard A. (2001). *Frontiers of Legal Theory*. Cambridge, MA: Harvard University Press.

Prebisch, Raul. (1950). *The Economic Development of Latin America and Its Principal Problems*. Lake Success, NY: United Nations.

PR Newswire, "Research on 'Spiritual Capital.'" Philadelphia, February 2006.

Putnam, Robert. (1993). *Making Democracy Work: Civic Traditions in Modern Italy*. Princeton, NJ: Princeton University Press.

Putnam, Robert. (1995). "Bowling Alone: America's Declining Social Capital." *Journal of Democracy*, 6:65–78.

Rashid, Mansoora, and Robert Townsend. (1992). "Targeting Credit and Insurance: Efficiency, Mechanism Design, and Program Evaluation." University of Chicago/World Bank Working Paper.

Reid, Joseph. (1976). "Sharecropping and Agricultural Uncertainty." *Economic Development and Cultural Change*, 24:549–76.

Reid, Joseph. (1977). "The Theory of Share Tenancy Revisited-Again." *Journal of Political Economy*, 85:403–7.

Robinson, Julia. (1951). "An Iterative Method of Solving a Game." *Annals of Mathematics*, 54:296–301.

Rodrik, Dani. (1995). "The Political Economy of Trade Policy." In *Handbook of International Economics*, ed. Gene Grossman and Ken Roghoff. Vol. 3. London: Elsevier Science.

Rodrik, Dani. (1996). "Coordination Failures and Government Policy: A Model with Applications to East Asia and Eastern Europe." *Journal of International Economics*, 40(1): 1–22.

Romer, David. (1995). *Advanced Macroeconomics*. New York: McGraw-Hill.

Rosenstein-Rodan, Paul. (1943). "Problems of Industrialization of Eastern and Southeastern Europe." *Economic Journal*, 53:202–11.

Rostow, W. W. (1960). *The Stages of Economic Growth*. Cambridge: Cambridge University Press.

Rotsko, Nicholas, and Benjamin Powell. (2005). "CAFTA 'Free Trade' Agreement is a Sweet Deal for Special Interests." *Sacramento Business Journal*, September 16, 2005.

Sadoulet, Elizabeth. (1992). "Labor-Service Tenancy Contracts in a Latin American Context." *American Economic Review*, 82(4):1031–42.

Sampson, Robert, Jeffrey Morenoff, and Thomas Gannon-Rowley. (2002). "Assessing 'Neighbor-hood Effects': Social Processes and New Directions in Research." *Annual Review of Sociology*, 28:443–78.

Samuelson, Larry. (1998) *Evolutionary Games and Equilibrium Selection.*Cambridge, MA: MIT Press.

Samuelson, Paul. (1969). "The Way of an Economist." In *International Economic Relations: Proceedings of the Third Congress of the International Economic Association*, ed. Paul Samuelson. London: Macmillan, pp. 1–11.

Saxenian, Annlee. (1996). *Regional Advantage: Culture and Competition in Silicon Valley*. Cambridge, MA: Harvard University Press.

Saxenian, Annlee. (2002). "Bangalore: the Silicon Valley of Asia?" In *Economic Policy Reforms and the Indian Economy*. ed. Anne Kruger. Chicago: University of Chicago Press.

Schelling, Thomas. (1960). *The Strategy of Conflict*. New York: Oxford University Press.

Shleifer, Andrei. (1994). "Establishing Property Rights." *World Bank Research Observer*, 93:94–5.

Shleifer, Andrei, and Robert Vishny. (1993). "Corruption." *Quarterly Journal of Economics*, 108(3):599–617.

Scott, James. (1976). *The Moral Economy of the Peasant*. New Haven, CT: Yale University Press.

Seabright, Paul. (1993). "Managing Local Commons: Theoretical Issues in Incentive Design." *Journal of Economic Perspectives*, 7(4):113–34.

Seabright, Paul. (1997). "Is Cooperation Habit-Forming?" In *The Environment and Emerging Development Issues*, ed. Partha Dasgupta and Karl-Gorän-Mäler. Oxford: Clarendon Press.

Shaban, Radwan. (1987). "Testing between Competing Theories of Sharecropping," *Journal of Political Economy*, 95(5):893–920.

Shapiro, Carl, and Joseph Stiglitz. (1984). "Equilibrium Unemployment as a Worker Discipline Device," *The American Economic Review*, 74(3):433–444.

Sharpe, Kenneth Evan. (1977). *Peasant Politics: Struggle in a Dominican Village*. Baltimore: Johns Hopkins University Press.

Silke, Andrew. (2004). "Courage in Dark Places: Reflections on Terrorist Psychology." *Social Research*, 70(1):178.

Singer, Hans. (1950). "The Distribution of Trade between Investing and Borrowing Countries." *American Economic Review*, 40:473–85.

Singer, Hans. (1987). "Terms of Trade and Economic Development." In *The New Palgrave: A Dictionary of Economics*. Vol. 4. London: Macmillan, pp. 626–28.

Singh, Nirvikar. (2000). "Theories of Sharecropping." In *Development Economics: Micro-Theory*, ed. Pranab Bardhan and Christopher Udry. Vol. 1. Cambridge, MA: MIT Press.

Sliwa, Maria. (2006). "A Gospel of Involvement: U.S. Pastor Frees Abducted Child Soldiers in Sudan and Uganda." *PRISM*, March–April, 22–25.

Smith, Adam. (1776). *An Inquiry into the Nature and Causes of the Wealth of Nations*. ed. Edwin Cannan. Chicago: University of Chicago Press, 1976 ed.

Sobel, Joel. (2006). "For Better or Forever: Formal vs. Informal Enforcement." *Journal of Labor Economics*, 24(2):271–98.

Sommers, Marc. (2002). *Children, Education and War: Reaching Education for All Objectives in Countries Affected by Conflict*. Washington D.C.: World Bank Publications.

Spar, Debora. (1994). *The Corporate of Edge: the Internal Politics of International Cartels*. Ithaca, NY: Cornell University Press.

Spar, Debora. (2006). "Continuity and Change in the International Diamond Market." *Journal of Economic Perspectives*, 20(3):195–208.

Staiger, Robert. (1995). "International Rules and Institutions for Trade Policy." In *Handbook of International Economics*. ed. Gene Grossman and Ken Roghoff. Vol. 3, London: Elsevier Science.

Staiger, Robert, and Kyle Bagwell. (1990). "A Theory of Managed Trade." *American Economic Review*, 80(4):779–95.

Staiger, Robert, and Kyle Bagwell. (1999). "An Economic Theory of GATT." *American Economic Review*, 89(1):215–48.

Stiglitz, Joseph. (1990). "Peer Monitoring and Credit Markets." *World Bank Economic Review*, 4:351–366.

Stiglitz, Joseph, and Andrew Weiss. (1981). "Credit Rationing in Markets with Imperfect Information." *American Economic Review*, 71(3):393–410.

Stolper, Wolfgang, and Paul Samuelson. (1941). "Protection and Real Wages." *Review of Economic Studies*, 9:58–73.

Su, Francis. (1999). "Rental Harmony: Sperner's Lemma in Fair Division." *American Math Monthly*, 106:930–42.

Sugden, Robert. (1986/2004). *The Economics of Rights, Cooperation, and Welfare*, London: Blackwell; 2nd ed., New York: Palgrave-Macmillan.

Temin, Peter. (2006). "The Economy of the Early Roman Empire." *Journal of Economic Perspectives*. 20(1):133–151.

Trackman, Brian, William Fisher, and Luis Salas. (1999). *The Reform of Property Registration Systems in Costa Rica: A Status Report*. Cambridge, MD: Harvard Institute for International Development, Central America Project Series.

U.S. Census Factfinder. (2000). *Demographic Profile on Race, Ethnic, and Ancestry Groups and Thomas Brinkhoff: City Population*. http://www.citypopulation.de.

U.S. Agency for International Development. (1998). *Haiti Country Report*. Washington DC.

Udry, Christopher. (1994). "Risk and Insurance in a Rural Credit Market: An Empirical Investigation in Northern Nigeria." *Review of Economic Studies*, 61(1):495–526.

Van Hezik, Cecile. (2002). "The Long-Term Economic Consequences of Overgrazing for the Extensive Livestock Production Sector in Mongolia." Graduate thesis, Wagenignen University, the Netherlands.

Van Rijckeghem, Caroline, and Beatrice Weder. (2001). "Bureaucratic Corruption and Rate of Temptation: Do Wages in the Civil Service Affect Corruption, and by How Much?" *Journal of Development Economics*, 65:307–32.

Van Tassel, Eric. (1999). "Group Lending under Asymmetric Information." *Journal of Development Economics*, 60(1):3–25.

Van Tilburg, Jo Anne. (1994). *Easter Island Archeology, Ecology, and Culture*. London: British Museum Press and Smithsonian Institution Press.

Von Neumann, John, and Oskar Morgenstern. (1943). *Theory of Games and Economic Behavior*. Princeton, NJ: Princeton University Press.

Wade, Robert. (1987). *Village Republics*. Cambridge: Cambridge University Press.

Wade, Robert. (1990/2004). *Governing the Market: Economic Theory and the Role of Government in East Asian Industrialization*. Princeton, NJ: Princeton University Press.

Wagener, Oliver. (2006). "Development Cooperation and Islamic Values in Bangladesh." GTZ, Federal Ministry for Economic Cooperation and Development, Government of Germany, June.

Weber, Max. (1905). *The Protestant Ethic and the Spirit of Capitalism*. London: Allen and Unwin.

Weibull, Jörgen. (1995). *Evolutionary Game Theory*. Cambridge: MIT Press.

Weingast, Barry. (1998). "Constructing Trust." in *Institutions and Social Order*, ed. Karol Soltan, Eric Uslaner, and Virginia Haufler. Ann Arbor: University of Michigan Press, pp. 177–99.

Weitzman, Martin. (1974). "Free Access Versus Private Ownership as Alternative Systems for Managing Common Property." *Journal of Economic Theory*, 8:225–34.

Wenner, Mark. (1995). "Group Credit: a Means to Improve Information Transfer and Loan Repayment Performance." *Journal of Development Studies*, 32(1):263–281.

Williamson, Oliver. (1975). *Markets and Hierarchies*. New York: Free Press.

Williamson, Oliver. (1985). *The Economic Institutions of Capitalism*. New York: Free Press.

Wilson, Edward. (1978/2004). *On Human Nature*. Cambridge, MA: Harvard University Press.

Wilson, James, and George Kelling. (1982). "The Police and Neighborhood Safety: Broken Windows." *Atlantic Monthly*, 127:29–38.

World Bank. (1998). *El Salvador: Rural Development Study*. Washington DC: World Bank.

World Bank. (2002). *The Last Straw: Integrating Natural Disaster Mitigation with Environmental Management*. World Bank Disaster Management Facility. Washington, DC: World Bank Publications.

World Bank. (2003). *Breaking the Conflict Trap: Civil War and Development Policy*. New York: Oxford University Press.

World Trade Organization. (2005a). "Understanding the WTO." www.wto.org., pp. 8–10.

World Trade Organization. (2005b). "Environmental Disputes IV: Mexico vs. The United States, Tuna/Dolphin." www.wto.org.

Wydick, Bruce. (1999a). "Can Social Cohesion Be Harnessed to Mitigate Market Failures? Evidence from Group Lending in Guatemala." *Economic Journal*, 109:463–75.

Wydick, Bruce. (1999b). "The Effect of Microenterprise Lending on Child Schooling in Guatemala." *Economic Development and Cultural Change*, 47(4):853–69.

Wydick, Bruce. (2001). "Group Lending under Dynamic Incentives as a Borrower Discipline Device." *Review of Development Economics*, 5(3):406–20.

Wydick, Bruce. (2002). "Affirmative Action in College Admissions: Examining Labor Market Effects of Four Alternative Policies." *Contemporary Economic Policy*, 20(1):12–24.

Yang, Bo. (2004). "OPEC Behavior: A Thesis in Energy, Environmental, and Mineral Economics." Ph.D. diss., Pennsylvania State University.

Yergin, Daniel, and Joseph Stanislaw. (1998/2002). *The Commanding Heights: The Battle for the World Economy*. New York: Simon and Schuster.

Young, Peyton. (1998). *Individual Strategy and Social Structure*. Princeton, NJ: Princeton University Press.

Young, Peyton. (2001). "The Dynamics of Conformity." In *Social Dynamics*, ed. Steven Durlauf and Young Peyton. Cambridge: MIT Press.

Zhao, Jinhua. (2005). "The Role of Information in Technology Adoption under Poverty." United Nations University Research Paper No. 2005/41.

Zimbardo, Phillip. (1969). "The Human Choice: Individual Reason and Order versus Impulse, De-individualization, and Chaos." In *The Nebraska Symposium on Motivation*, ed. William Arnold and David Levine, Lincoln, NE: University of Nebraska Press.

Index